The Treaty Prohibiting Nuclear Weapons

This book chronicles the genesis of the negotiations that led to the Treaty on the Prohibition of Nuclear Weapons (TPNW), which challenged the established nuclear order.

The work provides readers with an authoritative account of the complex evolution of the "Humanitarian Initiative" (HI) and the negotiation history of the TPNW. It includes a close analysis of internal strategy documents and communications in the author's possession which trace the tactical and political decisions of a small group of state actors. By demonstrating the unacceptable humanitarian consequences and uncontrollable risks that these weapons pose to everyone's security, the HI convinced many states to ban nuclear weapons and reject the policy of nuclear deterrence as unsustainable and illegitimate. As such, this book is a case-study of multilateral diplomacy and cooperation between state and civil society actors. It also contains a full discussion of both sides of the nuclear argument and assesses the extent to which the HI and the TPNW have moved the dial and presented opportunities for transformational change.

This book will be of much interest to students of nuclear disarmament, arms control and non-proliferation, diplomacy, global governance and international relations in general.

Alexander Kmentt is Director for Disarmament, Arms Control and Non-Proliferation in the Austrian Ministry for Foreign Affairs. From 2016–2019 he served as Austria's Permanent Representative to the Political and Security Committee of the European Union. He is one of the architects of the Humanitarian Initiative that lead to the TPNW.

Routledge Global Security Studies

Global Security Studies emphasizes broad forces reshaping global security and the dilemmas facing decision-makers the world over. The series stresses issues relevant in many countries and regions, accessible to broad professional and academic audiences as well as to students, and enduring through explicit theoretical foundations.

Series Editors: Aaron Karp and Regina Karp

Confrontational and Cooperative Regional Orders
Managing Regional Security in World Politics
Ariel Gonzalez Levaggi

Military Coercion and US Foreign Policy
The Use of Force Short of War
Edited by Melanie W. Sisson, James A. Siebens, and Barry M. Bleachman

Expanding US Military Command in Africa
Elites, Networks and Grand Strategy
Edited by Tshepo Gwatiwa and Justin van der Merwe

Nuclear Weapons Free Zones
A Comparative Perspective
Exequiel Lacovsky

Renegotiating the Nuclear Order
A Sociological Approach
Tarja Cronberg

The Treaty Prohibiting Nuclear Weapons
How it was Achieved and Why it Matters
Alexander Kmentt

For more information about this series, please visit: www.routledge.com/Routledge-Global-Security-Studies/book-series/RGSS

The Treaty Prohibiting Nuclear Weapons

How it was Achieved and Why it Matters

Alexander Kmentt

Routledge
Taylor & Francis Group
LONDON AND NEW YORK

First published 2021
by Routledge
2 Park Square, Milton Park, Abingdon, Oxon OX14 4RN

and by Routledge
52 Vanderbilt Avenue, New York, NY 10017

Routledge is an imprint of the Taylor & Francis Group, an informa business

© 2021 Alexander Kmentt

The right of Alexander Kmentt to be identified as author of this work has been asserted by him in accordance with sections 77 and 78 of the Copyright, Designs and Patents Act 1988.

All rights reserved. No part of this book may be reprinted or reproduced or utilised in any form or by any electronic, mechanical, or other means, now known or hereafter invented, including photocopying and recording, or in any information storage or retrieval system, without permission in writing from the publishers.

Trademark notice: Product or corporate names may be trademarks or registered trademarks, and are used only for identification and explanation without intent to infringe.

British Library Cataloguing-in-Publication Data
A catalogue record for this book is available from the British Library

Library of Congress Cataloging-in-Publication Data
A catalog record for this book has been requested

ISBN: 978-0-367-53194-2 (hbk)
ISBN: 978-0-367-53195-9 (pbk)
ISBN: 978-1-003-08087-9 (ebk)

Typeset in Times New Roman
by Apex CoVantage, LLC

For Rebecca

Contents

Acknowledgements ix
List of abbreviations xi

Introduction 1

PART I
The Humanitarian Initiative: 2010–2017: building momentum 7

1 The origins of the "Humanitarian Initiative" 9
2 The game needs to change 27
3 2015: the momentum gathers 52

PART II
The ban treaty is coming 87

4 2016: achieving a negotiation mandate 89
5 2017: negotiating the TPNW 110

PART III
The contest of arguments 139

6 Human security, empowerment and challenging the nuclear status quo 141
7 Countering the humanitarian initiative and the ban 155

PART IV
TPNW impact and outlook   185

8   What does the TPNW represent and what is its impact?   187

   Post scriptum: some final thoughts on constructive engagement and bridge building . . .   221

   Annex I Austrian Pledge   224
   Annex II Text of the Treaty on the Prohibition of Nuclear Weapons   227
   Index   237

Acknowledgements

I am privileged to work as a diplomat in an area that is as fascinating and of such truly fundamental importance as nuclear disarmament, arms control and non-proliferation. Through my work in the Austrian Foreign Ministry, I feel I have been able to make a contribution to solving the nuclear weapons issue. This is what the Humanitarian Initiative and the Treaty on the Prohibition of Nuclear Weapons are all about. In 2019, I was granted a leave of absence from the Austrian Foreign Ministry to take up a senior visiting research fellowship at King's College London, for which I am grateful. The time away from active diplomacy allowed me to write this book and record the history of the Humanitarian Initiative and the Treaty on the Prohibition of Nuclear Weapons.

My research fellowship at King's College London and hence the work on this book has been made possible with generous funding from the Carnegie Corporation New York. I received additional generous financial support for this book and a series of workshops from the Friedrich Ebert Foundation, Federal Republic of Germany. I am grateful for additional generous funding provided to me by the Austrian Red Cross. Through the kind recommendation of Kazumi Matsui, Major of the City of Hiroshima, I received further generous funding from Mr. Koji Matsuo, Chairperson of the NPO Music brings Peace and Counselor of Calbee, Inc. I am honoured by the confidence that these funding institutions have placed in me.

I am grateful for the permissions to use epigrams that were granted by Taylor & Francis, the Norwegian Academy of International Law (NAIL), the Friedrich-Ebert-Stiftung (FES), the International Campaign for the Abolition of Nuclear Weapons (ICAN), as well as from Lord Browne of Ladyton, Ambassador Jorge Lomonaco and Richard Lennane. I would also like to thank the Historical Archive of the Government of Norway.

I am indebted to a great number of people with whom I have cooperated closely. Behind the Humanitarian Initiative and the process leading to the TPNW are many remarkable individuals and personal relationships; too many to list all by name but my thanks goes to all of them.

I must, however, acknowledge my colleagues at the Austrian Foreign Ministry with whom I had the pleasure of working on this issue. Like myself, they are inspired by the opportunity to be able to make an important contribution to the goal of achieving a world without nuclear weapons. Their commitment, enthusiasm and effort are exceptional. In addition to Thomas Hajnoczi, former Austrian ambassador to Geneva, my successor as Director at the Disarmament Department at the Foreign Ministry in Vienna and whose contribution to the TPNW was pivotal, I would like to thank George-Willhelm Gallhofer, Robert Gerschner, Susanne Hammer, Jessica Herz, Jan Kickert, Hartmut Koller, Martin Krueger, Franz-Josef Kuglitsch, Alexander Marschik, Julia Peitl (now Eberl), Georg Pöstinger, Karl Prummer, Philine Scherer-Dressler, Nadja Schmid, Christian, Strohal, Ronald Sturm, Caroline Wörgötter and Thomas Zehetner.

My gratitude also goes to the following persons who either agreed to be interviewed for the book or helped me with their valuable advice. These are: Ray Acheson, John Borrie, Lyndon Burford, Tim Caugley, Jean Marie Collin, Michiel Combrink, Kjølv Egeland, Beatrice Fihn, Torbjørn Graff Hugo, Peter Herby, Dell Higgie, Daniel Högsta, the late Michael Hurley, María Antonieta Socorro Jáquez Huacuja, Rebecca Johnson, Daryl Kimball, Steffen Kongstad, Alfredo Labbé, Kathleen Lawand, Richard Lennane, Patricia Lewis, Jorge Lomónaco Tonda, Magnus Lovold, Lou Maresca, Thomas Markram, Zia Mian, Richard Moyes, Gaukhar Mukhatzhanova, Breifne O'Reilly, Grethe Østern, Guilherme de Aguiar Patriota, Benoît Pelopidas, Tariq Rauf, Nick Ritchie, Tilman Ruff, Michael Spies, Beyza Unal, Heather Williams, Ward Wilson, Elayne Whyte Gómez, Reto Wollenmann, Tim Wright, as well as a number of additional individuals who were interviewed for this book but prefer not to be named.

Disarmament diplomacy has dominated my professional life for the last 20 years, frequently taking me away from home and family for extended periods of time. This is only possible through the constant support, advice, patience, encouragement and considerable sacrifice of my wife Rebecca. I am very fortunate and grateful to her.

Abbreviations

ABM	Treaty Anti-Ballistic Missiles Treaty
APM	Convention Anti-Personnel Mine Ban Convention
ASEAN	Association of Southeast Asian Nations
BTWC	Biological Toxin Weapons Convention
BML	Broadly Likeminded Group
CARICOM	Caribbean Community
CCM	Cluster Munitions Convention
CELAC	Community of Latin American and Caribbean States
CEND	Creating an Environment for Nuclear Disarmament
CCW	Certain Conventional Weapons Convention
CSTO	Collective Security Treaty Organization
CTBT	Comprehensive Nuclear Test-Ban Treaty
CWC	Chemical Weapons Convention
FMCT	Fissile Material Cut-Off Treaty
IAEA	International Atomic Energy Agency
ICAN	International Campaign for the Abolition of Nuclear Weapons
ICBMs	Intercontinental Ballistic Missiles
ICRC	International Committee of the Red Cross
IHL	International Humanitarian Law
ILPI	International Law and Policy Institute
INF Treaty	Intermediate-Range Nuclear Forces Treaty
IPPNW	International Physicians for the Prevention of Nuclear War
JCPOA	Joint Comprehensive Program of Action
MAD	Mutually Assured Destruction
NAC	New Agenda Coalition
NAM	Non-Aligned Movement
NATO	North Atlantic Treaty Organization
NGO	Non-Governmental Organisation
NPDI	Non-Proliferation and Disarmament Initiative
NPT	Nuclear Non-Proliferation Treaty
NSG	Nuclear Suppliers Group
NWC	Nuclear Weapons Convention
NWS	Nuclear Weapon State

OEWG	Open-Ended Working Group
OPANAL	Agency for the Prohibition of Nuclear Weapons in Latin America and the Caribbean
PAROS	Prevention of an Arms Race in Outer Space
SSOD	Special Session on Disarmament of the United Nations General Assembly
START	Strategic Arms Reduction Treaty
SLBMs	Submarine-Launched Ballistic Missiles
TPNW	Treaty on the Prohibition of Nuclear Weapons
UK	United Kingdom
UN	United Nations
UNDP	United Nations Development Program
UNIDIR	United Nations Institute for Disarmament Research
US	United States of America
WEOG	Western European and Others Group
WILPF	Women's International League for Peace and Freedom
WMD	Weapons of Mass Destruction

Introduction

On 7 July 2017, 122 of the 193 member States of the United Nations (UN) adopted the Treaty on the Prohibition of Nuclear Weapons (TPNW). On 24 October 2020, the TPNW achieved its 50th ratification, triggering the conditions for the entry into force on 22 January 2021. The treaty was the result of the determined and at times, audacious, diplomatic effort of a group of States acting in concert and cooperation with disarmament academics and civil society organisations. The TPNW prohibits the only weapon of mass destruction not yet subject to a comprehensive prohibition under international law.[1]

The very first resolution adopted by the newly formed United Nations (UN) General Assembly in 1946 called "for the elimination from national armaments of atomic weapons and all other major weapons adaptable to mass destruction".[2] The process that resulted in the TPNW must be understood as a continuation of the 75 year struggle to deal with these problems. Apart from a short period in the immediate aftermath of the Cold War and despite promises made by the five nuclear weapons states[3] recognised under the Nuclear Non-Proliferation Treaty (NPT),[4] progress on nuclear disarmament up to this point, has been limited. The process built on long-standing efforts in multilateral diplomacy and numerous initiatives on the part of States and nuclear disarmament advocacy groups to extract more concrete actions and commitments from those few States that possess nuclear weapons and to persuade them to reconsider a security system that is based on nuclear deterrence.[5]

Around the year 2010, a small group of leading disarmament diplomats, academics and NGO experts began to devise a way to re-frame the discourse on nuclear weapons by focussing on the humanitarian impact of a nuclear weapon explosion. Through a variety of new and coordinated initiatives, they planned to challenge orthodox security thinking, break through the paralysis that existed in multilateral disarmament fora and create a strong sense of urgency for nuclear disarmament. Collectively, this approach became known as the "Humanitarian Initiative" and did indeed generate remarkable momentum. Just seven years later, the Humanitarian Initiative convinced the majority of the world's States to back a UN Mandate to negotiate a treaty to prohibit nuclear weapons. The treaty rejects nuclear deterrence as a foundation for our shared security and poses the most significant challenge to the legitimacy of the nuclear status quo[6] to date.

The TPNW was heralded as a historic achievement and a triumph of multilateralism and a sign of hope that an unequivocal prohibition of nuclear weapons would pave the way for the elimination of nuclear weapons. The International Campaign for the Abolition of Nuclear Weapons (ICAN) received the 2017 Nobel Peace Prize for its efforts to achieve this treaty. Reactions from the five nuclear weapon States and their allies however, ranged from dismissal of the new treaty to attempts to vilify it with claims that a prohibition of nuclear weapons "would risk ... plunging the world into chaos".[7]

The question of how to deal with nuclear weapons has indeed been one of the most contested and vexed global issues since the dawn of the nuclear age in 1945. Are nuclear weapons crucial to preserving peace and stability or are they morally unacceptable, placing the future of humanity in an unacceptable and uncontrollable level of jeopardy? Are nuclear weapons a *necessary* evil or are they the *ultimate* evil?

There are strongly held beliefs on both sides of the argument. For some, a world without nuclear weapons is only conceivable in a future security environment where they are no longer considered necessary. For others, nuclear disarmament is an urgent priority and any alleged security benefit for possessor States is far outweighed by the risks and dangers that these weapons and the practice of nuclear deterrence have for the security of all. Deterrence believers and disarmament supporters, *realists* and *idealists*, nuclear weapon States and non-nuclear weapons States, have exchanged arguments for decades. These arguments have dominated the relevant discourse in the UN and in the framework of the international treaties developed to address the nuclear weapons challenge, most notably the NPT. While nuclear weapons have always been the subject of strongly held views, the Humanitarian Initiative and the TPNW have brought the divide in the international community into even sharper focus.

Parts I and II of this book function as a history of the Humanitarian Initiative and the process leading to the TPNW. These sections also serve as a guide to all those interested in diplomatic tradecraft, as they reveal how a policy objective was successfully pursued against the determined opposition of the most powerful military States in the world. The history of the Humanitarian Initiative shows how unlikely shifts in international relations can be brought about through the strategy and close cooperation of a small group of committed States, academia and civil society organisations. This history details how this group developed policy objectives, pursued and promoted them, all the time steadily building support and gaining momentum. The process of building political momentum for and the subsequent negotiation of the TPNW is a remarkable chapter in diplomatic nuclear history and, more broadly, of international relations.

Re-framing the nuclear weapons discourse[8] to focus on the humanitarian consequences and risks based on new research and a better understanding of their interplay was the plan. The result was a strong set of arguments and questions challenging the veracity of current nuclear weapons policies and the legality and the legitimacy of a security system based on nuclear deterrence. The traditional "state-centred" security focus with which nuclear armed States dominate the nuclear weapons debate in existing multilateral fora was thus challenged to consider a global human security perspective.

Against the apparent unwillingness or inability of nuclear weapon States to take credible steps towards nuclear disarmament, these human security arguments generated an unexpectedly strong momentum. Rather than continue to demand disarmament from States that possess nuclear weapons, establishing an unequivocal legal norm that prohibits nuclear weapons emerged as a viable and concrete action for the non-nuclear weapon States. They felt compelled and able to pursue this themselves, without the support or participation of nuclear weapon States, and in the face of their very strong opposition.

Parts III and IV of this book analyse the various challenges to the established nuclear order that are the result of these developments. Chapters 6 and 7 look at the contest of arguments between the proponents and opponents of the TPNW. They examine why the human security approach was successful in generating momentum for the TPNW and how the opponents of the TPNW tried to derail this process. In Chapter 7, the arguments of the opponents of the TPNW are closely scrutinized as to their validity and their impact.

Since the TPNW was adopted, the overall picture with regard to nuclear weapons has not improved. On the contrary. The "return of geopolitics"[9] sees a deterioration of relations between NATO and Russia, the increasing competition between the US and China, and a number of regional tensions and conflicts involving nuclear armed States. North Korea's nuclear weapons and missiles program continues to grow, and following the US withdrawal in 2018, the nuclear agreement forged with Iran in 2015[10] is, at the time of writing, on the verge of collapse. Today we see a stronger focus on nuclear weapons and nuclear deterrence than at arguably any point since the Cold War. There is an increase in the use of dangerous nuclear rhetoric.[11] In all nuclear armed States, nuclear arsenals are being modernised and new nuclear weapons and related delivery systems are being developed. A new nuclear arms race is already underway.

What is then the impact of the TPNW and the human security approach on nuclear disarmament? Is it a determined but ultimately unsuccessful attempt to counter these above-mentioned developments or will it play a transformational role in bringing about a world without nuclear weapons? While the longer-term impact of the TPNW will only be determined over time, Chapter 8 discusses the significant influence that can already be discerned from these initiatives. The chapter also assesses the extent to which the Humanitarian Initiative and the TPNW have moved the dial on the nuclear weapons discourse and the opportunities for transformational change that could be the result. Finally, this chapter considers the possible longer-term impacts on the nuclear weapons regime and the overall prospects for multilateralism in this field.

A post scriptum offers some suggestions for both sides to engage constructively, should bridge-building efforts be undertaken in earnest.

The story of the Humanitarian Initiative and the TPNW is one of cooperation and partnership between States, academia, and civil society organizations. Without ICAN's advocacy there would be no TPNW, as rightly recognized by the 2017

Nobel Peace Prize. Similarly, without a small group of committed States pushing the humanitarian arguments and devising a number of diplomatic initiatives to generate momentum, the TPNW would also not have materialized. These efforts were informed and enhanced by contacts and discussions between individual diplomats, activists and experts over many years, and reflected in some cases, networks of trust developed in other previous humanitarian disarmament initiatives. The TPNW succeeded because both individual States and NGOs utilised their available resources and pathways to enact change. On complex and contested issues, diplomatic breakthroughs often occur when there is a convergence between the policies of States or a group of States and the actions of "outside voices" from civil society. The Humanitarian Initiative and the TPNW are a case in point, where such convergence and cooperation led to a remarkable result.

The history of the Humanitarian Initiative and the TPNW has already been examined from the perspective of civil society actors who focus on how ICAN devised an effective campaign to mobilise State support for the TPNW.[12] The role of civil society organizations, in particular ICAN, the International Red Cross and Red Crescent Movement, as well as academia and other experts was pivotal in this process. The role of the States that enacted the TPNW has thus far been underrepresented. This book focusses on the perspectives and motivations of State actors and is intended to provide a complement and counterpoint to civil society perspectives.

I am an Austrian diplomat, and this book reflects the motivations and actions taken in the name of that country. It is evident that Austria would support any legitimate means to generate momentum for progress on nuclear disarmament as it enjoys such long-standing political consensus on this issue. Austria has been deeply involved in other previous humanitarian disarmament[13] initiatives, and it was one of the leading States at the forefront of the Humanitarian Initiative and the TPNW process.

The book inevitably has a somewhat subjective perspective. From its outset, I was closely involved in the Humanitarian Initiative. I was responsible for the 2014 Vienna Conference on the Humanitarian Impact of Nuclear Weapons, devised and wrote the "Austrian Pledge" and led the Austrian delegation at the 2015 NPT Review Conference. I was also closely involved in the various UN General Assembly initiatives, such as the 2013 open-ended working group and the four resolutions delivered at the 2015 First Committee of the UN General Assembly. These anchored the Humanitarian Initiative within the UN framework and established the TPNW negotiations as a UN General Assembly mandated process.

As such, this history is written by someone centrally involved in the events it describes. It makes very extensive use of others' first-hand accounts as well as valuable, internal primary source material. The important role played by other individuals is, however, not described in this book, owing to the very contentious nature of the debate and the, in part, hostile reactions to the TPNW. Others might disagree with certain aspects of my characterization of events, but these are my recollections of the Humanitarian Initiative and TPNW. I hope they will inform the historical narrative and attempts to analyse what these "mean" in terms of lessons learned for the future formation of international law and policy.

At a human level, the events described in this book involve individual diplomats, civil society representatives and academic experts who found common cause and worked together constructively. The importance of the issue and the sense of purpose forged many lasting personal and professional relationships. These relationships and networks of cooperation between different actors proved essential. Throughout, I was struck by an impressive level of commitment, at times this came at considerable personal and professional risk.

Notes

1 Biological and chemical weapons are subject to comprehensive legally binding prohibitions in the 1972 Biological Toxin Weapons Convention (BTWC) and the 1990 Chemical Weapons Convention (CCW) respectively. For more information see "United Nations Office for Disarmament Affairs", available at www.un.org/disarmament/wmd/.
2 The very first General Assembly resolution, entitled, "Establishment of a Commission to Deal with the Problems Raised by the Discovery of Atomic Energy", was adopted on 24 January 1946 in London, available at https://undocs.org/en/A/RES/1(I).
3 "Nuclear weapons States" refers to China, France, Russia, the UK and the US who had developed nuclear weapons prior to the Nuclear Non-Proliferation Treaty (NPT) and are recognized by the treaty as such. All other State parties to the NPT (Status 2020: 186) are non-nuclear weapon States. India, Israel and Pakistan are nuclear weapons possessors outside of the NPT. North Korea has withdrawn from the NPT in 2003. The legality of this withdrawal is, however, not recognized.
4 Under the 1970 Treaty on the Non-Proliferation of Nuclear Weapons (NPT), the five nuclear weapon States agree to not transfer nuclear weapons and, under Article VI, to "Pursue Negotiations in Good Faith on Effective Measures Relating to Cessation of the Nuclear Arms Race at an Early Date and to Nuclear Disarmament". The non-nuclear weapon States agree not to develop these weapons and, in exchange, are given access to nuclear energy for civilian applications; for information on the NPT see "United Nations Office for Disarmament Affairs", available at www.un.org/disarmament/wmd/nuclear/npt.
5 For a history of the nuclear disarmament movement since 1945, see for example Lawrence S. Wittner, *Confronting the Bomb: A Short History of the World Nuclear Disarmament Movement*, Stanford University Press, 2009.
6 Nick Ritchie, *The Real "Problem with the Ban Treaty? It Challenges the Status Quo"*, Carnegie Endowment for International Peace, 3 April 2017.
7 Statement by Russia at the First Committee of the UN General Assembly on 3 October 2016; see also Chapter 7.
8 See for example John Borrie, "Humanitarian Reframing of Nuclear Weapons and the Logic of a Ban", in *International Affairs*, vol. 90, no. 3, May 2014, pp. 625–646, https://doi.org/10.1111/1468-2346.12130; see also Nick Ritchie, "Waiting for Kant: Devaluing and Delegitimizing Nuclear Weapons", in *International Affairs (Royal Institute of International Affairs 1944)*, vol. 90, no. 3, 2014, pp. 601–623, available at https://doi.org/10.1111/1468-2346.12129.
9 See for example Walter Russell Mead, "The Return of Geopolitics – The Revenge of the Revisionist Powers", in *Foreign Affairs*, May–June 2014, available at www.foreignaffairs.com/articles/china/2014-04-17/return-geopolitics.

10 The 14 July 2015 agreement between Iran and the E3/EU+3 on a Joint Comprehensive Plan of Action (JCPOA). The US announced its withdrawal from the JCPOA on 8 May 2018.
11 For a collection of such incidents between 2015–2019 involving US/NATO, Russia, Israel, North Korea, India and Pakistan, see "Nuclear Weapons Ban Monitor: Tracking Progress Towards a World Free of Nuclear Weapons", p. 22, available at https://banmonitor.org/.
12 For a comprehensive account on ICAN's role in bringing about the TPNW, see for example Ray Acheson, *Banning the Bomb, Smashing the Patriarchy*, Rowman & Littlefield Publishers, March 2021, forthcoming.
13 See Chapter 1.

Part I
The Humanitarian Initiative
2010–2017: building momentum

Part I

The Humanitarian Initiative

2010–2017: building momentum

1 The origins of the "Humanitarian Initiative"

"We cannot leave it to the nuclear weapon states alone to decide when it is time for them to do away with these weapons. Their destructive power would affect us all, if put to use – and their threat continues to affect us all – therefore they are everyone's business".[1]

Nuclear disarmament: a bleak picture

The final years of the Cold War and its immediate aftermath are sometimes referred to as the "golden age of nuclear arms control".[2] This period commenced with a nuclear détente between Ronald Reagan and Mikhail Gorbachev at the 1986 Reykjavík Summit and their joint statement in 1987 that "a nuclear war cannot be won and must never be fought".[3] The following years saw the conclusion of landmark nuclear weapons related agreements, both bi-lateral between the US and the Soviet Union/Russian Federation and multilateral.[4] In these years, it was hoped that the previous four decades of initiatives and efforts on the part of the international community, driven largely by non-aligned[5] States and activist campaigns to rid the world of nuclear weapons, would become a reality. By 2000, however, this golden age had already ended, and the new millennium ushered in a very challenging period for multilateral disarmament, arms control and non-proliferation efforts. Seemingly unbridgeable differences between those States that possess nuclear weapons emerged and multilateral nuclear disarmament, arms control and non-proliferation efforts came to a halt. From 1997 onwards, the Geneva-based Conference on Disarmament,[6] whose mandate is to negotiate multilateral treaties, was unable to agree on a programme of work.

In the spring of 2000, the Non-Proliferation Treaty (NPT) Review Conference appeared to inject some much-needed energy. The State parties agreed on a Final Document containing "thirteen practical steps for the systematic and progressive efforts to implement the disarmament obligation of Article VI of the NPT".[7] These steps included strong multilateral commitments to achieve the early entry into force of the Comprehensive Nuclear Test Ban Treaty (CTBT), a commitment to negotiations of a Treaty prohibiting the production of fissile material for nuclear weapons (FMCT) and a commitment to establish a forum in the Conference on Disarmament to deal with nuclear disarmament. The nuclear weapon States agreed to a number of specific commitments and steps towards nuclear disarmament and, importantly, to an "unequivocal undertaking . . . to accomplish the total elimination of their nuclear arsenals leading to nuclear disarmament, to which all States parties are committed under article VI".[8]

As part of a package to extend the NPT indefinitely beyond its original 25-year lifespan,[9] general nuclear disarmament principles were agreed upon at the NPT 1995 Review and Extension Conference. The NPT Review Conference in 2000 concretised them. Shortly afterwards, the Russian Federation ratified the CTBT and during the First Committee of the United National (UN) General Assembly in Autumn 2000 and in the Conference on Disarmament, many States expressed a hope that significant progress on nuclear disarmament would follow.

This optimism was short-lived. George W. Bush came into office in January 2001 and his neoconservative administration soon signalled a unilateralist approach to arms control: they viewed arms control as a concept, particularly in multilateral settings, with scepticism and often with open disdain. For neoconservatives, it was, in the words of John Bolton who served in the administration as Undersecretary of State for Arms Control and International Security, a "refuge for those who are uncomfortable with American Power or who are seeking to restrain U.S. power"[10] and not an effective means to address security issues but, "a tired, threadbare, legacy of the Cold War".[11] The inclusion of "rogue states"[12] in the negotiations of multilateral agreements "made them weak, or flawed or ineffectual".[13] In short, arms control was considered as "impossible when it would be important, but unimportant when it is possible".[14]

The new US administration announced that it would not submit the CTBT to the Senate for ratification, as it epitomized the ineffective and outdated approach of the "wider congregation of arms control True Believers" and "CTBT candle-lighters".[15] It would not support negotiations on an FMCT and would not be bound by the thirteen practical steps.[16] In December 2001, the US withdrew from the 1972 Anti-Ballistic Missile Treaty (ABM Treaty), in clear contravention of the 2000 NPT Review Conference Final Document.[17] In the same month, in a move that further demonstrated its approach to multilateral disarmament, arms control and non-proliferation efforts, the US forced the end of a seven-year negotiation process for a verification regime to the 1972 Biological and Toxin Weapons Convention (BWC).

With the 2003 US invasion of Iraq and its justification to prevent Iraq's possession of weapons of mass destruction, the US focus had shifted to "counter proliferation". In the same year, North Korea withdrew from the NPT and an undeclared nuclear program in Iran was revealed, putting further pressure on the NPT. Not surprisingly, the 2005 NPT Review Conference ended in acrimony and without consensus or any semblance of agreement on nuclear disarmament or the continued support of the *thirteen practical steps*. The US (and to a less visible degree, France) refused to accept them as a basis for the proceedings during the Conference.[18]

The "inalienable right for nuclear energy for peaceful purposes", enshrined in Article IV of the NPT[19] has always been considered a key element of the NPT's "grand bargain", whereby non-nuclear weapon States forgo a nuclear weapons capability in exchange for access to nuclear energy for civilian applications and the promise of nuclear disarmament by the nuclear weapon States. In July 2005, the US dealt another major blow to the credibility of the NPT regime by negotiating a "US-India Nuclear Agreement",[20] subsequently pushing through an exemption for India from the stringent nuclear export controls guidelines of the Nuclear Suppliers Group.[21] The exemption gave India access to civil nuclear cooperation, despite the fact that it was not a member of the NPT. In the eyes of many of the NPT non-nuclear weapons States, the US had *de facto* recognized India as a nuclear weapon State and rewarded India for having stayed outside the NPT.

For supporters of nuclear disarmament, the bleak outlook continued. In October 2006, North Korea conducted their first nuclear test explosion. While this highlighted the urgency for a norm against nuclear testing, the road to CTBT entry into force remained blocked, mainly due to the continued negative US stance. The revelations about the Iranian nuclear program demonstrated that it is very difficult to differentiate between peaceful nuclear uses, allowed under Article IV of the NPT, and military applications of nuclear energy and technology, that are prohibited under Article II.[22] From 2006 onwards, increasing pressure was brought to bear against Iran, through UN Security Council Resolutions and the imposition of severe sanctions,[23] to which Iran reacted with threats to withdraw from the NPT.[24] To this day, the Iranian nuclear issue continues to reveal the "double-standard" that is built into the NPT regime and the irony has not gone unnoticed that the E3/EU plus 3 States[25] who have led the non-proliferation efforts against Iran all "rely" on nuclear weapons for their own security, while insisting on their unacceptability for other States.[26] Iran has managed to use this "double standard" argument to obtain a degree of "protection" in multilateral meetings from fellow non-aligned States.[27]

All through this period, the stalemate in the Conference on Disarmament continued unchanged with a ritualistic annual meeting schedule but without the necessary consensus on a programme of work to actually initiate any negotiations. Owing to the lack of political will on the part of the main protagonists, the different strategic interests of nuclear weapons possessors, and also to the stringent rules of procedure of this forum, requiring consensus on all decisions, no negotiations took place on any topic on the agenda.

By 2008, the state of health of multilateralism in the field of nuclear disarmament, arms control and non-proliferation was bleak. The NPT was challenged on all fronts: on proliferation by the North Korean and Iranian nuclear programs, on its "grand bargain" on peaceful uses of nuclear energy by the India exemption and, most evidently, on nuclear disarmament with the lack of implementation of Article VI and the "disowning" of the thirteen practical steps of the 2000 NPT Review Conference by some nuclear weapon States. The multilateral fora, most notably the Conference on Disarmament, were blocked and dysfunctional. The legitimacy and credibility of both the existing multilateral instruments and institutions was being dangerously undermined. The "end of arms control",[28] which John Bolton declared a policy objective, seemed on the verge of becoming reality.

For non-nuclear weapons states, eager to see multilateral progress in this field, the concern and the frustration about the status quo increased and, with it, discussions on how and when forward movement could be possible.

Initially, the focus of these discussions was on the Conference on Disarmament itself and on finding ways to overcome the stalemate. Various attempts,[29] all ultimately futile, were made to balance the different political priorities of its member States on the "four core issues"[30] on the Conference on Disarmament agenda, to enable the adoption of a programme of work.

At the First Committee of the UN General Assembly in 2005, six countries, Brazil, Canada, Kenya, Mexico, New Zealand, and Sweden, presented a proposal[31] to establish four so-called "open-ended ad-hoc committees" on the "four core issues".[32] The Conference on Disarmament requires consensus; these committees would operate under the rules of procedure of the UN General Assembly and therefore not require consensus. There was some support for this circumventory move but also strong opposition from the nuclear weapon States[33] as well as from some non-aligned States, who opposed what they saw as a challenge to the established UN "disarmament machinery".[34] Although the draft resolution was not tabled for adoption by the First Committee, it "caused a stir and demonstrated creative problem solving to address the deadlock in the CD".[35] This innovative method of circumventing "veto-dynamics" through the more flexible UN General Assembly rules of procedure would be taken up again in 2011, playing a crucial role in the context of what became known as the "Humanitarian Initiative"[36] and the subsequent TPNW negotiations.

The humanitarian disarmament approach

Amidst this gloomy picture in the nuclear disarmament, arms control and non-proliferation fields, there were some successes. From the mid-1990s, in parallel with the emergence of the concept of *human security*,[37] the suffering caused by specific weapons systems received increased international attention.[38] The terrible impact of antipersonnel landmines on civilians and especially children, sometimes even decades after the end of armed conflicts, became widely known. In 1997, the Anti-Personnel Mine Ban Convention[39] (APM Convention) resulted in a comprehensive prohibition of these weapons on humanitarian grounds. This successful campaign was, to a large extent, the result of issue framing and advocacy of the International Campaign to Ban Landmines (ICBL) coordinated by Jody Williams, the International Committee of the Red Cross (ICRC), and field-based humanitarian organizations. The interest and involvement of prominent personalities, especially Diana Princess of Wales, also helped to draw public and political attention. Together, they highlighted these humanitarian concerns and worked closely with States committed to promoting the concept of human security in order to prohibit these weapons, including many States that were affected by the scourge of landmines.

The APM Convention was pursued through what became known as the "Ottawa-Process",[40] named after the city where the negotiation process was launched. While the major landmine producers, such as the US,[41] Russia, China, India and Pakistan[42] did not participate, there was a clear conviction on the part of the majority of States, and especially mine-affected States, that a complete prohibition was necessary. Prior to the negotiations of the APM Convention, the antipersonnel landmine issue had been on the agenda of the Conference on Disarmament without achieving agreement on negotiations. The issue was also addressed in the context of the Convention on Certain Conventional Weapons (CCW) where a protocol on the use of landmines[43] was negotiated in 1996. This, however, did not result in a full prohibition of these weapons, owing to the resistance of the major military powers.

The APM Convention can be considered the initiator of the humanitarian disarmament approach. It effectively harnessed a so-called humanitarian approach to a disarmament issue by emphasising the human suffering and environmental harm caused by certain classes of weapons and seeking to remediate and prevent it through the establishment of international legal norms.[44] In the case of landmines, a human-centred and "effects-based" assessment of the impact of these weapons on civilian populations, prevailed over military utility considerations.[45]

The work of implementing the APM Convention started after its entry into force in 1999. The contrast between the progress on landmines with the stasis in the nuclear weapons field and the procedural and/or political problems that plagued the Conference on Disarmament could not have been greater. The APM Convention was a "beacon of light",[46] a multilateral disarmament process where tangible progress was made. "Ottawa" was an "ideal-typical" process for those States who wanted to show how multilateralism and international cooperation can work. Several of the States that played a pivotal role in bringing about the APM Convention, later promoted the focus on the humanitarian consequences of nuclear weapons, among them Austria, Ireland, Mexico, Norway, South Africa and Switzerland.

The tension between a humanitarian "effects-based" approach, promoted by a varying number of small and medium sized States,[47] and the "military-utility" considerations of bigger military powers characterised the multilateral discussions and negotiations on conventional weapons in the subsequent years. With regard to the illicit trade of small arms and light weapons,[48] the negotiations on cluster munitions[49] and, to some extent, the 2013 Arms Trade Treaty,[50] the humanitarian disarmament approach was pursued by very similar coalitions of States and civil society actors. These processes refined the humanitarian disarmament approach and established precedents for close and successful cooperation between States and civil society actors, which was important in the context of the Humanitarian Initiative and the TPNW.

By 2010, a humanitarian approach had been applied successfully to different weapons categories. It was a tested approach that demonstrated that new, international legal norms can be established by focussing on the humanitarian consequences that weapons have, an effective outreach campaign and close collaboration between progressive governments, international humanitarian organisations and advocacy groups. In all cases, States had first tried to use the traditional multilateral fora for negotiations[51]; their consensus, hence veto-prone rules of procedure together with the strongly held view of the major military powers that disarmament should be primarily conditioned by "military utility" considerations, prevented substantive progress on these issues. As a result, this humanitarian approach, was pursued through independent – meaning outside the UN – negotiation processes. The downside of this is that not all States and, in particular, not all major military powers, participate. Nonetheless it resulted in strong legal norms based on humanitarian principles. It is hoped that a high legal standard will, in time, influence the behaviour of States that are not initially involved in these processes.

When US President Barack Obama took office in early 2009, expectations were high that the US would re-engage with the full range of multilateral disarmament, arms control and non-proliferation efforts. During his election campaign, Obama endorsed the most recent call for a world without nuclear weapons, published in an opinion piece for the *Wall Street Journal* by the bi-partisan, US security establishment grandees George Shultz, William Perry, Henry Kissinger and Sam Nunn.[52] For non-nuclear weapon States, President Obama's speech in Prague in April 2009[53] provided a much hoped for counterpoint to the Bush Administration. In this speech, President Obama put nuclear weapons back on the international agenda. He highlighted the danger that is inherent in the existence of nuclear weapons, rather than merely the danger of nuclear proliferation to "problematic countries" such as Iran or North Korea. Obama stated, "seeking peace and security of a world without nuclear weapons" as a clear political commitment of the United States, although he qualified that by saying "this goal will not be reached quickly – perhaps not in my lifetime". President Obama was clear in his message, that the consequences of the use of nuclear weapons would be devastating and a concern for all peoples. This progressive "Prague agenda", reclaiming a positive leadership role for the United States was well received by many non-nuclear States, hungry for overdue, positive movement on nuclear disarmament.[54] The subsequent summit-level meeting of the UN Security Council, adopting resolution 1887 (2009)[55] and the signature of the New Strategic Arms Reduction Treaty (New START) between Russia and the United States on 8 April 2010[56] furthered these expectations and provided a positive backdrop to the 2010 NPT Review Conference in May 2010.

The 2010 NPT Review Conference

Given Obama's commitment to a world without nuclear weapons, in the run-up to the NPT Review Conference of 2010, expectations on the part of non-nuclear weapons States were high. There was also a feeling that this would possibly be the last chance to bring credibility and urgency to the multilateral nuclear disarmament process.

Immediately before the 2010 NPT Review Conference, Jakob Kellenberger, President of the ICRC, addressed the diplomatic corps in Geneva, Switzerland. In this keynote address, he recalled the ICRC experience as the first international humanitarian organization present in the immediate aftermath of the bombing of Hiroshima in 1945. He highlighted the inadequate capacities to address the humanitarian emergencies that would result from any use of nuclear weapons and the human and societal destruction that would ensue. In light of the humanitarian consequences, Kellenberger reiterated the ICRC position that "the ICRC finds it difficult to envisage how any use of nuclear weapons could be compatible with the rules of international humanitarian law".[57] This speech by the President of the international organization recognised as the "guardian of international humanitarian law"[58] was intended as a contribution to the substantive discussions at the NPT Review Conference in May 2010. It turned out to be important and consequential for the Humanitarian Initiative.

On the final day of the 2010 NPT Review Conference and after four weeks of difficult negotiations, State parties agreed consensually on a "Final Document".[59] The fact that consensus on a substantive outcome was achieved was considered an important success in itself, especially after the acrimonious experience of the 2005 Review Conference. This had been a clear policy goal of the Obama administration.[60] The consensus did not extend to the full document. There was no agreement on the part of the document that reviewed the implementation of the NPT in the past five years. Consensus was reached on an action programme related to the longstanding issue of the establishment a Middle East zone, free of nuclear and all other weapons of mass destruction and their delivery systems.[61]

The other key consensus outcome contained in the Final Document was an "Action Plan" called "Conclusions and recommendations for follow-on actions". The "Action Plan" was preceded by a set of principles and objectives, the fifth of which states that

> The Conference expresses its deep concern at the catastrophic humanitarian consequences of any use of nuclear weapons and reaffirms the need for all States at all times to comply with applicable international law, including international humanitarian law.[62]

This reference to the "humanitarian consequences of any use of nuclear weapons" was the first in an agreed NPT document, since the notion of the "devastation visited upon all mankind by a nuclear war"[63] was included in the Treaty's preambular paragraph 1 in 1968. This is interesting and surprising.

Arguably, all efforts to prevent the proliferation of nuclear weapons and to move towards nuclear disarmament can be interpreted as originating from the recognition that the devastation of nuclear war must be prevented. In the immediate aftermath of the use of atomic weapons in Japan in 1945, the immense destructive force of these weapons and the deeply disconcerting findings about the impact of radiation alarmed scientists[64] and civil society activists.[65] These humanitarian concerns were taken up predominantly by the Non-Aligned Movement[66] and by States in Nuclear Weapons-Free Zones that were established in the Southern Hemisphere.[67] In the past decades, several multilateral treaties addressing different weapon categories, among them chemical weapons, explicitly refer to the humanitarian consequences of their use as key motivations for the need to regulate them.[68] It is hard to imagine a weapon system where a humanitarian focus would be more pertinent than for nuclear weapons. As such, the 2010 NPT Review Conference agreement on a "principle" explicitly addressing the catastrophic humanitarian consequences of nuclear weapons, represented a significant opening.

The innocuous and somewhat self-evident language regarding the humanitarian consequences of nuclear weapons and international humanitarian law was originally proposed for inclusion into the Final Document by Switzerland, following the speech by the President of the Geneva-based ICRC. In the opening debate of the Conference, the Swiss Foreign Minister stated that "Switzerland's aim is to bring the humanitarian aspect to the heart of the current debate on nuclear disarmament".[69] Norway also promoted a stronger humanitarian focus[70] and was instrumental in placing the text as a "principle" at the beginning of the Action Plan. The President of the Review Conference, the Ambassador of the Philippines Libran Cabactulan, convened informal meetings of a small group of States in the final negotiation stage of the Conference to discuss possible "deal breakers" for the Final Document.[71] Norway's Ambassador Steffen Kongstad chaired these discussions and facilitated the inclusion of the text. He argued that it should be included as a key reason as to "why we are doing the Action Plan" and as an embodiment of a preventive approach to nuclear weapons use. The US and the nuclear weapon States were not supportive of including this humanitarian language. France was most vocally opposed, calling for its complete deletion. It was retained in the final text, and the nuclear weapon States accepted it in order not to endanger the consensus outcome.

In its Action 1 of the Action Plan, the Review Conference also resolved that "all States parties commit to pursue policies that are fully compatible with the Treaty and the objective of achieving a world without nuclear weapons". This appears to be another self-evident statement but it, too, represents a significant shift. Action 1 underscores the responsibility for implementing the Action Plan and *achieving a world without nuclear weapons* as shared between nuclear weapon States *and* non-nuclear weapon States. There are specific nuclear disarmament steps that obviously only the former can take. These include the reduction and the dismantling of weapons, changes in nuclear doctrines, transparency measures etc. Focusing on the humanitarian consequences of nuclear weapons, to generate momentum for nuclear disarmament was one concrete action that non-nuclear weapon States could pursue to support *achieving a world without nuclear weapons*.

The expression of deep concern regarding the "humanitarian consequences" contained in the fifth Action Plan principle, in conjunction with Action 1, thus, served as the *de facto* mandate for non-nuclear weapon States to pursue the Humanitarian Initiative as a means to implement NPT Article VI itself.

While there was some debate regarding the inclusion of the "humanitarian consequences" principle, it was by no means a focus of attention at the 2010 NPT Review Conference.[72] Arguably, the nuclear weapons States saw it as one of the textual concessions that are typical in the final bargaining and negotiation phase of documents that are agreed by consensus. In this case, the humanitarian text was accepted by nuclear weapon States as aspirational, something to satisfy those non-nuclear weapon States who wanted strong references to disarmament. In my view, nuclear weapon States did not at the time anticipate how this principle could and would be operationalised into a specific Humanitarian Initiative.

When measured against the high expectations for the 2010 Review Conference, it is however, questionable to what degree the Action Plan in its entirety represented a significant leap forward. Austrian Ambassador Alexander Marschik, chair Subsidiary Body I,[73] was tasked with the preparation of the Action Plan. His objective had been to achieve a strong document that included, to the extent possible, quantifiable, measurable and time-bound actions.[74] This was achieved only to a limited extent. With the exception of some transparency measures to which the nuclear weapon States agreed, the nuclear disarmament action items were partly a "re-packaging" of the *thirteen practical steps* agreed in 2000 and/or weakened by qualifying language. The more progressive proposals for devaluing and eliminating nuclear weapons put forward during the Conference by non-nuclear weapon States did not make it into the consensus recommendations, owing to opposition by one or more of the nuclear weapon states in the closed negotiations in the final week.[75] Despite the more positive public rhetoric, mainly from the US delegation, the nuclear weapon States presented a united front in their objections to too concrete and too forward-leaning commitments, thus, demonstrating that their approach towards nuclear disarmament had not changed fundamentally. As Harald Mueller, one of the most experienced observers of the NPT summarized:

> Altogether, the nuclear disarmament part of the document is characterised by weak language: what had appeared in the drafts and working papers as undertakings, commitments, with the conference ''urging' or 'calling upon', was in the end presented as a mere option, with the use of verbs such as 'encourage' and 'invite' dominating. All this hardly represents a decisive breakthrough for either nuclear disarmament or non-proliferation.[76]

NPT State parties generally expressed cautious satisfaction with the outcome of the Review Conference and relief about the fact that a consensus had been achieved.[77] It was clear however that the actual implementation of the vague "Action Plan" would be the real measure of success. The NPT disarmament process had, at best, been given some breathing space. In the words of Mueller:

> If the NPT community fails to use that opportunity, the erosion of the regime will return with a revenge . . . the result does not guarantee a sustainable future for the NPT. This needs the active effort of members from the centre of the Treaty.[78]

No progress on the 2010 NPT action plan

In the aftermath of the 2010 NPT Review Conference, two developments took place in parallel, both of which were essential precursors and conditions for the

Humanitarian Initiative. The first development was the active engagement on the part of non-nuclear weapon States to promote the implementation of the Action Plan and push for progress.

Initially, non-nuclear weapons States focussed their initiatives on the situation in the Conference on Disarmament. On 24 September 2010, a high-level meeting on "Revitalizing the Work of the Conference on Disarmament"[79] took place, convened by the UN Secretary General to draw political attention to the stalemate of this forum. By the end of the 2010 Session of the Conference on Disarmament in September, the "success" of the 2010 NPT Review Conference in May had not resulted in any positive movement in Geneva, as demanded by the Action Plan. This high-level meeting did not generate any new momentum or new ideas to move forward. In the following First Committee of the UN General Assembly in October 2010, Austria introduced a resolution requesting a follow-up to the high-level meeting[80] and suggested, with the support of 48 States, a plenary debate of the UN General Assembly on this issue.[81] While this debate in July 2011 did not produce a breakthrough for the Conference on Disarmament either, more and more States started to question whether negotiations would not be better pursued outside the Conference on Disarmament entirely. By the time of this plenary debate, yet another complete Session of the Conference on Disarmament was almost over, without progress. Hopes that the 2010 NPT outcome would bring about into tangible progress and confidence that any forward movement could be achieved within the Conference on Disarmament, were waning rapidly. A more proactive search for alternatives was getting underway.

In this period, Austria, Mexico and other States convened several informal discussions among non-nuclear weapon States[82] in Geneva and New York. They explored how an "operational resolution" from the UN General Assembly could be used to break the deadlock and get negotiations, in line with the 2010 NPT Action Plan, going. Among the ideas discussed was a resolution establishing a working group in Geneva on the FMCT, and a resolution with a mandate either for an expert conference to revitalize the disarmament machinery or for specific topics such as FMCT, negative security assurances[83] and on nuclear disarmament.

A more progressive idea was to return to that resolution first proposed in 2004/2005, whereby the UN General Assembly would establish multilateral disarmament negotiations on the "four core issues"[84] either "pending an agreement in the Conference on Disarmament" or without any link to the Conference. At the 2011 First Committee of the UN General Assembly, Austria, Mexico and Norway introduced such a draft resolution entitled "Taking forward multilateral disarmament negotiations". In the case where an agreement on a programme of work in the Conference on Disarmament could not be reached,[85] the resolution aimed to establish open-ended working groups "on priority issues of nuclear disarmament, encompassing, inter alia, nuclear disarmament and the achievement of a world without nuclear weapons". As had been the case with the similar attempt in 2005, there was fierce opposition to this resolution.

Nuclear weapon States objected that this "will not help resolve the political problems that underlie the deadlock of the CD", but rather, "will enable them to persist, while diluting the pressure to overcome them".[86] Opposition from some non-aligned States invoked the duplication of structures and a risk of undermining the Conference on Disarmament. The co-sponsors Austrian, Mexico and Norway announced that, rather than watering the text down in pursuit of acceptance, they preferred to preserve its integrity, not press for adoption at this year's session and return with the resolution in the following UN General Assembly session, which they did in autumn 2012.

The second development and precursor to the Humanitarian Initiative between 2010 and 2012 was the growing recognition that the 2010 Action Plan was not quite the success the non-nuclear weapon States had hoped it would be. Civil society organisations, primarily Reaching Critical Will and the James Martin Center for Nonproliferation Studies, produced comprehensive reports[87] monitoring the Action Plan's implementation progress. These were updated regularly. In this sense, the 2010 Action Plan proved its usefulness, albeit not as intended. As much as it had been hoped it would be a tool to monitor progress on nuclear disarmament, the detailed monitoring of the Action Plan provided clearer proof than ever before of the lack of progress and implementation.

By 2012, Gaukhar Mukhatzhanova's monitoring from the James Martin Center concluded that "our assessment of implementation indicates that the overall progress since 2010 has been very limited and even appears to have slowed down since the 2012 NPT Preparatory Commission". Reaching Critical Will observed that

> progress on the 22 Action Plan items dealing with nuclear disarmament was the most eagerly anticipated but has, perhaps, been the most disappointing for a number of reasons. . . . Consequently, while three of the five [nuclear weapon States] have made some moves to reduce their arsenals, overall progress on disarmament has been dismal.[88]

In addition to the ongoing inaction in the Conference on Disarmament, some of the policy and financial decisions by nuclear weapons States were particularly troubling. In order to get US Senate approval of the New START Treaty with Russia in December 2010, the Obama administration committed 85 billion USD to modernize the US nuclear weapons infrastructure.[89] These funds had initially been intended to "smoothen" the later ratification of the CTBT by the US Senate. By making the New START Treaty politically and financially so costly, the Republican opposition succeeded in taking the wind out of the "Prague agenda" before it had a chance to take off properly.[90] Ultimately, the Obama administration committed to spending over one trillion USD over the next 30 years[91] to update its entire nuclear weapons arsenal and infrastructure, and never put the CTBT forward for ratification. Although expenditures paled when compared to the US, by 2012 it was evident that all other states possessing nuclear weapons were also engaged in nuclear weapons modernization programs. Ray Acheson, Director of Reaching Critical Will, concluded that

> The US is not alone in the pursuit of a modernized nuclear arsenal. In fact, China, France, India, Israel, Pakistan, Russia, and the United Kingdom – all

states with nuclear weapons – are planning to, or already are, modernizing their nuclear warheads, delivery systems, or related infrastructure. Their modernization programs have serious implications for disarmament. By investing in the extension, upgrading, and reinforcement of their arsenals and capacities, these governments are actively investing in the future of nuclear weapons, not in the future of disarmament.[92]

This further exacerbated the credibility and trust deficit felt by non-nuclear weapon States. Was nuclear disarmament an urgent objective that was shared by all? Would the 2010 Action Plan also be left largely unfulfilled just as the promises made in the NPT Review Conferences in 1995 and 2000?[93] The loss of impetus to Obama's vision of a world without nuclear weapons, helped galvanize the disarmament-minded States and civil society towards a different type of process and a goal they could achieve without, if necessary, the involvement of the nuclear-armed states.[94]

The conditions for making the Humanitarian Initiative into something operational and actionable were created over several years but the failure of implementation of the 2010 NPT Action was clearly a catalyst. Firstly, by the increasing credibility and trust deficit regarding nuclear disarmament commitments and secondly, by a growing recognition that more innovative ways must be pursued to overcome the inertia in the existing fora.

Notes

1 Jonas Gahr Støre, "Foreign Minister of Norway, Statement at a Conference of the Norwegian Atlantic Committee", 1 February 2010, available at www.regjeringen.no/no/dokumentarkiv/stoltenberg-ii/ud/taler-og-artikler/2010/disarmament/id592550/.
2 Michael Krepon, "The Golden Age of Nuclear Arms Control", in *Arms Control Wonk*, 22 April 2019, available at www.armscontrolwonk.com/archive/1207168/the-golden-age-of-nuclear-arms-control/.
3 Joint Statement by Reagan and Gorbachev of 7–10 December 1987, available at www.reaganlibrary.gov.
4 Chief among them, the 1987 Intermediate-range Nuclear Forces Treaty (INF), the 1991 Strategic Arms Reduction Treaty (START I), the 1992 Treaty on Open Skies, the 1995 Indefinite Extension of the 1970 Nuclear Proliferation Treaty (NPT) and the 1996 Comprehensive Nuclear Test-Ban Treaty (CTBT).
5 The Non-Aligned Movement (NAM) position on nuclear disarmament was first formulated in the Final Communiqué of the Asian-African conference of Bandung of 24 April 1955, available at https://mnoal.org/.
6 For an introduction to Conference on Disarmament, see available at www.unog.ch/cd.
7 See "2000 Review Conference of the Parties to the Treaty on the Non-Proliferation of Nuclear Weapons Final Document", p. 14, available at www.un.org/disarmament/wmd/nuclear/npt2000/final-documents.
8 Ibid.
9 See NPT 1995 Review and Extension Conference, "Principles and Objectives for Nuclear Non-Proliferation and Disarmament", NPT/CONF.1995/32 (Part I), Annex Decision 2, available at https://unoda-web.s3-accelerate.amazonaws.com/wp-content/uploads/assets/WMD/Nuclear/1995-NPT/pdf/NPT_CONF199501.pdf.
10 John Bolton, "Arms Inspection and the Man", in *Weekly Standard*, 26 June 2000.

11 Stephen E. Miller, "Skepticism Triumphant: The Bush Administration and the Waning of Arms Control", in *Revue Internationale et Strategique*, vol. 51, no. 3, January 2003, p. 2, 13, available at https://doi.org/10.3917/ris.051.0013.
12 In a speech entitled "Beyond the Axis of Evil" on 6 May 2002, then Undersecretary of State John Bolton added Cuba, Libya and Syria to the "axis of evil" States, Iran, Iraq and North Korea that President George W. Bush had named in his State of the Union speech on 29 January 2002, available at https://georgewbush-whitehouse.archives.gov/stateoftheunion/2002/index.html.
13 Miller, "Skepticism Triumphant", p. 5.
14 Ibid.
15 John Bolton, *Surrender Is not an Option: Defending America at the United Nations and Abroad*, Threshold Editions, Simon and Schuster, 2007, p. 84.
16 See also Alexander Kmentt, "The CTBT: Has Its Time Come?", in *Obama and the Bomb: A Vision of a World Free of Nuclear Weapons*, Heinz Gaertner (ed.), Peter Lang Internationaler Verlag der Wissenschaften, pp. 71–88.
17 Step seven of the *thirteen steps*: "The Early Entry into Force and Full Implementation of START II and the Conclusion of START III as Soon as Possible While Preserving and Strengthening the Treaty on the Limitation of Anti-Ballistic Missile Systems as a Cornerstone of Strategic Stability and as a Basis for Further Reductions of Strategic Offensive Weapons, in Accordance with Its Provisions".
18 Harald Müller, "A Treaty in Troubled Waters", in *The International Spectator*, vol. 40, no. 3, p. 34, available at https://doi.org/10.1080/03932720508457135.
19 See NPT Article IV 1, "Nothing in This Treaty Shall Be Interpreted as Affecting the Inalienable Right of All the Parties to the Treaty to Develop Research, Production and Use of Nuclear Energy for Peaceful Purposes Without Discrimination and in Conformity with Articles I and II of This Treaty".
20 Joint Statement Between President George W. Bush and Prime Minister Manmohan Singh on 18 July 2005, available at https://georgewbush-whitehouse.archives.gov/news/releases/2005/07/print/20050718-6.html.
21 For the Nuclear Suppliers Group, see www.nuclearsuppliersgroup.org/en/guidelines. The NSG agreed on India specific exemption to the NSG Guidelines in a meeting on 21–22 August 2006 and on 6 September 2006 agreed to grant India a waiver from its existing rules.
22 See NPT Article II, "Each Non-Nuclear-Weapon State Party to the Treaty Undertakes not . . . not to Manufacture or Otherwise Acquire Nuclear Weapons or Other Nuclear Explosive Devices".
23 UN Security Council Resolutions 1696 (31 July 2006): 1737 (23 December 2006); 1747 (24 March 2007); 1803 (3 March 2008); 1835 (27 September 2008), available at www.un.org/securitycouncil/content/resolutions-0.
24 Ian Traynor, "Tehran Threatens to Abandon Nuclear Treaty", in *The Guardian*, 14 February 2006.
25 E3/EU plus 3 refers to the European Union and France, Germany and the United Kingdom together with China, Russia and the United States which led the negotiations with Iran about its nuclear program.
26 Alexander Kmentt, "The Development of the International Initiative on the Humanitarian Impact of Nuclear Weapons and Its Effect of the Nuclear Weapons Debate", in *International Review of the Red Cross*, vol. 97, 2015, p. 709, available at https://doi.org/10.1017/S1816383116000059.
27 For example during the 2010 Review Conference; see Harald Müller, "The 2010 NPT Review Conference: Some Breathing Space Gained, But No Breakthrough", in *The International Spectator*, vol. 45, no. 3, 2010, p. 13, available at https://doi.org/10.1080/03932729.2010.519543.
28 Bolton, *Surrender Is not an Option*, p. 74.

29 For a detailed description of these initiatives, see John Borrie and Vanessa Randin, eds., *Alternative Approaches in Multilateral Decision Making – Disarmament as Humanitarian Action*, p. 86, UNIDIR, November 2005, available at www.unidir.org/files/publications/pdfs/alternative-approaches-in-multilateral-decision-making-disarmament-as-humanitarian-action-314.pdf.

30 The "four core issues" on the Conference on Disarmament agenda are: FMCT, Nuclear Disarmament, Prevention of an arms race in outer space (PAROS) and assurances to non-nuclear-weapon States against the use or threat of use of nuclear weapons (Negative Security Assurances); see also Introduction to the Conference on Disarmament, available at www.unog.ch.

31 Previously, in 2004, Austria prepared a similar draft resolution in which the General Assembly would call on the Conference on Disarmament to establish the ad-hoc committees on the "four core issues", thereby also circumventing the impasse through a General Assembly resolution. After consultations, Austria decided not to formally submit this draft due to strong resistance from nuclear weapons States and some non-aligned States.

32 See "Draft Elements of an UNGA60 First Committee Resolution Initiating Work on Priority Disarmament and Non-Proliferation Issues", presented by Brazil, Canada, Kenya, Mexico, New Zealand, and Sweden at the 2005 First Committee of the UN General Assembly, available at www.reachingcriticalwill.org/images/documents/Disarmament-fora/1com/1com05/documents/draftelementsinitiating.pdf.

33 See "Explanator Note on Proposed Resolution Initiating Work on Priority Disarmament and Non-Proliferation Issues", presented by the US at the 2005 First Committee of the UN General Assembly, available at www.reachingcriticalwill.org/images/documents/Disarmament-fora/1com/1com05/documents/explanatorynoteinitiating.pdf.

34 The term "disarmament machinery" refers to multilateral processes, procedures and practices, and relevant international bodies whose purposes are to deal with issues of disarmament, non-proliferation and arms control. See United Nations Disarmament Research Institute (UNIDIR), "Disarmament Machinery: A Fresh Approach", September 2010, available at https://unidir.org/publication/disarmament-machinery-fresh-approach.

35 Jennifer Nordstrom, "First Committee Monitor-Final Edition 2005", p. 1, available at www.reachingcriticalwill.org/images/documents/Disarmament-fora/1com/FCM05/FCM-2005-5.pdf.

36 According to Rebecca Johnson, the term "Humanitarian Initiative" was first coined by the Chair of the NPT meeting in April 2013, Ambassador Cornel Feruta of Romania. It loosely refers to a set of initiatives to focus on the humanitarian consequences of nuclear weapons, such as primarily international conferences on this issue and cross-regional joint statements. See Rebecca Johnson, "NPT and Risks to Human Survival: The Inside Story", in *openDemocracy*, 29 April 2013, available at www.opendemocracy.net/en/5050/npt-and-risks-to-human-survival-inside-story/.

37 See for example Encyclopaedia Britannica, "Human Security, Approach to National and International Security That Gives Primacy to Human Beings and Their Complex Social and Economic Interactions: The Concept of Human Security Represents a Departure from Orthodox Security Studies, Which Focus on the Security of the State", available at www.britannica.com/topic/human-security; The 1994 UNDP Human Development Report New Dimensions of Human Security first coined the term "human security" within the UN system. See www.un.org/humansecurity/human-security-milestones-and-history/.

38 For the history of references to humanitarian concerns in disarmament efforts see also Tim Caugley, "Tracing Notions About Humanitarian Consequences", in *Viewing Nuclear Weapons Through a Humanitarian Lens*, John Borrie and Tim Caughley (eds.), United Nations Institute for Disarmament Research Geneva (UNIDIR), 2013,

Origins of the "Humanitarian Initiative"

pp. 14–28, available at www.unidir.org/files/publications/pdfs/viewing-nuclear-weapons-through-a-humanitarian-lens-en-601.pdf.

39 See "1997 Convention on the Prohibition of the Use, Stockpiling, Production and Transfer of Anti-Personnel Mines and on Their Destruction", available at https://disarmament.un.org/treaties/t/mine_ban.

40 For a more comprehensive study of this process see Jody Williams, Stephen D. Goose, and Mary Wareham (eds.), *Banning Landmines: Disarmament, Citizen Diplomacy, and Human Security*, Rowman & Littlefield, 2008; see also www.apminebanconvention.org/ottawa-process/overview/

41 The US participated in one Conference.

42 International Campaign the Ban Landmines, "Landmine Monitor 1999 – Towards a Mine-Free World – Executive Summary", in *ICBL*, available at www.the-monitor.org/media/1757245/lm1999execsum.pdf.

43 See "Amended Protocol II on Prohibitions or Restrictions on the Use of Mines, Booby-Traps and Other Devices" as amended on 3 May 1996 to the Convention on Certain Conventional Weapons, available at https://disarmament.un.org/treaties/t/ccwc_p2a.

44 See "Humanitarian Disarmament – Armed Conflict & Civilian Protection Initiative", available at https://humanitariandisarmament.org/about/.

45 For a detailed study of humanitarian disarmament see for example John Borrie and Vanessa Martin Randin (eds.), *Disarmament as Humanitarian Action: From Perspective to Practice*, UNIDIR, 2006, available at https://unidir.org/files/publications/pdfs/disarmament-as-humanitarian-action-from-perspective-to-practice-288.pdf.

46 Alexander Kmentt, "A Beacon of Light: The Mine-Ban Treaty Since 1997", in *Banning Landmines: Disarmament, Citizen Diplomacy, and Human Security*, Jody Williams, Stephen D. Goose, and Mary Wareham (eds.), Rowman & Littlefield, 2008, pp. 17–30.

47 For example in the case of the APM Convention, the "core group" of States pushing for the Treaty consisted of Austria, Belgium, Canada, Ireland, Mexico, the Netherlands, Norway, the Philippines, South Africa and Switzerland. The core group was supported by a large group of mine-affected developing countries. See www.apminebanconvention.org/overview-and-convention-text/.

48 See "Programme of Action to Prevent, Combat and Eradicate the Illicit Trade in Small Arms and Light Weapons", available at www.un.org/disarmament/convarms/salw/programme-of-action/.

49 See "2008 Convention on Cluster Munitions", available at http://disarmament.un.org/treaties/t/cluster_munitions.

50 See "2013 Arms Trade Treaty", available at https://disarmament.un.org/treaties/t/att.

51 See "1980 Convention on Prohibitions or Restrictions on the Use of Certain Conventional Weapons Which May Be Deemed to Be Excessively Injurious or to Have Indiscriminate Effects (CCWC)", available at https://disarmament.un.org/treaties/t/ccwc.

52 George Shultz, William Perry, Henry Kissinger, and Sam Nunn, "A World Free of Nuclear Weapons", Op-ed in *Wall Street Journal*, 4 January 2007, see also Alexei Arbatov and Rose Gottemoeller, "New Presidents, New Agreements? Advancing U.S.-Russian Strategic Arms Control", in *Arms Control Today*, August 2008, available at www.armscontrol.org/act/2008-08/features/new-presidents-new-agreements-advancing-us-russian-strategic-arms-control.

53 Barack Obama, "Now, Understand, This Matters to People Everywhere: One Nuclear Weapon Exploded in One City – Be It New York or Moscow, Islamabad or Mumbai, Tokyo or Tel Aviv, Paris or Prague – Could Kill Hundreds of Thousands of People. And no Matter Where It Happens, There Is no End to What the Consequences Might Be – for Our Global Safety, Our Security, Our Society, Our Economy, to Our Ultimate Survival", speech in Prague on 5 April 2009, available at https://obamawhitehouse.archives.gov/the-press-office/remarks-president-barack-obama-prague-delivered.

54 For example Jacqueline W. Shire, "Taking Back the High Ground: Disarmament and Nonproliferation Under the Obama Administration", in *Georgetown Journal of International Affairs*, vol. 11, no. 1, pp. 81–90, available at www.jstor.org/stable/43133803.
55 See UN Security Council meeting on 24 September 2009; S/RES/1887 (2009), available at http://unscr.com/en/resolutions/1887.
56 See US Department of State, "The New Start Treaty", available at www.state.gov/new-start/.
57 Jakob Kellenberger, "Bringing the Era of Nuclear Weapons to an End", speech in Geneva on 20 April 2010, available at www.icrc.org/eng/resources/documents/statement/nuclear-weapons-statement-200410.htm.
58 See for example Yves Sandoz, "The International Committee of the Red Cross as Guardian of International Humanitarian Law", in *ICRC Homepage*, 31 December 1998, available at www.icrc.org/en/doc/resources/documents/misc/about-the-icrc-311298.htm.
59 See "Final Document of the 2010 NPT Review Conference", NPT/CONF.2010/50 (Vol. I), p. 19, available at www.un.org/en/conf/npt/2010/.
60 Hillary Rodham Clinton, US Secretary of State, Statement on 3 May 2010, available at www.un.org/en/conf/npt/2010/statements/pdf/usa_en.pdf.
61 This issue had also been one of the necessary conditions to achieve the indefinite extension of the NPT in 1995. See "Resolution on the Middle East", at the 1995 Review and Extension Conference of the Parties to the Treaty on the Non-Proliferation of Nuclear Weapons, available at www.un.org/disarmament/wmd/nuclear/npt1995/.
62 See "Final Document of the 2010 NPT Review Conference", p. 19.
63 NPT preambular paragraph 1 encapsulates this notion as the key motivation for pursuing the NPT: "Considering the devastation that would be visited upon all mankind by a nuclear war and the consequent need to make every effort to avert the danger of such a war and to take measures to safeguard the security of peoples".
64 See for example the "Russell-Einstein Manifesto" of 9 July 1955, available at http://pugwash.org/1955/07/.
65 For a comprehensive overview of the history of nuclear disarmament activism, see, Lawrence S. Wittner, *Confronting the Bomb: A Short History of the World Nuclear Disarmament Movement*, Stanford University Press, 2009; see also Ray Acheson, *Banning the Bomb, Smashing the Patriarchy*, Rowman & Littlefield Publishers, March 2021.
66 See for example the Final Communiqué of the Asian-African conference of Bandung of 24 April 1955; "The Conference considered that disarmament and the prohibition of the production, experimentation and use of nuclear and thermo-nuclear weapons of war are imperative to save mankind and civilisation from the fear and prospect of wholesale destruction"; available also at https://mnoal.org/.
67 See for example the preamble of the Treaty for the Prohibition of Nuclear Weapons in Latin America (Tlatelolco Treaty) 1967 "Convinced that the incalculable destructive power of nuclear weapons has made it imperative that the legal prohibition of war should be strictly observed in practice if the survival of civilization and of mankind itself is to be assured", available at www.opanal.org/; for more information on Nuclear Weapon Free Zones see "United Nations Office for Disarmament Affairs", available at www.un.org/disarmament/wmd/nuclear/nwfz/.
68 See for example in the "1980 Convention on Certain Conventional Weapons (CCWC); or the "1990 Chemical Weapons Convention", available at https://disarmament.un.org/treaties/t/cwc.
69 Micheline Calmy-Rey, Minister for Foreign Affairs of Switzerland, Statement on 3 May 2010, available at www.un.org/en/conf/npt/2010/statements/statements.shtml; The Swiss government also sponsored a publication highlighting the humanitarian and international humanitarian law dimension of the nuclear weapons issue, which was

important in the context of the Humanitarian Initiative. See Benoit Pelopidas, Patricia Lewis, Nikolai Sokov, Ward Wilson, and Ken Berry, "Delegitimizing Nuclear Weapons," in *Monterey Institute of International Studies CNS Occasional Papers*, 2010, available at www.eda.admin.ch/dam/eda/de/documents/aussenpolitik/sicherheitspolitik/Delegitimizing_Nuclear_Weapons_May_2010.pdf.
70 Statement by Norway on 11 May 2010: "we should also look how nuclear weapons relate to International Humanitarian Law. Nuclear Weapons are the most indiscriminate, disproportionate and inhumane weapons ever created", available at www.un.org/en/conf/npt/2010/statements/statements.shtml.
71 Based on interviews of the author with participants in these informal meetings. The five nuclear weapon States, China, France, Russia, UK and US, as well as Brazil, Cuba, Egypt, Germany, Indonesia, Iran, Ireland Japan, Mexico, and South Africa attended these meetings.
72 This is also evidenced also by the relatively limited NGO reporting about this issue during the Review Conference. Only in the last Report by the NGO "Reaching Critical Will", which followed the entire Review Conference is detail, is there a longer article about this specific issue. See John Burroughs, "Humanitarian Consequences, Humanitarian Law: An Advance in Banning Use of Nuclear Weapons", in *NPT News in Review Final Edition*, 1 June 2010, p. 8, available at www.reachingcriticalwill.org.
73 See also Chapter 2, p. 18.
74 Interview conducted by the author with Ambassador Alexander Marschik, on 17 October 2019.
75 Rebecca Johnston, "Assessing the 2010 NPT Review Conference", in *The Bulletin of the Atomic Scientists*, July–August 2010, p. 6, available at https://doi.org/10.2968/066004001.
76 Müller, "The 2010 NPT Review Conference", p. 9.
77 See for example the closing statement of the non-aligned movement (NAM) on 28 May 2010, available at www.reachingcriticalwill.org/images/documents/Disarmament-fora/npt/revcon2010/statements/28May_NAM.pdf.
78 Müller, "The 2010 NPT Review Conference", p. 17.
79 See "High-Level Meeting on Revitalizing the Work of the Conference on Disarmament and Taking Forward Multilateral Disarmament Negotiations", 24 September 2010, available at www.un.org/en/ga/65/meetings/disarmament.shtml.
80 See Resolution, "Follow-Up to the High-Level Meeting Held on 24 September 2010: Revitalizing the Work of the Conference on Disarmament and Taking Forward Multilateral Disarmament Negotiations", A/RES 65/93, adopted by consensus on 11 January 2011, available at www.reachingcriticalwill.org/disarmament-fora/unga/2010/resolutions.
81 Michael Spindelegger, Foreign Minister of Austria, Statement in the Conference on Disarmament (CD) on 28 February 2011: "if this organization is not able to deliver results, we must explore alternative working structures here in Geneva". "It is my firm view that unless work of the CD commences by the end of its current first session [note: until March 2011], the General Assembly in New York should have a Plenary Debate on the Follow-Up of the High Level Meeting and on the future of multilateral disarmament," available at https://documents-dds-ny.un.org/doc/UNDOC/GEN/G11/611/05/PDF/G1161105.pdf?OpenElement.
82 The group on non-nuclear weapon States that were most active comprised of Australia, Austria, Canada, Germany, Ireland, Japan, Mexico, New Zealand, Norway, Sweden, Switzerland and South Africa. Several other States also participated on occasion.
83 Negative Security Assurances (NSAs) are guarantees by a nuclear weapon state that it will not use or threaten to use nuclear weapons against non-nuclear weapon. A multilateral treaty on NSAs is a longstanding priority mainly of non-aligned States.
84 Ibid.

85 See Resolution, "Taking Forward Multilateral Disarmament Negotiations", A/C.1/66/L.21. Rev.1 submitted by Austria, Mexico and Norway on 13 October 2011, available at www.reachingcriticalwill.org/images/documents/Disarmament-fora/1com/1com11/res/L21Rev1.pdf.
86 See Reaching Critical Will, "First Committee Report 2011", final edition, p. 4, available at www.reachingcriticalwill.org/images/documents/Disarmament-fora/1com/FCM11/FCM-2011-5.pdf.
87 See for example, Gaukhar Mukhatzhanova, "Implementation of the 2010 NPT Action Plan, April 5", in *James Martin Center for Nonproliferation Studies (CNS)*, 2013, available at www.nonproliferation.org/wp-content/uploads/2016/07/130405_2013_cns_npt_monitoring_report.pdf and Reaching Critical Will, "The NPT Action Plan Monitoring Reports", available at www.reachingcriticalwill.org/resources/publications-and-research/publications/5456-npt-action-plan-monitoring-reports.
88 Ibid., pp. 3–4.
89 See White House Fact Sheet, "An Enduring Commitment to the U.S. Nuclear Deterrent", 17 November 2010, available at https://obamawhitehouse.archives.gov/the-press-office/2010/11/17/fact-sheet-enduring-commitment-us-nuclear-deterrent; see also Brian P. McKeon, "Recalling the Senate Review of New START", in *Arms Control Today*, October 2019, available at www.armscontrol.org/act/2019-10/features/recalling-senate-review-new-start.
90 See for example "The Era of Magical Thinking: Trying to Understand Republican Opposition to the New START Treaty", in *The Economist*, 22 November 2010.
91 Jon B. Wolfsthal, Jeffrey Lewis, and Marc Quint, "The Trillion Dollar Nuclear Triad", in *James Martin Center for Nonproliferation Studies (CNS)*, 1 January 2014, available at www.nonproliferation.org/wp-content/uploads/2016/04/140107_trillion_dollar_nuclear_triad.pdf.
92 Ray Acheson, "Modernization of Nuclear Weapons: Aspiring to 'Indefinite Retention'?", in *Bulletin of the Atomic Scientist*, vol. 68, no. 5, 1 September 2012, available at https://thebulletin.org/2012/09/modernization-of-nuclear-weapons-aspiring-to-indefinite-retention/.
93 Kmentt, "The Development of the International Initiative on the Humanitarian Impact of Nuclear Weapons and Its Effect of the Nuclear Weapons Debate", p. 706.
94 Rebecca Davis Gibbons, "The Humanitarian Turn in Nuclear Disarmament and the Treaty on the Prohibition of Nuclear Weapons", in *The Nonproliferation Review*, vol. 25, no. 1–2, 2018, p. 35, available at https://doi.org/10.1080/10736700.2018.1486960.

2 The game needs to change

"Nuclear weapon states will not engage in negotiations on a comprehensive nuclear disarmament treaty. Not now, not ever. The so-called step-by-step approach has got nowhere. This will not change. The NPT only legitimizes nuclear weapons and does nothing for disarmament. The civil society effort to abolish nuclear weapons is flailing. It's time to change the game".[1]

Norway's key role

The rumblings of a search for potential alternative ways forward were already audible at the 2010 NPT Review Conference. In their statements, practically all non-nuclear weapon states expressed their dissatisfaction with the status quo on nuclear disarmament.[2] Austria's foreign minister announced that "if there is no clear progress towards 'global zero", we will discuss with partners the feasibility of a global instrument to ban these weapons. . . . a static regime that has lost its vision may benefit from fresh ideas".[3] By 2011, when the reality regarding the implementation of the Action Plan started to sink in, the focus shifted in earnest to the humanitarian consequences of nuclear weapons.

In this phase, Norway played a significant leadership role.[4] Before the 2010 Review Conference, policy makers in Norway had already started to draw parallels between their experience in previous humanitarian disarmament initiatives and nuclear disarmament and argued for a humanitarian focus on nuclear weapons.[5] In February 2010 Norway's Foreign Minister Jonas Gahr Støre stated that "experience from humanitarian disarmament should guide us on how to pursue and negotiate disarmament issues in general and . . . that it might be a good idea to ban nuclear weapons, even if not all states agreed". He went on to say that

some maintain that consensus is vital when it comes to nuclear disarmament. I am not fully convinced. I believe it would be possible to develop norms against the use of nuclear weapons, and even to outlaw them, without a consensus decision, and that such norms will eventually be applied globally. We cannot leave it to the nuclear weapon states alone to decide when it is time for them to do away with these weapons. Their destructive power would affect us all, if put to use – and their threat continues to affect us all – therefore they are everyone's business.[6]

In 2011, when no tangible progress in the implementation of the Action Plan was visible, Norway took a number of steps that can be considered the operational launch of what became known as the Humanitarian Initiative. Firstly, and in line with the experience of the previous successful humanitarian disarmament processes, Norway provided significant funding to several civil society organisations and think tanks.[7] Among the organisations that received Norwegian funding were ICAN, the NGO "Reaching Critical Will", the NGO "Article 36" and the think tank International Law and Policy Institute (ILPI).[8] These funding decisions were based on the understanding that making the case for the humanitarian consequences of nuclear weapons would require an effective public campaign. Importantly, ICAN was able to set up an office in Geneva and the UK-based NGO Article 36, which had previously worked on the Cluster Munitions Campaign, and the NGO Norwegian People's Aid joined ICAN. Within the global network of ICAN-affiliated NGOs, those that received funding from Norway subsequently led the effort to restructure the organisation. By early 2013, and after intensive internal discussions, ICAN's strategic goal had shifted from the promotion of the comprehensive Nuclear Weapons Convention[9] (NWC) and consolidated behind a ban treaty approach.[10]

The Amersham strategy meeting

On 26–27 September 2011, an informal meeting, funded by Norway, was convened in Amersham, UK by the International Law and Policy Institute. I attended this meeting as one of a small group of diplomats, representatives from relevant international organisations, and NGOs numbering approximately 15 in total.[11] This meeting was the first of a series of such informal gatherings; they proved very important in the context of the Humanitarian Initiative.

The purpose of this meeting was to discuss ways in which the nuclear disarmament stalemate could be overcome and how a viable strategy for a progressive agenda could be developed and pursued. Based on input papers prepared by ILPI and Article 36, the discussion commenced around the pros and cons of a prohibition of nuclear weapons use, which was then widened to address a comprehensive prohibition of nuclear weapons. On this issue, the discussion remained inconclusive. The participants all shared the view that in the current multilateral framework, no real progress was possible. Therefore, the game needed to change. What made this meeting so consequential was the fact that, irrespective of an as yet clearly defined end goal, the participants engaged in a strategic discussion on what such game changers could be, how change could be enacted and what actors and elements would be needed. Much of what was discussed on those two days in 2011 in Amersham, later came about.

Strategic points in the discussion were as follows:[12]

- One way of changing the game and breaking out of the nuclear disarmament paralysis could be to simplify and concentrate the issues by focusing on a narrower target: an instrument rooted in international humanitarian law. It

would be quite straightforward and could be an important tool for mobilising public understanding of and support for such an explicit development of International Humanitarian Law.
- An attractive aspect of the humanitarian law approach is that it may sidestep the difficulties of negotiating phased reductions/elimination of nuclear weapons. Moreover, it would serve to challenge the perception, established through the NPT, that certain states are inherently entitled to have nuclear weapons. A humanitarian law approach could provide a platform for a discussion that is not based on the recognition of the special status of the States with nuclear weapons, or their version of the state of international affairs.
- Such an approach would be valuable, even without the participation of nuclear weapon States. It would nevertheless affirm the moral position that use of nuclear weapons is incompatible with concepts of "humanity", would build stigma against nuclear weapons and reinforce customary rejection of their use. Whilst success for such a movement cannot be guaranteed in producing change amongst states with nuclear weapons, it is probably only through the generation of such movement, that the deadlock can be broken. A process should not be opposed to the engagement of the nuclear weapons States, but they should not be in a position to dictate the terms. Only without the barrier of consensus would this be achievable.
- The basis for such a movement would need to be a compelling rationale, one that requires no positive responses from States with nuclear weapons. Generation of movement would require a process that can be led and controlled by States that reject nuclear weapons. This can empower those States and build recognition that they have a capacity to influence the nuclear weapons agenda. Most importantly, it can reduce the likelihood of a process being derailed or held hostage by nuclear weapons States opposed to any reform or change to the status quo.
- It is important to challenge some of the "old truths" such as the "deterrence myth", calling out a deterrence strategy that is neither credible nor based on weapons that are particularly useful.
- It is important to look at the actual effects of nuclear weapons but also of the likelihood of use/accidents.
- The question is what kind of vehicle, if any, would be needed: a campaign for a ban without focus on a legal instrument, or a draft legal instrument to get the campaign going?
- Civil society needs to become more of a player and a credible actor with better and clearer mechanisms for the coordination of NGO activity. ICAN is best placed for that, with different actions, different groups in different countries, working towards the same goal. This would create pressure.
- There would need to be a small group of States working intensively alongside a coordinated civil society campaign with global reach, with support from international organizations who share the same goal and who are willing to work together over a period of time. It is reasonable to spend time to build up

relationships within such a group and to develop a solid intellectual framework with facts, counterarguments etc.
- It will be challenging to articulate why such an instrument would be a positive step forward for humanity and the cause of disarmament if its binding impact on nuclear weapon States is limited in the near term.

The Amersham meeting was not a strategy discussion to bring about a ban treaty per se, nor did it set a fixed course in this direction. The picture is more nuanced. There was certainly a sense that a ban could be framed as a clear goal behind which civil society would rally. Participants found however that it would be better to allow for the exact nature of an international humanitarian law-based instrument end goal to emerge over time and in parallel with making the humanitarian case for such a norm. A specific legal objective should not be locked in too early. Changing the game and re-framing the discourse was the leitmotif of these discussions, however. In my assessment, most Amersham participants, at the time, saw a ban treaty as a proposition that could be put "out there", it having the potential to create a much-needed new dynamic and shake up the existing stasis. Years later, one of the participants at this first "Amersham Group" described a ban as a "twinkle in the eye" during these early discussions, a possibility for which a great many things would have to fall into place, but not yet a clearly defined direction of travel.[13]

Amongst those senior diplomats who were part of the "Amersham Group", the ambiguity over the desired outcome of a focus on the humanitarian consequences of nuclear weapons continued. ICAN, moved decisively, albeit with extensive internal discussions, to embrace a ban treaty as opposed to a Nuclear Weapons Convention, playing a key role in making the case that it would be a viable approach. For the diplomats, a ban treaty seemed an attractive but unlikely, disruptive idea and certainly a politically risky proposition, given the opposition that such an approach would trigger.[14] At the time, I concluded that an effective civil society campaign for a ban treaty together with a credible threat of a negotiation process, would create some pressure. The approach could leverage progress on nuclear disarmament, including the implementation of the 2010 NPT Action Plan.

The main objective of the Amersham discussion was therefore not a ban treaty, rather a re-framing and reinvigorating of the nuclear weapons discourse. At the end of the meeting, there was an understanding among participants that the best way forward was through focussing nuclear weapons discourse on the humanitarian consequences of nuclear weapons and the unacceptability of their use.

Seven months later, by the time of the next NPT Meeting in April 2012 in Vienna,[15] the focus had shifted decisively towards the humanitarian consequences of nuclear weapons. Firstly, in November 2011, the Red Cross and Red Crescent Movement adopted a resolution expressing the conviction

> that the International Red Cross and Red Crescent Movement has an historic and important role to play in efforts to create the conditions for a world without nuclear weapons . . . and calls on all components of the Movement,

utilizing the framework of humanitarian diplomacy . . . to raise awareness among the public, scientists, health professionals and decision-makers of the catastrophic humanitarian consequences of any use of nuclear weapons, the international humanitarian law issues that arise from such use and the need for concrete actions leading to the prohibition of use and elimination of such weapons.[16]

In February 2012, a memo was prepared in the Norwegian Foreign ministry with a proposal to host an international conference as "part of a broader effort to draw attention to the humanitarian impact of nuclear weapons".[17] Foreign Minister Støre took this proposal up and in a debate in the Norwegian Parliament on 17 April 2012, and again, two weeks later in the Norwegian opening statement at the NPT Meeting in Vienna, announced a Conference, to take place in March 2013.[18]

Also in April 2012, the International Physicians for the Prevention of Nuclear War (IPPNW) presented an important study on the global impact of a limited nuclear war.[19] This report built on recent research into the climate effects of the use of nuclear weapons and demonstrated that previous studies had significantly underestimated the "nuclear winter" and the subsequent global declines in food production and the number of people at risk of mass starvation. The study was presented at the Vienna NPT meeting and was widely discussed among States and civil society representatives.

Finally, in advance of the NPT meeting, Switzerland proposed the idea of a cross-regional statement specifically on the humanitarian consequences of nuclear weapons. This built on the humanitarian principle included in the 2010 NPT Review Conference Final Document. Sixteen States negotiated this statement and agreed to co-sign it.[20] For the next three years, a combined strategy of cross-regional "humanitarian" statements in multilateral fora with three international conferences on the humanitarian consequences were the most visible expressions of the Humanitarian Initiative.

The humanitarian statements

The first cross-regional "Joint Statement on the Humanitarian Dimension of Nuclear Disarmament" delivered at the NPT Preparatory Conference in April 2012 was carefully calibrated by the 16 States. It was deliberately non-political and focussed exclusively on the key humanitarian concerns. It highlighted the immeasurable suffering from any intentional or accidental use of nuclear weapons, the lack of response capabilities of relief organisations, the global climate change impact, the continued threat to the survival of humanity, the questionable utility of nuclear weapons to address current challenges and the important legal ramifications that any use of nuclear weapons would have. The statement concluded that "it is of utmost importance that these weapons never be used again, under any circumstances" and called especially on nuclear weapon states "to give increasing attention to their commitment to comply with international law, in particular international humanitarian law".[21]

In the period between April 2012 and May 2015, the group of 16 used subsequent NPT meetings and the annual First Committee of the UN General Assembly to issue a series of similar statements. With the help of effective lobbying by ICAN, an ever-increasing number of States co-signed these statements. At the First Committee meetings in 2012, 2013 and 2014, the Second Preparatory Committee for the NPT in 2013 and the 2015 NPT Review Conference, the number of States co-signing these Joint Statements increased to 34,[22] 80,[23] 125,[24] 155[25] and 159[26] respectively. This marked uptake, over a relatively short period, is evidence of the interest generated by the Humanitarian Initiative. It became a politically attractive proposition for States to be associated with the humanitarian statements.[27]

In this period, a peculiar "competition" ensued between two, different, humanitarian statements. At the First Committee of the UN General Assembly in 2013, Australia came forward with an "alternative humanitarian statement".[28] It was intended to give voice to the so-called "nuclear umbrella States", meaning US allies in the North Atlantic Treaty Organization (NATO) plus Australia, Japan and South Korea who are "under protection" by the US through extended nuclear deterrence. Those States presumably felt under pressure from the momentum created by the "original" humanitarian statement and wished to express themselves on the humanitarian issue in some way. The pressure was particularly palpable for Japan, where an active civil society campaign had been launched on this issue and it ended up co-signing both humanitarian statements.[29] The Australian-led statement argued for a "step-by-step" approach and "practical efforts towards effective nuclear disarmament". It stated that "banning nuclear weapons by itself will not guarantee their elimination without engaging substantively and constructively with those states with nuclear weapons and recognising both the security and humanitarian dimensions of the nuclear weapons debate". This is remarkable, as the original humanitarian statement had referred neither to a ban, nor to not engaging with nuclear weapon States. It is clear evidence of the growing concern among the nuclear umbrella States about a possible diplomatic process leading to a prohibition of nuclear weapons. This "competition" continued until the 2015 NPT Review Conference, where a cross-regional statement of the original group of 16 states was delivered by Austria's foreign minister, Sebastian Kurz, on behalf of 159 States.[30] The statement of the Australian-led group was supported by 24 States.[31]

The competition between the two statements and the growing number of co-signatories to the "original" statement is a good indicator of the momentum and the game-changing potential that the Humanitarian Initiative was generating. It is remarkable that within three years and after failing to explicitly and collectively address the humanitarian consequences of nuclear weapons for several decades, over 180 States felt compelled to express themselves on the humanitarian consequences of the use of nuclear weapons and the need to prevent such consequences through urgent progress on nuclear disarmament.

Challenging the consensus rule

As stated in 2011 when Austria, Mexico and Norway withdrew their draft resolution on "Taking forward multilateral disarmament negotiations",[32] the three co-sponsors reintroduced a resolution at the 2012 First Committee of the UN General Assembly.[33] The principle behind the draft of the previous year was retained, namely the establishment of an open-ended working group to meet in Geneva, through a mandate from the UN General Assembly. The new draft resolution was simplified and the mandate for the open-ended working group was more general "to develop proposals to take forward multilateral nuclear disarmament negotiations for the achievement and maintenance of a world without nuclear weapons". The mandate was no longer linked to action or inaction in the Conference on Disarmament. The open-ended working group was simply to meet in Geneva for up to three weeks and produce a report for the next UN General Assembly "reflecting discussions held and proposals made" and to transmit the report to the Conference on Disarmament.

After another year of stalemate in the Conference on Disarmament and with this simplified approach, Austria, Mexico and Norway were able to convince the more sceptical States in the non-aligned movement.[34] The main arguments were that this project would not be a "challenge to the disarmament machinery" but an open forum in which to discuss the issues that are currently blocked, and all of which were a priority for the non-aligned States. In my view, the negative attitude towards this resolution on the part of the nuclear weapon States contributed directly to increasing support from non-nuclear weapon States. The resolution was adopted with a convincing majority of 147 States supporting it, 31 abstentions and 4 states, France, Russia, the UK and the US, voting against.[35]

France, the UK and the US expressed their opposition to an initiative

> outside of the established fora". They expressed "grave concerns as to the preparatory aspects of this meeting, its rules of procedure and other working methods. . . . It is for these reasons that we are unable to support this resolution, the establishment of the [open-ended working group] and any outcome it may produce.[36]

Despite the opposition from nuclear weapon States, Austria, Mexico and Norway considered it a significant success to have obtained such resounding support for the resolution. At last there was broad acknowledgement that the strict consensus rule in the Conference on Disarmament was an impediment to progress. As the open-ended working group would be operating on the basis of UN General Assembly rules of procedure and be open to civil society participation, the "consensus rule/veto dynamic" was successfully challenged.

The co-sponsors of the resolution, Austria, Norway and Mexico, then set about organising the substantive aspects of the open-ended working group. This was a challenging and tricky task. Given its contested origins, it was of crucial importance that the viability of this initiative could be demonstrated. The open-ended working group met for three separate, week-long sessions in the spring and summer of 2013. Meanwhile, stalemate in the Conference on Disarmament continued. With much effort and the help of supportive states,[37] civil society organisations, and academics, substantive and interactive sessions were organised.[38] Despite many competing meetings in Geneva, participation, especially from developing countries, including from nuclear armed India and Pakistan, remained high throughout the meetings. Participants clearly appreciated the substantive contributions from experts and the interactive discussions that provided a stark contrast to the Conference on Disarmament meetings. On 3 September 2013, the working group was able to adopt a report[39] without having to vote, even though this would have been possible under its rules of procedure. This was a significant success. It underscored the value of a non-consensus rule process, which facilitates the building of agreement and consensus, as against the application of a strict consensus rule that often leads to a veto mindset, as demonstrated in the Conference on Disarmament.

The report reflected the discussions and proposals made during the three sessions. It drew attention to several "old" nuclear disarmament proposals, including those contained in the 2010 NPT Action Plan. The report also included some important new ideas. In the section on the role of international law to take forward multilateral nuclear disarmament negotiations, it referred to "options to fill the legal gaps in achieving the objective of a world without nuclear weapons, including in the current international legal framework". In this context, the report also referred to the option of a treaty banning nuclear weapons. Moreover, the report acknowledges a prohibition of the possession, stockpiling, development, or transfer of nuclear weapons as an element "necessary for maintaining a world without nuclear weapons once achieved".[40] This seemingly innocuous acknowledgement is noteworthy. It encapsulates the notion that a prohibition is, as such, not contentious and generally accepted as necessary for a world without nuclear weapons. The only area of contestation is, thus, not the need for such a measure, but the timing. Whereas nuclear weapon States argue that a prohibition is an *endpoint* of nuclear disarmament, non-nuclear weapon States increasingly supported the argument that a prohibition, as with chemical and biological weapons, should be a *starting point*.[41]

The working group report also notes that "all states have a responsibility . . . notably in the light of the catastrophic humanitarian consequences of nuclear weapons" and, importantly, that "non-nuclear-weapon states have a role in promoting global nuclear disarmament".[42] Much in this section is based on a working paper, submitted by Austria. The paper suggested various contributions that non-nuclear weapon States might make such as

> address(ing) nuclear weapons as a humanitarian and human security issue [and that] non-nuclear weapon States can play a key role in transforming and reframing the discourse into a human security debate which addresses the security concerns and needs of peoples and societies. . . . [To] consider the potential of a broad political discourse that challenges existing nuclear

weapons narratives [which] could include a critical analysis of the validity of nuclear deterrence, the threat perceptions used to justify the continued reliance on nuclear weapons, the special value that is attributed to nuclear weapons and the link between the retention of nuclear weapons and the proliferation of nuclear weapons [and to] put all these aspects in the context of the risk of inflicting unacceptable humanitarian consequences to all humankind.[43]

As the NGO Reaching Critical Will pointed out in its reporting on the open-ended working group:

the real value of the group is not the words in its final report – it achieved more than that. One of the main successes of the OEWG . . . was to empower non-nuclear weapon states . . . even if nuclear-armed states are not engaging constructively. . . . This is an important shift in approach to nuclear weapons and is possibly a signal that the traditional power dynamics between nuclear-armed and non-nuclear weapon states are changing.[44]

The absence of the nuclear weapon States from the open-ended working group turned out to be an unexpected benefit as it focussed the discussion amongst non-nuclear weapon States on what they, themselves, could do to further the nuclear disarmament.

Following the success of the open-ended working group, Austria, Norway and Mexico discussed during September 2013 how to proceed. There was considerable interest by other States[45] in continuing the open-ended working group in 2014 and to try to obtain another mandate for this in the upcoming UN General Assembly. However, Norway saw little value in a follow-on mandate and did not want to present another resolution on "Taking forward multilateral disarmament negotiations". Initially, Mexico agreed with this assessment. Austria was strongly in favour of a continuation. Given the difficulties of establishing this open and non-consensus-based forum, Austria argued, it would be important to maintain it given the continued stasis in the Conference on Disarmament, especially as it had been a positive and empowering exercise. Most importantly, however, Austria was of the opinion, that an established, open-ended working group would furnish a useful avenue for the pursuit of eventual negotiations in the future, depending on the further development of the Humanitarian Initiative. For this reason alone, it would be important to present another resolution. After intensive discussions between Vienna and Mexico City, the two countries, without Norway, agreed to submit a fresh resolution to the 2013 First Committee of the UN General Assembly. In line with the Mexican preference and somewhat to the disappointment of Austria, it did not contain a new mandate for reconvening the open-ended working group in 2014. However, the fact that the "Taking forward multilateral disarmament negotiations" resolution was kept on the agenda of the UN General Assembly in the following two years proved to be important for the negotiation of the TPNW. This will be discussed in the next chapter.

Three conferences on the humanitarian impact of nuclear weapons

Oslo, 4–5 March 2013

A conference on the humanitarian impact of nuclear weapons took place on 4–5 March 2013 in Oslo, Norway. In line with the discussions in Amersham of September 2012, and this groups' subsequent informal meetings, the conference was intended to provide a facts-based, rigorous, scientific background with which to re-frame the nuclear weapons discourse in a humanitarian direction. According to an internal Norwegian Ministry of Foreign Affairs memo, "nuclear weapons are shrouded in a series of old preconceptions that have largely been left unchallenged"[46]; the Conference was supposed to do just this. The new Norwegian minister of foreign affairs, Espen Barth Eide stated in his opening speech that

> Today's conference is an opportunity for states and other stakeholders to establish a sound understanding of what is meant by the NPT Review Conferences reference to 'catastrophic humanitarian consequences' . . . A two-day conference cannot give us all the answers. But raising these questions and discussing them is important in itself. It is a way of framing the discourse on nuclear weapons in a manner that properly reflects the danger that these weapons represent – to us all. The insights we gain can strengthen and inform our future debates about nuclear weapons.[47]

Delegates from 127 States, the relevant humanitarian UN organizations i.e. the UN High Commissioner for Refugees, the UN Office for the Coordination of Humanitarian Affairs, the UN Development Programme and the World Food Programme, as well as the International Red Cross and Red Crescent Movement, and civil society organisations attended the conference. Scientific expertise on the situation in the immediate aftermath of a nuclear detonation and the resulting health and medical needs was presented to the participants. Other presentations laid out the longer-term social and economic impacts, including on food security, health, the environment and development that nuclear weapons use would have. Finally, humanitarian relief organisations assessed the state of preparedness and the absence of an adequate humanitarian response to a nuclear weapon detonation.[48]

Minister Eide concluded the conference with a Chair's summary[49] stating that "this broad participation reflects the increasing global concern regarding the effects of nuclear weapons detonations, as well as the recognition that this is as issue of fundamental significance to all of us". In the chair's view, three key points were discerned from the conference:

- It is unlikely that any State or international body could address the immediate humanitarian emergency caused by a nuclear weapon detonation in an

adequate manner and provide sufficient assistance to those affected. Moreover, it might not be possible to establish such capacities, even if it were attempted.
- The historical experience from the use and testing of nuclear weapons has demonstrated their devastating immediate and long-term effects. While political circumstances have changed, the destructive potential of nuclear weapons remains.
- The effects of a nuclear weapon detonation, irrespective of cause, will not be constrained by national borders, and will affect States and people in significant ways, regionally as well as globally.[50]

The Conference highlighted the difference between talking about nuclear weapons in the context of *abstract* security policy concepts and looking, in *concrete* terms, at the consequences inflicted upon people and human society in the event of a nuclear detonation. The contrast to the discussions in traditional multilateral nuclear weapons fora, such as the Conference on Disarmament, was marked.

The nuclear weapon States collectively boycotted the Oslo conference. In an "ill-advised display"[51] of so-called "P5 solidarity",[52] they communicated to the Norwegian hosts that they would not attend the Oslo Conference as it would "divert discussion away from the practical steps to create the conditions for further nuclear weapons reductions".[53] In particular the absence of the US, the UK and France from a conference organized by a fellow NATO member State astonished quite a number of delegates. This was widely perceived as a very dismissive stance by the NPT nuclear weapon States and further proof of a lack of readiness to engage with issues of serious concern for non-nuclear weapon States. One of the reasons given for the boycott was grounded in legal considerations. In view of a possible future negotiation process for a ban-treaty, their absence from the Oslo Conference would establish their objection to any future norm becoming or being considered as customary international law.[54] In my view, a proactive and serious engagement by nuclear weapon States would have been welcomed and would probably have fundamentally changed the course of the Humanitarian Initiative. As such, the "P5 boycott" contributed to the politization of the initiative and strengthened the momentum towards a ban-treaty, exactly what the P5 sought to prevent.

Importantly, the Oslo Conference of 2013 provided a forum around which civil society groups could coalesce their activities. ICAN organized a civil society forum before the conference, bringing together hundreds of activists.[55] This was the largest civil society gathering devoted to nuclear disarmament for a long time. Following through on one of the conclusions of the first Amersham meeting, the Norwegian hosts designated ICAN as its official civil society partner, greatly enhancing ICAN's role vis-à-vis other nuclear disarmament NGOs. By the time of the Oslo Conference, ICAN had undergone an internal restructuring process and had shifted its strategic goal to achieving a ban-treaty.[56] ICAN used the Oslo Conference to consolidate itself as an effective campaign with clear messaging and a clear campaign objective, a ban-treaty. Over the next two years, the ICAN partner NGO Article 36 organized a series of small informal gatherings to discuss a strategy for a ban treaty process more concretely. Similarly to the "Amersham group", these so-called "Berkshire meetings"[57] were attended by only a handful of individuals from States, international organisations and civil society, all acting in their personal capacities.

The Oslo Conference with its visible and dynamic civil society presence created a vibrant atmosphere and amidst this, a heightened sense that something of relevance was happening. A few months after the Oslo Conference, in September 2013, a new government came into power in Norway, which changed its policy and withdrew its support for this initiative. It joined the fold of other nuclear umbrella States that were critical of the Humanitarian Initiative and opposed to a new legal instrument. However, the ball that Norway had been so instrumental in getting to move, continued to roll. At the closing session of the Oslo Conference, Mexico announced that it would convene a follow-up conference within one year.

Nayarit, 13–14 February 2014

A second conference on the humanitarian impact of nuclear weapons was organized by Mexico and took place in Nayarit in February 2014.[58] It followed the format of its predecessor and further expanded the scope of the discussion. *Hibakusha*, the survivors of the atomic bombs in Hiroshima and Nagasaki were given an entire session dedicated to their powerful testimonies. Nayarit reinforced some of the key findings of the Oslo Conference, namely the devastating short- and long-term consequences on human health, the climate, food security and social order but also on the financial and business sectors and the local economy, as well as the inadequacy of response capabilities. The United Nations Institute for Disarmament Research (UNIDIR) presented a study on the challenges for the entire United Nations humanitarian coordination and response system to the emergencies caused by a nuclear detonation. The study concludes inter alia that "(t)he United Nations is unlikely to be able to offer much humanitarian assistance in the immediate aftermath of a nuclear weapon detonation event, and it would take time for the humanitarian system to deploy".[59]

As an important, additional, focus, the Nayarit conference considered the element of "risk" associated with nuclear weapons, such as through accidents, miscalculation or human or technical error. The destructive impact of nuclear explosions is widely known, but the wider public considers the likelihood of a nuclear explosion to be rather remote. For many participants it was important to learn therefore about the potential vulnerabilities of nuclear command and control infrastructures, as well as about risky practices involving nuclear weapons and the history of near accidents. Chatham House, the UK-based Royal Institute of International Affairs, presented a study that examined historical cases of "near nuclear misses". One of its key findings is that

> since the probability of inadvertent nuclear use is not zero and is higher than had been widely considered, and because the consequences of detonations

are so serious, the risk associated with nuclear weapons is high. . . . For as long as nuclear weapons exist, the risk of an inadvertent, accidental or deliberate detonation remains.[60]

Other important contributions on nuclear risks came from US investigative journalist Eric Schlosser, who had recently published his book *Command and Control*[61] and from Bruce Blair, a former US nuclear launch officer and founder of the US disarmament NGO Global Zero. Blair explained, in detail, the possible risks involved in the practices and protocols of nuclear weapons decision-making, such as with respect to the targeting and alert status of nuclear weapons.[62] For the first time, many participants appreciated how narrowly on several occasion in the past, serious accidents and even nuclear war were avoided and the extent to which this was the result of luck. The discussion of risks associated with the possession of nuclear weapons was thus an important substantive contribution of the Nayarit Conference to the Humanitarian Initiative and to re-framing the discourse on nuclear weapons. The Mexican Chair's summary of the conference refers to these elements as follows:

- Today the risk of nuclear weapons use is growing globally as a consequence of proliferation, the vulnerability of nuclear command and control networks to cyber-attacks and to human error, and potential access to nuclear weapons by non-State actors, in particular terrorist groups.
- As more countries deploy more nuclear weapons on higher levels of combat readiness, the risks of accidental, mistaken, unauthorized or intentional use of these weapons grow significantly.[63]

Participation in Nayarit increased, with the presence of 146 States and many international organizations and NGOs whose participation was, upon the request of the Mexican hosts, again, coordinated by ICAN. Compared to the atmosphere in Oslo, this conference had a distinctly more political character, as many delegations wanted to make statements expressing concern on the humanitarian consequences of nuclear weapons and demanding progress on nuclear disarmament.[64] Most of the second day of the conference was set aside for general debate. States highlighted the relevance of the Humanitarian Initiative, stressed that this should give further political momentum to multilateral nuclear disarmament efforts and called on the nuclear weapon States to engage in the discourse. A large number of delegations also called for new initiatives, and to put humanitarian arguments at the centre of all such efforts. An increasing number of delegations explicitly endorsed the idea of a ban treaty.[65]

Although both the US and the UK seriously considered participating in the Nayarit conference, in the end, all Nuclear weapon States continued their boycott. The US allies found it hard to manoeuvre between an expression of support for discussing the humanitarian consequences of nuclear weapons, as demanded by an increasing civil society activity in their respective countries, and their role as nuclear umbrella States. These States spoke of the "security dimension" of nuclear weapons and the need to proceed with "realistic steps" and in an "inclusive manner", meaning, with the participation of nuclear weapon States. By Nayarit, their concern that the Humanitarian Initiative could develop into a diplomatic process aimed at the prohibition of nuclear weapons had further increased. Coinciding with the Nayarit Conference, the Australian foreign minister, Julie Bishop, published an op-ed entitled "We Must Engage not Enrage Nuclear Countries"[66] making these points. It caused significant irritation among the participants and the Mexican hosts, given that nuclear weapon States had been invited, but chose not to attend the conference.

Mexico concluded the conference with a Chair's Summary containing the substantive points raised in the panel presentations and the statements. In contrast with the Oslo summary, this document contained explicit points as to how the Humanitarian Initiative should be taken forward politically:

- We need to take into account that, in the past, weapons have been eliminated after they have been outlawed. We believe this is the path to achieve a world without nuclear weapons.
- In our view, this is consistent with our obligations under international law, including those derived from the NPT as well as from Common Article 1 to the Geneva Conventions. The broad-based and comprehensive discussions on the humanitarian impact of nuclear weapons should lead to the commitment of States and civil society to reach new international standards and norms, through a legally binding instrument.
- It is the view of the Chair that the Nayarit Conference has shown that time has come to initiate a diplomatic process conducive to this goal. Our belief is that this process should comprise a specific timeframe, the definition of the most appropriate fora, and a clear and substantive framework, making the humanitarian impact of nuclear weapons the essence of disarmament efforts. It is time to take action. The 70th anniversary of the Hiroshima and Nagasaki attacks is the appropriate milestone to achieve our goal. Nayarit is a point of no return.[67]

While it was clear that this was a non-negotiated and therefore non-binding conclusion from the Mexicans, it caused a considerable stir at the end of the Nayarit conference and beyond. Civil society and those States that had openly voiced support for a ban treaty were delighted. The nuclear umbrella States, however, complained that their views were not reflected in this conclusion and that the conference was supposed to be non-political and facts based. To their minds, that the two humanitarian conferences represented a "slippery slope" towards initiating a diplomatic process to negotiate a nuclear weapon ban treaty was confirmed. In Mexico's view, the chair had simply reflected the clear expressions of support for such an approach that had been included in many statements during the general debate.

Vienna, 8–9 December 2014

The political conclusions of Nayarit were a surprise not only to the nuclear umbrella States. They were not expected by Austria, who at the beginning of the

Nayarit Conference had announced that it would host a third, follow-up conference towards the end of 2014.[68] The intention and timing of this announcement at the start of the Nayarit meeting, signalled that the Humanitarian Initiative was going forward in a sustained and accelerated manner. By now, parallel but connected activities such as the humanitarian conferences, the joint statements in different multilateral forums had become widely identified as a distinct initiative, even if it was more unified in appearance than reality at times.

The possibility of hosting a third humanitarian conference in Austria evolved out of the informal strategic discussions amongst supporters of the Humanitarian Initiative, including in the Amersham and Berkshire meetings in the months before the Nayarit Conference. Originally, it was hoped that South Africa would host the third humanitarian conference at which, possibly, a negotiation process could be launched. South Africa was considered a very symbolic and suitable place for such a conference, especially as it had given up its own nuclear weapons capability. However, Pretoria would only consider a conference if it took place after the 2015 NPT Review Conference once the lack of progress on nuclear disarmament and the implementation of the 2010 Action Plan was fully demonstrated. At this, many were concerned that the gap from Nayarit, in early 2014, until late 2015 or early 2016, would be too long.

The original motivation therefore of the Vienna conference was to maintain the momentum of the Humanitarian Initiative until the 2015 NPT Review Conference and a possible subsequent South African conference. The aim of the Vienna conference was to intensify the focus on the humanitarian consequences and risks associated with nuclear weapons, without being explicit about a possible political direction or end result. The internal memo which I prepared in autumn 2013 on the rationale for hosting this conference explains that the result of the Vienna conference depends on the developments during 2014 and that there is momentum in two directions:[69]

- NPT-track: due to the concern of nuclear weapon States about the Humanitarian Initiative and a possible ban-process, the Vienna Conference increases the pressure on them to fulfil their disarmament commitments under the NPT. Non-nuclear weapon States gain leverage to request more concrete steps and not merely announcements. Substantive progress at the NPT Review Conference could be claimed as a success for the Humanitarian Initiative.
- Ban process: if, as expected, nuclear weapon States will yet again not implement their disarmament commitments, this creates further momentum for a ban process. The conference in Vienna would take place at a critical juncture.

A deliberate ambiguity over the final direction of travel of the Humanitarian Initiative, was identified for its usefulness in the initial Amersham meeting in September 2011 and had two motivations. Firstly, it made it more difficult to criticise the Humanitarian Initiative, as long as it was conducted as a fact-based discourse about the humanitarian impact of nuclear weapons. Secondly, while support for the initiative was clearly growing fast, it was felt that more time was needed and the final "proof" of a non-implemented NPT Action Plan, to build sufficient momentum among a majority of States for an alternative way forward. The explicitly political Nayarit conclusion that "the time has come to initiate a diplomatic process" created a complicated situation for the Austrian hosts, especially myself, as I was tasked with the preparation of the Vienna Conference on the Humanitarian Impact of Nuclear Weapons on 8–9 December 2014.[70]

In the months after Nayarit, nuclear umbrella States undertook frequent diplomatic démarches in Vienna,[71] seeking clarity about the planned content and outcome of the Vienna Conference. The opposition to a diplomatic/political outcome was made clear. Moreover, they asked for reassurance that "their views" would be adequately reflected in any summary document, otherwise they would have to reconsider their participation in the conference.

At the same time, civil society organizations, especially ICAN, pushed for the Vienna Conference to initiate a diplomatic process to negotiate a nuclear weapon ban, or at least make significant progress towards this goal.[72] Some of the States strongly supporting the idea of a ban communicated to me that the usefulness of the "facts-based" type of conference had been exhausted. They felt that this third conference should give a clear sense of where the Humanitarian Initiative was heading, and which political and legal conclusions should be drawn from it. Many States, on the other hand, remained undecided about the way forward for the Humanitarian Initiative.[73]

I tried to deal with these conflicting expectations in several ways.[74] Assurances were given that the Vienna Conference would not initiate a diplomatic process and that the chair would attempt to reflect all views appropriately. In addition, Austria emphasised the connection between the Humanitarian Initiative, the Vienna Conference, and the 2015 NPT Review Conference. We reiterated *ad nauseam* that the Humanitarian Initiative originated in the 2010 NPT Action Plan and that the issues raised are of high relevance and provide substantive input for the 2015 NPT. In the 2014 NPT preparatory meeting for the 2015 Review Conference, Austria pointed out that

> the broad based and comprehensive discussions on the humanitarian impact of nuclear weapons, which have taken place in Oslo and in Nayarit – and will take place later this year in Vienna, underscore a growing support to firmly anchor the humanitarian imperative in the discussions about nuclear weapons and nuclear disarmament. They build on the preamble of the NPT and pursue the treaty's goal of achieving a world without nuclear weapons as well as implementing the 2010 NPT Action Plan. Better awareness of the devastating humanitarian impact and consequences of nuclear weapons builds momentum for the urgency of achieving nuclear disarmament and results in greater understanding of the need to eliminate this risk.[75]

Other supporters of the Humanitarian Initiative argued along similar lines.[76] The Vienna Conference would, thus, aim to consolidate the substantive elements developed in the two preceding conferences, as input for the 2015 NPT Review

Conference. The clear substantive link to the NPT and the assurance about the objectives and foreseen conclusions of the Vienna Conference made it more difficult for the nuclear umbrella States to stay away.

At the same time, Austria undertook focused outreach to the NPT nuclear weapon States regarding their participation at the Vienna Conference, in particular to the United States. This was based on the calculation that the United States had realized that their "boycott policy" was politically harmful and seen as antagonistic by an ever- growing number of States. Given the objectives that President Obama had laid out in his Prague speech, the argument that a focus on the humanitarian consequences of nuclear weapons was a "distraction" from the NPT, had clearly begun to backfire within the wider NPT membership. Some of the advocates of a more proactive US disarmament approach seemed to look for a way back into the humanitarian discourse. Having largely ignored it before, the Washington-based US think tank community now started to pay more attention to the Humanitarian Initiative.[77] On 7 November, the US announced[78] that it would be attending the Vienna Conference. The UK immediately followed suit, as expected. The decision to participate did not represent a fundamental shift in policy. "Instead, it likely had more to do with their belated concern to be seen to be engaging, and to defend the step-by-step' process on nuclear disarmament, with a view to the 2015 NPT Review Conference looming six months hence".[79]

The Vienna Conference was attended by 158 States, international organizations, the Red Cross and Red Crescent movement and several hundred civil society representatives. A large civil society forum took place on the two days preceding the conference creating a dynamic atmosphere of activism and significant media interest. This was also partly due to the US participation.

The conference program was designed to consolidate the case for urgent action on nuclear disarmament, given the humanitarian consequences and risks of nuclear weapon use and possession. Participants heard the testimonies of victims of nuclear weapons testing, as well as further Hibakusha statements. New presentations highlighted the gender dimension of radiation exposure, whereby women are more vulnerable than men.[80] To demonstrate the trans-boundary dimension of nuclear weapons detonations, for example on Austria, a presentation calculated the impact of a nuclear explosion of 200 kilotons in northern Italy, based on the geographical coordinates of the NATO military base in Aviano where US nuclear weapons are stored.[81] The focus on risks associated with nuclear weapons was also deepened: participants heard expert presentations on nuclear doctrines, war planning and scenarios of nuclear conflict, cyber-risks, risk calculation of nuclear war and an assessment of the risk of nuclear weapons use from a systems perspective.

The Vienna Conference added an analysis of existing international law and its applicability to nuclear weapons to the discussion, an aspect not addressed at the two previous conferences. The implications of the humanitarian findings were examined by panels from the perspectives of environmental norms, the World Health Organization's international health regulations, and the principles of international humanitarian law. The extent to which humanitarian considerations are addressed in existing international law regulating arms was also examined, as well as the ethical and legal principles on which international law is based, and how they pertain to nuclear weapons.

The ethical dimension of the nuclear debate was the subject of a personal message from Pope Francis to the Vienna Conference. This message was further expanded upon in a Vatican position paper presented in Vienna, calling in to question the moral justification of nuclear deterrence, making a strong call for nuclear abolition and positing the "need to resist succumbing to the limits set by political realism". In the paper, the Vatican further elaborated its position on nuclear deterrence, arguing *inter alia* that:

> In the absence of further progress toward complete disarmament and without concrete steps toward a more secure and a more genuine peace, the nuclear weapon establishment has lost much of its legitimacy. . . . Since what is intended is mass destruction – with extensive and lasting collateral damage, inhumane suffering and the risk of escalation – the system of nuclear deterrence can no longer be deemed a policy that stands firmly on moral ground.[82]

In the general debate on the second day, the question of which political conclusions should be drawn from the various new substantive findings of the humanitarian discourse loomed large in the statements by States, international organisations and civil society. Most non-nuclear weapon States argued that by posing considerable risks of unacceptable and catastrophic consequences, the existence of nuclear weapons endangered their security. They found that the complete elimination of nuclear weapons was the only guarantee against these risks, and that the humanitarian focus should generate urgent progress on nuclear disarmament. A growing number of States called explicitly for a prohibition against nuclear weapons.

In contrast, the statements by the nuclear umbrella States, the US, and the UK, expressed understanding for the humanitarian concerns but underscored the role nuclear weapons played in their security concepts as well as the global security environment, which needed to be taken into account. They argued for the maintenance of nuclear deterrence and the continuation of the so-called "step-by-step" approach to nuclear disarmament, as against a ban treaty approach.

At the end of the conference, as agreed in advance, Austria presented a Summary[83] that reflected the different State perspectives, as expressed in their statements. The Chair's Summary also contained a consolidated compilation of the main humanitarian findings that had been developed in Vienna and at the two preceding Conferences:

- The impact of a nuclear weapon detonation, irrespective of the cause, would not be constrained by national borders and could have regional and even global consequences, causing destruction, death and displacement as well as profound and long-term damage to the environment, climate, human health and well-being, socioeconomic development, social order and could even threaten the survival of humankind.

- The scope, scale and interrelationship of the humanitarian consequences caused by nuclear weapon detonation are catastrophic and more complex than commonly understood. These consequences can be large scale and potentially irreversible.
- The use and testing of nuclear weapons have demonstrated their devastating immediate, mid- and long-term effects. Nuclear testing in several parts of the world has left a legacy of serious health and environmental consequences. Radioactive contamination from these tests disproportionately affects women and children. It contaminates food supplies and continues to be measurable in the atmosphere to this day.
- As long as nuclear weapons exist, there remains the possibility of a nuclear weapon explosion. Even if the probability is considered low, given the catastrophic consequences of a nuclear weapon detonation, the risk is unacceptable. The risks of accidental, mistaken, unauthorized or intentional use of nuclear weapons are evident due to the vulnerability of nuclear command and control networks to human error and cyber-attacks, the maintaining of nuclear arsenals on high levels of alert, forward deployment and their modernisation. These risks increase over time. The dangers of access to nuclear weapons and related materials by non-State actors, particularly terrorist groups, persist.
- There are many circumstances in which nuclear weapons could be used in view of international conflicts and tensions, and against the background of the current security doctrines of States possessing nuclear weapons. As nuclear deterrence entails preparing for nuclear war, the risk of nuclear weapon use is real. Opportunities to reduce risk must be taken now, such as de-alerting and reducing the role of nuclear weapons in security doctrines. Limiting the role of nuclear weapons to deterrence does not remove the possibility of their use. Nor does it address the risks stemming from accidental use. The only assurance against the risk of a nuclear weapon detonation is the total elimination of nuclear weapons.
- No State or international body could address in an adequate manner the immediate humanitarian emergency or long-term consequences caused by a nuclear weapon detonation in a populated area, nor provide adequate assistance to those affected. Such capacity is unlikely ever to exist. Coordinated preparedness may nevertheless be useful in mitigating the effects including of a terrorist event involving the explosion of an improvised nuclear device. The imperative of prevention as the only guarantee against the humanitarian consequences of nuclear weapons use was highlighted.
- Looking at nuclear weapons from a number of different legal angles, it is clear that there is no comprehensive legal norm universally prohibiting possession, transfer, production and use. International environmental law remains applicable in armed conflict and can pertain to nuclear weapons, although it does not specifically regulate these arms. Likewise, international health regulations would cover effects of nuclear weapons. The new evidence that

has emerged in the last two years about the humanitarian impact of nuclear weapons casts further doubt on whether these weapons could ever be used in conformity with IHL. As was the case with torture, which defeats humanity and is now unacceptable to all, the suffering caused by nuclear weapons use is not only a legal matter, it necessitates moral appraisal.
- The catastrophic consequences of a nuclear weapon detonation event and the risks associated with the mere existence of these weapons raise profound ethical and moral questions on a level transcending legal discussions and interpretations.[84]

The Chair's Summary was facts-based, in line with the assurances that Austria had given in advance of the Conference and to avoid the kind of criticism expressed about the Nayarit Chair's Summary. Austria nevertheless wanted to strengthen the Humanitarian Initiative and indicate what a future political process towards a legal norm, based on humanitarian principles, could look like. At the end of the conference, Austria presented a strictly national commitment, the "Austrian Pledge".[85] In this document, the Conference hosts drew the "inescapable conclusions" from the evidence and facts developed in the course of the Humanitarian Initiative. The Austrian Pledge, which will be discussed in more detail in Chapter 2, became an important milestone in the Humanitarian Initiative and a catalyst for political momentum for the TPNW.

By the end of the Vienna Conference, several key "Amersham Group" goals had been achieved: a compelling set of arguments had been gathered and consolidated around the unacceptable humanitarian consequences and risks associated with nuclear weapons; the heretofore dominant narrative which gives status and value to the possession of nuclear weapons had been challenged; a stigma that use, as well as the possession, of nuclear weapons is incompatible with concepts of "humanity" was established.

A large number of States responded enthusiastically to this re-framing of the nuclear weapons discourse and with a sense of empowerment. It had been demonstrated that a humanitarian focus on nuclear weapons can be pursued meaningfully, even if nuclear weapon States do not participate. The consensus rule had been successfully challenged in the open-ended working group, further challenging the "special status" of nuclear weapon States. And, maybe, most importantly, civil society organisations had been energised by the Humanitarian Initiative, consolidating around an effective and simple ban treaty campaign with ICAN the de facto coordinating organisation.

Notes

1 Wildfire message to States of 19 May 2013, available at www.wildfire-v.org.
2 The statements held during the 2010 NPT Review Conference are available at www.un.org/en/conf/npt/2010/statements/statements.shtml.
3 Michael Spindelegger, "Foreign Minister of Austria", statement at the 2010 NPT Review Conference on 3 May 2010, available at www.un.org/en/conf/npt/2010/statements/statements.shtml.

The game needs to change 47

4 For a comprehensive analysis of Norway's role see Kjølv Egeland, "Oslo's 'New Track': Norwegian Nuclear Disarmament Diplomacy 2005–2013", in *Journal for Peace and Nuclear Disarmament*, pp. 468–490, available at https://doi.org/10.1080/25751654.2019.1671145; A significant part of Egeland's research is based on internal MFA documents released on freedom of information requests. Egeland's findings are consistent with my own close dealing with Norwegian diplomats and civil society representatives in this period; see also John Borrie, Michael Spies, and Wilfred Wan, "Obstacles to Understanding the Emergence and Significance of the Treaty on the Prohibition of Nuclear Weapons", in *Global Change, Peace & Security*, 2018, p. 9, available at https://doi.org/10.1080/14781158.2018.1467394.
5 Espen Barth Eide, Deputy Defence Minister of Norway, Statement to the Conference on Disarmament on Geneva, 17 February 2009, available at www.unog.ch/80256EDD006B8954/(httpAssets)/D3B3E2EA6FA3314DC12575600053CC0C/$file/1124_Norway.pdf.
6 Jonas Gahr Støre, Foreign Minister of Norway, Statement at a Conference of the Norwegian Atlantic Committee, 1 February 2010, available at www.regjeringen.no/no/dokumentarkiv/stoltenberg-ii/ud/taler-og-artikler/2010/disarmament/id592550/.
7 Egeland, "Oslo's 'New Track'", p. 476. Several other governments also provided funding to these organisations but not at the level of Norway.
8 For more information about these organisations see, www.icanw.org/; www.reachingcriticalwill.org/; www.article36.org/ and www.ilpi.org/.
9 The model NWC was submitted to the General Assembly (A/62/650) by Malaysia and Costa Rica in 2007. It outlines all aspects of a prohibition of nuclear weapons, including a phased program for their elimination and a verification regime. It, thus, requires the participation of nuclear weapon States, who did not support the NWC. The ban treaty approach focusses only on the legal prohibition aspect and was therefore something that could be pursued without necessarily the participation of nuclear weapon States. For more information on the NWC, see International Association of Lawyers Against Nuclear Arms, International Network of Engineers and Scientists Against Proliferation and International Physicians for the Prevention of Nuclear War, "Securing our Survival (SOS): The Case for a Nuclear Weapons Convention", 2007, available at http://lcnp.org/pubs/2007-securing-our-survival.pdf.
10 Based on several conversations with ICAN representatives. See also see Borrie et al., "Obstacles to Understanding the Emergence and Significance of the Treaty on the Prohibition of Nuclear Weapons", p. 6; Rebecca Davis Gibbons, "The Humanitarian Turn in Nuclear Disarmament and the Treaty on the Prohibition of Nuclear Weapons", in *The Nonproliferation Review*, vol. 25, no. 1–2, 2018, p. 17, available at https://doi.org/10.1080/10736700.2018.1486960.
11 All individuals of the "Amersham Group" had longstanding multilateral experience and had been closely involved in previous humanitarian disarmament efforts. To allow for an open discussion, participation was in a "personal capacity" only, meaning that they were not representing their respective organisations but took part in the meeting as individual experts.
12 Author's personal notes and archive.
13 Conversation of the author with an Amersham participant on 24 October 2019.
14 See also Borrie et al., "Obstacles to Understanding the Emergence and Significance of the Treaty on the Prohibition of Nuclear Weapons".
15 First Preparatory Committee for the 2015 NPT Review Conference in Vienna, Austria, 30 April–11 May 2012, see www.un.org/disarmament/wmd/nuclear/npt2015/prepcom2012.
16 See Resolution 1, "Working Towards the Elimination of Nuclear Weapons", adopted by the Council of Delegates on the International Red Cross and Red Crescent Movement, Geneva Switzerland, 26 November 2011, available at www.icrc.org/en/doc/resources/documents/resolution/council-delegates-resolution-1-2011.htm.

17 Egeland, "Oslo's 'New Track'", p. 474.
18 Statement by Norway on 30 April 2012 in the General Debate at the First Preparatory Committee for the 2015 NPT Review Conference, available at www.un.org/disarmament/wmd/nuclear/npt2015/prepcom2012-statements/.
19 Ira Helfand, "Nuclear Famine: Two Billion People at Risk? Global Impacts of Limited Nuclear War on Agriculture, Food Supplies, and Human Nutrition", in *IPPNW and Physicians for Social Responsibility*, 2nd ed., November 2013, available at www.ippnw.org/nuclear-famine.html.
20 See "Joint Statement on the humanitarian dimension of nuclear disarmament" by Austria, Chile, Costa Rica, Denmark, the Holy See, Egypt, Indonesia, Ireland, Malaysia, Mexico, New Zealand, Nigeria, Norway, the Philippines, South Africa and Switzerland at the First Preparatory Committee for the 2015 NPT Review Conference, 2 May 2012, available at www.reachingcriticalwill.org/images/documents/Disarmament-fora/npt/prepcom12/statements/2May_IHL.pdf.
21 Ibid.
22 Joint Statement delivered by Switzerland on behalf of 34 States, 22 October 2012; all subsequent statements are available at www.reachingcriticalwill.org.
23 Joint Statement delivered by South Africa on behalf of 80 States, 24 April 2013.
24 Joint Statement delivered by New Zealand on behalf of 125 States, 21 October 2013.
25 Joint Statement delivered by New Zealand on behalf of 155 States, 20 October 2014.
26 Joint Statement delivered by Austria on behalf of 159 States, 28 April 2015.
27 See also Alexander Kmentt, "The Development of the International Initiative on the Humanitarian Impact of Nuclear Weapons and Its Effect of the Nuclear Weapons Debate", in *International Review of the Red Cross*, vol. 97, 2015, p. 688, available at https://doi.org/10.1017/S1816383116000059.
28 Joint Statement delivered by Australia on behalf of 17 States, 21 October 2013.
29 See Editorial in *Japan Times* on 11 May 2013, available at www.japantimes.co.jp/opinion/2013/05/11/editorials/preventing-use-of-nuclear-weapons/#.XjMK5GiTJPY, see also Press Statement by Japanese Ministry for Foreign Affairs on 22 October 2013, available at www.mofa.go.jp/press/release/press4e_000047.html.
30 Joint Statement delivered by Austria on behalf of 159 States, 28 April 2015.
31 Joint Statement delivered by Australia on behalf of 24 States, 30 April 2015, available at www.reachingcriticalwill.org.
32 See Chapter 1.
33 See Resolution, "Taking Forward Multilateral Nuclear Disarmament Negotiations", A/C.1/67/L.46 (A/RES/67/56), available at www.reachingcriticalwill.org/disarmament-fora/unga/2012/resolutions.
34 During the First Committee in October 2012, the three co-sponsors engaged in so-called informal consultations on the resolution with individual States or groups of States in which I participated.
35 This is the result of the vote on the resolution in the Plenary of the General Assembly on 3 December 2012.
36 See "Explanation of vote" by the UK on behalf of France, UK and the US on 6 November 2012, available at www.reachingcriticalwill.org/images/documents/Disarmament-fora/1com/1com12/eov/L46_France-UK-US.pdf.
37 In addition to the three original co-sponsors Austria, Norway and Mexico, also Chile, Costa Rica, Iceland, Ireland, Liechtenstein, New Zealand, Nigeria, Philippines, Trinidad and Tobago and Uruguay had co-sponsored the resolution in the 2012 First Committee and helped actively to prepare the three sessions. Some of the nuclear umbrella States, among them Australia, Canada, Germany, Japan, Netherlands, also played an active role in the preparations.
38 For more details see website of the United Nations Office Geneva, "Taking Forward Multilateral Nuclear Disarmament Negotiations", available at www.unog.ch/cd.

39 See "Report of the Open-Ended Working Group to Develop Proposals to Take Forward Multilateral Nuclear Disarmament Negotiations for the Achievement and Maintenance of a World Without Nuclear Weapons", adopted on 3 September 2013, available at https://documents-dds-ny.un.org/doc/UNDOC/GEN/N13/506/11/PDF/N1350611.pdf?OpenElement.
40 Ibid., para. 29.
41 This became also an important element of the discussions during the 2016 open-ended working group. See Chapter 3, p. 7 and the arguments made in the Brazilian Working paper.
42 Ibid., para. 41–42.
43 See "An Exploration of Some Contributions That Non-Nuclear Weapon States Could Engage in to Take Multilateral Nuclear Disarmament Forward", working paper A/AC.281/WP.5, submitted by Austria on 28 June 2013, available at http://daccess-ods.un.org/access.nsf/Get?Open&JN=G1361975.
44 See Reaching Critical Will, "Open-Ended Working Group on Nuclear Disarmament – Report 6", September 2013, available at www.reachingcriticalwill.org/disarmament-fora/oewg/2013/reports.
45 In particular Switzerland, New Zealand and Ireland expressed this in conversations with the author at the time. Several States and civil society organisations also voiced this expectation at a workshop "Outcomes and Future of the Open-Ended Working Group on Nuclear Disarmament" organised by the James Martin Center for Non-Proliferation Studies, Geneva Centre for Security Policy on 17 August 2013 at which Egypt, Germany, Mexico, Costa Rica, Ireland, Kirgizstan, Finland, Sweden, Austria and a number of NGOs were present.
46 Egeland, "Oslo's 'New Track'", p. 474.
47 Esper Bart Eide, Minister for Foreign Affairs of Norway, opening statement at the Conference on the Humanitarian Impact of Nuclear Weapons, Oslo, Norway 4–5 March 2013, available at www.regjeringen.no/en/topics/foreign-affairs/humanitarian-efforts/humimpact_2013/id708603
48 More information on the Conference, the Chair's Summary and the presentations and statements are available at www.regjeringen.no/en/topics/foreign-affairs/humanitarian-efforts/humimpact_2013/id708603.
49 A "Chair's Summary" reflects the conclusions drawn by the chair. It is not a negotiated outcome and is therefore not binding for the participants of the Conference.
50 Ibid.
51 See Reaching Critical Will, "Conference Report Humanitarian Impact of Nuclear Weapons", Oslo Norway, 4–5 March 2013, p. 5, available at www.reachingcriticalwill.org.
52 This refers to the practice that the 5 Permanent members of the UN Security Council (P5) who are also the 5 NPT nuclear weapon States tend to coordinate their positions, especially in advance of NPT Review Conferences but also vis-à-vis initiatives and/or demands of non-nuclear weapon States. See also Chapter 2, p. 11.
53 "Joint explanatory note by China, France, Russia, the United Kingdom and the United States" regarding their non- attendance at the Oslo Conference, 2013, available at www.reachingcriticalwill.org/images/documents/Disarmament-fora/oslo-2013/P5_Oslo.pdf.
54 For the importance of "persistent objection" during the formation of customary international law. See Steven Hill and David Lemétayer, "The Treaty on the Prohibition of Nuclear Weapons: A Legal View from NATO", in *NATO Legal Gazette*, no. 39, May 2019. See also Curtis A. Bradley, "International Law in the U.S. Legal System", 2015, p. 138, available at https://doi.org/10.1093/acprof:oso/9780190217761.001.0001.
55 See "Farewell Oslo ¡Hasta Mexico!", in *ICAN Civil Society Forum Report*, 14 March 2013, available at https://goodbyenukes.wordpress.com/.

56 For more detail see Gibbons, "The Humanitarian Turn in Nuclear Disarmament and the Treaty on the Prohibition of Nuclear Weapons", p. 18.
57 See Borrie et al., "Obstacles to Understanding the Emergence and Significance of the Treaty on the Prohibition of Nuclear Weapons", p. 13.
58 The substantive and organisational preparations of the Nayarit Conference were, to a large extent carried out by Mexican diplomat María Antonieta Socorro Jáquez Huacuja whose contribution to the Humanitarian Initiative and the TPNW are very important.
59 See also John Borrie and Tim Caughley, *An Illusion of Safety: Challenges of Nuclear Weapon Detonations for United Nations Humanitarian Coordination and Response*, United Nations Disarmament Research Institute (UNIDIR), 2014, available at www.unidir.org/files/publications/pdfs/an-illusion-of-safety-en-611.pdf.
60 Patricia Lewis, Heather Williams, Benoît Pelopidas, and Sasan Aghlani, *Too Close for Comfort: Cases of Near Nuclear Use and Options for Policy*, Royal Institute of International Affairs, April 2014, available at www.chathamhouse.org/publications/papers/view/199200.
61 Eric Schlosser, *Command and Control: Nuclear Weapons, the Damascus Accident, and the Illusion of Safety*, Penguin Press, 2013.
62 See also Global Zero Commission on Nuclear Risk Reduction, "De-Alerting and Stabilizing the World's Nuclear Force Postures", April 2015, available at www.globalzero.org/wp-content/uploads/2018/09/global_zero_commission_on_nuclear_risk_reduction_report_0.pdf.
63 The Chair's Summary, the presentations and selected statements of the Second Conference on the Humanitarian Impact of Nuclear Weapons (Nayarit Conference) are available at www.reachingcriticalwill.org/images/documents/Disarmament-fora/nayarit-2014/chairs-summary.pdf.
64 See Ray Acheson, Beatrice Fihn, and Katherine Harrison, "Report from the Nayarit Conference", available at www.reachingcriticalwill.org/disarmament-fora/hinw/nayarit-2014/report; see also Kmentt, "The Development of the Humanitarian Initiative", p. 692.
65 Reaching Critical Will counted at least 20 States explicitly calling for a ban and over 50 unequivocally calling for the total elimination of nuclear weapons and the achievement of a nuclear weapons-free world. See Acheson et al., "Report from the Nayarit Conference".
66 Julie Bishop, Australian Foreign Minister, "We Must Engage, not Enrage Nuclear Countries", in *Sydney Morning Herald*, 14 February 2014, available at www.smh.com.au/opinion/we-must-engage-not-enrage-nuclear-countries-20140213-32n1s.html.
67 See "Chair's Summary" Nayarit Conference.
68 Austrian Foreign Ministry, "Kurz: 'Paradigm Shift in Nuclear Disarmament is Overdue'", press release on 13 February 2014, available at www.bmeia.gv.at/en/the-ministry/press/announcements/2014/kurz-paradigm-shift-in-nuclear-disarmament-is-overdue/.
69 Author's personal notes and archive.
70 I remember vividly that most participants and especially NGOs, cheered loudly in Nayarit when the Mexican chair concluded the Conference. I was plunged into panic, wondering how I could possibly manoeuvre through the political challenge that the organization of the upcoming Vienna Conference had just become.
71 Being tasked with the preparations for the Vienna Conference, I received most of these demarches.
72 See for example ICAN, "Nayarit Point of No Return: Mexico Conference Marks Turning Point Towards Nuclear Weapon Ban", press release, 14 February 2014, available at www.lasg.org/press/2014/press_release_14Feb2014.html.
73 Based on conversations of the author with diplomats and civil society representatives in the period before the Vienna Conference on the Humanitarian Impact of Nuclear Weapons.

74 For the preparation of the Vienna conference see Kmentt, "The Development of the Humanitarian Initiative", p. 694.
75 Statement by Austria at the Third Session of the Preparatory Committee for the 2015 Review Conference of the NPT, 2 May 2014, available at www.un.org/disarmament/wmd/nuclear/npt2015/prepcom2014/.
76 Ibid., see for example the Statement by Ireland of behalf of the New Agenda Coalition (Brazil, Egypt, Ireland, New Zealand, Mexico and South Africa) on 30 April 2014.
77 See, for example, "Leading Nuclear Policy Experts and Organizations Call on the United States to Participate in International Conference on Humanitarian Impacts of Nuclear Weapons", Arms Control Association Press Release on 29 October 2014, available at www.armscontrol.org/pressroom/2014-10/leading-nuclear-policy-experts-organizations-call-united-states-participate.
78 Office of the Spokesperson of the US Department of State, "United States Will Attend the Vienna Conference on the Humanitarian Impact of Nuclear Weapons", media note, 7 November 2014, available at https://2009-2017.state.gov/r/pa/prs/ps/2014/11/233868.htm.
79 See Borrie et al., "Obstacles to Understanding the Emergence and Significance of the Treaty on the Prohibition of Nuclear Weapons", p. 12.
80 All documents, presentations and statements, as well as a recording of the Vienna Conference on the Humanitarian Impact of Nuclear Weapons are available at www.bmeia.gv.at/index.php?id=55297&L=1 or www.hinw14vienna.at/index.php?id=55297&L=1.
81 See Matthew McKinzie et al., "Calculating the Effects of a Nuclear Explosion at a European Military Base", available at www.bmeia.gv.at/fileadmin/user_upload/Zentrale/Aussenpolitik/Abruestung/HINW14/Presentations/HINW14_S1_Presentation_NRDC_ZAMG.pdf.
82 See, "Nuclear Disarmament: Time for Abolition", position paper from the Holy See for the Vienna Conference, available at www.bmeia.gv.at/index.php?id=55297&L=1 or www.hinw14vienna.at, For the more recent development of the Catholic Church position on nuclear deterrence see Joshua J. McElwee, "Pope Condemns Possession of Nuclear Weapons in Shift from Church's Acceptance of Deterrence", in *The National Catholic Reporter*, 10 November 2017, available at www.ncronline.org/news/vatican/pope-condemns-possession-nuclear-weapons-shift-churchs-acceptance-deterrence and the statements made by Pope Francis in Hiroshima and Nagasaki in August 2019, See for example www.japantimes.co.jp/news/2019/11/24/national/full-text-of-pope-francis-nagasaki/#.XjBL62iTJPY; see also Pope Francis, "Tutti Fratelli – Encyclical Letter on Fraternity and Social Friendship", 3 October 2020, para. 262–267, available at www.vatican.va/content/francesco/en/encyclicals/documents/papa-francesco_20201003_enciclica-fratelli-tutti.html.
83 See "Chair's Summary" of the Vienna Conference on the Humanitarian Impact of Nuclear Weapons, available at www.bmeia.gv.at/index.php?id=55297&L=1 or www.hinw14vienna.at.
84 Ibid.
85 See "Austrian Pledge", available at www.bmeia.gv.at/index.php?id=55297&L=1 or www.hinw14vienna.at.

3 2015

The momentum gathers

> "I did not expect that they would become a cartel. And that's exactly what has happened. . . . It was those countries who can barely talk to each other about anything else, coming together to excoriate the rest of the world about not understanding the value of nuclear weapons".[1]

Early 2015: preparing for the 2015 NPT Review Conference

Could or should the Humanitarian Initiative be translated into a diplomatic process, to negotiate a legal norm prohibiting nuclear weapons? After the Vienna Conference in December 2014, this question loomed large. ICAN's campaign was now consolidated around the idea of a ban treaty. By arguing against such a ban treaty, the nuclear weapon States, and the nuclear umbrella States provided evidence that this was also what they were expecting. The architects of the Humanitarian Initiative continued to discuss possible ways forward in a number of informal meetings in the early months of 2015.

Our thinking was as follows: firstly, it was not yet clear how large the support for a new legal instrument actually was among non-nuclear weapon States. We saw evidence of strong and growing support for a focus on the humanitarian consequences and risks of nuclear weapons, but this momentum did not necessarily mean there was as much political support for a new treaty, especially if the nuclear weapon States were opposed to it. Secondly, the key objective of the Humanitarian Initiative was to create pressure and momentum for more progress on nuclear disarmament itself. This sense of urgency and pressure would have to be brought to the upcoming NPT Review Conference in May 2015. It was unlikely that political momentum for a new treaty would be there before then. Thirdly, the different options regarding the structure of a prohibition treaty and the provisions it should contain had yet to be discussed in detail. It therefore seemed prudent to first seek detailed discussion of these different options and their respective pros and cons. We anticipated that one of the most hotly debated issues at the NPT Review Conference would be whether the NPT, with its little implemented Article VI, had left a "legal gap" and, as a consequence, whether a comprehensive prohibition in a new multilateral nuclear disarmament treaty was required. On this issue, the States of the "New Agenda Coalition"[2] took a leading role.

Making the case for "Effective Legal Measures" to prohibit and eliminate nuclear weapons

At the NPT Preparatory Committee meeting in April/May 2014, the "New Agenda Coalition" presented a comprehensive working paper on Article VI of the NPT.[3] This working paper stated in some detail that

> in contradistinction to the high number of initiatives and arrangements currently in place to support the Treaty's non-proliferation agenda, the Treaty's article VI disarmament agenda has not been accorded the requisite priority. . . . and that . . . it is not acceptable that, 44 years after the entry into force . . . the parties to the Treaty have not yet elaborated the 'effective measures' that article VI requires.[4]

The working paper went on to present a cogent case as to why the need to prevent the catastrophic humanitarian consequences of nuclear weapons demands a clear, legally-binding, multilateral commitment to achieve nuclear disarmament. The working paper calls on "all parties to the Treaty (to) pursue and elaborate 'effective measures' for the achievement of the Treaty's irreducible disarmament imperatives".[5] Some of the key provisions essential to any future treaty are also discussed, such as on prohibitions, verification and national implementation. Finally, the working paper elaborates in detail four different options for a future legal instrument

> for the achievement and maintenance of a world without nuclear weapons . . . which should now be explored, discussed and tested against the requirements of article VI.
>
> 1) A comprehensive Nuclear Weapons Convention, which, in setting out general obligations, prohibitions and an effective basis for time-bound, irreversible and verifiable nuclear disarmament, would complement the Chemical Weapons Convention and the Biological and Toxin Weapons Convention as an effective measure for the elimination of all weapons of mass destruction;
>
> 2) A Nuclear Weapons Ban Treaty, which would establish the key prohibitions necessary for the pursuit, achievement and maintenance of a world free of nuclear weapons; such a Treaty could, but need not, additionally set out the practical arrangements required for implementing and overseeing effective, time-bound, irreversible and verifiable nuclear disarmament;
>
> 3) A framework arrangement of mutually supporting instruments aimed at achieving and maintaining a world free of nuclear weapons. These would work in concert to establish the key prohibitions, obligations and arrangements for the achievement and maintenance of a world free of nuclear weapons;
>
> 4) A hybrid arrangement which might include elements of all or any of the above options, or new elements.[6]

The "New Agenda Coalition" working paper provided arguments and structure for a future discussion of four different options on "effective legal measures" to implement the nuclear disarmament obligation under NPT Article VI. The suggested discussion of four different options would make it less controversial for States to engage in this debate, even if they had not yet taken a definite decision as to whether they would support any of them. Most importantly, though, the working paper provided clear reasoning as to why the existing legal framework for multilateral nuclear disarmament (note: NPT Art. VI) is incomplete and therefore not viable, without the addition of a comprehensive legal norm, universally prohibiting nuclear weapons. In light of the humanitarian consequences and risks of nuclear weapons, this situation needed to be remedied with urgency. This reasoning and the conclusion on the need "to fill the legal gap" became the key rationale behind the "Austrian Pledge" as discussed below.

The "Austrian Pledge"

The "Austrian Pledge",[7] later renamed the "Humanitarian Pledge",[8] was introduced at the closing ceremony of the Vienna Conference on the Humanitarian Impact of Nuclear Weapons on 8 December 2014 as a strictly national commitment by Austria.[9] As a catalyst for the TPNW, the "Pledge" played a very significant role in the following two years. It provided an action-oriented commitment that States supporting the Humanitarian Initiative could associate themselves with. It also provided a highly effective campaign and public information tool with which ICAN could approach and lobby States and mobilise civil society. When the Nobel Committee in Oslo, Norway, announced its decision to award the 2017 Nobel Peace Prize to ICAN, it recognised the role played by the "Humanitarian Pledge". The Committee highlighted ICAN's "work to draw attention to the catastrophic humanitarian consequences of any use of nuclear weapons and for its ground-breaking efforts to achieve a treaty-based prohibition of such weapons". Furthermore, citing the key formulation of the "Humanitarian Pledge", the Committee stressed that

> ICAN has been a driving force in prevailing upon the world's nations to pledge to cooperate with all relevant stakeholders in efforts to stigmatise, prohibit and eliminate nuclear weapons. To date, 127 states have made such a commitment, known as the Humanitarian Pledge.[10]

My idea of presenting a national pledge, in addition to the Chair's Summary at the Vienna Conference, was born in the early planning stages of the Vienna conference in autumn 2013 and proposed in an internal memo in the Austrian Foreign Ministry.[11] States participating at the Vienna Conference would expect a factual Chair's Summary without political conclusions, which not all States may be in agreement with. The nuclear umbrella States, in particular, had made this expectation very clear to the Austrian hosts.[12] A political conclusion, charting or indicating a way forward for the Humanitarian Initiative, could therefore not be included in the Chair's Summary. Such conclusions could, however, be presented in the form of a national commitment. I wrote the text of the "Austrian Pledge" in collaboration with a small group of colleagues[13] in the Austrian Foreign Ministry in the days leading up to the Vienna Conference, once the conference programme was finalised and the level of participation by States confirmed. It was not shared with other delegations. In a meeting of the "Amersham Group"[14] shortly before the Vienna conference, I did however inform those present of the intention to issue such a national pledge at the end of the upcoming Vienna Conference.[15]

The "Austrian Pledge" was drafted deliberately in the format of a UN General Assembly resolution for two reasons: firstly, as States were familiar with this kind of document, it would make it easier, I hoped, for States to associate themselves with this document; similar to co-sponsoring a UN General Assembly resolution. Secondly, should it at a later stage become appropriate to introduce the "Austrian Pledge" to the General Assembly, the document would already be in the correct format of a resolution. This turned out to be the case, later in 2015.

The preambular paragraphs of the pledge set out the key arguments regarding the humanitarian consequences of nuclear weapons, the risks associated with these weapons, the lack of humanitarian response capabilities and the important role of international organisations, relevant UN entities, the Red Cross and Red Crescent Movement, elected representatives, academia and civil society in a humanitarian-focused debate on nuclear weapons. In the second part of the document, the operative paragraphs, the document set out key political commitments paving the way for the future negotiations of the TPNW, by pledging

> to identify and pursue effective measures to fill the legal gap for the prohibition and elimination of nuclear weapons, . . . to cooperate with all stakeholders . . . in efforts to stigmatise, prohibit and eliminate nuclear weapons in light of their unacceptable humanitarian consequences and associated risks.[16]

This pledge to "fill the legal gap" was, however, not an explicit endorsement for a particular legal outcome or format of a treaty but rather a commitment to push for "effective legal measures" as suggested by the "New Agenda Coalition". The new evidence of the humanitarian consequences and risks of nuclear weapons provided a compelling case for more urgency and more credible progress on nuclear disarmament. Effective legal measures "to fill the legal gap" are a crucial element of this. The exact format of these legal measures was secondary, the different options for them needed to be discussed, nonetheless. In the immediate aftermath of the Vienna Conference, when States were invited to associate themselves with the "Austrian Pledge", this position was encapsulated in an internal background note sent to all Austrian embassies worldwide:

> civil society organisations interpret the 'Austrian Pledge' as an expression of support for a ban-treaty. If asked, it should be clarified that Austria would support every legal approach that credibly promotes nuclear disarmament. Austria has not yet taken a decision as regards a particular legal approach

but is of the view that the discussion about such legal approaches should take place urgently and that the upcoming 2015 NPT Review Conference should take the long overdue steps in this regard.[17]

The US, the UK and nuclear umbrella States participating at the Vienna conference noted positively that the Chair's Summary included their perspectives on the nuclear weapons issue.[18] Australia, for example, declared itself "pleased to see a more balanced range of views in the Chair's Statement" than at the previous conference in Mexico".[19] In retrospect, it seems that the significance of the "Austrian Pledge" was initially underestimated. The main concern, namely that the Vienna Conference could launch a negotiation process towards a ban-treaty, had been averted. Evidence for this conclusion can be found in the cable sent from the Australian Mission in Vienna after the December 2014 Conference, containing the assessment that "the push for a ban on nuclear weapons had failed to gain the kind of traction that its proponents had hoped for". The cable dismissed the "Austrian Pledge" as amounting "to little more than a promise to take the outcomes of the conference to the 2015 NPT [Review Conference] and other relevant UN bodies".[20] In my view, a national commitment undertaken by a small country such as Austria was not considered particularly significant.

Austria now charged its diplomatic network worldwide with promoting and distributing the outcome of the Vienna Conference. All 193 member States of the United Nations were invited to associate themselves with the "Austrian Pledge" in order "to further strengthen the humanitarian arguments and findings in advance of the upcoming NPT Review Conference and to underscore the expectation of the international community for credible and urgent progress in this field".[21]

While we hoped that some States would respond positively to this initiative, and that civil society organisations would help to promote the "Austrian Pledge", it was by no means certain. The first indication that the pledge was gaining traction came a month later, at the Third Summit of the Community of Latin American and Caribbean States (CELAC) held in Costa Rica on 28–29 January 2015. Upon the initiative of Mexico and Costa Rica, an explicit endorsement of the "Austrian Pledge" on the part of the Heads of State or Government of 33 States of CELAC was included in a Special Declaration on the "Urgent Need for a Nuclear Weapon-Free World".[22]

In the subsequent months, Austria continued its own diplomatic outreach to encourage States to sign up to the pledge, but it was ICAN that turned the "Austrian Pledge" into the effective campaign tool that we had hoped for in the Austrian Foreign Ministry. ICAN understood the potential of the "Pledge" to create momentum behind the idea of the ban-treaty. ICAN's report of the Vienna Conference concluded that

> Vienna gave us a starting point. It gave us a Pledge to pursue a legal prohibition on nuclear weapons. But it also gave us a way forward in reconstructing how we think about and approach nuclear weapons. It is the most exciting

opportunity we have to deal with these weapons once and for all. We must seize it and ban nuclear weapons now.[23]

In one of the informal meetings of the "Berkshire Group"[24] in February 2015, the value of the pledge was described by ICAN as follows:

> The 'Austrian Pledge' is proving a very useful advocacy tool for ICAN in the period after Vienna. It provides campaigners around the world with an opportunity to ask their governments a political question: will your government work with others to fill the legal gap for the prohibition and elimination of nuclear weapons? The level of sign up to the Pledge will be the clearest indication yet of which states are ready to move forward in a diplomatic process.[25]

ICAN campaigners embarked on a large-scale global lobbying campaign in support of the "Austrian Pledge" and encouraged States to send diplomatic communications – so-called "Notes Verbales" – to the Austrian Foreign Ministry, formally expressing their wish to be associated with the pledge.[26] In the following months, the number of States that did this increased steadily, so that by the start of the 2015 NPT Review Conference,[27] 78 States had formally endorsed the "Austrian Pledge". A website was set up by the Austrian Foreign Ministry where the growing list of "pledge-supporters" could be traced.[28] This campaign continued during and after the Review Conference.

As a result of the Vienna Conference, both the substantive arguments and the political conclusions on how to proceed with the Humanitarian Initiative had thus taken shape: firstly, the substantive findings on the humanitarian consequences and risks of nuclear weapons had been built into a compelling case for urgency on nuclear disarmament progress. Secondly, a strong focus was brought to bear on the need to "fill the legal gap" with four options for such "effective legal measures" clearly laid out by the "New Agenda Coalition". Both elements were encapsulated in the "Austrian Pledge", which chartered a clear, political way forward for the Humanitarian Initiative and enjoyed growing support. Finally, all of this was complemented and supported by a highly effective ICAN campaign which focussed the attention on and argued in favour of a ban-treaty.

The immediate run-up to the 2015 NPT Review Conference

"Armed" with growing momentum and strong substantive arguments, the attention of the supporters of the Humanitarian Initiative now shifted to the upcoming 2015 NPT Review Conference. It was clear that the humanitarian consequences and the "effective legal measures to fill the legal gap for the prohibition and elimination of nuclear weapons", would be key issues.

As regards their implementation of the 2010 Action Plan, it was now quite clear that after five years, the nuclear weapon States had little to show for their promises.[29] Despite the ongoing reduction of deployed strategic nuclear weapons by the US and Russia under the new START Treaty, all five nuclear weapon States were modernizing their nuclear arsenals. This, and the significant budgetary resources committed to these modernization programmes, demonstrated that all the nuclear weapon States had plans of retaining their nuclear arsenals for many decades to come. Importantly, there were neither visible evidence of significant changes, nor plans for those changes, which would reduce the role of nuclear weapons in their doctrines. Moreover, the state of paralysis in the Conference on Disarmament continued unchanged and progress on the entry into force of the CTBT was nowhere in sight. In short, there was no discernible sign that nuclear weapon States had any intention of changing their approach to nuclear disarmament or pursuing this with any heightened sense of urgency.

The much heralded "P5 Process",[30] a dedicated forum for the nuclear weapon States, established in 2009 to discuss their responsibilities under the NPT, with a particular focus on nuclear disarmament had also yielded very little, bar a common reporting format for the nuclear weapon States and the development of a "Glossary of Key Nuclear Terms".[31] As much as non-nuclear weapons States made an effort to recognize the relevance of these steps, they could hardly be interpreted as signs of an urgent focus on nuclear disarmament. Much of the "P5 Process" discussion appeared to centre around their shared opposition to non-nuclear weapon States initiatives, such as the Humanitarian Initiative, rather than providing a common vision on how progress on nuclear disarmament could be achieved. Lord Desmond Browne of Ladyton, the former UK Secretary of State for Defence and initiator in 2009 of the "P5 Process" later commented

> I did not expect that they [note: the P5] would become a cartel. And that's exactly what has happened. . . . It was those countries who can barely talk to each other about anything else, coming together to excoriate the rest of the world about not understanding the value of nuclear weapons.[32]

The fact that the nuclear weapon States opposed or dismissed the initiatives undertaken by the non-nuclear weapon States so strongly and largely failed to engage in the debate on the humanitarian consequences of nuclear weapons, did not make the outlook for the NPT Review Conference any better.

The 2010 NPT Review Conference had already been considered by some non-nuclear weapon States as the last chance to give more credibility to the NPT nuclear disarmament dimension.[33] This view had only intensified in the intervening five years. Through its ambiguous formulations, permitting the adoption of a Final Document by consensus, the Action Plan of 2010 had once again "papered over" the fundamental differences regarding nuclear disarmament between non-nuclear and nuclear weapon States. By 2015, it was clear that this attempt had also failed to create momentum for nuclear disarmament. The fate of the 2010 Action Plan now looked very similar to that of the other previous nuclear disarmament "success stories": the 1995 "principles and objectives" and the 2000 "thirteen practical steps".[34] For the sake of agreeing to a final document at the end of the

NPT Review Conference, in 2010, a semblance of consensus had again been maintained on the issue of nuclear disarmament. In reality, there was no consensus, either about the urgency of nuclear disarmament, or on what constituted a credible implementation of the NPT's Article VI obligation. It was therefore doubtful whether the same approach, brushing over such fundamental divergences through ambiguous consensus language could work again.

The supporters of the Humanitarian Initiative concentrated on bringing the humanitarian focus to the 2015 NPT Review Conference with as much force and momentum as possible. The "Austrian Pledge" stated a need to

> present the facts-based discussions, findings and compelling evidence . . . to all relevant fora, in particular the NPT Review Conference 2015 and in the UN framework, as they should be at the centre of all deliberations, obligations and commitments with regard to nuclear disarmament.

In the early months of 2015, growing support for the Humanitarian Initiative was reiterated by many States in their statements to multilateral fora in advance of the NPT Review Conference, such as in the Conference on Disarmament in Geneva[35] and the UN Disarmament Commission in New York.[36]

Many non-nuclear weapon States prepared working papers on nuclear disarmament for the 2015 NPT Review Conference with an unprecedented focus on the humanitarian consequences of nuclear weapons. Such working papers are issued by States or groups of States to highlight their specific priority issues and are intended to provide recommendations for inclusion in a potential consensus Final Document of the Review Conference.

A group of the most active supporters of the Humanitarian Initiative comprising Austria, Chile, Costa Rica, Holy See, Indonesia, Ireland, Malaysia, Mexico, New Zealand, Philippines, Sweden and Switzerland, presented a joint working paper exclusively on the issue of the humanitarian consequences of nuclear weapons. It contained 12 specific recommendations for the way in which the humanitarian focus of the past five years should be referenced in a Final Document of the 2015 Review Conference. The working paper stated that

> the overwhelming call by the international community for urgent progress towards the total elimination of nuclear weapons as the only way to avoid the catastrophic humanitarian consequences of nuclear weapons is a fact that must be acknowledged. It is the motivating force to the destination promised in the NPT – a world without nuclear weapons.[37]

The recommendations in the working paper explicitly focused on a recognition of the findings and evidence regarding the humanitarian consequences and risks of nuclear weapons. The idea behind presenting this working paper[38] was to see and test the extent to which nuclear weapon States would be prepared to engage constructively on the substantive issues developed in the context of the Humanitarian Initiative. If, arising from the increased knowledge and concern for the humanitarian consequences and risks of nuclear weapons, a consensus could at least be found on the need for more urgency on nuclear disarmament, this would be a significant "win" for the Humanitarian Initiative and a positive outcome for the Review Conference. Several other working papers prepared by States or group of States also highlighted the humanitarian consequences of nuclear weapons and urged progress on nuclear disarmament.[39]

The call for "effective legal measures" to "fill the legal gap" for the prohibition and elimination of nuclear weapons" as contained in the "Austrian Pledge" was again put forward by the "New Agenda Coalition". This group submitted an update to their working paper of 2014[40] on "Article VI of the Treaty on the Non-Proliferation of Nuclear Weapons".[41] It stated that the

> members of the New Agenda Coalition believe that it is high time to elaborate the 'effective measures' relating to nuclear disarmament which are required by article VI . . . States parties must now engage in serious discussions on the legal framework for a world without nuclear weapons and advance the necessary preparatory work [which] will enhance the Treaty's credibility and rectify the imbalance in implementation between nuclear disarmament and nuclear non-proliferation [and] serve to give the Treaty's existing prohibitions additional normative support.

The "New Agenda Coalition" working paper expressed the belief "that work to advance article VI's 'effective measures' should now focus on enabling a choice between two legal approaches: the stand-alone comprehensive convention/ban treaty or the framework agreement of mutually supporting instruments". To this end, it recommended "for decisions to be taken [by the Review Conference] to advance 'effective measures' with appropriate follow-up in all disarmament forums, as well as by the General Assembly".[42] Several other working papers echoed the New Agenda Coalition call for initiating such a discussion.[43]

The main supporters of the Humanitarian Initiative, thus, came to the NPT Review Conference equipped with strong arguments and two main objectives: firstly, to promote the substantive findings on the humanitarian consequences and risks of nuclear weapons and, secondly, to push for a discussion of "effective legal measures" for nuclear disarmament. Their position was underpinned by a growing level of support by non-nuclear weapon States for these proposals, as evidenced in many statements, working papers and the increasing number of endorsements for the "Austrian Pledge", which encapsulated both objectives.

The 2015 NPT Review Conference

The NPT Review Conference was held in New York from 27 April to 22 May 2015 under the presidency of Ambassador Taous Feroukhi of Algeria. It was an acrimonious meeting. Among the contentious issues, the Middle East[44] was very much a focus of attention. However, the nuclear disarmament issue was arguably as contentious and of prime importance to a greater number of non-nuclear weapon

States. The following analysis focuses solely on the nuclear disarmament negotiations over the course of the four weeks of the Conference and, specifically, how they pertain to the further development of the Humanitarian Initiative. It is a necessarily subjective account and not a reflection of the entire breadth of discussions and negotiations on the multitude of issues discussed at the Review Conference.

The four-day opening plenary session provided ample evidence of the significant momentum that the Humanitarian Initiative had generated among non-nuclear weapon States since 2010.[45] According to the NGO Reaching Critical Will and its detailed reporting of the Review Conference,[46] 70 States used their respective opening national statements to highlight this initiative.[47] Austria's Foreign Minister Sebastian Kurz delivered the largest cross-reginal group statement on a specific topic in the history of the United Nations. The "Joint Statement on the Humanitarian Dimension of Nuclear Disarmament" had the support of 159 States, all of whom expressed their deep concern about the humanitarian impact of nuclear weapons and demanded that nuclear weapons never be used under any circumstances.[48] ASEAN, CARICOM, CELAC, the Organisation for the Prohibition of Nuclear Weapons in Latin America and the Caribbean (OPANAL) and the Non-Proliferation and Disarmament Initiative (NPDI) delivered additional group statements in the same vein. Meanwhile, the Australia-led group of 26, mostly nuclear umbrella States, presented its now familiar "alternative humanitarian statement", arguing for the consideration of both humanitarian and security dimensions.[49]

On the issue of "effective legal measures" and the need to "fill the legal gap", the position was similar. The New Agenda Coalition reiterated its call for discussions to commence on "effective legal measures" and many States echoed this call or explicitly expressed support for the "Austrian Pledge",[50] which by this time had 78 States endorsing it.

As in previous Review Conferences, after the four days of opening plenary sessions, the Review Conference moved to meet in three different Main Committees. Main Committee One dealing with nuclear disarmament, Main Committee Two with non-proliferation of nuclear weapons and Main Committee Three with peaceful uses of nuclear energy. Each of the three Committees is tasked with the production of a report reviewing the implementation of the Treaty in the past five years but also containing a forward-looking section, with decisions and recommendations that can be agreed upon in the future. At the end of the Review Conference, these three different reports are – if there is consensus – collated into one Final Document of the Review Conference. Following past practice, a further sub-committee, the so-called Subsidiary Body I, was established within Main Committee One. This body has the specific task of developing proposals for commitments and actions which NPT member States agree to undertake in the next five years, in order to discharge their nuclear disarmament obligations under the Treaty.

The procedure for developing the reports in the NPT Review Conference is as follows: the Chair of the respective Main Committee or Subsidiary Body prepares a first draft document based on the positions and recommendations States have expressed in their statements, working papers and in informal consultations with the Chair. The documents are then presented to States in the respective committee, where they provide further comments, after which another draft is prepared and then discussed and so on until, hopefully, a consensus text emerges.

This process was followed in 2015 in Subsidiary Body I. Whereas plenary sessions and meetings of the Main Committees are normally open for the participation of observers and registered civil society groups,[51] Subsidiary Body I is restricted to State representatives. Swiss Ambassador Benno Laggner, the Chair of Subsidiary Body I, presented his first draft report of forward-looking measures on how to implement NPT Article VI on 8 May 2015.[52] Laggner drew on the very strong support expressed for the humanitarian consequences of nuclear weapons and the many substantial contributions on "effective legal measures" in this first draft:

> • The Conference agrees that . . . the catastrophic humanitarian consequences of any use of nuclear weapons should underpin and lend urgency to efforts by all States leading to the total elimination of nuclear weapons. It is in the interest of the very survival of humanity that nuclear weapons are never used again, under any circumstances;
> • that awareness of the catastrophic humanitarian consequences of any use of nuclear weapons should serve as a unifying factor and compel urgent action for the full implementation of article VI.

The draft document called upon the nuclear weapons States to:

> • ensure that their policies address fully all risks associated with nuclear weapons, which are greater than previously assumed; [and]

> reaffirms and recognizes that the total elimination of nuclear weapons is the only absolute guarantee against the humanitarian risks by the continued existence of nuclear weapons, including the threat of use of nuclear weapons.

The issue of "effective legal measures" was addressed in the draft text as follows:

> Noting that a majority of States parties believe that a legal framework is necessary for the full implementation of article VI, the Conference encourages all States to engage, without delay, within the framework of the United Nations disarmament machinery, in an inclusive process to identify and elaborate the legal provisions required for the achievement and maintenance of a world without nuclear weapons.

The draft then went on to list the four options of "effective legal measures" as proposed by the "New Agenda Coalition". Finally, the draft encouraged the continuation and intensification of efforts to raise awareness amongst the public, including younger and future generations, of all topics related to nuclear disarmament and non-proliferation, including on the humanitarian impact of nuclear weapons.

If the criteria for drafting an NPT document are to reflect what has been put forward as working papers and said by States in their statements, Ambassador Laggner produced a good text. He had based his draft on the groundswell of support for the Humanitarian Initiative and for addressing the "legal framework for the full implementation of article VI". The text was certainly not as progressive as the strongest supporters for nuclear disarmament and the Humanitarian Initiative had hoped for. In terms of concrete nuclear disarmament commitments and clear timelines for their implementation, it was vague and nuclear weapon States were merely "being called upon" or "encouraged".

The reaction of the nuclear weapon States to this draft document was nevertheless very negative and forceful. In Main Committee I, all five spoke out firmly against this draft with France, UK and the US calling it "unacceptable" and not "a basis for further work or consensus" and demanded that the text be scrapped in its entirety.[53] In the closed meetings of Subsidiary Body I, the tone was even harsher, including some rather personal attacks against the Swiss ambassador himself.[54] The US opposed the notion of the existence of a legal gap in the NPT, stating that effective measures are not limited to multilateral, legally binding actions. "We can accept that the final phase in the nuclear disarmament process should be pursued within an agreed legal framework but nothing in Article VI requires time frames or specific requirements for achieving the final elimination of nuclear weapons".[55] The other nuclear weapon States argued along the same lines. The UK, for example, stated that

> we hear a majority of countries say that nuclear weapons should never be used again under any circumstances. While we respect that view, that is language which cannot command consensus because to sign up to it would contradict our policy of nuclear deterrence. We will not agree that there is a gap in the NPT to be filled or a framework to be established by a single legal instrument.[56]

Surprisingly, the nuclear weapon States also rejected the notion that the focus on humanitarian consequences and risks had brought forward any new relevant information, arguing that these issues had been known for a long time. France, in particular, claimed that there has been "no new information in decades". US and France also said they did not believe that there was any increased risk of use of nuclear weapons, a line of argument that non-nuclear weapon States found highly questionable.[57] It was particularly striking that those nuclear weapon States most vehemently opposed to engaging in the debate and who had not participated in any of the three humanitarian conferences, were now arguing that there was no relevant information. As Matthew Bolton put it,

> France's claim that there is 'no new information' sounds remarkably like what social psychologists would identify as a projection of fault onto others.

The claim that there is no new information is actually an admission that they do not listen to new information or wish there was no new information.[58]

ICAN criticised the nuclear weapon States'

> increasingly frantic opposition to any discussion of a legally-binding instrument on the prohibition and elimination of nuclear weapons is directed at the 80+ states that have joined the pledge from the Vienna conference to fill the legal gap, as well as the New Agenda Coalition, which has sought to advance thinking on how to fill this gap.[59]

Non-nuclear weapon States and supporters of the Humanitarian Initiative, as well as NGOs, fought back against these assertions. In their statements, they pointed to the new evidence on the humanitarian impact of nuclear weapons and the many risk drivers that had been identified and discussed in detail since 2010. Ireland, for example, responded by highlighting that

> we must acknowledge reality. What we have learned about the risks and consequences of any use of nuclear weapons no longer affords us the luxury of simply continuing with an ad hoc parallel process of voluntary disarmament outside the NPT. What we have learned has changed the parameters of our discussion forever. That is the new reality.

Ireland further stated that it "cannot accept an outcome from this Review Conference that closes off any options for elaborating effective measures for nuclear disarmament before they have been discussed".[60]

South Africa delivered a statement with a particularly sharp analysis of the state of nuclear disarmament in the NPT. It amounted to a stinging rebuke of the approach presented by the nuclear weapon States. The statement pointed out that the

> misuse of the 2010 outcome as a roadmap seems to give licence to an approach, which suggests that they have an indefinite right to possess nuclear weapons. It further suggests that if they get tired of talking to each other, then they take a rest stop, whilst they are armed with the most dangerous weapons. . . . The security considerations of the five are unilateral and imposed on all of us. And of course, as many states parties have pointed out over the decades, if the nuclear-armed states and their nuclear-dependent allies continue to promote the perceived 'security benefits' of nuclear weapons, they are essentially promoting proliferation.[61]

This powerful statement was delivered by Ambassador Abdul Minty of South Africa and to experienced delegates, it was recognised as a legacy statement from the veteran negotiator of the 1995 NPT Review and Extension Conference. After he finished speaking, the meeting room erupted into sustained applause.

Despite the defence mounted by many of the non-nuclear weapon States, subsequent revisions of Laggner's draft became weaker. After three weeks, a consensus on nuclear disarmament seemed a remote prospect. The various debates demonstrated a dismissive and, in part, overtly hostile approach from nuclear weapon States. This was directed especially towards the arguments of the Humanitarian Initiative and the concept of initiating a discussion on the "effective legal measures". It became obvious that the nuclear weapon States were neither willing to accept any urgent nuclear disarmament steps, nor any need for more progress, or more timebound actions on nuclear disarmament. Their approach was essentially the same as in previous NPT Review Conferences, namely, to accept – at best – ambiguous language in documents, obfuscating the fundamental differences concerning what nuclear disarmament should mean and how urgently it should be pursued. The UK ambassador actually captured this in his statement when he said "it is a consensus that we should be looking for. How can anything other than a consensual outcome strengthen this treaty? A non-consensual outcome would indicate that there were very different interpretations of the treaty or of its implementation".[62] The nuclear weapon States apparently failed to understand or did not want to accept the degree of disenfranchisement their approach to the nuclear disarmament obligations under the NPT was causing to non-nuclear weapon States. In the words of South African Ambassador Minty

> we simply see agreements being reached and then soon after, some of the five [note: nuclear weapon States] walk away from these agreements, when the ink is hardly dry. So, what are we to do with these kinds of agreements? What has happened to the 1995 agreement? What has happened to the 2000 outcome and other outcomes that we have had? Why do some still talk as if we do not have such agreements? Why do some only refer to certain aspects of the Treaty and not to the NPT regime as a whole?[63]

As the Conference progressed, the nuclear weapon States' approach became ever clearer; as a result, it became ever easier to make the case for the "Austrian Pledge". On 18 May 2015, the Austrian delegation informed Main Committee One that as 84 States now supported the pledge; it was necessary to clarify that the "Austrian Pledge" was "no longer a national pledge only but a pledge supported by almost half of the NPT membership".[64] A new document, the "Humanitarian Pledge"[65] was issued by the Austrian Foreign Ministry.[66] ICAN was very effective in promoting the "Pledge" and continued its lobbying work throughout the duration of the Review Conference. With more and more non-nuclear weapons States disillusioned and discouraged by the apparent unlikelihood of any meaningful progress on nuclear disarmament being achieved, by the end of the Review Conference, support for the "Humanitarian Pledge" increased to 107 States.

The "Focus Group"

As no consensus in Main Committee One was in sight at the beginning of the fourth and final week, the President of the Review Conference convened an informal "Focus Group" of 19 delegations.[67] The specific purpose of this group hosted in informal meetings in the Permanent Mission of Algeria was to try to find consensus language on nuclear disarmament. While small informal groups have also been convened in previous NPT Review Conferences, the practice itself is somewhat problematic. On what basis are the participants selected? No records exist for such meetings, and how do non-participants see this from the point of view of transparency of process and the legitimacy of any potential outcome? I was extended an invitation by the Review Conference President, specifically to represent the "humanitarian camp", given that Austria had coordinated the cross-regional statement supported by 159 States and the growing support for the "Humanitarian Pledge".

The discussions in the Algerian Mission were convened on four days from Monday 18 until Thursday 21 May 2015. They took place in a small, poorly air-conditioned, densely packed room. Two participants per delegation attended; the discussions lasted the whole of each day and late into the first two nights. The most contentious issues continued to be the Humanitarian Initiative, calls for more transparency by the nuclear weapon States, the meaning of "effective legal measures", and whether or not an additional legally binding instrument would be required to fully implement article VI of the NPT.

As Potter describes, recollections of what happened in those four days vary considerably between the different participants. "What was regarded as important and clear to some attendees, is not recalled by others, who may well have been focused on different matters of particular importance to their delegations".[68] In my, admittedly subjective recollection, these meetings in the Algerian Mission were intense, difficult and acrimonious. They confirmed my concerns about convening this kind of informal "Focus Group" and the legitimacy of the NPT process itself. From my perspective, there was a high degree of "harmony" among the nuclear weapon States in their joint quest to weaken practically all the text elements on nuclear disarmament that they did not like in Ambassador Laggner's draft text. Nuclear weapon States took turns in objecting forcefully to different elements of the text, assisted at times by the nuclear umbrella States present. The more progressive nuclear disarmament elements of the text began to melt away. This dynamic was extremely frustrating to observe.

I focused on defending the "humanitarian language" in Laggner's draft and arguing for the inclusion of key elements of the joint cross-regional humanitarian statement supported by 159 States and of the recommendations of Working Paper 30.[69] Given that these humanitarian elements were supported by an overwhelming majority of the NPT membership, I argued that these formulations must be the basis for the negotiations around which to form a consensus. The fact that only a few of the 159 delegations who share these humanitarian concerns were "selected" to attend the "Focus Group" should not deny or silence their positions on the issues. Negotiations focused inter alia on whether the document could state that nuclear weapons should never be used again "under any circumstances". Nuclear weapon States vehemently objected to this language as it would be incompatible with their nuclear deterrence postures, which rely on the threat of use of nuclear weapons. For the other camp, the catastrophic global humanitarian consequences and the risks of nuclear weapons provided an absolute imperative to prevent their use. This is the central case on which the Humanitarian Initiative was built. In the "Focus Group" negotiations, I did not feel able to agree giving up this key phrase from the cross-regional humanitarian statement. For their part, nuclear weapon States objected also to a compromise suggestion of simply stating that 159 States had expressed this view in a cross-regional statement. They did not want to accept that an NPT Final Document in any way referenced and documented the fact that more than four fifths of the NPT membership had expressed their opposition to the legitimacy of the practice of nuclear deterrence.

After experiencing the "dynamic" of the negotiations of these "Focus Group" meetings, my view on the NPT process and its integrity has changed: it appears that the preparations for the Review Conference, the input and the working papers, as well as the proceedings and statements during the early phase of the Conference have only limited relevance for the actual result of the Conference. These aspects of the official work of the Review Conference is what non-nuclear weapon States traditionally focus on in the – false – expectation that their input and proposals will be relevant for the actual result of the Review Conference. For the nuclear weapon States, it appears to be entirely different. What really matters to them, is the maintenance of full control of the formal NPT proceedings and to ensure that the status quo is preserved. Whenever proposals that they object to emerge in the *formal* NPT proceedings, they are effectively "killed" in the *informal* meetings and in consultations. Here, pressure is applied to the Conference President and the Committee Chairs and onto individual delegations, especially in small, unrecorded settings such as the "Focus Group". In those intense meetings, there is no record, no scrutiny and the pro-disarmament views of the majority of States are underrepresented. The tables are turned even more in favour of the nuclear weapon States who, when it comes to rejecting nuclear disarmament ideas and reducing text proposals to a lowest possible level, act in surprising and considerable harmony. In the quest to maintain the status quo, they are, regrettably, sometimes aided by nuclear umbrella States, as was the case in these "Focus Group" meetings. Nuclear weapon States appear to deliberately gear their approach towards these opaque and unrecorded avenues, on the side-lines of the official meetings. Nuclear weapon States have applied this approach "successfully" at NPT Review Conferences – and other multilateral disarmament processes for that matter – for a long time. They have more experience, field larger delegations and have a stronger institutional memory than non-nuclear weapon States and, as a consequence, usually get their way, as evidenced by the history of NPT Review Conferences. The four days of the "Focus Group" meetings, were a case in point, demonstrating how little weight the nuclear weapon States are prepared to give to the arguments and demands raised by the Humanitarian Initiative and to positions that had been expressed by four fifths of the NPT membership.

With just two days to go before the end of the Conference, further negotiations in the "Focus Group" were called off on the evening of Wednesday 20 May. The divide between nuclear and non-nuclear weapon States had increased rather than diminished and seemed insurmountable.[70] Instead, President Feroukhi announced that she would present a text representing her "best efforts" to the Review Conference, for adoption as a Final Conference Document.[71] It was a "last ditch – take it or leave it"[72] text prepared under her own responsibility. It was, thus, not a negotiated document, but an attempt by the President to deliver a text that no delegation would disapprove of, so much as to break a consensus on its adoption.

The disarmament section of this document was drafted by Swiss Ambassador Laggner and presented to the "Focus Group" for comments, but not negotiations, in the Algerian Mission on the morning of Thursday 21 May. The exact positions of States towards Laggner's text are not clear. When it was presented to the "Focus Group", the text was certainly not endorsed and "no action remotely resembling agreement on the paper was ever taken".[73] No delegation in the "Focus Group" explicitly endorsed or rejected it. This apparently continued to be the case in the subsequent consultations by the President with individual delegations.

From the perspective of States pushing for more progress on nuclear disarmament, the draft was disappointing. Disarmament references were weak and did not live up to the high level of expectation and the sense of urgency for progress, expressed by most non-nuclear weapon States. ICAN was scathing in its analysis of the draft text, calling it "a nuclear-armed state text [that] sells out nuclear disarmament and serves those who seek to preserve and embolden the false perception of legitimacy of nuclear weapons asserted by nuclear-armed and their nuclear allied states".[74]

One problematic aspect was that Ambassador Laggner retained a proposal he had made during the "Focus Group" meetings. The draft text proposed that the upcoming First Committee of the UN General Assembly should establish an open-ended working group "to identify and elaborate effective measures for the full implementation of article VI" and that this group would "conduct its work on the basis of consensus".[75] In the "Focus Group" discussions, the US delegation had been quite receptive to a consensus-based open-ended working group. The level of acceptance for this idea from the other nuclear weapon States remained unclear. The participants in the "Focus Group" from the New Agenda Coalition as well as from Austria, were highly sceptical towards the idea of establishing another consensus-rule based forum. Channelling the "frustration" of non-nuclear weapon States into another, consensus-based, prolonged discussion process, was unsatisfactory. In all likelihood, it would not have any better prospect of success than the stalled Conference on Disarmament.

The draft final conference document

The President's draft for the Final Conference Document was distributed to all NPT State Parties on Thursday 21 May. She called for a final plenary meeting on the afternoon of Friday 22 May, the last day of the Review Conference, and hoped that delegations would not object to her compromise proposal. She consulted with delegations and asked for support for her draft text.

Several non-nuclear weapon States, including Austria, seriously considered blocking the adoption of this Final Document, owing to dissatisfaction with the

2015: the momentum gathers 69

nuclear disarmament section. Discussions to this end took place with respective capitals and with other like-minded delegations. However, right until the end of the Conference, a breakthrough in the parallel negotiations on the issue of a Middle Eastern Zone free of Weapons of Mass Destruction seemed possible.[76] These negotiations were still ongoing until the very last plenary meeting. An agreement on this issue would have meant significant progress for the NPT. Building support for a group of States to jointly block the Final Document on nuclear disarmament, while there was still a chance for progress on the Middle East issue, was problematic. Rather than blocking the adoption of the Final Document, Austria decided to seek support from other non-nuclear weapon States for a joint statement which clarified that the Final Document proposed by the President was not a negotiated result, and that the section pertaining to disarmament was unsatisfactory. With this statement, these delegations would be able to disassociate themselves from the disarmament section of the Final Document, while not formally breaking consensus on a possible successful Conference result on the Middle East. At least one non-nuclear weapon State nevertheless had instructions to block the Final Document.[77]

In the end, shortly before the final plenary session of the Review Conference, the Middle East negotiations also failed to reach an agreement. In the final plenary, the US, supported by Canada and the UK, declared that there was no consensus on the issue of the Middle East and they were, thus, not in a position to support the Final Document prepared by the President. As had been the case in 2005, and earlier in 1980 and 1990, the 2015 NPT Review Conference, after four weeks of negotiations, failed to reach a consensus on a Final Document. The "formal" – and most widely reported – reason for the failure of the Conference was that these three States had blocked the adoption because of the Middle East. This view is too narrow.[78] It does not account for the profound disagreements on nuclear disarmament described above and that the nuclear disarmament text proposed for adoption by the President was certainly not a negotiated text. Without the Middle East issue, disagreements over the nuclear disarmament section would have resulted in a rejection of the Review Conference Final Report.

After four weeks of very intense negotiations on nuclear disarmament, the failure of the Review Conference on the Middle East was an anti-climactic outcome, to say the least, for those delegations who had focused on the nuclear disarmament dimension and the Humanitarian Initiative. However, this outcome did save these delegations from having to either block the Final Document themselves or to "swallow" a text on nuclear disarmament, in the pursuit of a consensus outcome, large segments of which they found deeply disappointing.

In the closing plenary session in the evening on Friday 22 May, many non-nuclear weapon States voiced their disappointment about the lack of progress on nuclear disarmament. I delivered a closing joint-statement for which the support of 49 States had been found in a matter of very few hours stating that

> the exchanges of views that we have witnessed during this review cycle demonstrate that there is a wide divide that presents itself in many fundamental

aspects of what nuclear disarmament should mean. There is a reality gap, a credibility gap, a confidence gap and a moral gap. . . . even the document before us shows the urgency to act upon the unacceptable humanitarian consequences of nuclear weapons, but then falls dramatically short of making credible progress on filling the legal gap in what should have been the forward-looking part.[79]

Thailand stated that

the humanitarian initiative represented at this Review Conference, a moment of clarity for an overwhelming majority of non-nuclear weapon states that the responsibility to disarm, rests on both nuclear and non-nuclear weapons states alike. Unfortunately, we were unable to commit, to beginning a process to negotiate a legally binding instrument that would have taken us substantially further in actually realizing a world free of nuclear weapons. . . . We deeply regret this shortcoming.[80]

Ireland noted that

serious efforts to identify and pursue effective measures for the implementation of Article VI are required as a matter of urgency. It seems clear to most that to be effective, these measures would require to be legally binding. As the NPT approaches 50 [years], work to achieve this must in our view begin immediately.[81]

The US delegation, while underlining its opposition to the Middle East part of the text,

acknowledged the sincere and shared concern of the humanitarian impact of nuclear weapons. It is precisely our understanding of the consequences of nuclear weapons use that drives our efforts to reduce – and eventually eliminate – nuclear weapons, and to extend forever the nearly 70-year record of non-use of nuclear weapons.[82]

The strategy for the 2015 general assembly

For proponents of the Humanitarian Initiative, the outcome – or lack thereof – at the Review Conference was somewhat ambivalent. On the one hand, it was deeply frustrating how little inroads had been made into the "phalanx" of nuclear weapon State opposition. On the other hand, as the Thai statement pointed out, the Review Conference had been "a moment of clarity". Nuclear-weapon States had demonstrated that they are simply not prepared or not able to move forward on nuclear disarmament and the basic bargain that underpins the NPT. Moreover, the approach, at least from some of the nuclear weapon States, "was at times hostile, at times ridiculing, towards non-nuclear-armed states that were calling for concrete measures to ensure implementation of disarmament obligations and commitments".[83]

If the momentum created over several years by the Humanitarian Initiative and evidenced in 159 States underwriting a historic cross-regional joint statement could not be translated into concrete and urgent progress and a shift in the nuclear weapons State approach, what else could non-nuclear weapon States do? As such, the failed NPT Review Conference 2015 also brought more *clarity* to the Humanitarian Initiative and further momentum to the "Humanitarian Pledge". At the closing of the 2015 NPT Review Conference, support by States for the Pledge had increased to 107. In the assessment of more and more non-nuclear weapons States, the lack of progress in the NPT context and the refusal of nuclear weapon States to engage on the Humanitarian Initiative's arguments validated the way forward suggested in the "Humanitarian Pledge": "to fill the legal gap for the prohibition and elimination of nuclear weapons . . . and to cooperate in efforts to stigmatise, prohibit and eliminate nuclear weapons in light of their unacceptable humanitarian consequences and associated risks". ICAN promoted this notion by stating

> the outcome from this Conference is the Humanitarian Pledge . . . 107 states . . . have highlighted this legal gap and have committed to fill it, by endorsing the Humanitarian Pledge issued by Austria. . . . Now these states . . . must use the pledge as the basis for a new process to develop a legally-binding instrument prohibiting nuclear weapons.[84]

The Washington Post called it an "uprising among civil society groups and the coalition of 107 states, which are seeking to reframe the disarmament debate as an urgent matter of safety, morality and humanitarian law".[85] In short, the key and palpable results of the 2015 NPT Review Conference were a yet further increased sense of disenfranchisement with the NPT disarmament process on the one hand, and increased momentum among the non-nuclear weapon States to move forward on the Humanitarian Initiative and the "Humanitarian Pledge" on the other.

Despite the momentum for the "Humanitarian Pledge" coming out of the NPT Review Conference, there was no clarity or clear plan among the main proponents of the Humanitarian Initiative on how exactly to proceed. In 2014, South Africa had indicated that it considered hosting a follow-up humanitarian conference, after the 2015 NPT Review Conference.[86] This would be the next big event for the Humanitarian Initiative and, especially ICAN, hoped that this would be the opportunity to launch ban treaty negotiations. But no decision to host a conference had thus far been taken in Pretoria.

To assess the state of play and discuss possible ways forward, another meeting of the "Amersham Group"[87] was convened on 25 June 2015, one month after the end of the NPT Review Conference. In my recollection, the mood at this meeting was sober. The negative atmosphere and the aggressive attitude displayed by some of the nuclear weapon States during the NPT Review Conference had been shocking to some of the participants. Others saw the Conference's failure as an opportunity for continued mobilisation around the Humanitarian Initiative. ICAN representatives at the meeting focused on the possible South African conference but seemed to have no plan B if this conference did not materialize. At the time it was only known that the issue was awaiting a cabinet-level decision in South Africa.[88] ICAN representatives found that the lack of clarity regarding a next international conference made the work of civil society more difficult, as such international meetings are crucial for keeping the momentum going. I recall a sense of exhaustion and uncertainty as to how the Humanitarian Initiative could and should be taken forward.[89] It seemed as if having pushed so far and hard up to and during the NPT Review Conference, the Humanitarian Initiative was in danger of running out of steam.

After this sobering meeting, I discussed the situation and the indecisive mood of the meeting with my colleague, Thomas Hajnoczi, the Austrian Ambassador in Geneva. We felt that an in-depth discussion between disarmament diplomats from the most active and like-minded States would have to take place urgently. We needed to gauge the extent to which there was a shared vision on possible next steps. The staunchest support for the Humanitarian Initiative at the NPT Review Conference and, especially in the "Focus Group" meetings had, in our view, come from Ireland, Mexico and South Africa. Consequently, we invited senior diplomats from these three States to an informal discussion in the Austrian Mission in Geneva on 9 July 2015.

In advance of this meeting, I prepared an internal memo for my foreign minister detailing the ways in which Austria could take the Humanitarian Initiative forward.[90] The memo drew attention to the growing risk of a return to a nuclear arms race and a (re-)emphasis on nuclear deterrence in Europe and the subsequent increased nuclear threats. It stressed that the original objective of the Humanitarian Initiative had been to generate momentum for progress on nuclear disarmament *within* the established UN disarmament architecture, in particular the NPT. In case, however, such progress proved impossible to achieve, the Humanitarian Initiative had now created sufficient momentum to initiate negotiations for a treaty prohibiting nuclear weapons. This momentum was evidenced by the support for the "Humanitarian Pledge". After the failed 2015 NPT Review Conference, the memo argued that this point had now been reached. A future prohibition norm of nuclear weapons would not be directed against the NPT, but complementary to it and necessary for the implementation of its Article VI obligation that is binding on all NPT State parties. This would be important for the credibility of the NPT and multilateral disarmament and non-proliferation efforts in general. To this end, the memo suggested continuing efforts to increase the support for the "Humanitarian Pledge" and to work with other like-mined States to develop a concrete strategy on when and how such a diplomatic process to negotiate a new legal instrument should be initiated. In light of its leading role as the initiator of the "Humanitarian Pledge" and the all-party domestic support that Austria's role in nuclear disarmament enjoyed, the memo suggested that Austria continue at the forefront of the Humanitarian Initiative. For Austria, the moment had arrived to operationalize the "Pledge" and commit fully to a process leading to negotiations for a treaty prohibiting nuclear weapons.

The meeting with senior diplomats from Ireland, Mexico, South Africa and Austria in the Austrian Mission in Geneva on 9 July 2015 is, in my view, the occasion on which one of the most important and strategic discussions on the way to the TPNW took place. We discussed several key questions in depth, such as what conclusions should be drawn from the failed NPT Review Conference and to what extent, in their view, States would now be ready to commit to initiating treaty negotiations, as well as what exactly the objective of such a process should be.[91]

The discussions centred around how the upcoming First Committee of the UN General Assembly in autumn 2015 should be approached. There was agreement among the participants that the First Committee would be an opportunity to strengthen the link between the Humanitarian Initiative and the UN. Most of the activities of the Humanitarian Initiative had thus far taken place either outside the UN framework, such as the three humanitarian conferences, or were limited to statements in NPT meetings or the UN General Assembly First Committee. In the discussion, the idea was supported to introduce several resolutions based on the humanitarian impact of nuclear weapons. As these resolutions would be voted upon by all UN member States, the level of support for the Humanitarian Initiative could be demonstrated. It was believed that bringing the Humanitarian Initiative to the UN General Assembly would lead to a greater "buy-in" from non-nuclear weapon States, in particular from the non-aligned movement. These States traditionally prefer disarmament negotiations to take place under UN auspices.

We shared an assessment that the increased support for the Humanitarian Initiative and the "Humanitarian Pledge" were the only positive outcomes of the 2015 NPT Review Conference. There was momentum and the sense of urgency needed to be retained. It was now important to clearly connect the Humanitarian Initiative with the "effective legal measures" discourse, in other words, that the humanitarian consequences and risk arguments give urgency to the pursuit of a prohibition of nuclear weapons. It would also be important to take a clear stance against the semblance of legitimacy of continued possession of nuclear weapons under the NPT. To this end, the moral and ethical dimensions of nuclear disarmament and the threat nuclear weapons pose to all humanity should be further developed. There was also a shared assessment that many countries were not yet ready to commit fully to negotiations for a legal instrument to prohibit nuclear weapons. The focus should therefore be on creating an opportunity for a serious discussion about "effective legal measures" to implement Article VI of the NPT, strongly underpinned by humanitarian consequences and risk arguments, as had been proposed by the "New Agenda Coalition".

A key aspect under discussion at the meeting was how to prevent a "consensus-based open-ended working group", that had been proposed in the (not adopted) Final Document of the 2015 NPT Review Conference. We shared an expectation that another State or group of States could try to revive this idea and propose such a consensus-based group in a resolution at the First Committee. It was thought likely candidates for such an initiative could be one or more nuclear umbrella States or possibly Sweden and Switzerland. All present at the 9 July meeting opposed a new consensus-based, open-ended working group. We discussed how we could pre-empt this ourselves by introducing a resolution establishing an open-ended working group that would not operate on the basis of consensus. Such a proposal would best be made in an amended version of the "Taking forward multilateral nuclear disarmament negotiations" resolution with which a first such non-consensus open-ended working group had been established in 2012 and which had convened in Geneva in 2013.[92]

The idea of four different "humanitarian" resolutions – three new ones and the revised "Taking forward multilateral nuclear disarmament negotiations" resolution – emerged in the discussion. Austria would present two resolutions as lead-sponsor: the first resolution to be based on the text of the cross-regional joint statement that had been supported by 159 States. Its aim would be to formalise the broad support for this text through a vote on the resolution. The second resolution would introduce the "Humanitarian Pledge", which was already written in the form of a UN General Assembly resolution. It was felt that some States which had not yet endorsed the "Humanitarian Pledge" would now vote in favour of the resolution in the UN General Assembly, thereby further increasing the number of supporters. South Africa would draft and be a lead-sponsor of a third resolution on the moral and ethical dimension of nuclear weapons and nuclear disarmament. Finally, Mexico would be the lead-sponsor of a reworked resolution on "Taking forward multilateral nuclear disarmament negotiations". This resolution would establish an open-ended working group to meet during the course of 2016 with a mandate to address "effective legal measures" on the basis of UN General Assembly rules of procedure and, thus, not be based on the consensus rule. It was further agreed that the four States would coordinate and work together in drafting these texts, would co-sponsor all four resolutions, would encourage wider co-sponsorship for these resolutions and work together to garner support for this approach from civil society. All four resolutions would be valid in their own right but, taken together, would constitute a comprehensive and forceful approach in pushing the Humanitarian Initiative forward.

After a brief period in the doldrums following the 2015 NPT Review Conference, the result of the 9 July 2015 meeting was a coherent strategy. The Humanitarian Initiative would be brought forward into the UN General Assembly through four complementary resolutions. Their combined objectives were to strengthen the arguments on the humanitarian consequences and risks, underscore, based on these arguments, the ethical rationale for nuclear disarmament, generate further momentum for the "Humanitarian Pledge" and, finally, launch discussions on "effective legal measures" to prohibit and eliminate nuclear weapons without a consensus straitjacket. All these objectives had been pursued in the 2015 NPT Review Conference but without success. The General Assembly was now the right forum to move this forward.

In the following weeks, Austria, Ireland, Mexico and South Africa cooperated closely, prepared the resolutions and undertook outreach activities with States and civil society organisations, in particular ICAN. In hindsight, the discussion and the strategy that emerged from this meeting in early July enabled the transition of the Humanitarian Initiative to transition into a formal negotiation process under the auspices of the UN General Assembly, ultimately leading to the TPNW.

The first committee of the 2015 UN general assembly

The United Nations First Committee in October 2015 proved to be – just as the NPT Review Conference in May of the same year – a rather contentious occasion. In the general debate, many States expressed disappointment at the failure of the NPT Review Conference in May, while stressing their continued support for the NPT.[93] The agreement reached on 14 July 2015 between Iran and the E3/EU+3 on a Joint Comprehensive Plan of Action (JCPOA) was widely welcomed as having strengthened the non-proliferation dimension of the NPT. The spotlight, however, was now clearly trained on nuclear disarmament; the Humanitarian Initiative was the defining topic of the First Committee in 2015. The 70th anniversary of the nuclear attacks on Hiroshima and Nagasaki in 1945 was referenced by a great number of States who stressed the importance of the focus on the humanitarian consequences of nuclear weapons. Many statements from States or groups of States, among them the African Group, ASEAN and CELAC called for a legal prohibition of nuclear weapons.[94] Nonetheless, nuclear umbrella States, such as for example Australia and Germany continued to underline the security dimensions of nuclear weapons and rejected the validity of a ban treaty approach.[95] The nuclear weapon States continued to rail against the direction the Humanitarian Initiative was taking. France argued for example that "disarmament cannot be based on an exclusively legal approach . . . and that the specific nature of nuclear weapons compared with other weapons of mass destruction needs to be taken into account".[96]

As planned by Austria, Ireland, Mexico and South Africa, four resolutions were submitted to the First Committee for consideration.[97] Austria introduced a resolution on the "Humanitarian consequences of nuclear weapons" that incorporated the cross-regional statement on the humanitarian consequences of nuclear weapons delivered at the 2015 NPT Review Conference on behalf of 159 States, reiterating, inter alia, the point that "it is in the interest of the very survival of humanity that nuclear weapons are never used again, under any circumstances".[98] The "Humanitarian pledge for the prohibition and elimination of nuclear weapons"[99] was the second resolution introduced by Austria.

The South African resolution on the "Ethical imperatives for a nuclear-weapon-free world"[100] outlined the ethical reasons for nuclear disarmament and that "given their indiscriminate nature and potential to annihilate humanity, nuclear weapons are inherently immoral". It further stressed that all states

> share an ethical responsibility to act with urgency and determination, with the support of all relevant stakeholders, to take the effective measures, including

legally binding measures, necessary to eliminate and prohibit all nuclear weapons, given their catastrophic humanitarian consequences and associated risks.

Mexico introduced the amended resolution "Taking forward multilateral nuclear disarmament negotiations"[101] that built on the open-ended working group held in Geneva in 2013.[102] This resolution was already on the agenda of the General Assembly because Austria and Mexico had introduced it in 2012, 2013 and again in 2014. Using an existing resolution to present a new proposal for an open-ended working group we knew to be advantageous. The resolution already had a strong and established track record of support from the years 2012–2014, when it had garnered the support of more than 130 States. Working with an existing, successful, resolution made it also easier to pre-empt and counter any alternative proposal for a "consensus open-ended working group" introduced by another State.

Two competing resolutions: again, all about consensus

The newly amended resolution proposed an open-ended working group with a mandate to "substantively address concrete effective legal measures, legal provisions and norms that will need to be concluded to attain and maintain a world without nuclear weapons". The second part of the mandate was to "address recommendations on other measures that could contribute to taking forward multilateral nuclear disarmament negotiations". The open-ended working group was to convene in Geneva for up to three weeks in 2016. Furthermore, the resolution encouraged all States to participate and "to make their best endeavours to reach general agreement". This call for "general agreement", however, did not mean a strict application of consensus. It merely stated that general agreement should be the objective of the open-ended working group. In case "general agreement" could not be reached, voting would be possible.

Contrary to expectations, it was Iran and not one of the nuclear umbrella States that took up the idea of a "consensus-based" open-ended working group. Iran presented a resolution, called "Effective measures on nuclear disarmament"[103] that proposed a two-year mandate for an open ended-working group in New York. Its mandate was very similar to the Mexican resolution, in all but one aspect: it stipulated that "the open-ended working group shall conduct its work on the basis of consensus".

Iran argued that there

> exits a unique opportunity for conducting a focused and serious discussion among member States to identify, elaborate and recommend effective measures on nuclear disarmament . . . and that the consensus-based approach was important to secure the active participation of nuclear weapons States.[104]

In my reading of this situation, Iran had other political motivations: the JCPOA had recently been concluded, imposing very strict verification obligations on

Iran. Having been subjected to unprecedented non-proliferation pressures, Iran appeared, thus, to be interested in assuming a leadership role on nuclear disarmament. Moreover, Iran calculated that the Mexican resolution would be strongly objected to by the nuclear weapon States. Iran could therefore put itself in a politically favourable position vis-à-vis those States that led the JCPOA negotiations and in particular the US, by presenting a less objectionable resolution to the one coming from the Humanitarian Initiative camp. Arguably, Iran saw an opportunity to play the mediator role on the contentious "effective legal measures" issue, could claim leadership on nuclear disarmament vis-à-vis the non-aligned States, and at the same time, gain some favour and goodwill with the P5, as "defender" of the consensus rule.

The First Committee was thus confronted with the peculiar situation of two competing and substantively very similar resolutions, that nevertheless differed fundamentally from one another owing to their different rules of procedure. This led to interesting situations where some States "praised" the constructive resolution on nuclear disarmament from Iran at the same time as criticising the "radical" and "divisive" approach of Austria, Ireland, Mexico and South Africa.[105] Very shortly after the JCPOA had been concluded, expressly to control Iran's nuclear program, this praise of Iran's approach to nuclear disarmament struck a very strange chord.

In any case, many States expressed understandable concern about the prospect of adopting two resolutions establishing two open-ended working groups, dealing with the same topic. There was a clear expectation to try to merge the two approaches, which resulted in intensive consultations between Mexico and its co-sponsors, and Iran. However, neither side was willing to compromise on the consensus/non-consensus issue. In my assessment, Iran calculated that the Mexican-led resolution would be either withdrawn or amended with a consensus provision, or one combined resolution would be drafted. In all these scenarios, Iran would have achieved its objectives. However, Iran did not seem to expect that Mexico and its co-sponsors would be prepared to risk the establishment of two open-ended working groups, by all accounts a rather non-sensical outcome. We, on the other hand, considered it essential to demonstrate that such an outcome, while regrettable, would be better than embarking on yet another consensus-based nuclear disarmament exercise. We were not bluffing.

There was maybe one key miscalculation on the part of Iran: while the nuclear weapon States and the nuclear umbrella countries clearly "preferred" the Iranian resolution, this did not mean that they would actively support it. Arguably, Iran thought that its resolution would be adopted without a vote,[106] once the Mexican resolution had been withdrawn or amended. However, as Mexico and its co-sponsors did not cave and did not withdraw their resolution, this plan did not work. A vote was requested on the Iranian resolution, thereby preventing it being adopted without a vote, changing the situation dramatically. Now the resolution could not "slip through" without a vote, rather, States would be "on record" with their vote. It is hard to imagine, for example, that the US delegation would have been able to vote anything other than "no". Endorsing an Iranian nuclear disarmament resolution would probably have been a (domestic) political step too far.

Nevertheless, on 5 November, in the last hours of voting in this First Committee session, things took a dramatic and unexpected turn. Just before the vote on the Mexican-led resolution, France delivered a statement on behalf of the five nuclear weapon States explaining why they would vote against the Mexican resolution. France said that

> productive results can only be ensured through a consensus-based approach. To ensure such an approach is genuinely inclusive and fully anchored in the security context, States must agree in advance on the key parameters of the process ahead. [This resolution] lacks all those vital components that would guarantee both a meaningful collaboration and a productive outcome as a result of concerted collective effort.

The statement continued by stating that the five States "remain open to other channels of discussion, not excluding an appropriately-mandated open-ended working group".[107] This was a "nod" in the direction of the Iranian resolution.

Shortly after the French statement, Iran took the floor and explained however that

> after listening to the statement . . . on behalf of the P5, it is evident that the nuclear weapon States are not willing at all to commit themselves to a consensus-based and inclusive approach. In the absence of such willingness . . . there will be no justification for keeping this resolution on the table.[108]

Iran then withdrew its resolution.

What may have transpired is that Iran asked the nuclear weapon States for their active support of its resolution but received negative or reluctant answers. Without the clear endorsement of the five nuclear weapon States, the political calculation for Iran did not hold up anymore. This seemed to surprise many in the room, including some of the nuclear weapon States. It left those States and the nuclear umbrella States in an uncomfortable situation. Two parallel open-ended working groups could have been played off against one another, with one being presented as more constructive than the other. The consensus-based group could have been controlled procedurally, thus, nothing the nuclear weapon States did not support could emerge from it. Since it was an Iranian initiative, they could have kept some distance from it and participation in its discussions could have been presented as a major concession. At the same time, the "Iranian" open-ended working group meeting in New York would have inevitably detracted to a considerable degree from the "Mexican" open-ended working group in Geneva, which would have struggled to generate the political momentum that we hoped to achieve. Diplomatic miscalculations, however, meant that now only the Mexican-led resolution was left to be voted on.

Immediately after the withdrawal of the Iranian resolution, the Mexican-led resolution on "Taking forward multilateral nuclear disarmament negotiations" was adopted with 138 votes for, 12 against and 34 abstentions, a result considered very "strong".[109] An open-ended working group without the consensus-rule straitjacket and with the mandate to "recommend effective measures on nuclear disarmament, including legal provisions . . . for the achievement and maintenance of a world without nuclear weapons"[110] was thus established.

The other three "humanitarian" resolutions achieved similar results. The resolution on the "Humanitarian consequences of nuclear weapons" was adopted with 144 votes for, 18 against and 22 abstentions. The "Humanitarian Pledge for the Prohibition and Elimination of Nuclear Weapons" achieved 139 votes for, 29 against and 17 abstentions and the resolution on the "Ethical imperatives for a nuclear-weapon-free world" was adopted by 132 votes for, 36 against and 16 abstentions.[111]

As such, the Humanitarian Initiative emerged greatly strengthened from the 2015 First Committee of the UN General Assembly. The overwhelming majority of UN member States supported the approach proposed in the four resolutions. By taking the Humanitarian Initiative to the UN General Assembly and by initiating an UN-mandated open-ended working group process, the path towards the negotiation of a legal instrument was now a UN process. A UN mandate enhanced the legitimacy and hence the buy-in from many States for any future negotiation process.[112]

The withdrawal of the Iranian consensus-based open-ended working group resolution removed the last significant obstacle. It was now possible to discuss "effective legal measures" in a forum that is not stifled by the consensus/veto dynamic. The voting results of the four resolutions are clear evidence that most States had now reached the conclusion that a new approach be tried, even if the five nuclear weapon States fiercely opposed it.

The strategy developed by the senior diplomats representing Ireland, Mexico, South Africa and Austria at our discussions in the Austrian Mission in Geneva on 9 July proved crucial. Also, the tactical foresight of keeping the "Taking forward multilateral nuclear disarmament negotiations" resolution on the agenda of the UN General Assembly in both 2013 and 2014,[113] in order to amend it in 2015 and promote a new non-consensus open-ended working group, was vital. An open-ended working group working on the basis of a consensus rule, as proposed by Iran, would probably have continued its deliberations on possible "effective legal measures" for years but with no real hope of reaching an agreement. The TPNW could not have emerged from such a forum.

Notes

1 Lord Desmond Browne of Ladyton, "A World Free of Nuclear Weapons: Is It Desirable? Is It Possible? How Could It Be Achieved?", in *OPANAL*, Luiz Filipe de Macedo Soares (eds.), 13 February 2017, p. 52, available at www.opanal.org/wp-content/uploads/2017/02/OPANAL_Seminar_2017.pdf.

2. New Agenda Coalition (NAC) consists of Brazil, Egypt, Ireland, Mexico, New Zealand and South Africa. It operates within the framework of the NPT and focusses on achieving progress on nuclear disarmament. It was established in 1998 and played a particular important role in negotiating the "Thirteen Practical Steps" at the 2000 NPT Review Conference.
3. "Article VI of the Treaty on the Non-Proliferation of Nuclear Weapons", working paper submitted by Ireland on behalf of the New Agenda Coalition (Brazil, Egypt, Ireland, Mexico, New Zealand and South Africa) to the Preparatory Committee for the 2015 Review Conference of the Parties to the Treaty on the Non-Proliferation of Nuclear Weapons, document: NPT/CONF.2015/PC.III/WP.18, available at www.un.org/disarmament/wmd/nuclear/npt2015/prepcom2014/; the working paper was to a large extent the work of the Irish diplomat Michael Hurley.
4. Ibid., p. 5.
5. Ibid., p. 7.
6. Ibid., p. 9.
7. For the "Austrian Pledge", see Annex I.
8. See below note 66.
9. See "Humanitarian Pledge", in Annex A.
10. Nobel Committee Press Release on 6 October 2017, available at www.nobelprize.org/prizes/peace/2017/press-release/.
11. Author's personal notes and archive, see also Chapter 1, p. 43.
12. See Chapter 2.
13. Thomas Hajnoczi, Georg Pöstinger, Ronald Sturm and Caroline Wörgötter.
14. Meeting of the "Amersham Group" in Zurich on 28 November 2014, author's personal archive.
15. I nevertheless received a phone call from a high US official shortly before the Conference about a "rumour" that Austria would be planning a second outcome to the Vienna Conference. The author explained that there would be a Chair's Summary and that Austria would issue a purely national statement and commitment at the end of the conference.
16. "Austrian Pledge" presented by Deputy Foreign Minister Michael Linhart, Vienna Conference on the Humanitarian Impact of Nuclear Weapons, see Annex I.
17. Author's personal notes and archive.
18. Based on my numerous conversations with participants from nuclear umbrella States as well as from the UK and the US.
19. See "Documents from the Australian Foreign Ministry Obtained by ICAN Australia Under the Freedom of Information Legislation", available at https://icanw.org.au/resources/foi/, see also Tim Wright, "Australia 'Worried' About 'Growing Momentum' Towards Global Treaty Banning Nuclear Weapons", September 2015, p. 3, available at https://icanw.org.au/wp-content/uploads/2015-September-ICAN-analysis-of-FOI.pdf.
20. Ibid.
21. Communications by the Austrian Foreign Ministry sent to 193 member States of the United Nations during the course of January 2015, personal archive of author.
22. See "Special Declaration of the Community of Latin American and Caribbean States (CELAC) on the Urgent Need for a Nuclear Weapon-Free World", which resulted from the Third Summit of CELAC, held in Belén, Costa Rica, on 28–29 January 2015, available at www.celacinternational.org.
23. Ray Acheson, "Filling the Gap", in *Reaching Critical Will Report of the Third Conference on the Humanitarian Impact of Nuclear Weapons*, p. 5, available at www.reachingcriticalwill.org/images/documents/Disarmament-fora/vienna-2014/filling-the-gap.pdf.
24. See Chapter 2.

25 ICAN representative at a meeting of the "Berkshire Group" on 17–18 February 2015, personal archive of the author.
26 One anecdote that cause quite some amusement within ICAN was the endorsement of Niue of the "Austrian Pledge". Tim Wright of ICAN Australia spoke by phone to a high-level representative of Niue about the "Austrian Pledge" who committed to supporting it. When Wright followed up a few weeks later, he was informed that Niue had to first establish diplomatic relations with Austria, via the Austrian Embassy in Canberra, in order to be able to send a formal diplomatic note endorsing the "Austrian Pledge" to Vienna. Mr. Wright was therefore able to boast as having been responsible for the establishment of diplomatic relations between Austria and Niue.
27 The 2015 Review Conference of the Parties to the Treaty on the Non-Proliferation of Nuclear Weapons (NPT) was held at the United Nations in New York from 27 April to 22 May 2015, more information is available at www.un.org/en/conf/npt/2015/.
28 See www.hinw14vienna.at or www.bmeia.gv.at/index.php?id=55297&L=1.
29 See for example, Gaukhar Mukhatzhanova, "Rough Seas Ahead: Issues for the 2015 NPT Review Conference", in *Arms Control Today*, April 2014, available at www.armscontrol.org/act/2014-04/rough-seas-ahead-issues-2015-npt-review-conference, see also Nuclear Threat Initiative, "2015 NPT Review Conference Backgrounder", 4 May 2014, available at www.nti.org/analysis/articles/2015-npt-review-conference-backgrounder/.
30 For more information see Maximilian Hoell, "The P5 Process: Ten Years on", in *European Leadership Network Policy Brief*, 25 September 2019, available at www.europeanleadershipnetwork.org/policy-brief/the-p5-process-ten-years-on/.
31 P5 Glossary of Key Nuclear Terms, April 2015, available at https://2009-2017.state.gov/documents/organization/243293.pdf.
32 Lord Desmond Browne of Ladyton, "A World Free of Nuclear Weapons".
33 See Chapter 1.
34 Ibid.
35 See for example the statements of Algeria, Austria, Brazil, Chile, Colombia, Costa Rica, Egypt on behalf of the Group of 21, Ethiopia, Ghana, Iraq, Ireland, Lebanon, Kenya, Mexico, Mongolia, South Africa and Sweden during the plenary sessions of the Conference on Disarmament between 28 January until 17 March 2015, available at www.unog.ch/cd.
36 See for example the statements by the Community of Latin American and Caribbean States (CELAC), the non-aligned Movement (NAM), the African Group, Austria, Brazil, Guatemala, Mexico at the session of the United Nations Disarmament Commission, 7 to 22 April 2015, available at www.un.org/disarmament/institutions/disarmament-commission/session-2015/.
37 Ibid., working paper 16 by NPDI and 44 submitted by the United States.
    Working paper 30 submitted by Austria, Chile, Costa Rica, Holy See, Indonesia, Ireland, Malaysia, Mexico, New Zealand, Philippines, Sweden and Switzerland, available at www.un.org/en/conf/npt/2015/pdf/NPT%20CONF2015%20WP.30_E.pdf.
38 I prepared the first draft of the working paper.
39 See working papers, 8, 9, 15, 16, 21, 22, 27, 29, 30, 39, 40, 42, 44, 52 of the 2015 Review Conference of the Parties to the Treaty on the Non-Proliferation of Nuclear Weapons (NPT), 27 April to 22 May 2015 (NPT), all working papers are available at www.un.org/en/conf/npt/2015/working-papers.shtml.
40 See above note 3.
41 Working paper 9 by Brazil, Egypt, Ireland, Mexico, New Zealand and South Africa to the 2015 Review Conference of the Parties to the Treaty on the Non-Proliferation of Nuclear Weapons, available at www.un.org/en/conf/npt/2015/working-papers.shtml.
42 Ibid.
43 See for example Working paper 40 by the States Parties to the Treaty for the Prohibition of Nuclear Weapons in Latin America and the Caribbean (Treaty of Tlatelolco)

and working paper 29 by Austria to the 2015 Review Conference of the Parties to the Treaty on the Non-Proliferation of Nuclear Weapons, available at www.un.org/en/conf/npt/2015/working-papers.shtml.

44 The issue was how to proceed with the longstanding issue of the establishment a Middle East zone free of nuclear and all other weapons of mass destruction and their delivery systems. The 2010 NPT Review Conference had agreed that a conference would be convened on this issue bringing together all actors in the region, including the non-NPT State party Israel. However, it had not been possible to convene this conference, despite intensive efforts in the period 2010–2015. See also William C. Potter, "The Unfulfilled Promise of the 2015 NPT Review Conference", in *Survival*, vol. 58, no. 1, 2016, p. 163, available at https://doi.org/10.1080/00396338.2016.1142144.

45 See for example, Nick Ritchie, "The Humanitarian Initiative in 2015: Expectations Are Building for the Need for Nuclear Disarmament Progress", in *ILPI-UNIDIR NPT Review Conference Services*, paper, no. 1, 2015, p. 3, box 2, available at www.unidir.org/files/publications/pdfs/the-humanitarian-initiative-in-2015-en-626.pdf.

46 The official documents and plenary statements of the NPT Review Conference are available on the UN website, available at https://undocs.org/NPT/CONF.2015/. The NGO Reaching Critical Will, a member of ICAN, maintains a comprehensive website www.reachingcriticalwill.org where also statements held in the NPT Main Committees as well as draft documents discussed during the course of the conference are available, in addition to day to day reporting of the proceedings during the NPT Review Conference.

47 See Reaching Critical Will, "NPT News in Review", vol. 13, no. 8, 12 May 2015, p. 1, available at www.reachingcriticalwill.org/disarmament-fora/npt/2015/nir; www.reachingcriticalwill.org. Individual statements highlighting the humanitarian consequences were made by Argentina, Australia Austria, Belgium, Brazil, Brunei Darussalam, Bulgaria, Colombia, Costa Rica, Cuba, Denmark, Finland, Germany, Ghana, Guatemala, Holy See, ICRC, Indonesia, Iraq, Ireland, Japan, Kazakhstan, Kyrgyzstan, Laos, Liechtenstein, Libya, Luxembourg, Malawi, Malaysia, Maldives, Malta, Marshall Islands, Mexico, Mongolia, Montenegro, Morocco, Myanmar, Netherlands, Niger, Nigeria, Norway, Oman, Palau, Panama, Papua New Guinea, Peru, Philippines, Poland, Portugal, Qatar, Samoa, Saudi Arabia, Senegal, Serbia, Singapore, Slovakia, Slovenia, Spain, Sri Lanka, Sweden, Switzerland, Tanzania, Ukraine, UAE, UK, Venezuela, Viet Nam, Yemen, Zambia, available at www.reachingcriticalwill.org/images/documents/Disarmament-fora/npt/NIR2015/No2.pdf.

48 See Chapter 2.

49 Ibid.

50 See Reaching Critical Will, "NPT News in Review", pp. 4–5; Statements on "effective legal measures" and/or the "Austrian Pledge" were made by the New Agenda Coalition, Austria, CARICOM, CELAC, Brazil, Colombia, Costa Rica, Guatemala, Iraq, Ireland, Kenya, Liechtenstein, Malawi, Malta, Palau, Papua New Guinea, Saudi Arabia and Zambia.

51 Unless a State or States specifically object(s) to this.

52 See "Report of Main Committee I: Chairman's Draft on Substantive Elements", 8 May 2015, available at www.reachingcriticalwill.org/images/documents/Disarmament-fora/npt/revcon2015/documents/MCI-CRP3.pdf.

53 See Reaching Critical Will, "NPT News", p. 1.

54 I witnessed some unwarranted comments putting into question the chair's integrity in the closed meetings of Subsidiary Body I.

55 Statement by US Delegation in Subsidiary Body 1 on 8 May 2015, available at www.reachingcriticalwill.org/images/documents/Disarmament-fora/npt/revcon2015/statements/8May_US_SBI.pdf.

2015: the momentum gathers 83

56 Statement by the UK Delegation in Main Committee One on 15 May 2015, available at www.reachingcriticalwill.org/images/documents/Disarmament-fora/npt/revcon2015/statements/15May_UK.pdf.
57 See Matthew Bolton, "No New Information on the Consequences of Nuclear Weapons?", in *NPT News in Review*, vol. 13, no. 10, 14 May 2015, p. 7, available at www.reachingcriticalwill.org/images/documents/Disarmament-fora/npt/NIR2015/No10.pdf.
58 Ibid.
59 Thomas Nash, "The Nuclear-Armed States, Hubris and Banning Nuclear Weapons", in *NPT News in Review*, no. 9, 13 May 2015, p. 9, available at www.reachingcriticalwill.org/images/documents/Disarmament-fora/npt/NIR2015/No9.pdf.
60 Statement by the Delegation of Ireland in Main Committee One on 15 May 2015, available at www.reachingcriticalwill.org/images/documents/Disarmament-fora/npt/revcon2015/statements/15May_Ireland_MCI.pdf.
61 Statement by South Africa, Subsidiary Body I, 13 May 2015, available at www.reachingcriticalwill.org/images/documents/Disarmament-fora/npt/revcon2015/statements/13May_SouthAfrica.pdf.
62 Statement by the UK Delegation in Main Committee One on 15 May 2015.
63 Statement by South Africa on 13 May 2015.
64 Statement by Austria in Main Committee One on 18 May 2015, available at www.reachingcriticalwill.org/images/documents/Disarmament-fora/npt/revcon2015/statements/18May_Austria_MCI.pdf.
65 During an informal discussion with ICAN member Thomas Nash on 17 May 2015, we talked about that some States had been reluctant to endorse a document that was called "Austrian" and would prefer a less country-specific title and I said that I was looking for a different name to "internationalize" the Pledge. Thomas Nash then suggested "Humanitarian Pledge", which I proposed to Vienna and made the announcement to Main Committee One on the following day.
66 "Humanitarian Pledge Document", available at www.hinw14vienna.at or www.bmeia.gv.at/fileadmin/user_upload/Zentrale/Aussenpolitik/Abruestung/HINW14/HINW14vienna_Pledge_Document.pdf. The text was identical to the "Austrian Pledge" except that all references to "Austria" were replaced by "We, the States supporting and/or endorsing this pledge"; see also Annex I.
67 The invited "Focus Group" consisted of the five NPT nuclear weapon States (China, France, the Russian Federation, the UK and the US) the six-country membership of the New Agenda Coalition (Brazil, Egypt, Ireland, New Zealand, Mexico and South Africa), as well as Austria, Australia, Cuba, Indonesia, Iran, Japan, the Netherlands and Sweden.
68 See Potter, "The Unfulfilled Promise of the 2015 NPT Review Conference", p. 158.
69 Working paper 30, see note 37.
70 Potter, "The Unfulfilled Promise of the 2015 NPT Review Conference", p. 158.
71 Working paper of the President on the Final Document, NPT/CONF.2015/WP.58, available at https://undocs.org/NPT/CONF.2015/WP.58.
72 This is how the President described the document in consultations with State party representatives, including at meetings I participated in.
73 Potter, "The Unfulfilled Promise of the 2015 NPT Review Conference", p. 158.
74 Ray Acheson, "Editorial", in *NPT News in Review*, vol. 13, no. 16, p. 1 see also "Draft Review", pp. 3–5, available at www.reachingcriticalwill.org/images/documents/Disarmament-fora/npt/NIR2015/No16.pdf.
75 Working paper of the President on the Final Document.
76 Potter, "The Unfulfilled Promise of the 2015 NPT Review Conference", p. 163.
77 Based on my informal discussions with diplomats from States supporting the Humanitarian Initiative in the aftermath of the Conference.

78 Potter, "The Unfulfilled Promise of the 2015 NPT Review Conference", p. 152.
79 Statement by Austria on behalf of 49 States, Closing Plenary on 22 May 2015, available at www.reachingcriticalwill.org/disarmament-fora/npt/2015/statements#closing.
80 Ibid., Statement by Thailand.
81 Ibid., Statement by Ireland.
82 Ibid., Statement by the US.
83 See Ray Acheson, "NPT News in Review", final edition, vol. 13, no. 17, 25 May 2015, p. 1, available at www.reachingcriticalwill.org.
84 See Reaching Critical Will, "2015 NPT Review Conference Outcome Is the Humanitarian Pledge", in *Pressenza*, 23 May 2015, available at www.pressenza.com/2015/05/2015-npt-review-conference-outcome-is-the-humanitarian-pledge/.
85 Dan Zak, "Nuclear Conference Collapses Over WMD Free Zone in the Middle East", in *Washington Post*, 22 May 2015, available at www.washingtonpost.com.
86 See Chapter 2.
87 See Chapter 2 for an explanation of this group, its aims and actions.
88 South Africa had concerns about the costs of such a meeting. As the Humanitarian Initiative was subsequently taken forward through the UN General Assembly (see below), the idea of the conference in South Africa was, in the end, not pursued. However, no formal decision either for or against the conference was taken in Pretoria. Interview by the author with a South African diplomat on 6 March 2020.
89 Meeting of the "Amersham Group" in Nyon, Switzerland on 25 June 2015, personal notes of the author.
90 Internal memo Austrian Foreign Ministry, personal archive of the author.
91 Personal notes of the meeting at the Austrian Mission on 9 July 2015 and archive of the author.
92 See Chapter 2.
93 See Mia Gandenberger, "First Committee Monitor", no. 2, 19 October 2015, p. 4, available at www.reachingcriticalwill.org/images/documents/Disarmament-fora/1com/FCM15/FCM-2015-No2.pdf; all statements delivered at the First Committee are also available at https://papersmart.unmeetings.org/ga/first/70th-session/statements/.
94 Ibid.
95 Ibid.
96 Statement by France on 19 October 2015, available at https://papersmart.unmeetings.org/ga/first/70th-session/statements/ or www.reachingcriticalwill.org.
97 All resolutions, documents and statements as well as a webcast of the 70th Session of the First Committee of the UN General Assembly can be available at https://papersmart.unmeetings.org/ga/first/70th-session/programme/; see also the relevant documents and the comprehensive reporting by the NGO Reaching Critical Will, available at www.reachingcriticalwill.org.
98 Ibid., Resolution A/C.1/70/L.37; "Humanitarian Consequences of Nuclear Weapons", available at https://papersmart.unmeetings.org/ga/first/70th-session/programme/.
99 Ibid., Resolution A/C.1/70/L.38; "Humanitarian Pledge for the Prohibition and Elimination of Nuclear Weapons", available at https://papersmart.unmeetings.org/ga/first/70th-session/programme/.
100 Ibid., Resolution A/C.1/70/L.40; "Ethical Imperatives for a Nuclear-Weapon-Free World", available at https://papersmart.unmeetings.org/ga/first/70th-session/programme/.
101 Ibid., Resolution A/C.1/70/L.13.Rev.1; "Taking Forward Multilateral Nuclear Disarmament Negotiations", available at https://papersmart.unmeetings.org/ga/first/70th-session/programme/.
102 See Chapter 2.

103 Ibid., Resolution A/C.1/70/L.28 Rev.1; "Effective Measures on Nuclear Disarmament", available at https://papersmart.unmeetings.org/ga/first/70th-session/programme/.
104 Statement by Iran on 5 November 2015, available at https://papersmart.unmeetings.org/ga/first/70th-session/statements/ or www.reachingcriticalwill.org.
105 For example, during some discussions at European Union coordination meetings that I attended.
106 According to the UN General Assembly rules of procedure, resolutions are adopted without a vote unless one or more member States request a recorded vote. In 2015, roughly half of the approximately 50 resolutions in the First Committee were adopted without a vote and the other half was voted on.
107 See "Explanation of Vote on Resolution L.13 Rev.1 of China, France, Russian Federation, United Kingdom and the United States," 2 November 2015, available at https://papersmart.unmeetings.org/ga/first/70th-session/statements/ or www.reachingcriticalwill.org.
108 Statement by Iran on 5 November 2015 before action on draft resolutions under the cluster of nuclear weapons; available at https://papersmart.unmeetings.org/ga/first/70th-session/statements/ or www.reachingcriticalwill.org.
109 For voting result see https://papersmart.unmeetings.org/ga/first/70th-session/documents/. All First Committee resolutions are first voted on in the First Committee and subsequently also put to a vote in the Plenary of the General Assembly where usually a slightly higher number of States is in attendance. The above number of the voting results of the four resolutions are based on the results obtained in the voting in the Plenary of the General Assembly.
110 Resolution A/C.1/70/L.13.Rev.1; "Taking Forward Multilateral Nuclear Disarmament Negotiations".
111 Ibid., the voting results are available at https://papersmart.unmeetings.org/ga/first/70th-session/programme/.
112 This was important as the proposed conference in South Africa did not materialise. At this conference, ICAN had hoped that a "stand-alone" negotiation process for a nuclear weapons ban – e.g. outside the framework of the UN – could have been launched by like-minded States. This was the model that had been used by the conventions prohibiting anti-personnel landmines and cluster munitions. Some states of the non-aligned movement had traditionally expressed hesitation towards disarmament negotiations to take place outside the UN and preferred to see such negotiations mandated by the UN General Assembly, as happened in the case of the TPNW.
113 See Chapter 2.

Part II
The ban treaty is coming

# 4 2016

Achieving a negotiation mandate

> "If any member does not participate in this forum it will be only because you have exercised your right not to, not because you have been prevented or denied participation.... the legitimacy of this Working Group comes from its origin, established by the universal body par excellence, and its mandate, consistent with the ethical imperative of nuclear disarmament".[1]

The 2016 open-ended working group on taking forward multilateral nuclear disarmament negotiations

The TPNW negotiations took place over four weeks in 2017, from 27 to 31 March and from 15 June to 7 July 2017. Much of these negotiations built upon the work and discussions of the three sessions of the open-ended working group in 2016[2] established by the First Committee of the UN General Assembly in 2015. In order to understand the negotiation history of the TPNW, the work of the open-ended ended working group in 2016 and the formal treaty negotiations in 2017 should be considered together.

The mandate of the open-ended working group was "to identify, elaborate and recommend effective measures on nuclear disarmament, including legal provisions and other arrangements that . . . are required for the achievement and maintenance of a world without nuclear weapons".[3] The second aspect of its mandate was to develop recommendations on "other measures that could contribute to taking forward multilateral nuclear disarmament negotiations", such as transparency measures, nuclear risk reduction and additional awareness raising. The open-ended working group's specific task was to "submit a report on its substantive work and agreed recommendations to the General Assembly at its seventy-first session [note: in 2016], which will assess progress made".[4]

After the contentious 2015 NPT Review Conference and the First Committee of the General Assembly in autumn 2015, the dividing lines in the international community regarding the Humanitarian Initiative were even more pronounced. What should be the way forward on nuclear disarmament and what, if any, "effective legal measures" for the prohibition and elimination of nuclear weapons should be pursued?

For the four States which initiated and co-sponsored the "Taking forward multilateral nuclear disarmament negotiations" resolution, Austria, Ireland, Mexico and South Africa and a growing number of the by now 139 States supporting the "Humanitarian Pledge",[5] a legally binding prohibition of nuclear weapons was the clear policy objective.[6] However, it was not yet clear how many States would already be prepared to commit initiating negotiations on a prohibition treaty, especially if the nuclear armed States objected to it. Furthermore, the nature and possible options[7] of such a treaty still needed to be discussed in more detail. The open-ended working group provided an opportunity to debate this and to develop – in a forum not necessarily stifled by the consensus rule – a broadly shared vision how such a treaty should look like and what main provisions it should contain.

The South African delegation expressed this expectation in the first session of the open-ended working group in February 2016, stating that

> our belief is that this meeting should strive to reach agreement on what is necessary for both legally-binding effective measures and interim measures in order to advance multilateral nuclear disarmament negotiations for the achievement and maintenance of a world free of nuclear weapons.[8]

Ireland stated that

> (w)e have an opportunity now that is denied us in the rest of our disarmament machinery, stalled for decades and preoccupied with process and procedure. We have an opportunity here for real and genuine debate, open to all and blockable by none.[9]

ICAN, at the same time, continued to drive home the message about the specific value and the feasibility of a ban treaty, even without nuclear armed States.[10] Such a treaty would be "a reinforcement to the legal and political infrastructure supporting the elimination of nuclear weapons . . . (and) is likely to be the most meaningful step that is within our reach today".[11]

The five NPT nuclear weapon States remained opposed to this initiative and decided not to participate in the open-ended working group despite several attempts on the part of the resolution's co-sponsors to encourage their participation. The US opined that the agenda and rules for the group's meetings "will not result in constructive dialogue on nuclear weapons or conditions under which nuclear disarmament can best be achieved".[12] The nuclear weapon States did not want to participate in a non-consensus-based forum and claimed that it was a non-inclusive process. Nuclear weapon States seemed intent on building a negative narrative regarding the open-ended working group. The other four nuclear weapon States outside of the NPT, India, Israel, Pakistan and North Korea, also did not participate.[13]

All the nuclear umbrella States participated in the open-ended working group. With the nuclear weapon States absent, it was left to them to express opposition to moving towards negotiations of a nuclear weapons ban treaty. Australia assumed an unofficial coordination role by convening meetings in Geneva of a so-called "Broadly Likeminded Group" (BLM),[14] with the aim to "refresh our narrative".[15] According to Australian Foreign Ministry documents obtained by ICAN under Freedom of Information legislation, the BLM met to coordinate participation in the (open-ended working group) "to provide a strong alternative viewpoint, notably against those states who wish to push a near-term ban treaty" and to either thwart movement towards a ban, or ensure that any such recommendation in the report of the open-ended working group would be as contested as possible.[16]

In order to coordinate the approach for the open-ended working group, another meeting of the "Berkshire Group"[17] was convened on 20 and 21 January 2016 and organised by the British NGO, Article 36. A small group of diplomats including those of the co-sponsors of the resolution, Austria, Ireland, Mexico and South Africa, representatives of ICAN and several independent experts participated. The key objectives for the open-ended working group that emerged from the informal discussion at this meeting were as follows:[18]

- To demonstrate validity of this process.
- To facilitate – as in 2013 – broadest possible participation of States as well as civil society and academia.
- To have a substantive discussion on "effective legal measures" (1st part of the mandate).
- To "home in" on the legal approach that enjoys the most support among participating States and to increase buy-in from States supporting the "Humanitarian Pledge".
- To use the group to formally introduce some of the substantive findings of the Humanitarian Initiative (nuclear weapons risk, transparency, the scope, complexity and interrelationship of humanitarian consequences etc.) into this UN General Assembly mandated process.
- To develop substantive recommendations on both parts of the mandate.
- To produce a final report that covers the breadth of the discussions, proposals and recommendations (even if not agreed by all participants) and that could be used to take forward multilateral nuclear disarmament negotiations.

A substantive push for the Ban

The chair of the open-ended working group, Ambassador Thani Thongpakdi of Thailand planned and ran the OWEG's sessions in an innovative and flexible format. Two points are notable about his approach. Firstly, civil society representatives, including from ICAN and its constituents, were permitted access as observers to the OEWG sessions. This cannot be taken for granted in multilateral disarmament fora, and the access allowed ICAN both to follow the work of the group and to interact directly with delegations in real time. Secondly, Ambassador Thongpakdi was determined to have a facts-based discussion, to the greatest extent possible, and so he convened panels of outside experts from academia and thinktanks. The presentations from these panels stimulated unusually interactive and engaging discussions on aspects of the open-ended working group's mandate.[19] These expert contributions enhanced the understanding and informed the views of the participating States to a significant degree. One example of this was a study produced by UNIDIR and ILPI, released in time for the OEWG's February 2016 meeting. This study assisted States in the OEWG by providing a

> comprehensive analysis of what a prohibition of nuclear weapons could mean, and what it could entail . . . what a prohibition of nuclear weapons could plausibly constitute, why and how it might be pursued, and (which) maps out the arguments both for and against doing so.[20]

Expert presentations and substantive discussions were not limited to the "effective legal measures" part of the mandate. The open-ended working group also worked intensively on its second part of the mandate, namely on "other measures that could contribute to taking forward multilateral nuclear disarmament negotiations". These discussions were productive and much less contested than those on the first part of the mandate. They resulted in several important recommendations on which consensus among participating States was actually achieved.[21] The main focus of attention, however, was on the first part of the mandate.

The quality of the expertise and the interactive character of the discussions gave the open-ended working group a different "feel" to other fora through "a lot of new intellectual input, the participation of a much higher number of states in the debates, but also of civil society and a strong interactivity".[22] Moreover, as Ireland put it, the testimonies of survivors from Hiroshima and Nagasaki at the open-ended working group "cut through all abstract debate to bring us a true understanding of the devastating reality of this terrible weapon".[23] As a result, the 2016 open-ended working group – despite or maybe even due to the boycott of the nuclear armed States – produced some highly significant substantive input, ultimately strengthening the political resolve of a majority of States to move towards negotiations of a prohibition of nuclear weapons. One supporter of the Humanitarian Initiative characterised the dynamic at the open-ended working group as "discussions evolved naturally into a binary choice: you were either for or against nuclear weapons".[24]

In addition to the expert presentations, this evolution was facilitated by several substantive working papers delivered by States or group of States, in particular on the issue of "effective legal measures", as stipulated in part one of the open-ended working group's mandate. They illustrate how the discussion of the mandate of the open-ended working group progressively led to a clear-cut political decision to recommend the initiation of ban negotiations, even without the participation of nuclear armed States.

Austria presented a working paper on the "legal gap", which argued inter alia that "The very structure of the NPT requires additional legal (and non-legal) measures for its full implementation. This applies to Article VI just as much as it applies to the non-proliferation obligations".[25] This reasoning was further developed into a later working paper that was co-sponsored by all States endorsing the "Humanitarian Pledge". It recommended

> to pursue an additional legal instrument or instruments with urgency and to support international efforts to prohibit and eliminate nuclear weapons, [and] to recall that all such efforts are aimed at contributing to the full implementation of Article VI of the NPT and the achievement and maintenance of a world without nuclear weapons.[26]

Brazil presented a much discussed and important working paper which mooted moving forward with a legal prohibition now and without the participation of the nuclear weapon States as valid and necessary. The working paper argued that

> universality can be either a precondition or an objective of any negotiating process. History shows that the latter is the most effective approach, at least in disarmament affairs. . . . The inability of States possessing nuclear weapons to genuinely engage with non-nuclear-weapon States (NNWS) in more ambitious initiatives on nuclear disarmament is mostly a product of their inability to go beyond a confrontational security mindset and instead support a collective approach to security, predicated on cooperation and dialogue. . . . This points to the wider gap between the majority of States which see nuclear weapons as a threat to international security and those who believe such weapons increase their security, and, more worryingly, that such a state of affairs can be relied upon indefinitely. This gap, which transcends geopolitical rivalries, reveals a cognitive gap, a deep-seated difference in the understanding of nuclear weapons, and has been the most powerful obstacle to moving forward with the disarmament agenda.

The Brazilian working paper then drew the conclusion that

> the key to unlocking this impasse lies therefore in identifying the approach which will either allow the vast majority of the international community to . . . engage with [nuclear weapon States] in a meaningful way or to proceed at first without their necessary involvement and in fact pave the way for their future adherence. . . . The most viable option for immediate action seems to be the negotiation of a treaty prohibiting nuclear weapons, establishing general interdictions and obligations, and an unambiguous political commitment to completely eliminate nuclear weapons. . . . A prohibition on nuclear weapons followed by the negotiation of protocols on elimination and other relevant issues would be the best possible option available and could be immediately pursued.

Finally, Brazil proposed "that the final report of the open-ended working group recommends the immediate commencement of negotiations on a treaty for the prohibition of nuclear weapons, which would establish the main prohibitions and obligations associated with that goal".[27]

The reasoning put forward by Brazil in the working paper was influential in generating momentum for the ban, especially as it represented a change to Brazil's own position. For the first time, Brazilian officials were publicly advocating a legal prohibition (only) in a UN forum. The logic of *prohibition now, elimination and verification later* rationalised the ban treaty as a component of and step towards a future comprehensive Nuclear Weapons Convention. This was important to convince a number of non-aligned States (NAM) who had in the past supported a Nuclear Weapons Convention and had been reluctant to get behind the idea of a ban treaty.

Malaysia and Costa Rica – the architects of the Nuclear Weapons Convention at a diplomatic level – made a similar point in their joint working paper, arguing that

> norms [do not] require universal support in order to be established. Indeed, norms can and do affect the behaviour of a State even in cases where the State explicitly rejects the norm or denies its existence or applicability. . . . A joint approach of continuing to focus on the humanitarian and moral/ethical aspects of nuclear weapons, coupled with development of a legally-binding absolute prohibition on nuclear weapons (even of limited membership), would offer a high likelihood of building an effective norm over time. It would also provide a practical and realistic means by which developing countries could start to redress some of the imbalances in current multilateral approaches to nuclear disarmament and international security, where the interests of powerful nuclear-armed States and their allies are given disproportionate weight.[28]

Austria provided a second working paper the main aim of which was to counter the misleading assertion by nuclear weapon States and nuclear umbrella States, namely that the Humanitarian Initiative does not take "security considerations" with regard to nuclear disarmament sufficiently into account.[29] The paper stated that

> to the contrary, it puts the security at the centre of the debate and raises very serious issues and questions that challenge the narrower security perspective of States relying on nuclear weapons. Not only does the humanitarian perspective raise valid concerns from the non-nuclear weapon States perspective as to the degree to which their own and their population's security may be threatened by the existence of these weapons in nuclear armed States. It equally raises questions to what extent the very security argument used by States that rely on nuclear weapons holds up to scrutiny.[30]

A significant and important feature to emerge during the open-ended working group was that several States, traditionally less vocal on nuclear disarmament issues, came forward with strong and determined positions. A case in point was the joint working paper by Fiji, Nauru, Palau, Samoa and Tuvalu. These five Pacific States argued that

> Pacific islanders have suffered greatly as a result of half a century of nuclear testing in our region. The lived experience of our people informs our policies on nuclear disarmament and motivates us to contribute substantively to the work of bodies such as this. . . . It is a common error to assume that our challenge is limited to persuading the nuclear-armed States to alter their behaviour. In reality, a larger number of States contribute to nuclear dangers and impede progress towards disarmament through policies and practices that endorse the indefinite retention and potential use of nuclear weapons. A treaty banning nuclear weapons would aim to bring these States into line with the mainstream of the international community and, in so doing, to influence also the behaviour of nuclear-armed States.[31]

At the May 2016 session, Argentina, Brazil, Costa Rica, Ecuador, Guatemala, Indonesia, Malaysia, Mexico, Philippines and Zambia, representing all regions in which nuclear weapon free zones have been established,[32] submitted a joint working paper. This paper rounded up the "effective legal measures" discussion as seen from the perspective of States supporting the Humanitarian Initiative. It underlined that

> a legally-binding instrument prohibiting nuclear weapons would be a contribution in itself to nuclear disarmament. But, in order to reach our ultimate goal of achieving and maintaining a world free of nuclear weapons, other legally binding instruments, set of instruments or protocols to the legally binding instrument prohibiting nuclear weapons shall be negotiated. The legally binding instrument prohibiting nuclear weapons does not need to include measures leading up to the elimination of nuclear weapons. Measures to negotiate the destruction of nuclear weapons in an irreversible, verifiable and transparent manner would be the subject of future negotiations. . . . In light of the above, we propose that the Open-Ended Working Group, in its report, includes the following recommendations to the General Assembly: Convene a Conference in 2017, open to all States, international organizations and civil society, to negotiate a legally-binding instrument to prohibit nuclear weapons.[33]

The arguments for the "progressive status quo"

The nuclear umbrella States tried to counter the strengthening momentum towards a ban treaty. Under Australian coordination, the BLM group of States presented a working paper that outlined a so-called "progressive approach" as an alternative to the ban treaty.[34] It argued that a prohibition of nuclear weapons would be possible only as the final building block, once all the other "effective practical measures" have been implemented. These measures refer to transparency, risk reduction, reduction of the role of nuclear weapons in security doctrines, disarmament verification, the entry into force of the CTBT, and negotiations of a FMCT. The paper argued that

> The reality is that there will be no quick fixes if our goal is effective, verifiable and irreversible nuclear disarmament. Nor can the legitimate security concerns of States be brushed aside. Only by addressing both the security as well as humanitarian dimensions of nuclear weapons can we take the incremental but necessary steps that will enhance security for all and provide the best chance of reaching a world without nuclear weapons.[35]

The Netherlands and Canada each presented working papers addressing the "legal gap". Canada, for example, stated that

> the mere fact that a law or legal norm has not been imposed does not necessarily mean there is a legal gap. . . . (By) definition, the absence of a ban on nuclear weapons' use and possession can only constitute a legal gap if such use and possession is inherently illegal, based on applicable international law. Again, while this is an understandable aspiration, the reality is that under current customary international law, the use and possession of nuclear weapons is not illegal.[36]

The Canadian paper then went further and referred to

> strategic implications of precipitous negotiations on a ban on nuclear weapons. . . . It is quite possible that the premature negotiation of a ban would intensify existing rifts among states on nuclear issues, creating a less conducive environment for pursuing negotiations in good faith on nuclear disarmament. Similarly, it is possible that the imposition of a ban might have the unintended consequence of imperilling the stability achieved under the NPT.[37]

A main focus of the arguments presented by the nuclear umbrella States against a ban treaty was on "inclusivity" and "effectiveness". The gist of this reasoning was that the open-ended working group was not *inclusive*, since the nuclear armed States chose not to participate and that banning nuclear weapons, without the participation of the nuclear armed States, would not be *effective*. These points were repeated multiple times in the open-ended working group. Germany, for example, stated that "it is not realistic to expect that 'effective' nuclear disarmament can advance without engaging those States that possess nuclear weapons".[38] Italy, in the same vein, argued that

> we firmly believe that the hard, practical work necessary to bring us closer to a world free of nuclear weapons must be conducted on the basis of humanitarian concerns but also with a view to preserving the adequate conditions of

stability and security in the international environment. In addition, we reiterate that eliminating nuclear weapons will be possible only through substantive and constructive engagement with nuclear weapons States.[39]

This line of argument failed to get much traction among the other States participating in the open-ended working group. The "inclusiveness" argument backfired badly, as the nuclear weapon States had themselves decided not to engage in a discussion that was mandated by the UN General Assembly and supported by the overwhelming majority of States. Any accusation of a "lack of inclusiveness" should, thus, be directed rather to the non-participating nuclear weapon States, many felt. They saw the absence of the nuclear-armed States from the OEWG as regrettable and even as disrespectful, since the UN mandate constituted an invitation in good faith for all governments to participate, whatever their stance on nuclear weapons. Mexico's ambassador Jorge Lomonaco captured this sentiment when he stressed that

> if any member does not participate in this forum it will be only because you have exercised your right not to, not because you have been prevented or denied participation. For some, the legitimacy of the work that begins today [note: the first meeting of the open-ended working group] depends on the participation of certain members, with which they intend to grant them a right to veto ex ante [note: before the event] on the results of the initiative. None of that: the legitimacy of this Working Group comes from its origin, established by the universal body par excellence [note: the UN General Assembly], and its mandate, consistent with the ethical imperative of nuclear disarmament.[40]

Moreover, the absence of the nuclear armed States and the manner in which the nuclear umbrella States – widely perceived as acting as their proxies – operated in the OEWG complicated their arguments against the *effectiveness* of a ban treaty. On the one hand, the nuclear umbrella States argued that a ban of nuclear weapons would be ineffective and irrelevant without the participation of the nuclear armed States. At the same time, they expressed concern about the disruptive and detrimental impact of the ban treaty to international peace and security, which exposed their fears that it might indeed be effective.[41] This apparent contradiction only served to underscore the arguments in favour a ban treaty as being, indeed, "the only effective nuclear disarmament measure that could be pursued without nuclear weapon States, namely a prohibition".[42]

One diplomat described how the nuclear umbrella States arguments "backfired" as follows

> around the halfway point of the open-ended working group, it became a funnel, and the options began to narrow. This was a combined effect of the expert presentations, the impact of civil society, the statements in the room and the fact that the "nuclear umbrella States – which was painful to listen to – were speaking so strongly in defence of nuclear weapons. However, their

statements were too scripted, reiterating the same points over and over again. They did not seem to have the agility to move with the arguments that were put forward in the discussions and were not equipped for such an interactive setting.[43]

Another participant referenced "a key moment in the whole process when Brazil put forward a brilliant argument [note: in the above-referenced Working paper] that sold the ban treaty to the [non-aligned movement] as a component of and step towards the Nuclear Weapons Convention".[44] Another diplomat concurs

the open-ended working group discussions were fantastic. This was when the numbers started to add up, when States like Kenya and Sri Lanka etc. came forward to support the ban, stating that this would not be inconsistent with non-aligned movement positions [note: support for a comprehensive Nuclear Weapons Convention]. This was when I believed that it [note: the ban] would happen.[45]

The chair of the open-ended working group, Ambassador Thongpakdi, attempted to reflect the divergent views of the pro and contra ban treaty camps in an even-handed way. In the first draft report of the open-ended working group, the relevant paragraph in the "conclusion and recommendations" section reads as follows:

The Working Group recommended that additional efforts can and should be pursued to elaborate concrete effective legal measures, legal provisions and norms that will need to be concluded to attain and maintain a world without nuclear weapons. . . . In this regard, a *majority of States supported* (emphasis added) the convening by the General Assembly of a conference in 2017, open to all States, international organizations and civil society, to negotiate a legally-binding instrument to prohibit nuclear weapons, leading towards their total elimination. *A group of States* (emphasis added), however, considered that such negotiations would be premature in light of the current international security environment, stressed the need for any process to take forward multilateral disarmament negotiations to address national and international security considerations and supported the pursuit of practical building blocks consisting of parallel and simultaneous effective legal and nonlegal measures.[46]

While this clearly appeared to reflect the balance of positions that States expressed in the open-ended working group, Australia challenged the notion that there was "a majority" of States supporting the recommendation to convene ban treaty negotiations in 2017.[47] This challenge proved to be another example of nuclear umbrella States tactics backfiring. Mexico requested a so-called "roll-call" – an informal poll among delegations – to check whether there, indeed, was such a majority. Subsequently, the countries of the Association of Southeast Asian States

(ASEAN), the Latin American and Caribbean States (CELAC), the African Group, as well as Austria, Ireland, Liechtenstein, San Marino, Fiji, Palau and Samoa all took the floor to express themselves in favour of initiating such negotiations. These statements representing the positions of well over 100 States, demonstrated to everyone in the room that the chair had accurately described the situation and that there was a clear majority among the participating States.

To vote or not to vote

During the August 2016 session of the open-ended working group, intensive negotiations took place regarding the final report to the UN General Assembly, the aim being adoption without a vote. This would have been the preferred outcome, certainly for the initiators of the open-ended working group: a forum that allows voting creates more of an incentive to actually negotiate and find a consensus, thus making voting unnecessary, whereas a forum that applies a strict consensus rule often creates a "veto-mindset" which makes a consensus result less likely.

The key issue in the negotiations remained how the positions pro and contra a recommendation to initiate negotiations on a prohibition of nuclear weapons would be should be reflected in the report. On 18 August 2016, the evening before the last day of the open-ended working group, the chair invited several "opposing" delegations to his residence for a working dinner. Dinner, he said, would only be served after an understanding and agreement on the relevant paragraph in the report had been found, that would satisfy both camps and that could be presented to the open-ended working group the next day for adoption. After some discussion, the supporters of initiating ban negotiations agreed to a weaker formulation on the understanding that this would result in an adoption of the report without a vote. The relevant paragraph in the report would be weakened to only state that the Working Group "recognised" that there was a recommendation to convene a negotiation conference in 2017 which had received "widespread support".[48] All around the table accepted this proposal by the chair and pledged to recommend it to their Capitals for acceptance. Dinner was served and "all shook hands and broke bread. This was as close to honour as one could get".[49] In diplomatic practice it happens very rarely that a respective Foreign Ministry decides against the recommendation of the ambassador leading the negotiations. The participants went home that night thinking that the open-ended working group would be able to conclude without the contentious *consensus – no consensus* issue coming into play.

On the next morning, Friday, 19 August 2016, however, Australia, whose ambassador had been present at the dinner on the day before, informed Ambassador Thongphakdi that he had received instructions not to agree, after all, to the report and demanded a vote. This was not only an embarrassment for the Australian delegation and a challenge for the chair, it also created some confusion, as all delegations had expected the report to be adopted without a vote. Immediately after Australia's intervention, Guatemala requested that the changes agreed informally at the dinner the day before should be replaced with the stronger language of the previous version. There was a danger that the situation would unravel. South Africa called for a short recess. The group of ban-supporting States then agreed in an impromptu discussion that only minimal changes to the report would be requested, to avoid a chaotic situation and allow for the speedy adoption of the report.

When the meeting reconvened after the recess, a vote was called to strengthen the relevant paragraph to say that "(t)he Working Group recommended, with widespread support, (emphasis added) the convening, by the General Assembly, of a conference in 2017 . . . to negotiate a legally binding instrument to prohibit nuclear weapons, leading towards their total elimination".[50] This was followed by the adoption of the report as a whole by a vote.[51]

It is not entirely clear why Australia broke away from the informal agreement on the report achieved over dinner the day before. A spokesperson at the Foreign Ministry stated that "it was the most effective way to register our opposition to a recommendation to start negotiations on a ban treaty. A consensus report was not possible in the circumstances".[52] Other diplomats speculated that Australia may have calculated on things falling apart if a vote were called. Many States would not have instructions on how to vote and/or there would then be not enough time to deal with possible amendments and other procedural issues.[53]

Some of the other nuclear umbrella States were apparently blindsided by Australia's new stance, after the apparent agreement on the text the night before. Japan, for example did not like to be put in the situation of having to vote negatively on a report on nuclear disarmament and had, thus, been very keen to avoid a vote.[54]

The over-night change of stance seemed incongruous to many in the open-ended working group in light of Australia's credentials on engagement in nuclear disarmament at the multilateral level. However, there appears to have been a political calculation, extending beyond solely the report of the open-ended working group. Had the report been adopted without a vote, the boycott of the nuclear weapons States against participation that was based on the consensus rule argument would have looked even more unjustified.

During the course of the open-ended working group, it became increasingly clear that the recommendation for ban treaty negotiations could not be prevented. The number of States in support of this was too great and their level of determination had, if anything, increased. Unable to avert this unwanted outcome, the "next best alternative" for the ban treaty opponents was, thus, to attempt to undermine the outcome of the open-ended working group in its entirety and to the greatest extent possible.

As constructive and supportive multilateral actors normally do, Australia and the other nuclear umbrella States might well have adopted the report without a vote, as long as their position was adequately reflected in it. It appears, however, that Australia acted as a proxy for the US, with whom it had been in close contact throughout the open-ended working group.[55] Australia hoped to show that the open-ended working group had been divisive, non-inclusive and therefore not a valid process, that the nuclear weapon State boycott of it had been justified. This is the narrative that the opponents of the ban treaty have built and promoted ever since.[56]

Had a recommendation to the UN General Assembly to start such negotiations been agreed without a vote, the political challenges for the nuclear umbrella States would have increased further. ICAN's campaign in support of the ban treaty argued strongly for engagement and participation in a future negotiation process. The combined effect of this campaign in nuclear umbrella States, media coverage and parliamentary debates may have compelled more of those States to participate in a future negotiation process.

Arguably, the call for a vote was, thus, also intended to draw a line in the sand, forcing the nuclear umbrella States to vote against the open-ended working group report. If these States voted against such negotiations now, they would be "immunised" against voting for any ban treaty negotiations at a later point. The vote on the open-ended working group report exposed the nuclear umbrella States ambivalent or duplicitous stance on nuclear weapons, as it revealed their role as de facto guardians of the nuclear status quo. At the same time, it brought a degree of clarity: in voting against the report, the nuclear umbrella States began to build their case for staying away from negotiations. Future ban treaty negotiations would only be conducted by those States that really wanted to achieve a legally binding prohibition.

Despite the last-minute "vote drama", the open-ended working group's recommendation for UN mandated treaty negotiations in 2017, to prohibit nuclear weapons, was considered an important accomplishment by the States that had supported the report.[57] In the closing plenary, Mexico, for example, referred to the recommendations as "the most significant contribution to nuclear disarmament in two decades".[58] The Thai chair praised that "we have achieved an historic outcome today and that we are a step closer to achieving and maintaining a world without nuclear weapons. It is now up to the UNGA to take this forward".[59] After many years of paralysis, this outcome was a breakthrough for the non-nuclear weapon States. The absence of the consensus straitjacket had allowed them to develop their priorities and formulate policy recommendations on nuclear disarmament, which had been frustrated for decades in the Conference on Disarmament and in the NPT. This time, at least, the positions of the vast majority of non-nuclear weapon States had prevailed and were documented as an unqualified and clear policy recommendation to the UN General Assembly. On 1 September 2016, the report of the open-ended working group was submitted to the UN General Assembly for further consideration in its upcoming 71st Session.[60]

2016 UN general assembly: a ban treaty is coming

During the month of September 2016, a new draft of the resolution "Taking forward multilateral nuclear disarmament negotiations" was prepared by the original group of co-sponsors of the resolution, Austria, Ireland, Mexico and South Africa, enlarged by Brazil and Nigeria. The aim of the resolution was to obtain the formal decision by UN General Assembly to convene a conference in 2017 to negotiate a legally binding instrument to prohibit nuclear weapons, as recommended by the report of the open-ended working group. On 14 October, Austria formally introduced the new resolution "Taking forward multilateral nuclear disarmament negotiations" on behalf of those six States.[61] In addition to the decision to convene a diplomatic conference in 2017, the resolution also called upon "States participating in the conference to make their best endeavours to conclude as soon as possible a legally binding instrument to prohibit nuclear weapons, leading towards their total elimination". Austria argued

> this would represent not only a major step forward, a core contribution towards nuclear disarmament and an important step towards regaining balance in the currently uneven implementation of NPT obligations. It would also constitute the basis on which the necessary system to ensure the complete and verified implementation of the ultimate objective of a world free from nuclear weapons could subsequently be established.[62]

The discussions at the First Committee of the UN General Assembly in 2016 were dominated by this resolution and the divide that had opened up on the ban treaty.[63] The nuclear weapons States and the nuclear umbrella States continued to criticize the open-ended working group and the manner in which it reached a report, the subsequent resolution and the validity of any ban treaty agreement that might emerge. Russia warned that the ban treaty would "fundamentally break the established algorithm of multilateral work on nuclear disarmament".[64] The US delegation stated that a ban

> would abandon an approach to reductions which builds upon decades of pragmatic steps to reduce the role and number of nuclear weapons. . . . Such a path is polarizing and forsakes long-standing principles of credible nuclear disarmament, such as verifiability.[65]

The exchanges during a debate on 14 October 2016 designated for Ambassador Thani Thongphakdi to present the report of the open-ended working group report, became particularly heated. Germany accused the open-ended working group of "one-sided highlighting" of pro-ban positions.[66] Australia referred to the ban as "potentially dangerous" and stressed the benefits of extended nuclear deterrence.[67] Similarly, Canada, Estonia and Turkey criticised the "divisiveness" of the ban treaty approach.[68] France referred to the open-ended working group and the ban treaty as "illegitimate processes".[69] One diplomat remembered this session as "a couple of countries responded to (Thai Ambassador) Thani in a very antagonistic way, even though he was the chair of the process and had not forced anybody to any conclusions. That also backfired badly".[70] The UK dismissed a ban as having "no-normative effect" and demanded that the promotors of the ban treaty should observe the principle of "do no harm"; meaning not go down the route of a ban.[71] In the same statement, the UK pointed out that Britain's parliamentarians had recently voted to renew its nuclear armed submarines, stating that this was, however, not damaging to the NPT.[72] The UK reference to "do no harm" in the context of the ban treaty discussion was seen as particularly antagonistic in light of the testimonies of the hibakusha and the rationale of the ban treaty to prevent the humanitarian consequences – harm – of nuclear weapon explosions. The scene afterwards is described as follows:

> after the UK statement the US ambassador came over to "high-five"; they were very happy with themselves. Almost everybody in the room felt so uncomfortable. The tone and the wording was so wrong. People were absolutely appalled, also from the machismo of it.[73]

The supporters of ban negotiations countered these assertions in this session and throughout the First Committee. A number of statements highlighted that a prohibition of nuclear weapons would be fully consistent with and complementary to the NPT.[74] ASEAN found this "an unprecedented opportunity to infuse momentum in achieving the next critical steps to move the nuclear disarmament agenda forward".[75] The African Group welcomed the report of the open-ended working group and "strongly supports the call for banning nuclear weapons, the only WMD not prohibited by an international legal instrument".[76] Many States rejected the notion that the security considerations of some States are more important than those of others, or the assertion that a ban on nuclear weapons would be detrimental to international security and stability.[77] The Holy See criticised "nuclear deterrence and the threat of mutually assured destruction that cannot be the basis for an ethics of fraternity and peaceful coexistence".[78] In the General Debate at the start of the First Committee the African Group, the Caribbean Community (CARICOM), the Community of Latin American and Caribbean States (CELAC) and a large number of individual statements by non-nuclear weapon States made similar points.[79]

However, despite all the contestation and at times heated exchanges, the proponents of the resolution on "Taking forward multilateral nuclear disarmament negotiations" felt the outcome was not in any doubt. According to Austrian Ambassador Thomas Hajnoczi,

> the First Committee was relative smooth sailing, and everything was clear. Because the break [note: the Australian call for a vote at the open-ended working group] had happened beforehand, it was clear what we would present, it was clear who would vote against. The nuclear weapon States did not make many inroads against the vote to start negotiations.[80]

Both before and during the First Committee, the nuclear weapon States undertook an intensive lobbying campaign[81] repeating their opposition to the ban treaty and urging a vote against the initiation of ban negotiations. There are no public records of these "diplomatic demarches"[82] or less formal communications between the governments concerned. States are generally reluctant to admit that they have been at the "receiving end" of pressure campaigns.

Nevertheless, based on informal conversations, I am aware that France, Russia and the US were very active, particularly in African, Asian and Latin American and Caribbean States. The success of these actions was, however, limited. On this issue, the position of most ban supporting non-nuclear weapons States was by then firmly established and had been expressed in joint statements from various regional groups, such as the African Group, CELAC and ASEAN. This fact, as well as active lobbying from ICAN, the support expressed by the International Committee of the Red Cross and the Holy See, made it easier to withstand the pressure of the nuclear weapon States. Moreover, owing to the Australian call for a vote at the open-ended working group, non-nuclear weapon States, had already recorded a formal vote in favour of the recommendation to initiate ban negotiations.

The pressure and lobbying by the US were maybe most successful vis-à-vis its own allies. In a leaked communication from its NATO Mission in Brussels dated 17 October 2016, the US circulated a document to its allies "strongly encouraging you to vote 'no' on any vote at the UN First Committee on starting negotiations for a nuclear ban treaty" and that "efforts to negotiate an immediate ban on nuclear weapons or to delegitimize nuclear deterrence are fundamentally at odds with NATO's basic policies on deterrence and our shared security interests". The document also highlighted some possible military implications (for NATO) of a nuclear ban, which "could make it impossible to undertake nuclear planning or training" and which "could and are designed by ban advocates to – destroy the basis of US nuclear extended deterrence".[83]

This US "warning" to the nuclear umbrella States was effective, all of whom voted against the resolution, with the exception of the Netherlands, which abstained. However, the arguments put forward in the US communication also had unintended consequences. They in fact refuted the assertions by the nuclear weapon States that a ban treaty would be ineffective and inconsequential. The US document confirmed that the ban treaty and the de-legitimisation of nuclear weapons and nuclear deterrence would have a significant impact.

On 27 October 2016, the resolution "Taking forward multilateral nuclear disarmament negotiations" was adopted by the First Committee with a majority of 123 States voting yes, 38 no and 16 abstentions. When the voting results were displayed on the screen, applause erupted in the conference room with civil society representatives and many diplomats cheering. Representatives of the nuclear weapon States also reacted strongly. France, for example, expressed "dismay" and Russia warned (somewhat hyperbolically) that a ban treaty would be "destructive", "catastrophic", and "treacherous". In a joint statement, France, the UK and the US argued that banning nuclear weapons will render consensus at the next NPT Review Conference "impossible".[84] The angry reactions of the nuclear weapons States, however, did little to dampen the feeling of the majority of States that something significant had been achieved. For the first time since the UN General Assembly had adopted its very first resolution on 24 January 1946 calling "for the elimination from national armaments of atomic weapons",[85] the aspiration of the majority of States and their peoples had prevailed. After many years of frustrating stasis on multilateral nuclear disarmament, 2017 would see the start of negotiations for the prohibition of nuclear weapons. There was also an undeniable sense of satisfaction, that the control of multilateral proceedings on nuclear weapons, enjoyed for so long by the nuclear weapon States, had been successfully challenged. ICAN described this as "a revolt of the vast majority of states against the violence, intimidation, and injustice perpetuated by those supporting these weapons of mass destruction".[86]

Notes

1 Statement by Mexico on 22 February 2016, available at www.unog.ch/802 56EDD006B8954/(httpAssets)/D76F9FEB15ECACABC1257F68005CEE19/$file/Mexico+OEWG_desarmenuclear_intervencion_20feb16.pdf.
2 The three session in 2016 were in February (22–26), May (2–4 and 9–13) and August (5, 16, 17 and 19): see "Report of the Open-Ended Working Group Taking Forward Multilateral Nuclear Disarmament Negotiations", available at https://documents-dds-ny.un.org/doc/UNDOC/GEN/N16/276/39/PDF/N1627639.pdf?OpenElement.
3 Resolution, "Taking Forward Multilateral Nuclear Disarmament Negotiations", available at https://undocs.org/A/C.1/70/L.13/Rev.1.
4 Ibid.
5 See Chapter 3; 127 States had formally supported the "Humanitarian Pledge" and a further 12 States voted in favour of the "Humanitarian Pledge" resolution at the 2015 First Committee of the UN General Assembly.
6 See for example statements during the 2015 NPT Review Conference and the 2015 First Committee of the General Assembly as discussed in Chapter 3.
7 As identified in the working paper of the "New Agenda Coalition" discussed in Chapter 3.
8 Statement by South Africa on 22 February 2016 in the Open-Ended Working Group on Nuclear Disarmament 2016, available at www.reachingcriticalwill.org/disarmament-fora/oewg/2016/february/statements.
9 Statement by Ireland on 22 February 2016, available at www.unog.ch/8025 6EDD006B8954/(httpAssets)/E6D73F48B6373272C1257F6F004C4428/$file/Ireland+OEWG+Opening+Session.pdf.
10 See for example Mia Gandenberger and Ray Acheson, "Prohibition Takes Centre Stage Again During Second Day of the OEWG", in *OEWG Report*, vol. 2, no. 3, 23 February 2016, available at www.reachingcriticalwill.org/disarmament-fora/oewg/2016/february/reports/10759-oewg-report-vol-2-no-3.
11 Statement by "Article 36" on 23 February 2016, available at www.reachingcriticalwill.org/images/documents/Disarmament-fora/OEWG/2016/Statements/23Feb_Article36.pdf.
12 See Kingston Reif, "U.S. Will Skip Disarmament Meetings", in *Arms Control Today*, March 2016, available at www.armscontrol.org/act/2016-03/news-briefs/us-skip-disarmament-meetings.
13 India, for example, explained its non-participation in the conference on Disarmament on 23 February 2016 along similar lines, available at https://undocs.org/en/cd/pv.1376.
14 The "Broadly Likeminded Group" (BLM) consisted of Australia, Belgium, Bulgaria, Canada, Croatia, the Czech Republic, Estonia, Finland, Germany, Greece, Hungary, Italy, Japan, Lithuania, Luxembourg, the Netherlands, Poland, Portugal, Slovakia and Spain.
15 Freedom of Information document from the Australian Foreign Ministry obtained by ICAN Australia, available at https://icanw.org.au/wp-content/uploads/2015-September-ICAN-analysis-of-FOI.pdf, p. 1.

16 Freedom of Information document from the Australian Foreign Ministry obtained by ICAN Australia, available at https://icanw.org.au/wp-content/uploads/2016-October-ICAN-analysis-of-FOI.pdf.
17 See Chapter 2.
18 Meeting of the "Berkshire Group" on 20 and 21 January 2016, personal archive of the author.
19 The expert presentations are available at www.unog.ch/__80256ee600585943.nsf/(httpPages)/0ee296104d287e88c1257fb7002fc9f0?OpenDocument&ExpandSection=1#_Section1, as well as available at www.reachingcriticalwill.org/disarmament-fora/oewg/2016/february/documents.
20 See "A Prohibition of Nuclear Weapons: A Guide to the Issues", in *United Nations Institute for Disarmament Research (UNIDIR) and International Law and Policy Institute (ILPI)*, February 2016, available at www.unidir.org/files/publications/pdfs/the-2016-open-ended-working-group-en-660.pdf.
21 These recommendations, which were included in the Final Report of the open-ended working group addressed issues such as "transparency measures related to the risks associated with existing nuclear weapons", "Measures to reduce and eliminate the risk of accidental, mistaken, unauthorized or intentional nuclear weapon detonations" and "additional measures to increase awareness and understanding of the complexity of and interrelationship between the wide range of humanitarian consequences that would result from any nuclear detonation", see "Report of the Open-Ended Working Group Taking Forward Multilateral Nuclear Disarmament Negotiations", Doc. Nr. a/71/371, p. 12, available at http://daccess-ods.un.org/access.nsf/Get?OpenAgent&DS=A/71/371&Lang=E.
22 Statement by Austria on 5 August 2016, available at www.reachingcriticalwill.org/images/documents/Disarmament-fora/OEWG/2016/Statements/05August_Austria.pdf.
23 Statement by Ireland on 4 May 2016, available at www.unog.ch/80256EDD006B8954/(httpAssets)/7F38228A00F266DBC1257FC300576367/$file/2016May+Wrap+up_Ireland.pdf.
24 Interview conducted by the author on 31 March 2020 with a diplomat participating in the open-ended working group sessions.
25 "The 'Legal Gap', the Treaty on the Non-Proliferation of Nuclear Weapons and Different Approaches on Taking Forward Nuclear Disarmament Negotiations", working paper submitted by Austria on 22 February 2016, available at http://daccess-ods.un.org/access.nsf/Get?Open&JN=G1603259.
26 "The 'Legal Gap': Recommendations to the Open-Ended Working Group on Taking Forward Nuclear Disarmament Negotiations", working paper submitted on behalf of 127 States on 4 May 2016, available at http://daccess-ods.un.org/access.nsf/Get?Open&JN=G1609102.
27 "Effective Measures, Legal Norms and Provisions on Nuclear Weapons: A Hybrid Approach Towards Nuclear Disarmament", working paper submitted by Brazil on 9 May 2016, available at http://daccess-ods.un.org/access.nsf/Get?Open&JN=G1609311.
28 "Developing and Strengthening Norms for Attaining and Maintaining a World Without Nuclear Weapons", working paper submitted by Costa Rica and Malaysia on 26 February 2016, available at http://daccess-ods.un.org/access.nsf/Get?Open&JN=G1603754.
29 See also Chapter 7.
30 "Nuclear Weapons and Security: A Humanitarian Perspective", working paper submitted by Austria on 22 February 2016, available at http://daccess-ods.un.org/access.nsf/Get?Open&JN=G1603259.
31 "Elements for a Treaty Banning Nuclear Weapons", working paper submitted by Fiji, Nauru, Palau, Samoa and Tuvalu on 3 March 2016, available at http://daccess-ods.un.org/access.nsf/Get?Open&JN=G1604164.

32 For more information on nuclear weapon-free zones, see UN Office for Disarmament Affairs, available at www.un.org/disarmament/wmd/nuclear/nwfz/.
33 "Addressing Nuclear Disarmament: Recommendations from the Perspective of Nuclear-Weapon-Free Zones", working paper submitted by Argentina, Brazil, Costa Rica, Ecuador, Guatemala, Indonesia, Malaysia, Mexico, Philippines and Zambia on 11 May 2016, available at http://daccess-ods.un.org/access.nsf/Get?Open&JN= G1609546.
34 "A Progressive Approach to a World Free of Nuclear Weapons: Revisiting the Building Blocks Paradigm", working paper submitted by Australia, Belgium, Bulgaria, Canada, Croatia, Estonia, Finland, Germany, Greece, Hungary, Italy, Japan, Latvia, Lithuania, Netherlands, Norway, Poland, Portugal, Romania, Slovakia, Slovenia, Spain and Turkey on 24 February 2016, available at http://daccess-ods.un.org/access.nsf/ Get?Open&JN=G1603478.
35 Ibid.
36 "Is There a Legal Gap for the Elimination and Prohibition of Nuclear Weapons?", working paper submitted by Canada on 27 April 2016, available at http://daccess-ods. un.org/access.nsf/Get?Open&JN=G1608662.
37 Ibid.
38 Statement by Germany on 22 February 2016, available at www.unog.ch/__ 80256ee600585943.nsf/(httpPages)/5ee5df8a4a4bfd97c1257fb60054c6ce?OpenDocument&ExpandSection=3%2C2#_Section3.
39 Statement by Italy on 4 May 2016, available at www.unog.ch/80256EDD006B8954/ (httpAssets)/74A042775B328D8AC1257FAB003A4E17/$file/2016May+Panel+III_ Italy.pdf.
40 Statement by Mexico on 22 February 2016.
41 See Mia Gandenberger, "OEWG Report", vol. 2, no. 11, 10 May 2016, p. 3, available at www.reachingcriticalwill.org/images/documents/Disarmament-fora/OEWG/2016/ reports/OEWG2.11.pdf.
42 See Gandenberger and Acheson, "Prohibition Takes Centre Stage Again During Second Day of the OEWG".
43 Interview with a diplomat conducted by the author on 31 March 2020.
44 Email sent to the author on 26 September 2020.
45 Interview with a diplomat conducted by the author on 25 February 2020.
46 See "Draft Report of the Open-Ended Working Group Taking Forward Multilateral Nuclear Disarmament Negotiations", 28 July 2016, available at www. reachingcriticalwill.org/images/documents/Disarmament-fora/OEWG/2016/ Documents/A_AC.286_L.1.pdf.
47 Statement by Australia on 5 August 2016, available at www.unog.ch/80256ED D006B8954/(httpAssets)/A81EF20654018B18C125800A00585F87/$file/Aug+5+ Aus.pdf
48 See "Draft Report of the Open-Ended Working Group Taking Forward Multilateral Nuclear Disarmament Negotiations", 19 August 2016, available at www. reachingcriticalwill.org/images/documents/Disarmament-fora/OEWG/2016/ Documents/A-AC.286-CRP.3.pdf.
49 Interview with a diplomat conducted by the author on 31 March 2020.
50 See "Report of the Open-Ended Working Group Taking Forward Multilateral Nuclear Disarmament Negotiations", Doc. Nr. A/71/371, para. 67, p. 19.
51 The report was adopted with 68 yes, 22 no and 13 abstentions.
52 Michael Slezak, "Australia Attempts to Derail UN Plan to Ban Nuclear Weapons", in *The Guardian*, 21 August 2016, available at www.theguardian.com/world/2016/ aug/21/australia-attempts-to-derail-un-plan-to-ban-nuclear-weapons.
53 For example, interview with a diplomat conducted by the author on 31 March 2020.
54 Slezak, "Australia Attempts to Derail UN Plan to Ban Nuclear Weapons".

108 *The ban treaty is coming*

55 Regarding the Australian coordination with the US, see Tim Wright, "Australia's Role at the UN Working Group on Nuclear Disarmament in 2016", Freedom of Information document from the Australian Foreign Ministry obtained by ICAN Australia, available at https://icanw.org.au/wp-content/uploads/2016-October-ICAN-analysis-of-FOI.pdf.
56 This is discussed in more detail in Chapter 7.
57 The Australian call for a vote meant that also the recommendations on the second part of the open-ended working group's mandate, namely on "other measures that could contribute to taking forward multilateral nuclear disarmament negotiations" were voted on. This is particularly regrettable since consensus on these recommendations had been achieved.
58 See Reaching Critical Will, "OEWG Report 19", vol. 2, no. 19, August 2016, p. 4, available at www.reachingcriticalwill.org/images/documents/Disarmament-fora/OEWG/2016/reports/OEWG2.19.pdf.
59 Ibid.
60 See Note by the Secretary-General, "Taking Forward Multilateral Nuclear Disarmament Negotiations", Doc. Nr. A/71/371, 1 September 2016, available at https://documents-dds-ny.un.org/doc/UNDOC/GEN/N16/466/69/PDF/N1646669.pdf?OpenElement.
61 Resolution, "Taking Forward Multilateral Nuclear Disarmament Negotiations", available at https://undocs.org/A/C.1/71/L.41.
62 Statement by Austria on 14 October 2016 introducing the resolution "Taking Forward Multilateral Nuclear Disarmament Negotiations" on behalf of Brazil, Ireland, Mexico, Nigeria, South Africa and Austria, available at www.reachingcriticalwill.org/images/documents/Disarmament-fora/1com/1com16/statements/14Oct_Austria.pdf; the following States later also co-sponsored the resolution: Chile, Costa Rica, Democratic Republic of the Congo, Ecuador, El Salvador, Guatemala, Honduras, Indonesia, Jamaica, Kenya, Liechtenstein, Malawi, Malta, Namibia, Nauru, New Zealand, Palau, Panama, Paraguay, Peru, Philippines, Samoa, Sri Lanka, Swaziland, Thailand, Uruguay, Venezuela and Zambia, subsequently also joined by Angola, the Bahamas, Belize, Burundi, Cabo Verde, the Dominican Republic, Egypt, Fiji, Grenada, Guinea Bissau, Liberia, Libya, Malaysia, the Marshall Islands, Mauritania, Papua New Guinea, Saint Lucia, Saint Vincent and the Grenadines, San Marino, Sierra Leone, Trinidad and Tobago, Tuvalu and Viet Nam.
63 See Ray Acheson, "First Committee Monitor", no. 4, 24 October 2016, p. 6, available at http://reachingcriticalwill.org/images/documents/Disarmament-fora/1com/FCM16/FCM-2016-No4.pdf.
64 Statement by Russia on 3 October 2016; all statements as well as a webcast of the First Committee are available at www.un.org/disarmament/meetings/firstcommittee-71/ as well as available at https://papersmart.unmeetings.org/ga/first/71st-session/statements/.
65 Ibid., Statement by the US on 3 October 2016.
66 Ibid., Statement by Germany of 14 October 2016; see also First Committee Monitor No. 3 of 17 October 2016 for the debate on 14 October 2016, available at http://reachingcriticalwill.org/images/documents/Disarmament-fora/1com/FCM16/FCM-2016-No3.pdf.
67 Ibid., Statement by Australia on 14 October 2016.
68 Ibid., Statements by Canada, Estonia and Turkey on 14 October 2016.
69 Ibid., Statements by France on 14 October 2016.
70 Interview with a diplomat conducted by the author on 31 March 2020.
71 Ibid., Statement by the UK on 14 October 2016.
72 Ibid.
73 Interview with a diplomat conducted by the author on 31 March 2020; see also ICAN – UK "UK and US Ambassadors 'Fist-Bump' After Speech Against Banning Nuclear Weapons", 17 October 2016, available at http://uk.icanw.org/action/

2016: achieving a negotiation mandate 109

uk-and-us-ambassadors-fist-bump-after-speech-against-banning-nuclear-weapons/; recollections among participants vary on whether it was a "high-five" or a "fist-bump".

74 See statements as well as a webcast of the First Committee and also First Committee Monitor no. 3 of 17 October 2016 for the debate on 14 October 2016.
75 Ibid., Statement by Philippines on behalf of ASEAN on 14 October.
76 Ibid., Statement by Nigeria on behalf of the African Group on 14 October 2016.
77 Ibid,
78 Ibid., Statement by the Holy See on 14 October 2016.
79 Ibid., Statements by the African Group and CARICOM on 3 October 2016, by CELAC on 7 October 2016.
80 Interview with Austrian ambassador Thomas Hajnoczi conducted by the author on 14 April 2020.
81 See Kingston Reif, "UN Approves Start of Nuclear Ban Talks", in *Arms Control Today*, vol. 46, November 2016, p. 25, available at www.armscontrol.org/system/files/Dec_ACT_Color_reduced.pdf.
82 A Demarche is "a formal diplomatic representation of one government's official position, views, or wishes on a given subject to an appropriate official in another government or international organization". See available at https://projects.iq.harvard.edu/files/hks-communications-program/files/pp_sri_kulkarni_and_yotam_goren_4_10_17.pdf.
83 See NATO, "United States Non-Paper: 'Defense Impacts of Potential United Nations General Assembly Nuclear Weapons Ban Treaty; Note by the Secretary'", AC/333-N(2016)0029 (INV), 17 October 2016, annex 2, available at www.icanw.org/wp-content/uploads/2016/10/NATO_OCT2016.pdf; the expression "non-paper" usually refers to a "discussion paper" that is not part of formal business.
84 These statements are available at the First Committee webcast of the First Committee available at www.un.org/disarmament/meetings/firstcommittee-71/ and https://papersmart.unmeetings.org/ga/first/71st-session/programme/.
85 See Resolution, "Establishment of a Commission to Deal with the Problems Raised by the Discovery of Atomic Energy", was adopted on 24 January 1946, in London.
86 See Ray Acheson, "Editorial: Revolt", in *First Committee Monitor*, no. 5, 31 October 2016, p. 3, available at http://reachingcriticalwill.org/images/documents/Disarmament-fora/1com/FCM16/FCM-2016-No5.pdf.

5 2017
Negotiating the TPNW

"Nuclear weapons have always been immoral. Now they are also illegal".[1]

The 2017 TPNW negotiations

Having come so far, in the face of such determined opposition by the world's militarily most powerful States, the challenge for the ban treaty supporters now was how to set up an effective negotiation process that would result in a credible prohibition treaty of nuclear weapons. Until this moment, the momentum for the Humanitarian Initiative and a ban treaty was catalysed by the opposition on the part of the nuclear weapons States and the nuclear umbrella States. Non-nuclear weapon States from all regions of the world, supported by civil society organisations led by ICAN, had worked together effectively. Now, the supporters of the ban treaty would have to negotiate amongst themselves and on their own, given that nuclear weapons States and the nuclear umbrella States had made clear that they would not participate in the negotiations.[2] How could a common sense of purpose continue throughout the negotiations, when different stakeholders held different visions for the ban treaty and had divergent priorities for its scope and individual provisions? ICAN now turned its focus to lobbying States participating in the negotiations to promote their positions on what the ban treaty should or should not regulate. Friction among the negotiating States and between States and ICAN, as well as within ICAN and within civil society organisations more generally, was now on the cards.

Setting up the negotiation process

The "Taking forward multilateral nuclear disarmament negotiations" resolution required negotiations to take place in New York, between 27 and 31 March and again from 15 June to 7 July 2017 and be held under the rules of procedure of the UN General Assembly, unless otherwise agreed on by the conference (i.e. no consensus rule). International organizations and civil society representatives were invited to participate and contribute. Furthermore, it mandate also required a one-day organizational meeting to be convened in New York as soon as possible.

It also decided that the conference was to submit a report on its progress to the General Assembly in autumn 2017, in order to assess the progress made in the negotiations and decide the way forward. This latter provision is evidence that the co-sponsors of the resolution, Austria, Brazil, Ireland, Mexico, Nigeria, South Africa, did not necessarily expect the negotiations to conclude in 2017 but anticipated that a renewed mandate for their continuation in 2018 may need to be sought. As there were no additional instructions in the mandate, the initial planning and setting up of the negotiation process was driven by these States, which would become the so-called "core group" for the treaty negotiations, with support from the UN Secretariat.

The core group States approached Ambassador Elayne Whyte Gómez of Costa Rica with the suggestion to serve as President of the negotiation conference. They felt that a distinguished (female) diplomat from a country of the Global South with a strong multilateral track record and credentials on disarmament issues would be a suitable choice to preside over the negotiations. Moreover, Costa Rica is one of 27 States whose request for membership in the Conference on Disarmament has been blocked as part of the overall stasis of this forum.[3] Electing a President of one of these States would, thus, underscore the approach of the Humanitarian Initiative, namely that nuclear weapons are a concern for all humanity and that the discourse these weapons needs to be broadened and made more inclusive.

On 23 January 2017, Ireland hosted an informal brainstorming meeting in Dublin for a small group of States that had been most supportive of the Humanitarian Initiative, including from the six core group States, to discuss expectations for the negotiations and ideas for the content of the new treaty. This discussion did not lead to any formal understanding with regard to the subsequent negotiations. Nonetheless, it was an important occasion on which some of the key supporting States achieved some alignment as far as expectations and challenges for the next few months were concerned. A shared assessment at the meeting emerged on aiming "to keep the future treaty as simple as it could be and try to avoid making it as complicated as it could become".[4] Other considerations focused on the need for a strategic communication to the effect that the treaty is explicitly intended to support the NPT and is, hence, fully compatible with it. Furthermore, there should be nothing in the treaty that would serve as an easy excuse for non-participation. Participants also discussed the importance of the preamble to convey and clearly anchor the treaty in humanitarian and human security considerations. This should be formulated in a way that a wider public would be able to relate to. The time factor was also widely held to be a challenge, as the mandate only allowed for a relatively short negotiation period.[5] However, participants felt that they have the momentum now and should try to aim for an agreement by July 2017, rather than extending the negotiations to the following year.

The procedural preparations for the negotiations followed the script for other treaty making conferences under the aegis of the UN. The mandated organizational meeting on 16 February, thus, confirmed Ambassador Whyte Gómez as President and dealt with other administrative arrangements and the rules of procedure for the negotiations,[6] including the issue of participation. Despite the crucial role that civil society had played in the process of getting to the point of negotiations, some States, notably Iran and Syria, wanted to limit the participation of NGOs. Most States, however, strongly supported NGO participation.[7] More difficult was the issue of participation of the UN observer States.[8] This issue could not be finalised at the organizational meeting and was only resolved on the second day of the negotiations, essentially by admitting both observer States to the negotiations as full participants.

The negotiation session in March 2017

With these procedural hurdles out of the way, the first session of the negotiations to prohibit nuclear weapons could get under way. At the opening plenary session, State representatives laid out their general views and expectations for the negotiations. Many delegations invoked the sense that these negotiations were an important and historical opportunity.

A message by Pope Francis was delivered to the conference in which he referred to the (future) treaty as being

> inspired by ethical and moral arguments. [. . . and hoped that] the efforts of this conference may be fruitful and provide an effective contribution to advancing an ethic of peace and of multilateral and cooperative security, which humanity very much needs today.[9]

The President of the ICRC, Peter Maurer stressed that "the historical importance of the Conference cannot be overstated. [. . . and] appeal(ed) to delegates to work with urgency and determination, to adopt a clear an unambiguous prohibition of nuclear weapons grounded in international humanitarian law".[10]

Many States echoed these sentiments. Ireland underlined that "we are taking the opportunity to write a new history and in so doing to create a new, more stable, more security and more equal future for all".[11] ASEAN expressed the view that "this conference is a vital step in the path toward nuclear disarmament [which] complements and reinforces that treaty's [note: the NPT's] goals and objectives".[12] Algeria called the Conference a

> historical juncture [. . . and] a necessity we owe it to the world, and a huge majority has decided to open this path for everyone's sake and in the name of the very reason we are here at the United Nations: promote peace, prevent war through multilateral endeavours.[13]

The African Group called the conference "historic, the result of which will constitute an important contribution to global nuclear disarmament".[14] South Africa echoed this by referring to the conference as "a major milestone in the history of nuclear disarmament and the only reason for our presence here today is to negotiate an instrument that will prohibit nuclear weapons".[15] The Community of Latin American and Caribbean States (CELAC) reiterated the Continent's "desire for meaningful progress towards achieving a world free of nuclear weapons. . . . and encourage(d) others to join us on this path".[16] ICAN reminded delegations of their responsibility to "establish a clear, new, international standard . . . to declare, in no uncertain terms, that nuclear weapons are illegitimate, immoral and illegal".[17]

Not everyone shared this positive view of the negotiations or the sense of historical opportunity these offered. US Ambassador Nikki Haley orchestrated a press briefing outside the UN meeting room in which the rest of the international community had gathered for the negotiations. She was accompanied by representatives from the UK, France and other nuclear umbrella States who, looking rather uncomfortable, each said their countries would not participate in these negotiations but "wanted to have our voices heard".[18] The US ambassador said that

> as a mother, as a daughter, there is nothing I would like more than a world without nuclear weapons [but] in this day and time we can't honestly say that we can protect our people by allowing the bad actors to have them and those of us that are good, trying to keep peace and safety, not to have them.[19]

Ambassador Haley closed by "thanking the States that will not be attending [the negotiations] today for their commitment to their people, their commitment to their countries and their commitment to safety, freedom and peace in the future".[20]

For the States sitting inside the negotiation chamber and listening at that time to Pope Francis' message, this "staged public boycott . . . with a ragtag band of about 20 diplomats"[21] was a strange spectacle. One delegate remembered it as "being absurd for the delegations inside the room. There had been nothing of the sort before. The fact that States that could join in negotiations stand outside the room and say we will not enter . . . absurd!"[22] Another diplomat recalled it as "a lost representative of a superpower looking impotent. It looked ridiculous. But it brought media attention and added value for the negotiations and clearly motivated many delegations to participate. For the negotiations, it was only a win".[23] ICAN was scathing, pointing out that the US ambassador had essentially said, "I don't think nuclear weapons should be banned because I'm a mom and I care about my family".[24] Vanessa Griffen, an ICAN activist from the Pacific region, observed that "Pacific women – mothers and non-mothers alike – have spoken out against nuclear weapons repeatedly and want them banned [and] . . . (a)nyone who knows the impact of nuclear weapons knows their effects on women, and on children".[25] ICAN Executive Director Beatrice Fihn remarked that "normally we NGOs stand outside of negotiation halls. Today, we are inside and the representative . . . Now the US is standing outside and protests. The whole world is upside down".[26]

Among the negotiating States, the focus of attention shifted quickly onto the different expectations and what delegations wished to see in the future ban treaty. One defining feature of the negotiations and the result of the long process of getting to this point, was the "considerable confluence"[27] that already existed in the positions. The States that took part in the negotiations, by and large, wanted to achieve a successful outcome and knew that they had a unique opportunity to do so, which should not be squandered. Nevertheless, the level of preparation varied considerably among delegations. At the March session, many delegations were "only ready to discuss their positions on the provisions at a general level of detail".[28]

This fact was taken into account by the President of the conference and the March session was structured accordingly. There were no actual negotiations on the treaty text, rather interactive panels and expert presentations on the key aspects for the future treaty, giving delegations the opportunity to outline either their general approach to the negotiations or, for the better prepared delegations, to present their detailed positions and expectations. This approach made a virtue out of necessity and helped clarify the key issues for delegations. It also provided Ambassador Whyte Gómez with the substantive basis upon which to prepare the first draft of the treaty text. It gave experts from academia, civil society and the ICRC a significant opportunity to impact the negotiations and to "clarify a number of complex and potentially contentious issues, including on approaches to verification, nuclear testing, the transit of nuclear weapons through national territory and adherence to the treaty by states possessing nuclear weapons".[29] The contribution of these expert panels and interactive sessions to the negotiation momentum and the subsequent successful outcome cannot be overstated.

The President presented her first draft of the treaty on 22 May 2017 in Geneva.[30] Based on the "many common elements and aspirations that had emerged"[31] during the March session, she attempted to "synthesize the many areas where the views of States converged". Her goal was to prepare a "constructive starting point" for the negotiations in June and July. The draft thus included the elements which the President considered to be "ripe, well considered and deemed to constitute a basis for building consensus". Issues that she considered not yet fully developed, she set aside for the second round of negotiations. These included the preamble, general obligations, safeguards, positive obligations (such as victim assistance and environmental remediation), and implementation and final provisions. The President listed the following four overarching principles for the draft: 1) *complementarity* with existing instruments (especially the NPT), 2) *reinforcement* (avoid loopholes to evade existing non-proliferation norms), 3) *simple and non-discriminatory nature* (reflecting a clear and strong prohibition of nuclear weapons and 4) be a *basis for the future* by providing pathways and frameworks for future accession of nuclear weapon States, thus promoting the achievement and maintenance of a world without nuclear weapons.[32]

The negotiation session in June and July 2017

Now the first draft of the treaty was available, the scene was set for the decisive phase of negotiations taking place between 15 June and 7 July 2017. Time pressure was a significant factor. It was a tall order to attempt the negotiations of this treaty in the short time allotted. On the other hand, this, arguably, provided the necessary focus and the opportunity to achieve a historic result. There was no time to waste and success would depend on all stakeholders living up to the occasion and being ready to show the necessary focus, flexibility, and readiness to compromise. One of the key reasons why this goal was ultimately achieved was owed to the fact that there was a high unity of purpose among the negotiating States, as most of the sceptics and opponents boycotted the negotiations. The atmosphere was, as Acheson observed,

> mostly constructive and always dynamic. Delegations supported and built off each other's suggestions, engaging in debate about the merits of particular proposals. It was more open and relaxed than most other UN conferences; activists were welcomed in most of the meetings and most delegations were clearly genuinely committed and excited to be doing this work.[33]

That is not to say, however, that the negotiations made for plain sailing. Far from it. There were also many low points, arguments, infighting and robust exchanges about individual articles and tough, at times acrimonious, negotiations and searches for compromise solutions: in short, all the usual hallmarks of multilateral treaty negotiations.

Negotiating the key provisions

The TPNW that emerged from the negotiations in June and July 2017 is the result of very fast-paced negotiations. This is something that is often invoked by the opponents of this endeavour when criticising the treaty. When the Conference resumed on 15 June 2017 for the final negotiation phase, the first few days were dedicated to delegations commenting on the President's first draft, and to making proposals for revisions. While most delegations praised the draft as a good basis for the negotiations, it was clear from the comments that many issues still needed time and intensive negotiations before they could be resolved. The President subsequently organised interactive sessions and panel discussions with experts to discuss some of the difficult issues. On 27 June, the President presented a revised draft of the treaty[34] and a new methodology for the negotiations.[35] She appointed facilitators to help finalise the open issues. Negotiations on Article 1 (general obligations) were led by the President herself; Articles 2–5 (transparency, stockpile destruction and verification) were facilitated by Helena Nolan from Ireland; Articles 6–7 (national implementation and positive obligations such as victim assistance and environmental remediation) were facilitated by Ambassador Alfredo Labbé from Chile; the final clauses of the treaty were facilitated by Ambassador Virachai Plasai from Thailand and the negotiations on withdrawal and the relationship with other treaties by Ambassador Hasan Kleib from Indonesia. Ambassador Pedro Commissario from Mozambique facilitated the negotiations on transit and on withdrawal. The remainder of the negotiations were conducted partly in so-called "closed meetings", in which only State delegations could participate, and partly in a plenary format, both formal and informal. The result of the small group negotiations was put into a second revised draft treaty and presented by the President on 3 July.[36] After a final review of the text on 5 July, the Conference adopted the TPNW on 7 July 2017.[37] One hundred twenty-two States voted in favour of the TPWN, Singapore abstained and the Netherlands, which had requested a vote, voted against the treaty.

The following section examines the major issues and proposals addressed during the negotiations.[38]

The preamble

The preamble of the TPNW contains 23 paragraphs and describes the motivation of the States negotiating the treaty and the rationale behind its adoption. Given the pivotal role that the Humanitarian Initiative played in generating the political momentum for the TPNW, the preamble received a lot of attention and is the place where the humanitarian/human security approach underpinning the entire enterprise is reflected most prominently. It was felt that the first draft submitted by the President on 22 May 2017, did not adequately reflect all humanitarian aspects and many delegations requested various changes to strengthen the text.[39] On 20 June 2017, the President presented a revised preamble document which was further negotiated and finalised in the following week.

In the final document, ten of the preamble's 24 paragraphs explicitly refer to facts and conclusions drawn directly from the Humanitarian Initiative. The preamble highlights deep concern about the humanitarian consequences from any use of nuclear weapons, the risks posed by their continued existence and that these risks concern the security of all humanity. It also states the lack of response capabilities, the fact that these consequences transcend national borders and pose grave implications for human survival, the environment, socio-economic development, the global economy, food security and the health of current and future generations. The preamble stresses the disproportionate impact of nuclear weapons on women and girls and references the experiences of the *hibakusha* and those affected by nuclear tests, including the disproportionate impact on indigenous people. It also underlines the ethical imperative for nuclear disarmament. Moreover, the preamble refers to the principles and rules of international humanitarian law and its application to nuclear weapons. Finally, it reaffirms that any use of nuclear weapons would be abhorrent to the principles of humanity and the dictates of public conscience, the so-called "Martens Clause".[40] These strong humanitarian references anchor the TPNW firmly as a humanitarian disarmament instrument and provide a cogent rationale for the prohibition of nuclear weapons and the rejection of nuclear deterrence.

In addition, the preamble refers to the longstanding goal of a world without nuclear weapons and the limited progress on nuclear disarmament. In this regard, the preamble reaffirms that "there exists an obligation to pursue in good faith and bring to a conclusion negotiations leading to nuclear disarmament in all its aspects under strict and effective international control".[41] The last paragraphs of the preamble reference the importance of the NPT as the cornerstone of the nuclear disarmament and non-proliferation regime, the importance of the CTBT, the contributions of nuclear-weapon-free zones, the importance of gender balance, of disarmament education and, finally, the importance of the efforts on the part of the United Nations, the International Red Cross and Red Crescent Movement and civil society.

Article I: the prohibitions

The TPNW contains prohibitions in its Article I of the "development, production, testing, acquisition, stockpiling, transfer, possession, stationing, as well as the use and threat of use" of nuclear weapons. State Parties of the TPNW undertake "never under any circumstances" to perform any of these prohibited acts, "nor assist, encourage or induce in any way anyone to engage in any prohibited activity, nor shall a State Party seek or receive assistance to so engage". Furthermore, any stationing, installation or deployment of any nuclear weapons in its territory or at any place under its jurisdiction or control is prohibited.

The prohibitions of "development, production, acquisition, possession, and stockpiling" were included in the President's first draft and remained unchanged during the negotiations. The most intensely debated prohibitions were 1) the threat of use of nuclear weapons, 2) nuclear weapons testing, 3) military preparations for nuclear weapons use, 4) the transit of nuclear weapons and 5) the financing of nuclear weapons related activities, of which the latter three were not included in the final treaty.[42]

The use and threat of use of nuclear weapons

The first draft of Article I only contained a prohibition of the *use* of nuclear weapons. However, many States[43] as well as several NGOs supported the inclusion of the *threat of use*. South Africa had argued already at the March session that the inclusion of the threat of use "would be key to the effort to delegitimise nuclear deterrence".[44] Contrary to this, Mexico and Austria argued against the inclusion, with the argument that there is already a general prohibition on the threat of (armed) force in the UN Charter.[45] Incorporating the threat of use "could be seen as calling into question the validity of the more general norm".[46] Given the strong support by many delegations, the prohibition of "use or threat to use nuclear weapons or other nuclear devices" was included in the draft of 3 July and remained in the final treaty.

Nuclear testing

The first draft of the treaty prepared by the President included a prohibition of "any nuclear weapon test explosion or any other nuclear explosion", which is a direct quote from the CTBT. Some States[47] argued that the CTBT does not prohibit so-called subcritical testing[48] and that the TPNW would provide an opportunity to close this loophole, however this was opposed by many States who were concerned about creating an inconsistency with or a competing norm to the

CTBT.[49] Other States opposed a prohibition of testing with the argument that any form of testing, including subcritical tests, would be covered by the prohibition to develop nuclear weapons. Some States[50] wanted to include direct references to the CTBT. The negotiations on this issue became rather heated and continued in a small group format. The solution around which an agreement could be found was proposed by New Zealand Ambassador Dell Higgie, namely, to simply add the word "test" to the list of prohibitions. A prohibition of nuclear testing was, thus, included in the TPNW, but the simple formulation together with the clear reference to the vital importance of the CTBT in the TPNW preamble prevents any consistency issues with the CTBT.

Military preparations for nuclear weapons use

Article 1 (1)e of the TPNW contains a prohibition on assisting, encouraging or inducing activities that are prohibited by the treaty. In the negotiations, highly vexed questions had arisen around whether an explicit prohibition of *planning and preparations for the use of nuclear weapons* should also be included and the extent to which such acts are already covered by the assistance prohibition. This matter is highly relevant to the question of how the TPNW relates to States in military alliances such as NATO and also the Collective Security Treaty Organization (CSTO), as both include the possible use of nuclear weapons as part of their collective defence doctrines. Given the integrated defence cooperation within NATO in particular, it would be very difficult to determine which acts of military preparation would fall under such a prohibition and which would not.[51] In the case of NATO, Belgium, Germany, Italy, the Netherlands and Turkey cooperate for example in forward deployment and nuclear weapons stationing relationships with the US. These would fall under the explicit prohibition of "allow(ing) any stationing, installation or deployment of any nuclear weapons" contained in Article 1 (1)g. However, NATO allies also cooperate in training and exercises, overflights, port visits, targeting exercises etc. and other activities in the context of NATO's Nuclear Planning Group. A NATO ally/nuclear umbrella State wanting to join the TPNW would, thus, face the challenge of having to change NATO policy and doctrine with regard to nuclear deterrence, in order to ensure that the NATO membership is compatible with the TPNW. This issue posed a significant political challenge for the treaty negotiations. Several States strongly supported an explicit prohibition of military planning of nuclear weapons use, as did the ICRC and ICAN,[52] which would have made the prohibition norm more encompassing and comprehensive. Austria opposed this, based on the rationale of not giving NATO members a too easy excuse not to join the TPNW, and also that planning and preparation of nuclear weapons use would be covered by the prohibition on assisting, encouraging or inducing activities. In the final text, the explicit prohibition of planning and preparation was not included.

Nevertheless, given the different perspectives expressed during the negotiations, the scope and the interpretation of the prohibition of Article 1 (1)e and whether or not membership of a self-professed "nuclear alliance"[53] such as NATO is compatible with the TPNW, this is likely to remain one of the most contested articles of the treaty. As Casey-Maslen details in his legal commentary, a number of activities that NATO allies/nuclear umbrella States regularly undertake could fall under the prohibitions of assistance, encouragement or inducement of activities prohibited under the TPNW.[54]

More clarity on how precisely individual State parties interpret the provision Article 1 (1)e will emerge during the implementation of the TPNW. Austria, for example, has stated that

> assisting, encouraging and inducing is to be understood as referring to measures taken by state parties with the object and purpose of actively supporting, in particular, the possession, use, or threat to use of nuclear weapons. [. . . and that] the mere fact of belonging to a military alliance together with nuclear weapon States or of participating in military manoeuvres with such states, without actively assisting in, encouraging or inducing the deployment of nuclear weapons does not fall under the prohibition of Art. 1(1)e of the Treaty.[55]

In examining the possible TPNW implications for Norway, a NATO member, Nystuen et al, concluded that Norway would have to adjust some of its current practices to comply with Article 1 (1)e.

> Specifically, Norway would have to refrain from "encouraging" or "inducing" the possession and use of nuclear weapons by its allies. Norway's unqualified support for NATO's current strategic concept (2010) and Deterrence and Defence Posture Review (2012) would appear to fall foul of this provision. By actively supporting NATO's policy of extended nuclear deterrence, Norway "encourages" the nuclear-armed allies to retain their nuclear arsenals. . . . After accession, Norway would have to desist from endorsing any NATO documents containing positive references to the potential use of nuclear weapons. Norway would either have to block the adoption of alliance documents containing such language or disassociate itself from such statements through interpretive declarations or "footnotes".

However, the authors conclude that "NATO member states bear no legal obligation to support extended nuclear deterrence or the retention of nuclear weapons. From a legal point of view, accession to the TPNW is compatible with NATO membership".[56]

Transit of nuclear weapons

The negotiations regarding a specific prohibition *of transit of nuclear weapons* through the national territory, maritime waters and the airspace of state parties were equally difficult. Such a prohibition was strongly supported by many States, especially from CELAC, as well as Iran, Kazakhstan, Nigeria and by ICAN. On the other hand, Austria, New Zealand and member States of the Southeast Asian Nuclear Weapon Free Zone[57] argued that the implementation of such a prohibition would be difficult to enforce and should be left out, given that transit was also covered by the prohibition on assistance.[58] This issue became one of the most contentious issues in the plenary debates, with no solution in sight. Negotiations on transit continued in a small "closed format" group facilitated by Ambassador Pedro Commissario of Mozambique, which were equally heated.[59] He consulted and proposed several possible formulations to address this issue. Since none generated the necessary consensus, he concluded that the issue of transit should best be left out of the text. No specific prohibition on transit was included in the final text of the TPNW.[60]

Financing of nuclear weapons

One of ICAN's main objectives was the inclusion of a prohibition against the *financing of nuclear weapons*. As a prohibition would "be significant in terms of putting pressure on the companies currently running the nuclear weapon labs . . . [and] critical for impeding 'modernisation' programmes and diverting human and economic resources away from weapons and towards meeting social needs".[61] Furthermore, as PAX, a Dutch NGO and member of ICAN, argued

> one way to extend the impact of norms outside the treaty is to promote the understanding that the financing of prohibited acts is prohibited. This is one way to effectively pre-empt the argument against the efficacy of a treaty banning nuclear weapons on those states that have nuclear weapons.[62]

Indonesia proposed including a prohibition of financing and was supported by many States, including Thailand, Kazakhstan, Guatemala, Ecuador, Egypt, Peru, Philippines, Iran and Cuba.[63] However, the members of the core group, South Africa, Austria, Ireland, Mexico, supported inter alia by Mozambique, Sweden and Switzerland argued against this, with the argument that such a prohibition would be difficult to implement and that direct financing for nuclear weapons programs would be covered by the prohibition of assistance in Article 1 (1)e. One diplomat from a core group country remembers

> the objective was not to have a 'look good' treaty but a treaty where the national implementation must be possible. How could such a prohibition be implemented in a common capital market? The Finance Ministry would have never agreed to this.[64]

Casey-Maslen also concludes that a legal "distinction exists between buying shares in (i.e. investing in) a company that has some involvement in a nuclear weapons programme, and specifically financing a programme to develop, produce or maintain nuclear weapons".[65] In the final text of the TPNW, there is no explicit prohibition of financing. The extent to which financing is covered by the prohibition of Article 1 (1)e will also undoubtedly be one of the key issues for discussion during the implementation of the TPNW.

Article 3: safeguards

The provisions on safeguards became "one of the most heavily debated and amended provisions during the negotiations".[66] Safeguards in this context are agreements concluded between States and the International Atomic Energy Agency (IAEA), which enables the Agency to verify that States comply with their international legal obligations to use nuclear materials and technology exclusively for peaceful purposes.[67] NPT non-nuclear weapon States are obliged to conclude such safeguards agreements. NPT nuclear weapon States, however, are not obligated and have only concluded so-called "voluntary offer" safeguards agreements that are limited in scope. Many non-nuclear weapon States have also concluded a so-called "Additional Protocol" with the IAEA, which are voluntary but provide for the currently highest standard of IAEA verification activities.

The negotiations on safeguards were made more difficult by the opposition of the nuclear weapon and nuclear umbrella States. The President sent an official letter of invitation to IAEA Director General Yukio Amano for the IAEA to participate in the TPNW negotiation conference. Ambassador Whyte Gómez and the supporters of the ban negotiations noted that IAEA participation would be important because a) the subject matter of the negotiations in New York is of direct relevance to the IAEA's statutory competence to apply safeguards, b) that the negotiations are mandated by the UN General Assembly and c) that the IAEA's participation would contribute to ensuring that the new treaty reinforces the disarmament and non-proliferation regime, including safeguards.[68]

Such was the evident sensitivity of the issue and even though the decision on IAEA participation in international conferences is entirely in the purview of the Director General and does not "require" approval, Amano submitted the invitation for discussion at the IAEA Board of Governors on 15 June 2017. Not surprisingly, the nuclear weapon States and several nuclear umbrella States on the Board objected vociferously to the ban negotiations at what became a heated meeting. Amano was sufficiently intimidated that he decided the IAEA would not attend the negotiations. As such, the episode raises some disturbing issues. Opponents of the TPNW had deterred the international organization in charge of nuclear safeguards from attending and providing expert advice to an inter-governmental negotiation on matters directly related to the Agency's work. These were the same States that later pressed their public "concern" that the TPNW safeguard provisions are, in their view, unsatisfactory.[69] It is hard to see how their actions does them or the IAEA credit.

Some States wanted to use the TPNW negotiations to strengthen the IAEA Additional Protocol by making it compulsory under the TPNW. Switzerland, Sweden and the Netherlands were particularly supportive of this.[70] Other States simply wanted to mirror NPT language on safeguards in order to avoid any accusation of creating a competing norm. Some States that had not (yet) concluded an Additional Protocol were strongly opposed to making it compulsory in the TPNW. Most vocal among those States was Brazil, but also Egypt, Iran and Venezuela. At the same time, there was a broad agreement that the IAEA safeguards system should be strengthened, if possible.

The negotiations conducted by the President in plenary settings and the draft version submitted on 27 June 2017 did not bring the issue closer to a resolution. It was again the negotiations in "closed meetings", this time facilitated by Helena Nolan of Ireland, which managed to resolve this protracted issue and produced a text that became Article 4 of the TPNW. The compromise text "locks in" the IAEA safeguards obligations each State has at the time of its ratification of the TPNW. For the majority of States this already *is* the Additional Protocol.[71] The text does not make the conclusion of an Additional Protocol compulsory for States that do *not yet* have one. The TPNW, thus, provides a higher safeguards standard than the NPT, although not as high as some States and many experts would have liked.[72] Article 3 (2) further obliges a State Party that has not yet done so, to conclude and bring into force an IAEA comprehensive safeguards agreement.[73]

Article 4: dealing with the elimination of nuclear weapons

During the open-ended working group in 2016, many States coalesced around a "prohibition-only" approach, thus leaving the issue of eliminating of nuclear weapons for a future, additional, instrument and a time when (some) nuclear weapon States would be ready to participate in such an endeavour. During the negotiations in 2017, the elimination issue resurfaced however with a number of States arguing that the treaty should also outline a detailed disarmament process. The TPNW ended up containing both a comprehensive set of prohibitions and some provisions regarding the elimination of nuclear weapons. This was owed to the desire of negotiators to give nuclear weapons possessor States two "avenues" to join the treaty, should they wish to. These avenues (discussed below) allowed States to either join the TPNW once they destroyed their nuclear weapons or to join the TPNW and follow a procedure for the subsequent verifiable elimination of nuclear weapons. The first option, popularized among States participating in the 2016 OEWG in part by ILPI and UNIDIR studies, is referred to as "destroy and join" and the second as "join and destroy".[74]

The negotiations on these provisions were difficult. The first draft of the treaty on 22 May 2017 only reflected a "destroy and join" option and was widely seen as unsatisfactory and requiring significant additional negotiations. Some States, including Austria, Ireland, Mexico, New Zealand and South Africa, argued that accession to the treaty should be as open as possible, including by providing for a "join and destroy" option. Finally, a detailed South African proposal combined both avenues in one Article and provided the solution around which support coalesced. In difficult small group negotiations, facilitated by Helena Nolan of Ireland, the approach suggested by South Africa, albeit with significant modifications, became Article 4 of the TPNW.

The "destroy and join" option, Article 4 (1) of the TPNW, obliges a State Party that owned, possessed or controlled nuclear weapons and *has* eliminated its nuclear weapons programme, including the irreversible conversion of all nuclear weapons related facilities, to cooperate with a "competent international authority" to verify this. This authority is to be designated by the TPNW State Parties (at a Meeting of State Parties or a Review Conference) in the future. The obvious candidate for this role is the International Atomic Energy Agency. However, there were two reasons why the IAEA was not explicitly tasked with this role by the TPNW and why this provision ended up in the slightly awkward formulation of a "competent international authority". Firstly, there was the strong opposition of the nuclear weapon States and other IAEA Board Members, such as nuclear umbrella States to the ban treaty negotiations. They had already objected to any role of the IAEA, as discussed earlier in this chapter. Secondly, as argued by Casey-Maslen, "it is not possible under international law to bind the Agency in an international treaty to which it is not party".[75] However, Article 4 (1) does oblige a State Party that has eliminated its nuclear weapons programme to conclude a Safeguards Agreement with the IAEA. Through such an agreement, the IAEA would be tasked to control the non-diversion of declared nuclear material and the absence of undeclared nuclear material.

The "join and destroy" avenue was first included in the draft treaty on 27 June 2017. In the formulation of language, it was essential to ensure that nuclear armed States would not be able to drag out the elimination of their nuclear weapons, thereby effectively circumventing the treaty. This could be solved by an approach similar to that of the Chemical Weapons Convention[76] where State Parties are bound by its prohibitions while undertaking an agreed disarmament/elimination process. The "join and destroy" avenue is enshrined in Article 4 (2) of the TPNW and specifies that States are required to

> immediately remove them [nuclear weapons] from operational status, and destroy them as soon as possible but not later than a deadline to be determined by the first meeting of States parties, in accordance with a legally binding, time-bound plan for the verified and irreversible elimination of that State Party's nuclear weapons programme.

This was a compromise since some States, such as for example Mexico, wanted to determine a fixed deadline for the elimination of nuclear weapons. Ireland argued against this by stating that "it would not be feasible in the time available . . . to negotiate detailed arrangements for the elimination of nuclear weapons now".[77] Article 4 (4) also requires State Parties with nuclear weapons from another State on its territory to ensure the prompt removal of such weapons, as soon as possible but not later than a deadline to be determined by the first meeting of States Parties.

Article 4 of the TPNW ended up dealing with the elimination of nuclear weapons in much more detail than most stakeholders expected, following the discussions on the scope of the treaty in the 2016 open-ended working group. Once it became clear that most States supported both a "destroy and join" and a "join and destroy" avenue, a higher degree of detail became necessary. Subsequently, this section of the TPNW has nevertheless been criticised by its opponents for not being detailed and clear enough.[78] However, given the boycott of the negotiations by nuclear weapons possessor States, it was important to set out parameters for a process whereby such States could join the TPNW. The details of the actual verifiable elimination of nuclear weapons will, however, require the participation of nuclear weapon States. By providing such avenues without prescribing the elimination process in too much detail, the TPNW negotiators acted prudently in my view.

Article 6 and 7: victim assistance, environmental remediation and international cooperation and assistance

In line with the humanitarian approach upon which the TPNW process was built, civil society organisations, the ICRC and many governments wanted to ensure that the rights of victims of nuclear weapons explosions, including the provision of assistance, would be adequately reflected in the Treaty. This was also in recognition of the pivotal role played by *hibakusha* and victims of nuclear testing in generating the momentum for the ban.

The negotiations focused on the issue of responsibility. Some States[79] argued that the prime responsibility for assistance to victims should lie with those States that have caused the damage to victims in the first place. However, other States, ICAN and the ICRC argued that the primary responsibility for providing assistance to victims lies with States in whose jurisdictions and control they are.[80] The TPNW ended up following this second view, which is also in line with similar provisions taken in other humanitarian disarmament treaties, such as on antipersonnel landmines, cluster munitions and in Protocol V of the Convention on Certain Conventional Weapons.[81]

On environmental remediation, the situation was not dissimilar. Anti-nuclear NGOs and some States wanted to include provisions to redress damage and destruction to the environment caused by nuclear explosions, some pushed for more far-reaching measures such as decontamination, threat assessments and risk reductions measures.[82] The Marshall Islands, supported by Fiji, called for a strong provision, including enforcing the responsibility of those States that had used or tested nuclear explosive devices.[83] The solution that was found and became Article 6 (2) of the TPNW was that State Parties "shall take necessary and appropriate measures towards the environmental remediation of [contaminated] areas [under its jurisdiction or control]".

The responsibilities of State Parties that have tested or used nuclear explosive devices were thus not addressed in Article 6, which deals only with responsibilities of those States Parties in whose jurisdiction and control the victims live or the damaged environment is located. The responsibility of the "user" is tackled in Article 7 (6). It specifies that "a State Party that has used or tested nuclear weapons ... shall have a responsibility to provide adequate assistance to affected States

Parties, for the purpose of victim assistance and environmental remediation". This was the result of small group negotiations under the facilitation of Ambassador Alfredo Labbé of Chile, which also had been difficult. While it was important for the TPNW negotiations to agree on the principle of reflecting the responsibility of the "user" to redress the humanitarian consequences it has caused, Casey-Maslen points out "some drawback to this provision, as drafted". He rightly criticises, inter alia, that there is "no causal link between the testing and the responsibility towards any particular affected state party".[84] Moreover, the States that have tested nuclear explosive devices are unlikely to adhere to the TRPNW any time soon.

Article 17: withdrawal

An unexpected difficulty arose in the final stage of the negotiations on the issue of withdrawal from the Treaty. Article 17 stipulates that the Treaty should be of unlimited duration (paragraph 1) but provides, in paragraph 2 for a right to withdraw if a State Party "decides that extraordinary events related to the subject matter of the Treaty have jeopardised the supreme interest of its country". Paragraph 3 qualifies that the withdrawal shall only take effect a year after notice of the withdrawal is received but that the withdrawing State Party continues to be bound by the Treaty if it is party to an armed conflict.

Many states,[85] as well as ICAN, felt that having a withdrawal clause ran counter to the whole purpose of the Treaty. Other humanitarian disarmament treaties, such as on antipersonnel landmines or cluster munitions, do not foresee a withdrawal based on "supreme interests", an ultimately unclear and subjective criterion. Indeed without a specific withdrawal clause in the TPNW, the general withdrawal clause of the Vienna Convention on the Law of Treaties would have been applicable.[86] Others, among them Iran, Sweden, Egypt and Switzerland[87] argued in favour of retaining the clause.

At the end of an intensive plenary debate on 5 July 2017, the President suggested the removal of paragraphs 2 and 3 of Article 17 from the text. However, the States that wanted them to be retained objected. Ambassador Whyte Gómez then tried to get agreement on the Article as it stood. The States that had called for a removal of the Article decided to let it pass in order to not hold up the conclusion of the treaty.[88]

This was the last substantial issue to be resolved. After this plenary debate, the negotiations were closed and the draft treaty was moved to the UN translation services for translation into the six official UN languages.[89] On Friday 7 July 2017, the Conference reconvened for the TPNW's adoption. The day before, the Netherlands delegation informed the President that they would be requesting a recorded vote. With a no-vote by the Netherlands looming, it would be important to ensure that as many States as possible would be present to participate in the vote. With the help of overnight phone campaigns by ICAN and some States including Austria, 124 States gathered in the conference room at the allotted hour of the session. The President of the Conference then moved to the adoption of the Treaty and the recorded vote resulted with 122 States voting yes, Singapore abstaining and the

Netherlands voting no. The TPNW was, thus, adopted to a standing ovation of (most) of the participants.

Many delegations then asked to speak to give so-called "explanations of vote". Most delegations referred to the TPNW as a historic achievement and as a triumph of multilateralism.[90] Delegations expressed their hope that it would pave the way for the elimination of nuclear weapons and highlighted, for example by Trinidad and Tobago, that the TPNW had "shattered the chronic stalemate" in nuclear disarmament and non-proliferation, or by Chile, that "democracy is possible in the international system".[91] Many delegations also underlined the pivotal role played by civil society to get to this point.[92]

Ominously for their prospects of joining the TPNW in the near future, Sweden and Switzerland had both voted yes but delivered explanations of vote in which they drew attention to aspects of the Treaty with which they had concerns, as did the Netherlands referring to the obligations of the TPNW as being incompatible with its NATO membership.[93] However, this surprised no-one. Instead, perhaps the most memorable closing statement of the session was delivered on behalf of ICAN by Setsuko Thurlow, a hibakusha from Hiroshima. Thurlow said that she had "waited for this moment for seven decades and (was) overjoyed that it has finally arrived. This is the beginning of the end of nuclear weapons. . . . Nuclear weapons have always been immoral. Now they are also illegal".[94]

The different groups and stakeholders who negotiated the TPNW

Within the negotiation dynamic, there were several stakeholders among States and civil society organisations whose approaches, contributions and different perspectives for the negotiations particularly shaped the negotiation dynamics and, hence, the final outcome of the TPNW.

In 2016, Austria, Brazil, Ireland, Nigeria, Mexico and South Africa had submitted the resolution that mandated the ban treaty negotiations. This group of States formed what was known as the "core group" of States for the negotiations. The core group discussed and coordinated their approach in frequent informal meetings in Geneva and during the negotiations in New York. Other states that had also strongly supported the Humanitarian Initiative and the open-ended working group sometimes participated in these meetings and were closely consulted. These included in particular Indonesia, Malaysia, Philippines, Thailand, New Zealand and Chile, this constituted what was referred to as the "core group plus".

When compared to other multilateral treaty negotiations processes,[95] this core group was probably less closely knit and coordinated in their attempts of steering the process.[96] Some within the core group wanted the group to play a stronger and more visible role, including by making text proposals as the core group. Others argued for a looser approach. A more closely coordinated core group can be very effective in steering negotiations. It requires a fully shared perspective on the key provisions of the future treaty and a very close coordination with the President of the Conference. In the case of the TPNW both aspects were not fully there.

On some substantive issues, members of the core group had partly differing views. Also, while the core group's contact with the President was close, there was only a limited degree of coordination, especially in the early phase of the negotiations. Members of the core group had concerns about several aspects of the first draft of the treaty and were, at times, worried that the process could falter, especially given the time pressure. In the later phase of the negotiations, the cooperation between the President and core group intensified and facilitated a successful outcome. In hindsight, some difficulties during the negotiations could have been averted, especially if more cooperation had taken place with the President in the preparation of the first draft. At the same time, it may have been beneficial for the transparency of the negotiation process that the relationship between the President and the core group did not appear to be too "hand in glove".

The members of the core group nevertheless played a crucial role in consolidating agreement around many difficult issues. Core group members South Africa and Nigeria consulted closely with the African Group, ensuring that as many delegations as possible were present and expressed support for the negotiations and consensus solutions. Mozambique played a particularly active role in the negotiations. The same was true for Latin America and the Caribbean. The strong positions on nuclear disarmament by CELAC and the active role of core group delegations from Brazil and Mexico, as well as Chile, Cuba, Ecuador, Guatemala, Jamaica and Peru among others, made sure that this region played a very significant role in bringing the negotiations to a successful conclusion. The fact that the President of the Conference came from this region also contributed to this. The core group members Austria and Ireland continued to play a leading role, cooperated closely and had very similar objectives for the negotiations. The small group facilitation by Helena Nolan from Ireland on some of the most protracted issues is particularly noteworthy. Austria coordinated the core group and was active on all fronts in trying to facilitate a positive outcome. Liechtenstein was also very active in the negotiations and supported similar positions as Austria and Ireland.

In the Asian region, the active role and participation of Indonesia, Malaysia, Philippines, Thailand and Viet Nam was particularly crucial. These States had a clear vision for the negotiations, were very active and constructive throughout the negotiations and wanted to achieve a strong and credible prohibition treaty.

Among the other strongly supportive delegations whose contribution should be stressed are particularly New Zealand, as well as Algeria, Kazakhstan and the Pacific Island States, with Fiji amongst them playing the most active role. In addition to the message from Pope Francis at the opening of the Conference, the Holy See participation in the Conference, with its clearly expressed support for the negotiations, provided many other participating States with an important validation. The same can be said for the role of the ICRC. As "guardian of International Humanitarian Law",[97] its strong support for the prohibition of nuclear weapons and detailed proposals on some key issues helped convince many delegations.

Sweden and Switzerland formed a specific group of their own. Their position can be described as generally very supportive of nuclear disarmament and the humanitarian approach in the nuclear weapons debate. However, in both States, the full spectrum of nuclear weapons discourse is present from strong support for nuclear disarmament to a rather pro-nuclear deterrence position. Both States were supportive of the negotiations but not fully convinced of a prohibition, without the nuclear weapon States. The collective NATO boycott rather strengthened the hand of the ban-sceptics in these two States. They were referred to as the "sceptically constructive" States[98] who put particular emphasis on the relationship with the NPT, as well as on the nuclear safeguards issue. During the negotiations, nuclear testing also became a major issue for them. Some members of the core group referred to the Swedish and Swiss positions as "too inflexible, sticking to their opening positions and not moving with or reacting to the negotiations".[99] As a result, both States only played a relatively minor role in the negotiations. They had both very much hoped that more of the nuclear umbrella States would decide to participate. When this was not the case, their approach to the negotiations was driven by the wish to achieve a text which would, to the extent possible, facilitate a future participation of these States. A certain degree of frustration was expressed afterwards and informally at the fact that very few of the Swedish and Swiss proposals were taken up. Privately, officials from these countries grumbled that their national positions appeared to be "de-prioritized" in the negotiations compared to others – even those seemingly of non-aligned hardliners.[100]

Otherwise, participation from Europe was disappointing and all NATO States absent, apart from the Netherlands. Even Norway, which had instigated the first humanitarian conference in Oslo in 2013, did not attend the negotiations. The Netherlands was in a singular position among the participating States. It was the only State from the nuclear umbrella States that decided to take part in the negotiations. This was not the result of a change of position by the government regarding the ban, but due to significant and successful ICAN pressure[101] and a parliamentary debate urging the government to participate in negotiations. During the negotiations, the Netherlands made proposals, especially with regard to its NATO membership, which were at odds with the text that the other delegations were negotiating. Some delegates observed that the Netherland's objective was not to make the treaty better, but to demonstrate that the outcome was something they could fully disassociate themselves from and which they could criticise. "The Netherland's delegation absolutely did not want to end up being implicated with any aspect of the treaty", was the analysis of one diplomat.[102] Another core group diplomat stated that

> getting the additional Protocol in [note: into the treaty text] would have been the only deliverable that was worthwhile for the US and nuclear umbrella States, such as the Netherlands. Other than this, there was only a negative agenda for these negotiations which they saw as an anti-nuclear deterrence exercise.[103]

The role of the Dutch was widely considered as awkward and their uncomfortable diplomatic position was palpable to others during the negotiations. At the end of the negotiations, the Netherlands was the delegation that called for a vote and was the only State that voted against adoption of the TPNW.

Cuba, Egypt and Iran played a very active role during the negotiations. For some members of the core group, there had been some level of concern whether these States – important members of the group of non-aligned States with pronounced positions on nuclear disarmament – might choose to be obstructive. In the end, all three States, for their specific reasons, participated constructively and decided, by and large, to go along with the momentum of the negotiations. Cuba traditionally supported a comprehensive nuclear weapons convention but came around to accepting a ban as a step towards this objective and was bound by the pro-ban positions that had been agreed within CELAC. It also wanted to support a President who came from its region. Iran initially raised again the issue of consensus and also the scope of the future treaty, expressing its preference for a comprehensive prohibition treaty that would include provisions on the elimination of nuclear weapons. Even though it may not have been convinced of the ban treaty approach, Iran was active during the negotiations and did not play a disruptive role. The precarious situation of the Iran nuclear agreement (JCPOA) and the looming threat of the US withdrawing from it,[104] may have contributed to Iran's stance during the negotiations. "Iran understood that politically it cannot be the spoiler in these negotiations",[105] was how one diplomat from the core group interpreted Iran's approach. Egypt, too, was a very active participant with many proposals on different aspects of the treaty and was a constructive actor in the negotiations.

ICAN, of course, was an influential observer in the negotiations and through its advocacy work had done much to pave the way for States to reach this point. Maybe one of the most important contributions was their public outreach, in terms of raising awareness about these negotiations. ICAN was very present, especially on social media and its performance was highly effective and professional. Importantly, ICAN "worked the phones" and encouraged smaller delegations to participate in the negotiations and provided much needed background and information for delegations with less capacity and expertise on nuclear weapons issues. Keeping as many States as possible actively engaged was a key contribution on the part of ICAN.

Regarding the substantive contributions of ICAN to the negotiations themselves, the picture is more nuanced, owing to the fact that ICAN is itself composed of many individual NGOs. ICAN activists pushed for the strongest possible treaty and were involved and present with different actors at all levels of the negotiations. However, as is typical of international negotiations in which civil society can attend and observe but do not have negotiating rights, some of its positions and proposals did not make it into the final text. Having worked closely with many government representatives to generate the momentum to get to the negotiations, the cooperation with the same States became more difficult during the negotiations as they were now at the receiving end of ICAN lobbying activities. This is an entirely normal development during negotiations but poses a strategic challenge for NGOs. Does the partnership that was so instrumental in the road to the treaty survive the negotiations, or is it the job of NGOs to always push governments forward, no matter what? The partnership model would require a readiness by NGOs to accept tactical considerations and compromises, even from their vantage point unsatisfactory ones, for the sake of achieving the overall objective. The more activist approach will lead civil society representatives to promote specific positions and to exert pressure even on States with whom there had been close cooperation before. ICAN also faced these challenges.[106]

While ICAN, as a coalition, had a negotiation position and specific "asks" for the outcome, its large coalition was arguably not so well equipped to deal with the changing negotiation dynamics and opposition from States to some of ICAN's proposals and positions. This was the case in particular on the issues of financing, transit, threat of use, environmental remediation or victim assistance. Some actors within ICAN, especially from its steering committee, were more open to accept the assessment of their closest State partners on why a particular issue should be pushed only so far. Other ICAN members, which favoured the activist approach wanted to push issues further leading to robust discussions within ICAN on which approach to follow. On many issues, ICAN had to resort internally to voting to reach decisions. Some NGOs that are part of ICAN at times "continued to propose their own ideas and pursue their own tactics independently".[107] One core group diplomat remembered that

> it seemed difficult for the ICAN leadership to keep things together at the beginning. Different ICAN activists promoted partly different agendas and priorities during negotiations. With many States picking up on these points to support ICAN, we ended up having many more open points in the negotiations than expected. There was a message control problem with ICAN at times.[108]

Over the course of the negotiations and with the final outcome taking shape, this situation improved. One contributing factor for this was that in the final phase, the negotiations moved in part to so-called "closed meetings" in which civil society representatives were not admitted. While this led to considerable frustration within ICAN,[109] it was necessary in light of the time pressure and in order to focus delegation's minds on identifying the achievable compromises necessary to bring the negotiations to a successful close. Even though the TPNW does not contain all the positions and proposals that ICAN as well as individual ICAN NGOs had advocated for, the NGO coalition that had done so much to make the TPNW a reality, rallied strongly behind the treaty once it was achieved.

Reflections on the negotiations process

Perhaps the biggest accomplishment was the relatively swift conclusion of the TPNW negotiations. This was certainly owed to a large extent to the fact that almost all participating states wanted to achieve a ban treaty. Nevertheless, the negotiation process was at times difficult, and success was not guaranteed. In hindsight, one of the key difficulties was the time factor. The TPNW was negotiated at speed, with only four weeks of formal negotiations. Of those, a significant part was devoted to more general discussions and expert presentations. While these were of excellent quality, they point to the fact that many delegations had come to the negotiations with a general idea about the objective they wanted to achieve but not with detailed and legally sound prepared positions on the individual provisions that would have to be negotiated.

Here, the comparison with other humanitarian disarmament processes is instructive. The process leading to the 2009 Cluster Munitions Convention stretched over one and a half years from the Oslo Conference in February 2007 until the two-week negotiation conference in Dublin in May 2008.[110] Between these, there were additional preparatory conferences in Lima, Vienna and Wellington. At all these meetings, the actual legal text of the future convention was further developed and further consolidated and had reached a fairly high level of maturity when States convened in Dublin to finalise the text. A similar length of time and amount of deliberation had been required, a decade earlier, for the Anti-Personnel Mine Ban Convention.

In terms of substantive preparation, the TPNW process lacked this kind of gradual maturation. The discussions in the open-ended working group in 2016 had been useful in sketching an outline of what should and could be contained in a ban treaty, but they did not substitute a more comprehensive preparatory process.[111] The reasons for this are partly practical and partly political. The processes for the cluster munitions and landmine conventions took place outside the UN and were financed independently, largely by Western States. Of those resources, Norway had shouldered a particularly significant portion, used to sponsor the participation of developing countries. Such funds were not available for the TPNW process,[112] which was mandated by the UN General Assembly and had a budget for a limited number of meetings.

Moreover, the fragility of the entire process, given the strong opposition against this endeavour, also played a role. Many participants felt that the window of opportunity to get this treaty done was very small and an "extension of the negotiations into 2018 may have become extremely difficult, especially after the election of US President Trump".[113] The time factor and absence of formal preparations gave all participants, States and civil society alike, little time to transition from generating momentum and defending the idea of a ban treaty against its opponents, into a mindset for treaty negotiations amongst themselves.

There has also been some criticism of how the President and her team structured the negotiations, especially in the early phase of the negotiations and with the preparation of the first draft of the Treaty. Some delegates felt that valuable time for the negotiations was lost, which made the "endgame" more difficult and more pressured.[114]

As a result of these various factors, negotiations had to be done under considerable time pressure and some of the provisions could have profited from longer consideration in order to refine them further. Moreover, the fact remains that the negotiations took place without the participation of nuclear armed states. Some of the aspects of the TPNW therefore, could only provide a framework, a pathway for these States to engage with the Treaty, should they decide to do so in the future. The TPNW would have undoubtedly looked different in some articles, such as for example safeguards and elimination, had nuclear armed states decided to participate in the negotiations in good faith. As one UN official put it "the end result is always as good as you can make it at the time and with the people that are in the room".[115]

Even if some provisions of the TPNW could have been refined more, the TPNW "end result" is a strong and unequivocal prohibition of nuclear weapons. It is as such, a major diplomatic accomplishment and what the negotiating States wanted to achieve. A clear "legal line in the sand" has been drawn by the TPNW. The "legal gap" for the prohibition of nuclear weapons – the only weapon of mass destruction not unequivocally prohibited – has been filled. For the states that wanted to outlaw nuclear weapons and the concept and practice of nuclear deterrence because of the humanitarian consequences and risks of nuclear weapons, the TPNW provides a solid and comprehensive legal basis for it. States that want to keep nuclear weapons and continue to think they need to rely on the precarious practice of nuclear deterrence, will for these reasons, find and continue to find issue with the TPNW, how it came about and how it was negotiated.

Notes

1. Statement by Setsuko Thurlow on behalf of ICAN on 7 July 2017, see TPNW webcast archive available at www.un.org/disarmament/tpnw/webcast.html.
2. With the exception of The Netherlands, which, apparently under pressure from Parliament and civil society action, decided to participate in the TPNW negotiations. For more information see also available at www.icanw.org/netherlands
3. See for example "Report of the Conference on Disarmament to the General Assembly of the United Nations", Doc. Nr. CD?2179, 13 September 2019, available at www.unog.ch/80256EDD006B8954/(httpAssets)/850B8631E9B65126C12584CC005B3649/$file/CD_2179_E.pdf.
4. Interview conducted by the author on 17 June 2020 with a diplomat who had participated in this meeting.
5. This was the case largely because securing the budget for the TPNW negotiations had been a considerable challenge. In the end, the costs for the negotiations were taken from the unused budget allocation to the Conference on Disarmament. However, these unused funds were limited allowing only for a certain number of negotiation days and not for additional preparatory meetings, which would normally be the case with treaty negotiations.
6. When the Rules of Procedure of the Conference were adopted, Iran initially insisted on all decisions being taken by consensus (see also Chapter 3) but this was not accepted.
7. A compromise was found whereby States would have the (theoretical) possibility to veto the participation of individual NGOs, which, however, did not happen.
8. Two UN observer States The Holy See and Palestine wanted to participate in the negotiations. The contentious issue, which comes up frequently in the context of UN conferences, are the participatory rights of the delegation of "The State of Palestine" given

that Palestine is recognized as a State by 137 and not recognized by 48 States UN member States (status September 2020), see "Permanent Observer Mission of the State of Palestine to the United Nations New York", available at https://palestineun.org/.
9. Pope Francis, Message by to the President of the Conference on 27 March 2017. This message as well as all statements delivered at and the documents of the conference are available at https://papersmart.unmeetings.org/ga/71st-session/united-nations-conference-to-negotiate-a-legally-binding-instrument-to-prohibit-nuclear-weapons-leading-towards-their-total-elimination/statements/; another very comprehensive resource for statements and documents as well as reports is available at www.reachingcriticalwill.org/disarmament-fora/nuclear-weapon-ban.
10. Ibid., Statement by ICRC President Peter Maurer on 27 March 2017.
11. Ibid., Statement by Ireland on 27 March 2017.
12. Ibid., Statement by ASEAN on 27 March 2017.
13. Ibid., Statement by Algeria on 27 March 2017.
14. Ibid., Statement by the African Group on 27 March 2017.
15. Ibid., Statement by South Africa on 27 March 2017.
16. Ibid., Statement by the Community of Latin American and Caribbean States (CELAC) on 27 March 2017.
17. Statement by ICAN on 28 March 2017, available at www.reachingcriticalwill.org/images/documents/Disarmament-fora/nuclear-weapon-ban/statements/28March_ICAN.pdf.
18. See for example Michelle Nichols, "U.S., Britain, France, Others Skip Nuclear Weapons Ban Treaty Talks", in *Reuters*, 27 March 2017, available at www.reuters.com/article/us-nuclear-un/u-s-britain-france-others-skip-nuclear-weapons-ban-treaty-talks-idUSKBN16Y1QI.
19. Ibid.
20. Ibid.
21. Zia Mian and M.V. Ramana, "Ending Nuclear Lawlessness", in *The Hindu*, 13 April 2017, available at www.thehindu.com/opinion/lead/ending-nuclear-lawlessness/article17960731.ece.
22. Interview with a diplomat on 14 April 2020 who participated in the negotiations in New York.
23. Interview with a diplomat conducted by the author on 1 April 2020 who participated in the negotiations in New York.
24. Ray Acheson, *Banning the Bomb, Smashing the Patriarchy*, Rowman & Littlefield Publishers, March 2021, forthcoming.
25. Ibid., cited Letter to ICAN campaigners from Pacific supporter Vanessa Griffen, 28 March 2017.
26. In a conversation with Austrian Ambassador Thomas Hajonoczi.
27. See Stuart Casey-Maslen, *The Treaty on the Prohibition of Nuclear Weapons: A Commentary*, Oxford University Press, 2019, p. 49.
28. John Borrie, Michael Spies, and Wilfred Wan, "Obstacles to Understanding the Emergence and Significance of the Treaty on the Prohibition of Nuclear Weapons", in *Global Change, Peace & Security*, 2018, p. 15, available at https://doi.org/10.1080/14781158.2018.1467394.
29. Ibid.
30. See "Draft Convention on the Prohibition of Nuclear Weapons", presented by the President on 22 May 2017, available at https://s3.amazonaws.com/unoda-web/wp-content/uploads/2017/05/A-CONF.229-CRP.1.pdf.
31. Remarks by the President on 22 May 2017, available at https://s3.amazonaws.com/unoda-web/wp-content/uploads/2017/05/Letter-from-the-Chair_May-24-2017.pdf.
32. Ibid.
33. Acheson, *Banning the Bomb, Smashing the Patriarchy*.

134 *The ban treaty is coming*

34 See "Draft Treaty on the Prohibition of Nuclear Weapons", submitted by the President on 27 June 2017, available at https://s3.amazonaws.com/unoda-web/wp-content/uploads/2017/06/A-CONF.229-2017-CRP.1-Rev.1.pdf.
35 See also John Borrie, Michael Spies, and Wilfred Wan, "Obstacles to Understanding the Emergence and Significance of the Treaty on the Prohibition of Nuclear Weapons", in *Global Change, Peace & Security*, 2018, p. 17, available at https://doi.org/10.1080/14781158.2018.1467394.
36 See "Draft Treaty on the Prohibition of Nuclear Weapons", submitted by the President on 3 July 2017, available at www.undocs.org/en/a/conf.229/2017/L.3.
37 See "Treaty of the Prohibition of Nuclear Weapons", Doc. Nr. A/CONF.229/2017/8, adopted on 7 July 2017, available at https://undocs.org/A/CONF.229/2017/8.
38 For comprehensive legal commentary of the TPNW as well as a history of the negotiations see, Casey-Maslen, *The Treaty on the Prohibition of Nuclear Weapons*.
39 See Reaching Critical Will, "Nuclear Ban Daily", vol. 2, no. 2, 16 June 2017, p. 3, available at www.reachingcriticalwill.org/images/documents/Disarmament-fora/nuclear-weapon-ban/reports/NBD2.2.pdf.
40 The Martens Clause recalls that "in cases not covered by the law in force, the human person remains under the protection of the principles of humanity and the dictates of public conscience" (1977 Additional Protocol II to the Geneva Conventions), see for example available at www.weaponslaw.org/glossary/martens-clause.
41 This language is taken from the 1996 Advisory Opinion of the International Court of Justice, "Legality of the Threat or Use of Nuclear Weapons", 8 July 1996, available at https://web.archive.org/web/20171118183503/www.icj-cij.org/files/case-related/95/7497.pdf.
42 See below and see also Casey-Maslen, *The Treaty on the Prohibition of Nuclear Weapons*, p. 132.
43 For example, Indonesia, Algeria, Brazil, Chile, Kazakhstan and Thailand in the Plenary meeting on 16 June 2017.
44 Statement by South Africa on 29 March 2017, available at http://statements.unmeetings.org/media2/14683384/south-africa.pdf.
45 See "UN Charter" Article 2 (4) "All Members shall refrain in their international relations from the threat or use of force against the territorial integrity or political independence of any state, or in any other manner inconsistent with the Purposes of the United Nations". The Charter of the United Nations was signed on 26 June 1945, in San Francisco, at the conclusion of the United Nations Conference on International Organization, and came into force on 24 October 1945, available at www.un.org/en/charter-united-nations/.
46 Statements by Mexico and Austria on 29 March 2017, available at http://statements.unmeetings.org/media2/14683372/mexico.pdf; http://statements.unmeetings.org/media2/14683377/austria.pdf.
47 For example, Cuba, Ecuador, Egypt, Iran, Venezuela and Viet Nam.
48 This refers to nuclear testing where no self-sustaining nuclear fission chain reaction happens, as would be the case with a detonation of a nuclear explosive device.
49 Mexico, Austria, Ireland and Sweden.
50 For example, Switzerland and the Netherlands.
51 See for example "Strategic Concept for the Defence and Security of the Members of the North Atlantic Treaty Organization", 2010, available at www.nato.int/strategic-concept/index.html.
52 For example, Indonesia, supported by Thailand, Iran, Mozambique, Venezuela, Uganda, Palestine and Bangladesh suggested the inclusion of such a paragraph, see "Nuclear Ban Daily", vol. 2, no. 3, 19 June 29, p. 8, available at www.reachingcriticalwill.org/images/documents/Disarmament-fora/nuclear-weapon-ban/reports/NBD2.3.pdf; for the ICRC see "Comments of the International Committee of the Red Cross on Key Provisions of the Draft Convention on the Prohibition of Nuclear

Weapons", 14 June 2017, available at https://s3.amazonaws.com/unoda-web/wp-content/uploads/2017/06/A-CONF.229-2017-CRP.2-ICRC-second-paper.pdf.
53 As expressed in "Active Engagement, Modern Defence: Strategic Concept for the Defence and Security of the Members of the North Atlantic Treaty Organisation" adopted by "NATO Heads of State and Government in Lisbon", 23 May 2012, available at www.nato.int/cps/en/natolive/official_texts_68580.htm.
54 See Casey-Maslen, *The Treaty on the Prohibition of Nuclear Weapons*, p. 158.
55 Communication sent by Austrian Ambassador Thomas Hajnoczi on 19 April 2017, cited in Casey-Maslen, *The Treaty on the Prohibition of Nuclear Weapons*, p. 165; this is based on an interpretative analysis prepared by the Office of International Law of the Austrian Foreign Ministry for the ratification of the TPNW by the Austrian Parliament on 21 March 2018, see available at www.parlament.gv.at/PAKT/VHG/XXVI/I/I_00009/index.shtml#tab-ParlamentarischesVerfahren.
56 Gro Nystuen, Kjolv Egeland, and Torbjorn Graff Hugo, "The TPNW and Its Implications for Norway", in *Norwegian Academy of International Law*, September 2018, p. 5, available at www.researchgate.net/publication/335834495_The_TPNW_and_its_implications_for_Norway.
57 See "Treaty on the Southeast Asia Nuclear Weapon-Free Zone", available at http://disarmament.un.org/treaties/t/bangkok.
58 See "Nuclear Ban Daily", 19 June 2017.
59 For example, the delegate from Ecuador walked out of a meeting in protest to the discussions on transit.
60 Cuba and Ecuador clarified that they will interpret the treaty that transit is prohibited by the prohibition of Article 1 (1)e. For example interpretative statement by Cuba upon its ratification of the TPNW, text available at UN Treaty Section available at http://bit.ly/2AlahjS.
61 See Ray Acheson, "Confronting Profits and Legacies of Nuclear Violence", in *Nuclear Ban Daily*, vol. 2, no. 8, 27 June 2017, available at www.reachingcriticalwill.org/images/documents/Disarmament-fora/nuclear-weapon-ban/reports/NBD2.8.pdf.
62 "Banning Investment: An Explicit Prohibition on the Financing of Nuclear Weapons Producers", working paper submitted by PAX, A/CONF.229/2017/NGO/WP.5, 17 March 2017, available at www.reachingcriticalwill.org/images/documents/Disarmament-fora/nuclear-weapon-ban/documents/NGOWP.5.pdf.
63 See "Nuclear Ban Daily", 19 June 2017, p. 3.
64 Interview conducted by the author with a diplomat from a core group State on 14 April 2020.
65 See Casey-Maslen, *The Treaty on the Prohibition of Nuclear Weapons*, p. 167.
66 Ibid., p. 181.
67 For more explanation see, "IAEA Safeguards Agreements", available at www.iaea.org/topics/safeguards-agreements.
68 Statement delivered by Brazil on behalf of 30 States in the IAEA Board of Governors on 15 June 2017, personal archive of the author.
69 See also Chapter 7.
70 See for example "Need for Verification Mechanism at This Stage for a Treaty Prohibiting Nuclear Weapons", working paper 6 submitted by Sweden, together with Chile and Uganda, 10 May 2017, available at https://undocs.org/A/CONF.229/2017/WP.6.
71 At the time of writing (autumn 2020), 136 States have concluded an Additional Protocol, see available at www.iaea.org/topics/additional-protocol.
72 See also Chapter 7 which discusses the criticism that was voiced against this solution by opponents of the TPNW.
73 IAEA comprehensive safeguards agreement (INFCIRC/153 Corrected); for more information, see "IAEA Comprehensive Safeguards Agreements", available at www.iaea.org/topics/safeguards-legal-framework/more-on-safeguards-agreements.

74 ILPI and UNIDIR, "A Prohibition on Nuclear Weapons: A Guide to the Issues", 2016, pp. 38–40, available at https://unidir.org/publication/prohibition-nuclear-weapons-guide-issues. See also Tim Caughley and Gaukhar Mukhatzhanova, *Negotiation of a Nuclear Weapons Prohibition Treaty: Nuts and Bolts of the Ban*, 2017, available at https://unidir.org/publication/negotiation-nuclear-weapons-prohibition-treaty-nuts-and-bolts-ban.
75 See Casey-Maslen, *The Treaty on the Prohibition of Nuclear Weapons*, p. 194.
76 See Articles III and IV of the Convention on the Prohibition of the Development, Production, Stockpiling and Use of Chemical Weapons and on their Destruction, available at http://disarmament.un.org/treaties/t/cwc.
77 See "Nuclear Ban Daily", vol. 2, no. 4, 20 June 2017, p. 2, available at www.reachingcriticalwill.org/images/documents/Disarmament-fora/nuclear-weapon-ban/reports/NBD2.4.pdf.
78 See Chapter 7.
79 See for example Statement by Sweden om 27 June 2017, supported by Cuba, Thailand, Venezuela and Viet Nam.
80 See for example ICRC, "Comments of the International Committee of the Red Cross on Key Provisions of the Draft Convention on the Prohibition of Nuclear Weapons", 14 June 2017, available at https://s3.amazonaws.com/unoda-web/wp-content/uploads/2017/06/A-CONF.229-2017-CRP.2-ICRC-second-paper.pdf.
81 Ibid.
82 See for example, Article 36 "Environmental Remediation in the Nuclear Weapon Ban Treaty: A Comprehensive and Detailed Approach", June 2017, available at www.article36.org/wp-content/uploads/2017/06/ER-short-paper-final.pdf.
83 See Statement of the Marshall Islands on 18 June 2017, "Nuclear Ban Daily", vol. 2, no. 5, 21 June 2017, available at www.reachingcriticalwill.org/images/documents/Disarmament-fora/nuclear-weapon-ban/reports/NBD2.5.pdf; the "polluter pays" principle was also supported by other States, including Cuba, Ecuador, Egypt, Iran, Nigeria as well as Sweden.
84 See Casey-Maslen, *The Treaty on the Prohibition of Nuclear Weapons*, p. 224.
85 For example, Brazil, Mexico, Mozambique, Chile, Liechtenstein, Ecuador, New Zealand, South Africa, Ghana, Guatemala, Indonesia and Palestine, in "Nuclear Ban Daily", vol. 2, no. 13, 6 July 2017, p. 9, available at www.reachingcriticalwill.org/images/documents/Disarmament-fora/nuclear-weapon-ban/reports/NBD2.13.pdf.
86 See Article 56 of the Vienna Convention on the Law of Treaties, available at https://legal.un.org/ilc/texts/instruments/english/conventions/1_1_1969.pdf. According to this provision a withdrawing state needs to prove that "it is established that the parties intended to admit the possibility of denunciation or withdrawal . . . or that a right of withdrawal may be implied by the nature of the treaty".
87 Ibid.
88 See also Ray Acheson, "And the Text Goes to Translation", in *Nuclear Ban Daily*, 6 July 2017, p. 1.
89 Arabic, Chinese, English, French, Russian and Spanish.
90 The statements are available at www.reachingcriticalwill.org/images/documents/Disarmament-fora/nuclear-weapon-ban/reports/NBD2.15.pdf; see also webcast archive available at www.un.org/disarmament/tpnw/webcast.html.
91 Ibid.
92 Ibid.
93 See "Explanation of Vote", by Sweden, Switzerland and the Netherlands on 7 July 2017, available at www.un.org/disarmament/tpnw/statements.html.
94 See *Nuclear Ban Daily*, vol. 2, no. 15 as well as also webcast archive available at www.un.org/disarmament/tpnw/webcast.html.

95 Such as for example in the processes leading to the Antipersonnel Landmine Convention, the Cluster Munitions Convention and the Arms Trade Treaty.
96 See also Borrie et al., "Obstacles to Understanding the Emergence and Significance of the Treaty on the Prohibition of Nuclear Weapons", p. 16.
97 See for example Yves Sandoz, "The International Committee of the Red Cross as Guardian of International Humanitarian Law", in *ICRC Homepage*, 31 December 1998, available at www.icrc.org/en/doc/resources/documents/misc/about-the-icrc-311298.htm.
98 Argentina and Colombia as well as Singapore also belonged to the more sceptical participants.
99 Interview conducted by the author with a diplomat from the core group on 27 April 2020.
100 Interview conducted by the author with a diplomat on 24 June 2017. "Non-Aligned Hardliners" refers in this context primarily to Iran and Cuba.
101 See for example, "The Netherlands Should Actively Negotiate an International Nuclear Weapons Ban Treaty", by the Dutch NGO PAX, 19 May 2016, available at https://nonukes.nl/netherlands-actively-negotiate-international-nuclear-weapons-ban-treaty/.
102 Interview conducted by the author with a diplomat from the core group on 1 April 2020.
103 Interview conducted by the author with a diplomat from the core group on 30 April 2020.
104 The US announced its withdrawal from the Joint Comprehensive Plan of Action (JCPOA) on 8 May 2018.
105 Interview conducted by the author with a diplomat from the core group on 27 April 2020.
106 For an interesting description of the internal challenges for ICAN, see also Acheson, *Banning the Bomb, Smashing the Patriarchy*.
107 See also Borrie et al., "Obstacles to Understanding the Emergence and Significance of the Treaty on the Prohibition of Nuclear Weapons", p. 18.
108 Interview conducted by the author with a diplomat from the core group on 1 April 2020.
109 See Acheson, *Banning the Bomb, Smashing the Patriarchy*.
110 For a comprehensive history of the Cluster Munitions Convention, see John Borrie, *Unacceptable Harm: A History of How the Treaty to Ban Cluster Munitions was Won*, UNIDIR, 2009, available at www.unidir.org/publication/unacceptable-harm-history-how-treaty-ban-cluster-munitions-was-won.
111 See also Borrie et al., "Obstacles to Understanding the Emergence and Significance of the Treaty on the Prohibition of Nuclear Weapons", p. 14.
112 Especially after the withdrawal of support to the Humanitarian Initiative by Norway after the change of government in 2013.
113 For example, interview conducted by the author with a diplomat of the core group on 25 February 2020.
114 See Acheson, *Banning the Bomb, Smashing the Patriarchy*.
115 Interview conducted by the author with a UN official on 22 June 2020.

Part III
The contest of arguments

Part III

The contexts of arguments

6 Human security, empowerment and challenging the nuclear status quo

"An expression of collective resistance to those aspects of nuclear hegemony, nuclear hierarchy, and practices of nuclear control that legitimize and perpetuate the existence of nuclear weapons, the practice of nuclear deterrence, and the risks of catastrophic nuclear violence".[1]

Contestation has always characterised the discourse on nuclear weapons and nuclear disarmament. Ever since the Non Proliferation Treaty entered into force in 1970, and even well before, the non-nuclear weapon States – the "nuclear have nots" – have demanded more credible progress on nuclear disarmament from the five nuclear weapon States. These demands usually culminate at the NPT Review Conferences, held every five years. The definition of a successful disarmament outcome at a NPT Review Conference is usually one where these demands are met by the nuclear weapon States, reluctantly, accepting some – albeit strongly qualified – commitments on nuclear disarmament. This happened in 1995, 2000 and 2010.[2]

The process leading to the negotiations and the adoption of the TPNW can be seen as a decisive break from this established pattern. The nature of the discourse in the Humanitarian Initiative and the fact that the five nuclear weapons States boycotted it, changed the dynamic. Instead of voicing demands of what *you* – the nuclear weapon States – should do, we looked to what *we* – the non-nuclear weapon States – could or even need to do ourselves to further the case of nuclear disarmament. This sense of agency of the non-nuclear weapons States is a consequence of their loss of trust in any disarmament process led by the nuclear weapon States. The TPNW, thus, represents a profound shift from the traditional nuclear disarmament discourse within the NPT. It is an expression of the "crisis of legitimacy"[3] detected in the NPT-based nuclear disarmament framework.

Since 2010, a dynamic process of – relative – empowerment of the non-nuclear weapon States has taken place, challenging the control and dominance of the multilateral nuclear weapons sphere, that the nuclear weapons States traditionally enjoyed. The most visible expressions of this process are the Humanitarian Initiative and the TPNW itself. The nuclear weapon States and their allies have reacted to the change in different ways, ranging from initially dismissing the development, to opposition, to outright hostility. This chapter traces the development of the arguments that were employed in the Humanitarian Initiative and the process leading to the TPNW.

The humanitarian initiative 2011–2017: why was it effective?

As discussed in Chapter 1, a key motivation behind the Humanitarian Initiative was the wish to re-frame the nuclear weapons discourse. The parameters of this discourse have traditionally been set by the nuclear weapon States, based on their own overarching priorities of preventing the further spread of nuclear weapons to other States and maintaining strategic stability – meaning a "stable" nuclear deterrence relationship – between themselves. The NPT itself epitomises these priorities. Nuclear disarmament was never *their* priority. The vague nuclear disarmament obligation in Article VI of the NPT was the "price" to be paid to get the non-nuclear weapon States[4] to agree to the NPT and its stringent non-proliferation obligations. Within the parameters set by the nuclear weapon States, these weapons in the hands of *other* actors are a problem that must be prevented. In their *own* hands, however, they are a guarantor of global stability and security, at least for the foreseeable future.

Arguably, in the eyes of the five NPT nuclear weapon States, who are also the five permanent members of the UN Security Council, the multilateral nuclear disarmament, arms control and non-proliferation regime with the NPT at its core is a *de facto* extension of the UN Security Council. The NPT itself is also a representation of these hierarchical parameters. Nuclear weapons are the ultimate currency of power, given their unprecedented destructive power. Their possession – at least as per the NPT – is limited to just five actors, who are also the five permanent members of the UN Security Council with "primary responsibility for the maintenance of international peace and security".[5] Multilateral fora dealing with nuclear weapons are set up in a way that decisions are taken generally by consensus. This provides a guarantee to the nuclear weapon States of always being able to prevent unwanted developments and maintain the status quo. In Ritchie's analysis

> the core structure of global nuclear order is an international security structure that aligns the positions of NPT NWS [note: nuclear weapon States] with those of permanent membership of the UN Security Council in an oligarchic security hierarchy in which some are structurally advantaged and others are structurally disadvantaged.[6]

As a consequence, it can be argued that any nuclear disarmament debate in which non-nuclear weapon States demand progress on disarmament from the nuclear weapon States within the hierarchical structure of the NPT treaty framework, contributes to the perpetuation of this power distribution. As Harrington concludes in 2009 "arguments for nuclear disarmament unintentionally participate in the construction of nuclear fetishism by reproducing the association between nuclear weapons and power".[7]

The Humanitarian Initiative and the resulting TPNW, challenged the parameters of the nuclear weapons discourse in an "an expression of collective resistance to those aspects of nuclear hegemony, nuclear hierarchy, and practices of nuclear control that legitimize and perpetuate the existence of nuclear weapons, the practice of nuclear deterrence, and the risks of catastrophic nuclear violence".[8] Re-framing the nuclear weapons discourse around the humanitarian consequences and risks of nuclear weapons was effective in generating momentum for the TPNW because this focus countered the nuclear weapon States' narrative on the security, responsibility and legitimacy of the nuclear status quo. This re-framing is demonstrated by the substantive conclusions developed in the context of the Humanitarian Initiative. They form the basis of the Humanitarian Pledge, the humanitarian-focussed statements and working papers at the 2015 NPT Review Conference, the humanitarian resolutions adopted by the First Committee of the UN General Assembly in 2015,[9] the work of the 2016 open-ended working group. They underpin the TPNW negotiations and are reiterated in the TPNW's preamble.

Human security, responsibility and legitimacy

As regards the humanitarian consequences of nuclear weapons, the following key arguments were put forward:

- That the immediate mid- and long-term consequences of a nuclear weapon explosion are significantly graver than previously known.
- That the complexity of and interrelationship between these consequences on health, environment, infrastructure, food security, climate, development, social cohesion and the global economy that are systemic and potentially irreversible.
- That they will not be constrained by national borders but have regional or even global effects, potentially threatening the survival of humanity.
- That no national or international response capacity exists that could adequately respond to the human suffering and humanitarian harm that would result from a nuclear weapon explosion in a populated area, and that it would be unlikely that such a capacity could be established, even if attempted.[10]

These perspectives on the transboundary global consequences, across a wide range of sectors, and the lack of response capability to the human suffering, placed the discussion on nuclear weapons and their effects firmly in a *human security* context.[11] The Humanitarian Initiative thus promoted a globalist and comprehensive view of security. This is in direct juxtaposition to the "state-centred" security arguments of nuclear weapon States, who stress that nuclear weapons are essential for their and their allies' security, owing to the deterrence value of nuclear weapons and the consequent ability to maintain a strategic stability between themselves. Even if the threat vis-à-vis a potential aversary may be justifiable, how can the threat of inflicting such global consequences be considered legitimate and justified by national security considerations? In short, the Humanitarian Initiative asserted that States arguing for nuclear weapons and relying on nuclear deterrence defend a narrower and self-serving, but ultimately short-sighted perspective of security, which comes at the expense of the security of all.

The nuclear weapon States and nuclear umbrella States have yet to rebut the above-mentioned conclusions effectively and provide satisfactory answers on how to address the humanitarian consequences. Their key arguments are that there is no relevant new information and that the humanitarian consequences have been known for decades, as well as that the threat of inflicting these unacceptable consequences is exactly what makes nuclear deterrence effective.[12]

The second key aspect of the human security argument raised by the Humanitarian Initiative is the element of risk. The arguments are that

- The risk of nuclear explosions is significantly greater than previously assumed and increasing with proliferation, the lowering of the technical threshold for nuclear weapon capability, the ongoing modernisation of nuclear weapon arsenals in nuclear weapon possessing states, and the role that is attributed to nuclear weapons in the nuclear doctrines of possessor states.
- The risks of accidental, mistaken, unauthorized or unintentional use of nuclear weapons are evident due to the vulnerability of nuclear command and control networks to human error and cyber-attacks, the maintaining of nuclear arsenals on high levels of alert, forward deployment and their modernization.
- That there are many circumstances in which nuclear weapons could be used in view of international conflicts and tensions, and against the background of the current security doctrines of States possessing nuclear weapons. As nuclear deterrence entails preparing for nuclear war, the risk of nuclear weapon use is real.[13]

These conclusions on nuclear weapons risks, emphasise the point that it is the very policies and the collective behaviour of States possessing nuclear weapons that create and increase the risk of nuclear weapons use, either intentionally or out of some form of accident or miscalculation. The "human security" of the international community and indeed the entire planet is, thus, put at grave risk by these practices. Nuclear weapons States may think that they can control these risks but have yet to provide proof of this to the international community. While the probability of nuclear weapons explosions may be low, the risks remain and given the potentially global consequences, they may be too high and unacceptable. Viewed from the Humanitarian Initiative perspective, the aggregated risks from nuclear weapons and of the practice of nuclear deterrence by all nuclear weapons possessing States are perceived as a direct threat to the security of all States and all peoples.[14] The combination of arguments on the humanitarian consequences and the risks associated with nuclear weapons, both *significantly greater than previously known*, challenges the assertions of nuclear weapons as a guarantor of security. Whose security and what kind of security is being talked about in the context of nuclear weapons and does the security calculation hold up to scrutiny?

From the human security perspective, ensues the question of *responsibility*. Can the threat of not only mutually assured destruction between adversaries but also the risk of inflicting global catastrophic consequences, possibly threatening the survival of humankind be considered as a responsible policy? Nuclear weapon States like to assert that they are *responsible*[15] but in light of the potential global consequences and risks of these weapons, for what and to whom exactly are they responsible? These States claim that they are rational and responsible enough to handle nuclear weapons and assert that nuclear deterrence works because it leads to rational and – hopefully responsible – behaviour of all actors involved in this equation. This, however, is a circular argument From the Humanitarian Initiative and human security perspective, a security approach that relies on nuclear weapons and the possible infliction of devastating global consequences looks like an irresponsibly high risk-taking gamble, based on an illusion of safety[16] and security.

The *responsibility* arguments put forward by the Humanitarian Initiative, contained another dimension: if nuclear armed States are apparently trapped in a vicious circle, justifying their own need to have nuclear weapons with the possession of nuclear weapons by other nuclear armed States, what is then the *responsibility* of non-nuclear weapon States? The consequences and risks of nuclear weapons are grave, and the nuclear armed States have no satisfactory answers to address these human security concerns. What actions can therefore be taken by non-nuclear weapon States to help the international community potentially break free from this high-risk dynamic? The human security arguments about humanitarian consequences and risks of nuclear weapons, thus, leads to an appeal to the sense of *responsibility* of all States and to a call for action to strengthen the normative framework of the nuclear disarmament and non-proliferation regime. This is in stark contrast to the lack of credible leadership on this issue by the States who possess nuclear weapons and who, as permanent members of the UN Security Council, should live up to their special responsibility for the collective security of all States. By extension, this line of argument also applies to the nuclear umbrella States, whose ambiguous stance of professed support for nuclear disarmament while "enjoying" the benefits of extended nuclear deterrence has come increasingly into focus during the Humanitarian Initiative.

Finally, the re-framing of the perspectives of *security* and *responsibility* following from the arguments on the humanitarian consequences and risks of nuclear weapons gives new impetus to the long-standing concerns about the *legitimacy* of the NPT-based nuclear disarmament and non-proliferation regime.

The very nature of the NPT with its division into "nuclear haves" and "nuclear have nots" has been criticised as discriminatory ever since the treaty came into being; a point reiterated in many NPT statements, in particular by the non-aligned movement.[17] As Egeland concludes,

> What the disarmament commitment [note: NPT Art.VI] did do, was to publicly and in formal terms counteract the NPT's apparent breach with the principle of the equality of states. By casting the NPT as a step towards disarmament, article VI allowed the non-nuclear weapon States to describe

themselves not simply as 'inferior' or 'unequal', but as 'equal in waiting'; the hierarchy enshrined by the treaty would be temporary.[18]

For the non-nuclear weapon States, the NPT disarmament provisions of Article VI – part of the "grand bargain" of the NPT[19] – were always also intended to counter the discriminatory nature of the treaty and underscore the notion that "the nuclear weapon States would gradually deconstruct the nuclear hierarchy".[20]

As discussed in Chapter 1, the credibility of the NPT "grand bargain" was increasingly undermined and reached a new low point in the unconvincing implementation record of the 2010 NPT Action Plan in the years from 2010 to 2015. This fuelled the motivation of non-nuclear weapon States to look for alternative approaches. The Humanitarian Initiative added and further accentuated arguments to challenge the *legitimacy* of the nuclear status quo and the existing multilateral frameworks tasked to deal with the nuclear weapons issue.

How can the *legitimate* security concerns of non-nuclear weapon States be addressed effectively in a multilateral NPT treaty framework that is inherently discriminatory against them? Who addresses their concerns about the humanitarian consequences and risks of nuclear weapons? Moreover, who would be responsible for remedial actions or compensation after a nuclear explosion, whether by accident or design, given the breadth of consequences on health, the economy, migratory movements etc.? This *human security* perspective is the basis from which non-nuclear weapon States wish to discuss these weapons. The Humanitarian Initiatve provided non-nuclear weapon States with a set of strong and new arguments to challenge the legitimacy of the nuclear status quo. It opened up the traditional, narrower, state-centred, security approach with which nuclear armed States dominate the nuclear weapons debate in existing multilateral fora. The focus on the humanitarian consequences and risks of nuclear weapons questions the "normalization"[21] of nuclear weapons and nuclear deterrence in the security policy discourse of nuclear weapon States and demands a re-assessment of what constitutes *responsible* behaviour. This focus raises pertinent questions on the *legitimacy* of the existing nuclear disarmament and non-proliferation regime.

Moreover, the humanitarian foundation of this argument and the expressed concern for the integrity of the nuclear disarmament and non-proliferation regime, links the nuclear weapons issue to international justice and a fair, rules-based, international system. As Matthew Bolton writes:

> The genius of this strategy – often called the Humanitarian Initiative – has been to use the language of international humanitarian law and human rights, rather than the dominant techno-strategic discourse, to challenge the great powers. The humanitarian discourse – which suggests that 'civilized nations' abstain from using 'barbaric' ways of killing – has condemned chemical weapons, cluster munitions, and landmines as "Other weapons" that are beneath the dignity of the chivalrous military officer.[22]

The nuclear weapon States and their allies have failed to give coherent answers and counterarguments regarding the humanitarian consequences and risks of nuclear weapons and this has certainly been a contributary factor in strengthening the resolve for a ban treaty. They have not properly addressed the specific humanitarian consequences and risk arguments except to say that nuclear deterrence works *because* of the threat of unacceptable consequences.[23] In their rendering, there are are no risks or if there are, they can be managed and, anyway, the information about the humanitarian consequences is not new and has been known for a long time.[24] The key questions on how to address the unacceptable humanitarian consequences and risks of nuclear weapons are either dismissed or remain unanswered. Supporters of the Humanitarian Initiative came to recognise that nuclear weapon States are unable to provide satisfactory answers to these questions and that their argumentation must, perforce, be entirely subordinated to maintaining the nuclear status quo and the doctrine of nuclear deterrence.

In the period 2011–2017, non-nuclear weapons States increasingly supported the Humanitarian Initiative, aided by civil society pressure and a growing number of studies and substantive contributions[25] that developed and strengthened the humanitarian arguments and focused a humanitarian lens[26] on the nuclear weapons issue. The humanitarian arguments reinforced the reasoning that it is the *responsibility* and in the *legitimate security* interest of non-nuclear weapon States to take matters into their own hands, given the unwillingness or inability of nuclear weapon States to take more credible steps towards nuclear disarmament. The Humanitarian Initiative was, thus, a direct challenge to the hierarchrical structure of the nuclear status quo and the "power currency value" of nuclear weapons.

Rather than continue to merely demand disarmament progress from nuclear weapon States, a legal prohibition of nuclear weapons emerged as the one concrete action that non-nuclear weapon States were able to effect themselves. ICAN's forceful and effective campaign was essential in generating the necessary momentum for the TPNW. It motivated States to support the Humanitarian Pledge and helped move them towards the conclusion that they could actually do something about this issue. The Humanitarian Initiative provided a forum in which a multitude of voices and actors from States and civil society were empowered, could underscore their own perspectives on nuclear weapons, and challenge the dominant, established discourse and conclusions of the five nuclear weapon States and their allies.

The "Wildfire"-factor

Shortly after the Oslo Conference on the humanitarian impact of nuclear weapons in March 2013, a new and unusual actor arrived on the disarmament scene in Geneva who would go on to have an important impact on building the case in favour of a ban treaty, albeit with methods that were highly unconventional for multilateral disarmament diplomacy. On 19 May 2013, disarmament diplomats, NGOs and think tanks received an email with the following text:

> Nuclear weapon states will not engage in negotiations on a comprehensive nuclear disarmament treaty. Not now, not ever. The so-called step-by-step approach has got nowhere. This will not change. The NPT only legitimizes

nuclear weapons and does nothing for disarmament. The civil society effort to abolish nuclear weapons is flailing. It's time to change the game.[27]

"Wildfire" was launched.

Wildfire was initially an anonymous website, designed in black and intended to look like a conspiratorial and anarchistic medium. Its opening page called for "no more commissions, no more pontificating windbags, . . . no more whining wishing and waiting, change the game". This looked like something new. The messages on the Wildfire website were confrontational, mocking, hilarious, humorous and certainly very undiplomatic. The website was quickly picked up on social media and widely shared in the so-called "disarmament community". In particular, the question of who the anonymous author of Wildfire was, was the subject of intensive speculation.[28]

While the creative flair and mystery around the anonymous website was a clever way of getting attention, the relevance of Wildfire lies in the way in which it deconstructed the nuclear weapons rhetoric as practiced by States and civil society in the traditional multilateral fora. Wildfire described its approach as "using mockery and satire in digital media to jolt governments into recognising the potential of new approaches to nuclear disarmament".[29] As such, Wildfire's messaging and running commentary on the nuclear weapons discourse was often borderline or beyond for multilateral diplomatic processes, but certainly effective and innovative.

For example, Wildfire coined the derogatory label "nuclear weasel states" for the nuclear umbrella States, which, according to Wildfire, "typically claim to support nuclear disarmament, but will also be observed undermining disarmament initiatives that look too promising. They will generally defend the interests of their nuclear-armed patron".[30] A typical Wildfire method was also to use quotes of statements made by the nuclear weapons States or nuclear umbrella States to

> highlight the absurdity, double standards and pointlessness of the existing approaches and processes, . . . and the potential of a ban treaty. . . . Often this required no more than picking out and highlighting the nuclear weapon States and "weasels" own words.[31] When stripped of the covering verbiage, the absurdity was stark and clear.[32]

For the diplomats from non-nuclear weapon States there was a certain degree of pleasure and satisfaction gained from reading these humorous and biting postings, as they accentuated some of the contradictions and frustrations in the nuclear weapons discourse in a manner that diplomats cannot employ.

The real target of the Wildfire campaign, however, were the non-nuclear-weapon states, with the aim of getting them to realise

> that the current nuclear disarmament approach would never work; indeed were designed to never work; that the nuclear umbrella States (the "weasels") were not their allies but were a key obstacle to nuclear disarmament in their

own right and that a ban treaty that included only non-nuclear weapon States could be effective and should be pursued.[33]

A case in point was Wildfire's statement at the 2014 Vienna Conference on the Humanitarian Impact of Nuclear Weapons, with its highly undiplomatic framing of what non-nuclear weapons should do:

> Nobody can force an alcoholic to stop drinking. And nobody can force the nuclear-armed states to disarm. Only they can choose to give up their weapons. But you, the sober members of the family of nations, can stop enabling them. You can remove the ambiguity that supports their habit. You can make clear where you stand, and what you will not accept. You can negotiate, and adopt, and bring into force a treaty banning nuclear weapons. . . . It's your future and your choice. You can sit and wait and whine, or you can take control, and negotiate a treaty banning nuclear weapons.[34]

While it is difficult to quantify the impact of the Wildfire campaign on States' ultimate decision to move forward with negotiations for the TPNW, I think it was considerable. Firstly, it provided a humorous and satirical counterpoint to the sometimes very contentious nuclear disarmament discourse. The palpable irritation of the nuclear weapon States and the nuclear umbrella States at being at the receiving end of mocking and scorn from Wildfire was amusing to observe. As such, the Wildfire postings and actions received a lot of attention within the disarmament community.

More importantly, however, Wildfire's postings, comments and actions may have been provocative, preposterous[35] and undiplomatic, but they were very articulate and intellectually coherent. Wildfire brought a different perspective to the nuclear weapons debate, introducing doubt into the prevailing narrative and arguing in a clear manner for an alternative way of addressing this issue. Wildfire's "over the top" presentation of pertinent observations "gave diplomats from States supporting the Humanitarian Initiative additional 'ammunition' in their interactions with each other and with their colleagues in capital",[36] which was a significant contribution to building momentum towards a ban treaty. Moreover, not being a part of ICAN, Wildfire's articulate way of making the case for a ban treaty and its "nuanced and sophisticated understanding of diplomatic and nuclear weapons related issues was a morale booster for the new forces within ICAN"[37] who had shifted their strategy from supporting a comprehensive nuclear weapons convention to a simple prohibition/ban treaty.[38]

Culmination of a decades-long struggle

The Humanitarian Initiative and the process leading to the conclusion of the TPNW negotiations in 2017 can be characterised as a period in which a strong set of arguments was created, re-framing the nuclear weapons discourse in a humanitarian direction. This, and the resulting challenge to the nuclear status quo, was achieved through cooperative and complementary activities by State and civil society actors, using their respective available fora and strengths effectively. The combination of arguments around human security, responsibility and legitimacy generated significant momentum for change and a stronger sense of agency for non-nuclear weapon States.

Certainly, this momentum was limited to non-nuclear weapon States, disenfranchised by the NPT process, and who looked for new ways to strengthen the nuclear disarmament and non-proliferation regime. The Humanitarian Initiative created a sense of empowerment for these States and provided a cogent new representation of their longstanding nuclear disarmament priorities. Moreover, the fact that the Humanitarian Initiative could be pursued without the *sanctus* of the nuclear weapon States, who usually exert full control over proceedings on this issue, was attractive. These factors, together with the excitement and expectation generated by the ICAN campaign, created a funnel effect, as more and more non-nuclear weapon States embraced the idea of supporting a ban treaty.

Moreover, the boycott of and lack of engagement in the Humanitarian Initiative by the nuclear weapon States, and the not very convincing counterarguments (discussed in the following section) added rather than sap momentum towards ban negotiations. They not only underscored the pertinence of the arguments and conclusions that the Humanitarian Initiative had developed. Their vehement and sometimes over-the-top opposition to the ban idea also *de facto* served as a potent antidote for the still sceptical non-nuclear weapon States that a ban that did not include the nuclear weapon States would make no difference. As a consequence,

> the more the nuclear-weapon states dismissed humanitarian perspectives and their allies sought to apply the brakes on the slippery slope toward prohibition negotiations, the more it appeared to strengthen the ICAN narrative, underlining the dissonance between those states' statements in support of a nuclear-weapon-free world with their lack of progress toward it.[39]

The adoption of the TPNW on 7 July 2017 represents a culmination of a decades-long struggle for nuclear disarmament. This was expressed in the many statements on that day i.e. "groundbreaking, historic, a triumph for multilateralism and a significant step forward".[40] At the Signing Ceremony for the TPNW at the United Nations in New York on 20 September 2017,[41] after speeches by the UN Secretary General, the President of the UN General Assembly, the President of Costa Rica, the President of the International Committee of the Red Cross and the Executive Director of ICAN, 50 States signed and three, Thailand, the Holy Sea and Guyana ratified the TPNW.[42] UN Secretary General Antonio Guterres welcomed the treaty as an "historic milestone towards the elimination of nuclear weapons . . . [and urged that] we cannot allow these doomsday weapons to endanger our world and our children's future". ICRC President Peter Maurer called the TPNW "a light for all humanity".[43]

For ICAN, the unrivalled recognition was the 2017 Nobel Peace Prize. The Norwegian Nobel Committee decided to award ICAN the Peace Prize for

> its work to draw attention to the catastrophic humanitarian consequences of any use of nuclear weapons and for its ground-breaking efforts to achieve a treaty-based prohibition of such weapons. . . . The coalition has been a driving force in prevailing upon the world's nations to pledge to cooperate with all relevant stakeholders in efforts to stigmatise, prohibit and eliminate nuclear weapons. To date, 127 states have made such a commitment, known as the Humanitarian Pledge.[44]

The award ceremony on 10 December 2017 was a worthy celebration and recognition of a dramatic change achieved in a relatively short period of time. The ICAN Nobel lectures were jointly delivered by Beatrice Fihn, ICAN Executive Director, and Setsuko Thurlow, Hibakusha survivor of the atomic bombing of Hiroshima. Fihn stated that

> Nuclear weapons, like chemical weapons, biological weapons, cluster munitions and land mines before them, are now illegal. Their existence is immoral. Their abolishment is in our hands. The end is inevitable. But will that end be the end of nuclear weapons or the end of us? We must choose one. We are a movement for rationality. For democracy. For freedom from fear.

Thurlow urged "To every president and prime minister of every nation of the world, I beseech you: join this treaty; forever eradicate the threat of nuclear annihilation".[45]

The Nobel Peace Prize Award in 2017 was undoubtedly also the high point in terms of public recognition of the TPNW and the humanitarian arguments that underpin it. While the negotiations and the adoption of the TPNW received relatively limited coverage in the media, the Nobel Peace Prize was globally reported, including by practically all so-called mainstream media.[46]

Amidst the jubilation about the Nobel Peace Prize came the news that France, UK and US would not send their ambassadors to attend the ceremony in Oslo "to express their reservations towards ICAN and the global treaty to ban weapons of mass destruction".[47] This quite unprecedented diplomatic move on the part of the three Western nuclear weapon States, vis-à-vis the Norwegian Nobel Committee hosts, did not spoil the celebrations but was a reminder that the Humanitarian Initiative, the TPNW and, more generally, nuclear disarmament, remained fiercely contested. With the TPNW adopted and ICAN awarded the Nobel Peace Prize, the opposition against this challenge to the nuclear status quo would only become more determined.

Notes

1 See Nick Ritchie, "A Hegemonic Nuclear Order: Understanding the Ban Treaty and the Power Politics of Nuclear Weapons", in *Contemporary Security Policy*, 2019, available at https://doi.org/10.1080/13523260.2019.1571852.

2 See Chapter 1.
3 Kjølv Egeland, "The Road to Prohibition: Nuclear Hierarchy and Disarmament, 1968–2017", doctoral thesis, Department of Politics and International Relations, University of Oxford, December 2017, p. 210.
4 Together with the right to peaceful uses of nuclear energy enshrined in NPT Article IV.
5 See Article 24 of the Charter of the United Nations, available at www.un.org/en/sections/un-charter/un-charter-full-text/.
6 Ritchie, "A Hegemonic Nuclear Order".
7 See Anne Harrington de Santana, "Nuclear Weapons as the Currency of Power: Deconstructing the Fetishism of Force", in *Nonproliferation Review*, Vol. 16, No. 3, November 2009, available at https://doi.org/10.1080/10736700903255029
8 See Ritchie, "A Hegemonic Nuclear Order".
9 See Chapter 4.
10 See Chair's Summary of the Vienna Conference on the Humanitarian Impact of Nuclear Weapons and "Humanitarian Pledge", available at www.bmeia.gv.at/index.php?id=55297&L=1 or www.hinw14vienna.at.
11 For human security, see Chapter 1.
12 See also Chapter 7 and Chapter 8.
13 See Chair's Summary of the Vienna Conference on the Humanitarian Impact of Nuclear Weapons and "Humanitarian Pledge".
14 See also Chapter 8.
15 See for example UK Statement on 8 July 2017, available at www.gov.uk/government/news/uk-statement-on-treaty-prohibiting-nuclear-weapons.
16 See also John Borrie and Tim Caughley, *An Illusion of Safety: Challenges of Nuclear Weapon Detonations for United Nations Humanitarian Coordination and Response*, United Nations Disarmament Research Institute (UNIDIR), 2014.
17 For past NAM statements and position papers on nuclear disarmament see James Martin Centre for Non-Proliferation Studies, "Non-Aligned Movement Disarmament Database", available at http://cns.miis.edu/nam/.
18 See Egeland, "The Road to Prohibition", p. 59.
19 See Chapter I; NPT Nuclear weapon States do not proliferate, non-nuclear weapon States do not seek these weapons and, in exchange, are given access to nuclear energy for civilian applications.
20 See Egeland, "The Road to Prohibition", p. 87.
21 Ritchie, "A Hegemonic Nuclear Order", p. 12; see also J. Ikenberry and C. Kupchan, "Socialization and Hegemonic Power", in *International Organization*, vol. 44, 1990, pp. 283–315.
22 See Matthew Bolton, *Caliban and the Nuclear Ban: Decolonising Politics of the Bomb*, First Committee Monitor, no. 4, 24 October 2016, available at http://reachingcriticalwill.org/images/documents/Disarmament-fora/1com/FCM16/FCM-2016-No4.pdf,
23 Julie Bishop, "We Must Engage, not Enrage Nuclear Countries", op-ed in *Sydney Morning Herald*, 14 February 2014, available at www.smh.com.au/opinion/we-must-engage-not-enrage-nuclear-countries-20140213-32n1s.html.
24 See Chapter 3.
25 Among the many publications, the author would highlight the following studies as having been maybe the most influential in strengthening the momentum behind the Humanitarian Initiative and for the TPNW: International Campaign for the Abolition of Nuclear Weapons (ICAN), "Catastrophic Humanitarian Harm", 2012, updated 2015, available at www.icanw.org/catastrophic_humanitarian_harm; John Borrie and Tim Caughley (eds.), *Viewing Nuclear Weapons Through a Humanitarian Lens*, United Nations Institute for Disarmament Research Geneva (UNIDIR), 2013, available at www.unidir.org/files/publications/pdfs/viewing-nuclear-weapons-through-a-humanitarian-lens-en-601.pdf; John Borrie and Tim Caughley, *An Illusion of Safety:*

Challenges of Nuclear Weapon Detonations for United Nations Humanitarian Coordination and Response, UNIDIR, 2014, available at https://unidir.org/publication/illusion-safety-challenges-nuclear-weapon-detonations-united-nations-humanitarian; Patricia Lewis, Heather Williams, Benoît Pelopidas and Sasan Aghlani, *Too Close for Comfort: Cases of Near Nuclear Use and Options for Policy*, Royal Institute of International Affairs, April 2014, available at www.chathamhouse.org/publications/papers/view/199200; ICRC, "The Human Cost of Nuclear Weapons", in *International Review of the Red Cross*, vol. 97, no. 899, Autumn 2015, available at https://international-review.icrc.org/reviews/irrc-no-899-human-cost-nuclear-weapons; Maya Brehm, Richard Moyes and Thomas Nash, "Banning Nuclear Weapons", Article 36, February 2013, available at www.academia.edu/7343889/Banning_nuclear_weapons?email_work_card=view-paper; Ira Helfand, "Nuclear Famine: Two Billion People at Risk? Global Impacts of Limited Nuclear War on Agriculture, Food Supplies, and Human Nutrition", in *IPPNW and Physicians for Social Responsibility*, 2nd ed., briefing paper, November 2013, available at www.ippnw.org/nuclear-famine.html.
26 See Borrie and Caughley, *Viewing Nuclear Weapons Through a Humanitarian Lens*.
27 Email launching Wildfire of 19 May 2013, available at www.wildfire-v.org.
28 Wildfire remained anonymous until 6 March 2014, when Richard Lennane, a former Australian diplomat and longstanding Geneva-based disarmament expert, revealed himself as Wildfire's "Chief Inflammatory Officer".
29 See video, "The Wildfire Approach to Nuclear Disarmament", available at https://youtu.be/8_0jz__Buio.
30 See http://wildfire-v.org/Weasel_flyer.pdf.
31 As an example, Wildfire juxtaposed the statement by the UK in the Conference on Disarmament on 5 March 2013, "We will take every opportunity to pursue our resolute commitment to a world without nuclear weapons", with the statement by the UK Prime Minister on 3 April 2013, "We need our nuclear deterrence as much today as we did when a previous British Government embarked on it over six decades ago"; see available at www.wildfire-v.org/news2013.html#31July13; Another example was when Wildfire produced a poster with a photo of a victim of the Hiroshima bombing with the text of a statement by the Australian Foreign Minister Julie Bishop saying that "the horrendous humanitarian consequences of nuclear weapons are precisely why deterrence has worked"; see available at http://wildfire-v.org/HINW14vienna/WL_rollups_s.pdfcircular.
32 Email to the author from Richard Lennane on 29 April 2020.
33 Ibid.
34 Statement by Wildfire at the Vienna Conference on the Humanitarian Impact of Nuclear Weapons on 9 December 2014, available at https://youtu.be/qrTk567QRxM as well as available at www.bmeia.gv.at/fileadmin/user_upload/Zentrale/Aussenpolitik/Abruestung/HINW14/Statements/HINW14_Statement_Wildfire.pdf.
35 See "A Treaty Banning Nuclear Weapons? Preposterous!", available at www.wildfire-v.org/NPT2015/Preposterous1.pdf.
36 Interview by the author on 1 May 2020 with a disarmament expert and longstanding observer of Wildfire's activities.
37 Ibid.
38 See Chapter 2.
39 See John Borrie, Michael Spies and Wilfred Wan, "Obstacles to Understanding the Emergence and Significance of the Treaty on the Prohibition of Nuclear Weapons", in *Global Change, Peace & Security*, 2018, p. 12, available at https://doi.org/10.1080/14781158.2018.1467394.
40 See also Chapter 5.
41 See webcast of the Signing Ceremony for the Treaty on the Prohibition of Nuclear Weapons on 20 September 2017; available at http://webtv.un.org/search/

154 The contest of arguments

      signing-ceremony-for-the-treaty-on-the-prohibition-of-nuclear-weapons/5581928964001/?term=Signing+Ceremony+for+the+Treaty+on+the+Prohibition+of+Nuclear+Weapons.&sort=date#.WcLVMqwUSOs.facebook.
42 Ibid.
43 Ibid., see also the report by the NGO Article 36, "Treaty on the Prohibition of Nuclear Weapons Opens for Signature at the UN in New York", 20 September 2017, available at www.article36.org/weapons/nuclear-weapons/tpnw-opens-sig/.
44 See press "The Nobel Peace Prize for 2017", in *Nobel Media AB 2020*, available at www.nobelprize.org/prizes/peace/2017/press-release/.
45 See Nobel lecture 2017 by Beatrice Fihn and Setsuko Thurlow, "ICAN receives Nobel Peace Prize 2017", available at www.icanw.org/nobel_prize.
46 For a representative collection of the media reporting in relation to the 2017 Nobel Peace Prize, see *New York Times*, available at www.nytimes.com/2017/10/06/world/nobel-peace-prize.html; BBC, available at www.bbc.co.uk/news/world-europe-41524583; *USA Today*, available at https://eu.usatoday.com/story/news/world/2017/10/06/ican-just-won-nobel-peace-prize-what-ican/738744001/; CNBC, available at www.cnbc.com/2017/10/06/international-campaign-to-abolish-nuclear-weapons-wins-the-nobel-peace-prize.html; CNN, available at https://edition.cnn.com/2017/10/06/world/nobel-peace-prize/index.html; *TIME* magazine, available at https://time.com/4971956/nobel-peace-prize-2017-ican-why/; *El Pais*, available at https://elpais.com/internacional/2017/10/06/actualidad/1507271462_313212.html; *Le Monde*, available at www.lemonde.fr/prix-nobel/article/2017/10/06/le-prix-nobel-de-la-paix-decerne-a-la-coalition-internationale-pour-l-abolition-des-armes-nucleaires_5197010_1772031.html; *Frankfurter Allgemeine Zeitung*, available at www.faz.net/aktuell/wissen/nobelpreise/friedensnobelpreis-geht-an-anti-atomwaffen-kampagne-ican-15233815.html; *Al Jazeera*, available at www.aljazeera.com/news/2017/10/anti-nuclear-weapons-campaign-ican-wins-nobel-peace-prize-171006065955247.html; *Japan Times*, available at www.japantimes.co.jp/news/2017/10/07/national/nobel-peace-prize-also-hibakusha-ican-chief/; *China Daily*, available at www.chinadaily.com.cn/world/2017-10/06/content_32917561.htm; *The Hindu*, available at www.thehindu.com/news/international/2017-nobel-peace-prize-awarded-to-international-campaign-to-abolish-nuclear-weapons/article19807322.ece; *Russia Today*, available at www.rt.com/news/405859-nobel-peace-prize-winner/; *The Daily Nation*, available at www.nation.co.ke/news/world/-ICAN-wins-Nobel-Peace-Prize/1068-4127984-346fyjz/index.html; *24 Brazil*, available at www.24brasil.com/mundo/campanha-contra-armas-nucleares-ganha-nobel-da-paz-2017/215703-noticias.
47 See for example Tony Robinson, "Nuclear Weapons States to Boycott Nobel Peace Prize Ceremony", in *Pressenza*, 1 December 2017, available at www.pressenza.com/2017/12/nuclear-weapons-states-boycott-nobel-peace-prize-ceremony/.

7 Countering the humanitarian initiative and the ban

"The objections appear more of a sideshow, a diversion from the main issue, rather than actual criticisms of the TPNW. Instead of clarifying the debate, such objections end up masking the most important political fault line of the debate, namely a profound disagreement over the acceptability of nuclear weapons and the legitimacy of nuclear deterrence".[1]

This chapter investigates the counterarguments against the Humanitarian Initiative and the TPNW. How has the political "messaging" evolved, both inside the various multilateral fora and also in the outside world? Which arguments are employed, by whom and when, and which "narrative" is successful?

The early phase

It took the nuclear weapon States some time to recognise that the increased focus on the humanitarian consequences was a serious development with the potential to pose a challenge to their nuclear hegemony. When a paragraph expressing concern about the humanitarian consequences on the use of nuclear weapons was included in the 2010 NPT Review Conference Final Report,[2] the nuclear weapon States did not like it but accepted it. It is likely that they did not consider this a very significant paragraph let alone an actionable one. At that time, references to the humanitarian consequences of nuclear weapons by States were still infrequent.[3] At the 2012 NPT Preparatory Committee for the 2015 Review Conference, this began to change. This meeting saw the first of the cross-regional humanitarian statements supported by 16 States,[4] the announcement by Norway of the Conference on the humanitarian impact of nuclear weapons[5] to be held in 2013, the presentation of the International Physicians for the Prevention of Nuclear War (IPPNW) study on the global impact of a limited nuclear war,[6] and significantly more States and NGOs referring to this issue. I remember a somewhat annoyed reaction by the US and UK delegations to the 16 States cross-regional statement in a meeting of the so-called Western European and Others Group (WEOG) in the margins of the NPT meeting.

The 2012 First Committee of the UN General Assembly brought a further increase in focus on the humanitarian consequences of nuclear weapons, when 34 States supported a second cross-regional statement on this issue.[7] When Swiss ambassador Laggner read this statement to a completely silent conference room, there was a tangible feeling among diplomats and civil society representatives that something of significance was happening. Civil society enthusiastically reported at the time that "(t)his powerful joint statement may have concluded the thematic debate on nuclear weapon issue but it will set the stage for renewed action on achieving disarmament".[8]

The increasingly vibrant atmosphere surrounding this issue and the upcoming 2013 Oslo Conference may have been the moment when the nuclear weapon States began to realise the potential – or from their perspective the *danger* – of this development. Alarmingly, things started to resemble the blueprint of previous successful humanitarian disarmament campaigns, such as those against antipersonnel landmines and cluster munitions.[9] Most of the same States that had been at the forefront of these earlier campaigns were behind the joint cross-regional statements. The same States were now actively promoting humanitarian arguments concerning nuclear weapons and NGOs were increasing their focus and targeting activities around this approach. The nuclear weapon States' concern was heightened by the adoption by the First Committee of the UN General Assembly in 2012 of the resolution "Taking forward multilateral nuclear disarmament negotiations", which established a first open-ended working group to meet in Geneva. The nuclear weapon States had fiercely opposed this resolution but were unable to stop it.[10] By late 2012, both initiatives – the establishment of the open ended working group and the increasing humanitarian focus – were now understood by the nuclear weapon States as a concerted challenge to the nuclear status quo.

In early 2013, when the Conference on Disarmament reconvened in Geneva for another unproductive session, the irritation on the part of the nuclear weapon States about the new developments was clear. This was expressed in several critical statements underlining the primacy of the Conference on Disarmament, the consensus rule and the need to stick to the agreed 2010 Action Plan.[11] By the time 127 States gathered in Oslo on 3–4 March 2013 for a conference on the humanitarian impact of nuclear weapons, the push-back by the nuclear weapons States was coordinated.[12]

In their "Joint explanatory note" to the Norwegian hosts, the five nuclear weapon States explained their non-attendance of the Conference by stating that they "understand the serious consequences of nuclear weapons use and will continue to give highest priority to avoiding such contingencies". The concrete reasons for the conference boycott were identified as

> (w)e remain concerned that the Oslo Conference will divert discussion away from practical steps to create conditions for further nuclear weapons reductions. The practical, step-by-step approach that we are taking has proved to be the most effective means to increase stability and reduce nuclear dangers.[13]

In a notable variation of language used in the cross-regional humanitarian statement of 2012, which stated that "it is of utmost importance that these weapons never be used again, under any circumstances",[14] the "Joint explanatory note" stated: "It is in the interest of all nations to assure that nuclear war should never be fought, for there can be no winners in such a conflict".[15]

At the plenary meeting of the Conference on Disarmament of 5 March 2013, one day after the Oslo Conference, the nuclear weapon States felt compelled to provide additional explanations. Russia expressed concern about the

> trend of moving away from the agreed Action Plan, attempts to reinterpret it or take a selective approach to its implementation, including the imposition of additional obligations, and delegitimization not only of the use but also of the very possession of nuclear weapons.[16]

The UK said it respected

> those who campaign against nuclear weapons, but we disagree on the issue of the legitimacy of nuclear weapons and that a ban on such weapons is the right way to move us closer to the complete elimination of nuclear weapons. We are concerned that the Oslo event will divert attention and discussion away from what has proven to be the most effective means of reducing nuclear dangers – a practical, step-by-step approach that includes all those who hold nuclear weapons.[17]

The French ambassador criticised non-consensual resolutions by the UN General Assembly and expressed concern "that the conference will divert attention from the discussions on practical measures that will allow new progress in nuclear disarmament to be made".[18] The US delegation recognized

> that many in this chamber, whether they be Member States, observers or our civil-society partners, will have divergent opinions. Let me underline our commitment to the vision of a world without nuclear weapons, even if we have a different road map of moving toward that goal.[19]

The Chinese delegation made similar points about the step-by-step approach and expressed concern about weakening "the authority of the aforementioned mechanisms, divert(ing) valuable resources and throw(ing) the international nuclear disarmament process into disarray, without effectively carrying forward the nuclear disarmament process".[20]

By the time of the Oslo Conference in 2013, the general nuclear weapon States' approach towards countering the Humanitarian Initiative had thus taken shape: the gist of their arguments was questioning the validity and legitimacy of the Humanitarian Initiative as it threatened the established (nuclear) order of things. As the Humanitarian Initiative gathered further momentum, the nuclear weapon

States' counterarguments focussed more specifically and almost exclusively on criticising the idea of a ban treaty. Once the TPNW was negotiated in 2017, their arguments shifted to a criticism of the content of the treaty specifically. The various arguments underpinning the nuclear weapon States' positions will be analysed in the following.

The tactics of the opponent

Deflection

One notable aspect of the nuclear weapon States approach is very limited engagement on the actual issue of humanitarian consequences of nuclear weapons, at no stage going further than a general acknowledgement that these consequences exist and to affirm their "resolve to prevent such an occurrence from happening".[21] The nuclear weapon States have not provided answers or commented in any detail on the key Humanitarian Initiative conclusions, i.e. on the transboundary and potentially global consequences across a wide range of sectors and the lack of response capability to address the contingency of a nuclear weapon explosion. This absence of substantive engagement on the actual issues was complemented by questioning whether the conclusions on the humanitarian consequences and risks of nuclear weapons were, in fact, relevant or new. The contestation about the veracity of the humanitarian conclusions was particularly striking at the 2015 NPT Review Conference with some heated exchanges during the negotiations.[22]

In this context, the participation of the US and the UK at the 2014 Vienna Conference on the humanitarian impact of nuclear weapons can be scrutinised usefully. After an intense internal debate and outreach by Austria, the US had decided to attend the conference, soon followed by the UK. Both broke with the heretofore "P5 solidarity" of boycotting such conferences.[23] At the time, there was much anticipation about this engagement with the Humanitarian Initiative, especially on the part of the US. However, neither the US nor the UK actually spoke to the issues discussed at the conference.[24]

The US statement at the Vienna Conference acknowledged the moving "personal stories on the humanitarian impacts of nuclear weapons use". However, the only "substantive nod" in relation to the humanitarian consequences and risks was their reference to the "increased investments to ensure the safety and security of our nuclear arsenal and our enterprise". The rest of the statement was essentially a typical NPT statement, listing various disarmament related steps the US has taken or would be willing to consider in the future.

Similarly, the UK only agreed that "devastating humanitarian consequences could result from the use of nuclear weapons"[25] but then moved on to ask what conclusions should be drawn from this, namely avoiding the use of nuclear weapons, preventing their spread and keeping them secure. This was followed by declaring that a ban of nuclear weapons "fails to take account, and therefore jeopardises, the stability and security which nuclear weapons help to ensure",[26] underscoring the value of the step-by-step approach through the NPT and the importance of the

UN Disarmament Machinery. Finally, the UK said it would "work to create the conditions in which nuclear weapons are no longer needed but would maintain a minimum credible nuclear deterrent for as long as it is needed".[27]

The lack of engagement with the issues on the agenda of the Vienna Conference made the participation of these two nuclear weapon States, which had been so widely welcomed, look uncomfortable and out of step with the discourse that the vast majority of States wanted to have.

One explanation for the avoidance of addressing the arguments on the humanitarian consequences and risk of nuclear weapons is, of course, the absence of valid counterarguments. Such a conversation would inevitably entail admitting that the humanitarian consequences of nuclear weapons explosions affect not only one's own and the adversary's populations, but also the populations of innocent bystander States. As such, it would reveal a willingness to accept these effects on third States and, indeed, on all of humanity, as a "necessary collateral" to maintaining a nuclear deterrence-based notion of security and stability.

Moreover, there are also no convincing counterarguments to be made regarding the absence of humanitarian response capabilities and the lack of credible plans for such contingencies. Instead, nuclear weapon States "bank" on the belief that the threat of using nuclear weapons and inflicting unacceptable consequences is enough to *deter* anyone from using them, and therefore these contingencies will not be required. Nuclear risks, to the extent that they are even acknowledged, can be managed and are worth taking given the deep-seated belief that the "horrendous humanitarian consequences of nuclear weapons are precisely why deterrence has worked".[28] Arguably, nuclear weapon States did not and do not see any advantage in engaging in such discussions. Deflection is the much better approach.

This disconnect characterised the entire Humanitarian Initiative. The vast majority of non-nuclear weapon States actively wanted the nuclear weapon States to engage on the humanitarian consequences and risks issues, in order to see that their concerns are taken seriously and lead to a shared sense of urgency for nuclear disarmament. The nuclear weapon States' responses to these points, however, were either not forthcoming or not very substantive. It can be argued that the nuclear weapons discourse in these countries is so firmly embedded in an exclusively military and state-centred security approach, that it becomes almost impossible to even countenance a different, *human* security, perspective. Whenever the humanitarian consequences and risks were raised, the response of the nuclear weapon States – and of the nuclear umbrella States – was to criticise a possible ban treaty.

The lack of, or at best very limited, engagement by the nuclear weapon States on the issues themselves also represented "a blatant act of disrespect"[29] for the concerns and priorities of non-nuclear weapon States. Consequently, their overall boycott of non-nuclear weapon States' initiatives meant that ever more of these States came around to supporting the idea of a ban. In my view, this stance ended up underscoring the pertinence of the arguments and conclusions that the Humanitarian Initiative was developing and added rather than subtracted momentum to them.

Distraction and division

Two counterarguments often used in tandem by nuclear weapon States and nuclear umbrella States were that a ban treaty would *distract* from the established nuclear disarmament approach and that it would be *divisive*. The US statement on the day of the adoption of the TPNW put it succinctly: "At best it [the TPNW] is a distraction from those efforts. At worst, it will deepen political divisions".[30] Similar "distraction" points have been made on many occasions since the 2013 Oslo Conference.

The "division" allegedly introduced into the nuclear weapons discourse by the Humanitarian Initiative and the TPNW has been lamented by nuclear weapon States and reiterated by nuclear umbrella States on many occasions.[31] Australia, for example, worried that "a ban treaty could create parallel obligations and thus ambiguity and confusion and would deepen divisions between nuclear and non-nuclear weapons states".[32] In Russia's view, the TPNW "provokes deep disagreements among members of the international community".[33] The US went further stating that a ban treaty "risks creating an unbridgeable divide between states, polarizing the political environment on nuclear disarmament".[34]

From the perspective of the TPNW supporters, these arguments are not only unjustified but also a quite offensive distortion of the facts.

Firstly, given the severity of the humanitarian consequences and risks of nuclear weapons for the entire planet, the "distraction" argument is, per se, highly problematic. Moreover, the point presupposes that great attention was given by the nuclear weapon States to implementing the "practical step-by-step approach" agreed upon in the framework of the NPT over several decades and Review Conferences. As explained in Chapters 1 and 2, this is not the case and the approach had been seriously undermined by 20 years of inaction in multilateral nuclear disarmament. The nuclear weapon States had a very poor track record of implementing any of these agreed steps, let alone taking actual steps away from a reliance on nuclear weapons.

The Humanitarian Initiative and the subsequent TPNW were never intended or presented by its supporting States as a panacea for the solution of the nuclear weapons issue, nor as a reason to stop the implementation of other nuclear disarmament steps. On the contrary. The idea was to underscore the urgency of taking further necessary and effective measures, such as inter alia the pursuit of a FMCT, the entry into force of the CTBT, de-alerting measures or negative security assurances. Moreover, it is certainly not these States which are the cause of the various obstacles to progress on any of the agreed disarmament commitments under NPT Article VI. TPNW promoters are not the ones blocking the entry into force of the CTBT, FMCT negotiations in the CD, or the ones failing to reduce stockpiles or engage in negative security assurances or de-alerting measures.

The promoters of the TPNW have always emphasized the importance of progress on all aspects of nuclear disarmament and non-proliferation, as contained notably in the NPT 2010 Action Plan. Some of these issues, such as the CTBT, are also explicitly referenced in the preamble of the TPNW. The new treaty does not *distract* from these other issues, but rather aims at creating new momentum for nuclear disarmament efforts by providing a strong(er) legal basis for all these other important measures. Moreover, focusing on the humanitarian consequences of nuclear weapons and further strengthening the legal norm against a weapon that they have already forsaken, was and is a way for the non-nuclear weapon States of implementing the NPT itself.[35] It is not clear how this should be a "distraction".

The "division" argument is an interesting confusion of cause with effect. Clearly, divisions about nuclear disarmament have existed since 1945. However, it is the lack of progress in the implementation of the nuclear disarmament obligation of Article VI of the NPT that has increasingly deepened divisions and is certainly one of the elements that promoted the Humanitarian Initiative and the process leading to the TPNW. The divisions exist *because* of the loss of credibility in the implementation of Article VI on the part of the nuclear weapon States and not because of initiatives to help remedy this.[36] Nuclear weapon States have steadfastly refused to entertain this conclusion.

Moreover, it must be reiterated that the nuclear weapon States boycotted the humanitarian conferences, the open-ended working group and the treaty negotiations. This is, of course, the sovereign right of any State. It is, however, perplexing that those same States complain about a divisive approach when they themselves are not prepared to engage in inclusive discussions and processes initiated by non-nuclear weapon States. Hegemonic and discriminatory aspects are embedded in the NPT and this is where, arguably, the five nuclear weapon States have honed their odd stance: whenever they do not agree and choose not to engage with a discussion and a process, then – by definition – the discussion and processes, rather than the refusal to engage with them, must be divisive. Moreover, the nuclear weapon States do not like the TPNW because it is divisive, but it is only divisive because they do not like it. The redundancy of their argument is striking.

When the US warned that the ban treaty (meaning its supporters) "risk(s) creating an unbridgeable divide between states, . . . and effectively limiting any future prospect for achieving consensus",[37] it was further evidence of this thinking. It can hardly be disputed that, for a large part of the international community, the Humanitarian Initiative and the TPNW are expressions of long-held views and priorities as regards nuclear disarmament. For the first time, non-nuclear weapon States were able to follow through on these priorities by generating momentum through the Humanitarian Initiative and devising a UN General Assembly based negotiation process. What the US statement essentially says is that because *you* – the non-nuclear weapon States – have dared to actually pursue your long-standing policy priority, *we* – the nuclear weapon States – threaten any consensus in the future. In short, the only chance for consensus is the continuation of the status quo and the "price" for any future consensus would be the disregard of non-nuclear weapon States' positions and a continuation of the "fudging" of the fundamental differences that exist on nuclear disarmament.[38]

While it is of course legitimate to make these points, both the "distraction" and the "division" arguments are grounded in an approach that seeks to protect the established "nuclear order", rather than on any actual substantive position.

Refuting the arguments against the TPNW

The inefficacy argument

It surprises no one that the five States that officially possess nuclear weapons are the main objectors to the TPNW. Along with the nuclear umbrella States, they continue to challenge the efficacy of a treaty which was negotiated without them.

For example, France, UK and the US, issued a joint press statement after the adoption of the TPNW stating that they "do not intend to sign, ratify or ever to become party to it. . . . A purported ban . . . cannot result in the elimination of a single nuclear weapon and will not enhance any country's security, or international peace and security".[39] France stressed that "without the participation of the nuclear weapon States, no nuclear weapon would be eliminated",[40] and that the TPNW was "not only an 'ineffective' measure on the path to nuclear disarmament, but is also fraught with risks".[41] Russia conceded that "the effort to ban nuclear weapons might carry some weight if all nuclear-weapon States were willing to participate, but there was no such willingness nor would there be".[42] The US highlighted that "there is no 'quick fix' to achieving nuclear disarmament. There is no path other than the hard, daily work of verifiable step-by-step disarmament".[43] This is just a small selection of many statements that echoed these points.

Some NATO partners have traditionally sought for themselves the role of "bridge builders" between the three Western nuclear weapon States and the many non-nuclear weapons States who push for more progress on nuclear disarmament. The nuclear weapon States' boycott of the Humanitarian Initiative, especially on the part of the US, put these allies in the difficult and unfamiliar position of having to "defend" the nuclear status quo against the challenge of a possible ban treaty. This was contrary to the pro-nuclear disarmament self-image that these States carefully cultivate.

The idea of creating a legal norm which prohibits nuclear weapons, without the possessors of these weapons, seemed particularly counterintuitive, uncomfortable and possibly dangerous to those States under the NATO nuclear umbrella. This was not just due to their own reliance on extended US nuclear deterrence, but also because it challenged their own traditional nuclear disarmament narrative. Nuclear umbrella States, thus, invoked the "ineffective" argument with fervour.

Germany, for example, stated that "it is not realistic to expect that 'effective' nuclear disarmament can advance without engaging those States that possess nuclear weapons".[44] Australia argued "that an effective measure is one that includes those stakeholders whose behaviour we most want to influence" and that "we need to take into account existing political/security considerations".[45] The Polish delegation underlined that

> any process that can effectively lead us to a world free of nuclear weapons will by necessity be an inclusive one. . . . As nuclear weapons possessors don't want to engage (at least not all of them) we should think how to attract them. Or to make them feel being obliged to.[46]

The Netherlands echoed this point but with an interesting nuance on the responsibility of the nuclear weapon States

> The principle of effectiveness requires nuclear weapon possessors are involved in further steps towards Global Zero. In turn, these countries have a duty to lead. The apparent inability of the nuclear-weapon states to effectuate further progress threatens the credibility of our existing disarmament and non-proliferation structures.[47]

Frequent points used to challenge the efficacy of a ban were also that "simply banning nuclear weapons will not lead to their elimination"[48] and that "there are no short-cuts"[49] that can result in an effective, verifiable and irreversible nuclear disarmament.

Indeed, pursuing a ban on nuclear weapons against the opposition of nuclear armed States is, at first glance, counterintuitive. Many non-nuclear weapon States deliberated long and hard before they felt ready to back this approach. The ban treaty emerged as a route, only after many decades of fruitless pleading and exhausting all other approaches and initiatives.

In terms of substantive merit, the "inefficacy" counterargument is interesting for several reasons. Firstly, this argument is made by States, that possess or rely on nuclear weapons, as a reason why they will not join the TPNW. In terms of logic, this connection of cause and effect is circular: States with nuclear weapons are not willing to join the TPNW because, in their view, it will not eliminate a single nuclear weapon. Of course, the TPNW cannot eliminate a single weapon in itself, as long as nuclear weapon States are not joining. But apart from this point of logic, this argument misses the point that a legally binding non-discriminatory prohibition of nuclear weapons creates the legal basis for their elimination and a practical measure towards this objective. This was the case with the Biological as well as the Chemical Weapons Conventions. The pressure and momentum created by the TPNW for progress on nuclear disarmament as well as on non-proliferation, is intended to facilitate reductions of nuclear weapons and establish potential pathways, once countries possessing these weapons are ready, to abandon them.

On several occasions, nuclear weapon States have worried about the profound implications of the TPNW for the legitimacy of nuclear weapons and the practice of nuclear deterrence. Maybe the most telling example is the communication sent by the US to all NATO allies entitled "Defense Impacts of Potential United Nations General Assembly Nuclear Weapons Ban Treaty".[50] This urged allies to vote against the resolution to mandate negotiations in 2016. The premise of the document is that "the effects of a nuclear weapons ban treaty could be wide-ranging" and "could impact non-parties as well as parties". The document lists several ways in which the ban could be effective. The document draws attention to the likelihood of a ban limiting nuclear-weapons-related planning, training, and transit or allowing allies to use, plan, or train to use nuclear weapons. According to the document, a ban could also limit the use of nuclear-capable delivery systems and nuclear-weapons-sharing practices.[51] Unwittingly, this iteration of points where the ban treaty *could* have an impact, provided a particularly strong vindication of the effectiveness of the norm-setting approach behind the TPNW. Challenging the legality and the legitimacy of nuclear weapons and nuclear deterrence may not in itself eliminate nuclear weapons, but clearly has the potential to impact current nuclear weapons related practices and nuclear deterrence. From the point of view of the Humanitarian Initiative, this is exactly why the TPNW is valid.

Another argument frequently invoked by Western nuclear weapon States and nuclear umbrella States is that the TPNW, through its humanitarian narrative and its support from civil society, applies much more pressure on democratic than on autocratic states. France, for example, worried that a ban would be "destabilising because it would generate uneven pressure on the different nuclear-weapon States, particularly those that, like France, have already taken significant steps towards nuclear disarmament".[52] It is certainly true that civil society engagement and campaign pressure does not yet seem to have had much impact on the public discourse in autocratic states. The TPNW supporters are thus implicitly accused of inadvertently playing into the hands of autocracies at the expense of democratic states.

The TPNW, however, is directed against nuclear weapons as such and not against any States or alliances currently relying on them. It sets a non-discriminatory norm which has the aspiration of becoming universal over time. Certainly, governments of different States will face differing degrees of domestic pressure to accede to the TPNW and, naturally, the public discourse in an open society is, by definition, more vibrant, and sometimes very contested. This argument has nothing to do with the issue of nuclear weapons or the TPNW; it is a natural function of democratic political systems. It is to be expected, and must indeed be hoped for, that democratic systems will have open societal discussions on the issue of nuclear weapons, including the humanitarian consequences and risks associated with them. Democratic states also have more intense discussions on issues such as human rights and climate change. Indeed, progress and change on these and other issues is expected to spring more from democratic debates and decision-making processes, than from closed and autocratic political systems.

It is expected that the three Western nuclear weapon States and the nuclear umbrella States will face a more open discussion about the fact that the majority of States in the world consider their insistence on nuclear weapons incompatible with Article VI of the NPT. Their citizens must assess the extent to which this undermines a self-image as defenders of the global rule of law and of effective multilateralism.

The threat perceptions among nuclear weapon States that underpin their current belief in the need for nuclear deterrence are intrinsically interrelated and mutually reinforcing. Reliance on nuclear deterrence and today's concept of strategic stability, based on these weapons, may appear as a closed system of argumentation, but this can change. Once some of the protagonists of the current nuclear deterrence belief system are ready to take steps away from it, the parameters also start to change for the other actors. If democratic systems are more likely to initiate and enact this change, this should be considered a strength rather than a weakness.

Broader societal discussions on all issues lead to more legitimate and possibly more progressive policy choices.

Not taking the "security environment" into account

Another frequently invoked criticism of a ban treaty is that it does not take security considerations into account. This point was and continues to be made in different variations by opponents of the TPNW. The US, for example, stated "(r)ejecting security considerations related to nuclear weapons leaves no room for discussion on 'effective measures' needed to sustain nuclear disarmament progress, thereby discouraging, not promoting, needed dialogue". A ban treaty "runs the risk of undermining regional security" and that "it is unrealistic to ask non-nuclear weapon states and nuclear weapon states alike to reject their current security arrangements without addressing the underlying security concerns that led them to seek such arrangements in the first place".[53] France stated that "it would be dangerous to think that it is possible to disconnect nuclear disarmament issues from the security context", while at the same time highlighting that nuclear disarmament processes "were decided upon and implemented for the benefit of the security of all".[54] Nuclear weapon States urged "to accept that the hard practical work necessary to bring us closer to a world free of nuclear weapons must still be done, including a focus on not just humanitarian but also security considerations. There are no short cuts".[55] Some critical statements can also be characterised as somewhat hyperbolic. In 2015, for example, the US warned that "proposals such as a nuclear weapons ban . . . risk creating a very unstable security environment, where misperceptions or miscalculations could escalate crises with unintended and unforeseen consequences, not excluding the possible use of a nuclear weapon".[56] Russia even opined that the ban treaty "would risk . . . plunging the world into chaos".[57]

After the adoption of the TPNW, France, UK and the US jointly complained that

> (t)his initiative clearly disregards the realities of the international security environment. Accession to the ban treaty is incompatible with the policy of nuclear deterrence, which has been essential to keeping the peace in Europe and North Asia for over 70 years.[58]

Russia declared that "the conceptual framework for the negotiating process was unacceptable to us, as it essentially disregarded the strategic context and approached the elimination of nuclear weapons in isolation from objective realities".[59] More recently and in a similar vein, the supporters of the TPNW were accused of

> sidestep(ing) the messy business of having to worry about what would happen in a world without nuclear deterrence, or about otherwise trying to manage, ameliorate, or overcome competitive geopolitics. Such an approach also

sidesteps the awkward question of what competitive politics might look like after disarmament.[60]

These views are underpinned by two major doctrinal sentiments. Firstly, the imperative, from the perspective of the five nuclear weapon States, that their views and dominant roles on global security issues are safeguarded and not put into question. Secondly, the deeply entrenched belief that nuclear deterrence is and remains of fundamental importance for international security and stability. The ban treaty challenges both.

In response, it can be easily documented that any premise that nuclear deterrence increases security and therefore should not be delegitimized, was far from being universally accepted, already well before the Humanitarian Initiative and the TPNW. It is also incorrect to infer that non-nuclear weapon States have accepted this premise explicitly or implicitly through the NPT or through its indefinite extension. The positions expressed by non-nuclear weapon States in conjunction with agreeing to the package of decisions providing for the 1995 indefinite extension of the NPT, as well as at the subsequent NPT Review Conferences and on many other occasions, make this very clear. Non-nuclear weapon States neither accepted the indefinite extension of the possession of nuclear weapons, nor of a right to such possession, nor of the practice of nuclear deterrence. Rather, the differences in these conflicting interpretations have been "papered over" with ambiguous language.[61]

The assertion that the TPNW supporters only highlight a *humanitarian* perspective and do not take *security* considerations into account is an interesting spin but also misleading, especially when looking at the history of the nuclear weapons discourse. Non-nuclear weapon States had to take the security perspective of States that believe in nuclear deterrence into account for the past decades. The NPT and the nuclear disarmament and non-proliferation regime built around the NPT is, itself, an expression of the security priorities of the nuclear weapon States. The security perspectives of non-nuclear weapon States regarding nuclear disarmament and the implementation of NPT Article VI have been expressed also for decades but not been considered to the same degree. The threat perceptions of non-nuclear weapon States, stemming from the concern about the humanitarian consequences and risks of nuclear weapons are thus not merely a *humanitarian* perspective but based on equally valid and pertinent *security* considerations. It is these security considerations that have not been taken into account adequately, rather than the other way around.

When principles such as "benefits of the security of all"[62] or "undiminished security for all"[63] are invoked to criticise the TPNW and its supporters, nuclear weapon States should consider that these principles apply not only for the security relations between States that possess or rely on nuclear weapons, but also for non-nuclear weapon States. After all, the overwhelming majority of States has chosen not to be protected by nuclear deterrence because they see their national security better served without reliance on nuclear weapons. The process leading to the TPNW, and the treaty itself, are merely the expression and consolidation of the views of the majority of non-nuclear weapon States on security, nuclear weapons and the understanding of what Article VI of the NPT means. While opponents of the TPNW are perfectly entitled to their views, they neither own the exclusive right to interpret the NPT nor are they the sole arbiter of whose security perspectives are more valid than others.

Proponents of the TPNW have never disputed the difficult security challenges facing the international community today or argued that nuclear disarmament should be seen in isolation from the global security environment, nor have they advocated the ban as a panacea for achieving a world without nuclear weapons. All disarmament, arms control and non-proliferation efforts, including the eventual elimination of nuclear weapons must inevitably proceed in the face of ongoing security challenges, during times of international crises and some form or another of geopolitical competition. From the perspective of the TPNW, the challenging international security environment, coupled with the continued and possibly rising reliance on nuclear weapons by the nuclear possessor States, make nuclear disarmament efforts, if anything, even more urgent.

The argument that one must wait for a future security environment in which nuclear deterrence is no longer necessary, as a precondition for nuclear disarmament is disingenuous. There will always be real or perceived security imbalances between States, which, if one follows this line of argument, will provide excuses in perpetuity to not alter the nuclear status quo. Such ideal circumstances are unlikely ever to exist. Similarly, the often-invoked argument of the need to retain nuclear weapons as an "ultimate insurance policy"[64] against unknown threats, is an argument to justify nuclear weapons forever. The future will always be uncertain and hold new and unknown threats.

The prohibition norm of the TPNW provides one key legal measure. From this, additional steps to implement Article VI of the NPT needed to attain and maintain a world without nuclear weapons should be taken. This includes the steps promoted in the "progressive approach", that opponents of the TPNW say they favour. Moreover – and that is a key conceptual advantage of the TPNW – such additional measures, including deep cuts in nuclear arsenals and disarmament verification, will in fact become easier and, indeed maybe only possible, when they are based on a strong and comprehensive prohibition of nuclear weapons. States are more likely shun a weapon if this weapon is morally unacceptable and legally prohibited, than in a situation where the alleged "virtues" of these weapons continue to be highlighted at every opportunity. For TPNW supporting states, this logic is compelling and firmly based on security considerations.

There is one additional argument, related both to the "security environment" as well as to the NPT-TPNW relationship (discussed in the next section) that nuclear weapons states like to omit. Their assertion that nuclear weapons are *necessary* for the security of States has created a big impression. Nuclear weapon States and nuclear umbrella States do not tire of highlighting this point and have done so in particular to express their opposition to and as an argument against the TPNW. There are, however, many non-nuclear weapon States who could justifiably claim that their security environment is at least as challenging as the security environment of States "relying" on nuclear weapons. Why would that argument not count for other states? By underscoring the challenging security environment and the *necessity* to keep replying on nuclear weapons because of it, nuclear weapon States and nuclear umbrella States only highlight a striking double standard as regards the concept of security.

There are thus several arguments that can be made to refute the accusation that the TPNW is *only* based on a humanitarian perspective and does not take security considerations into account. In truth, conflicting security approaches underpin the respective arguments. One that posits that nuclear weapons and nuclear deterrence are required to guarantee national security and preserve international stability – until an unspecified future – and one that considers that very practice as a fundamental threat to the security of humanity. The extent to which there is scope to bridge this divide, or at least address these perspectives constructively, is a key challenge for the future of the nuclear disarmament and non-proliferation regime and will be discussed in the next chapter. It is deeply problematic to witness the security concerns of non-nuclear weapon States supporting the TPNW being dismissed or belittled and to be accused of naively undermining international security, by the very same States who hold the weapons, the possession of which is the origin of an existential global security threat.

Undermining to the NPT

Opponents of the TPNW accuse it of undermining the NPT and the entire disarmament and non-proliferation regime. Before the TPNW was negotiated, the opponents warned of a negative impact of the TPNW on the NPT. Once the TPNW was concluded, the tone got harsher and several aspects of the treaty were identified as allegedly being detrimental to the NPT.

The accusations include for example that a ban treaty "would undermine existing non-proliferation and disarmament regimes . . . could impact other aspects of the NPT, including strengthening cooperation in the peaceful applications of nuclear energy or ideas to reinforce the non-proliferation pillar"[65] or that the treaty could create parallel obligations to the NPT, which could lead to "forum shopping"[66] and "impeding the effective functioning of the NPT regime – and perhaps even by enticing defections from the NPT".[67] After adoption, the TPNW was accused of "undermining and weakening the NPT, which has played an unparalleled role in curtailing the nuclear arms race",[68] or, that it departs from previous NPT agreements.[69]

For supporters of the Humanitarian Initiative and the TPNW, the accusations of harming the NPT are considered particularly offensive, disingenuous and unjustified. As Austrian Ambassador Thomas Hajnozci points out

> the negotiations of the TPNW were marked by the utmost care to make the TPNW a new legal instrument in line with the existing disarmament and non-proliferation regime. The treaty explicitly and structurally fits into the

framework created by the NPT and constitutes a necessary measure for the implementation of its Article VI.[70]

The States at the forefront of this process have been among the strongest supporters of the NPT and enjoy an unblemished record of implementation. They are all longstanding promoters of various initiatives in support of nuclear disarmament and non-proliferation. To accuse, for example Ireland, which is considered as having invented the NPT,[71] or South Africa, which actually disarmed its nuclear weapons and joined the NPT as a non-nuclear weapon State, of undermining the NPT must be considered grossly confrontational.

These accusations come primarily from those States whose own lacklustre NPT implementation records on nuclear disarmament were the reason why the Humanitarian Initiative and the TPNW process were initiated in the first place. From the outset, supporters of these initiatives pointed to the need to give urgency to the implementation of Article VI and to strengthen and shore up support of the NPT. This, as well as their own obligations under the NPT and for the wider regime, were key motivations to pursue the TPNW. It is thus

> a good faith effort by 122 countries to act on their NPT responsibility to take effective measures on nuclear disarmament . . . [given that] the NPT's normative potential had been exhausted in unleashing dramatic nuclear disarmament measures because the nuclear nine were caught in the trap of basing their nuclear policies solely within national security paradigms.[72]

An unequivocal pro-NPT stance is enshrined in the "Humanitarian Pledge" which called

> on all states parties to the NPT to renew their commitment to the urgent and full implementation of existing obligations under Article VI, and to this end, to identify and pursue effective measures to fill the legal gap for the prohibition and elimination of nuclear weapons.

Consequently, the preamble of the TPNW contains a reaffirmation of the NPT's role as a cornerstone of the nuclear disarmament and non-proliferation regime. It reaffirms prohibitions in place already in the NPT (Article 2) and establishes two avenues (Article 4) for nuclear armed States to implement their nuclear disarmament obligations under NPT Article VI.

Nuclear weapon States and nuclear umbrella States assert the need to keep nuclear weapons for their security and this has an important bearing on the assessment of whose actions undermine the NPT and the nuclear disarmament and non-proliferation regime. By underscoring the challenging international security environment and the *necessity* to keep replying on nuclear weapons, nuclear weapon States and nuclear umbrella States promote the *value* of nuclear weapons and, thus, encourage proliferation. One can even argue that such promotion is, in fact, an act of proliferation. It may not be proliferation in its literal sense, but it is nevertheless the proliferation of the *concept* of nuclear weapons as a desirable "guarantee" of security.

This stance is especially problematic at a time when the cohesion among NPT State Parties is fractured and support for the NPT is threatened by the weak implementation record on Article VI and the ambiguous position of nuclear umbrella States on nuclear disarmament. How can the proliferation of nuclear weapons be countered effectively in the long run, while simultaneously stressing their *necessity* and *desirability*? Without strong counterarguments, the view that nuclear weapons are *necessary* will only gain in attractiveness. The challenge posed by the North Korean nuclear weapons programme is a case in point. As Ramesh Thakur aptly observes "having instrumentalized the NPT as a solely non-proliferation tool instead of a reciprocal disarmament obligation, the nuclear powers were trapped in their own hypocrisy in dealing effectively with the challenge from North Korea".[73]

The TPNW provides an unequivocal counterargument, which the NPT is unable to do, given its discriminatory nature and in-built double standard. By legally prohibiting these weapons and declaring them morally indefensible and detrimental to the *undiminished security for all*, the TPNW creates a real taboo against both the possession of nuclear weapon and the practice of nuclear deterrence. At a time when security challenges are on the rise and without credible leadership on nuclear disarmament by States that rely on these weapons, the TPNW provides much needed normative reinforcement of nuclear non-proliferation efforts. In my view, it is the double-standard in the NPT and the lacklustre implementation of its Article VI that weakens it, not the TPNW with its new normative standard to redress exactly those weaknesses.

The regulation of nuclear safeguards

One NPT-related aspect which received particular criticism, was the way the TPNW dealt with the issue of IAEA Safeguards.[74] The TPNW is criticised because it "contains a safeguards standard that even in this day is not sufficient for the IAEA to draw a conclusion about the absence of undeclared nuclear activities",[75] or more antagonistically that the "ban drafters' choice to tie non-proliferation verification to a demonstrably obsolete measure strikes a blow against the existing verification standard".[76]

This criticism does not hold up to scrutiny, as the TPNW ensures that States maintain, as a minimum, their existing IAEA safeguards obligations. The majority of States have IAEA Additional Protocols[77] in place. Consequently, the TPNW legally secures the Additional Protocol as the current standard of non-proliferation verification, which is a higher standard than the one stipulated by the NPT. The TPNW thus, "goes beyond the NPT, by obliging States Parties to maintain, as a minimum, their existing Safeguards standards, thus making the Additional Protocol mandatory for states that are bound by it when the TPNW enters into force".[78]

For States that currently do not have an Additional Protocol, the TPNW set the IAEA Comprehensive Safeguards Agreement[79] as the minimum requirement, the same as in the NPT. The TPNW also explicitly refers to the possibility of strengthening these obligations in the future.

States that already have an Additional Protocol in place were largely in favour of making it mandatory in the TPNW. However, during the negotiations, some States argued that establishing the Additional Protocol as mandatory in the TPNW would change the nature of the Additional Protocol, which is optional. This would have exceeded the TPNW negotiation mandate. According to a diplomat from a State that objected to making the Additional Protocol mandatory,

> it was a false argument made by those States that are themselves not open to disarmament obligations. These States were angry that their non-proliferation objective was not included in a treaty they did not like and did not participate in. This shows the paradox of the nuclear weapons debate. It was an argument made to split and to divide.[80]

Importantly, and omitted by the critiques, the TPNW also goes beyond the NPT in relation to nuclear armed States. When joining the TPNW, they are obliged to negotiate, conclude, and maintain an adequate Safeguards agreement. Today, nuclear weapon States "are under no such obligation under the NPT, although they do have voluntary arrangements in place regarding safeguards for some of their nuclear material".[81]

Moreover, there is a distinctly disingenuous aspect to the criticism of the safeguard provisions, given that opponents of the TPNW expressly prevented the participation of the IAEA, the international organization in charge of nuclear safeguards, at the TPNW negotiations. The IAEA had been invited by the President of the negotiations with the explicit purpose of helping ensure that the treaty provisions reinforce the NPT and the IAEA safeguards regime.[82]

Notwithstanding this, the TPNW provides a higher safeguards standard than the NPT on some aspects, and in others hews as closely as possible to the NPT approach, precisely to avoid diverging from this standard. This was recognised by the UN High Representative for Disarmament Affairs, Izumi Nakamitsu, when she referred to the TPNW Safeguards provisions as having "reinforce(d) and complement(ed) the NPT and that you [note: the States] designed a new treaty that ensures that no States can evade the basic safeguards that underpin the NPT".[83]

Will the TPNW promote "forum shopping" or "defections"?

It is difficult to address the arguments of possible "forum shopping"[84] or "defections" (i.e. withdrawal) from the NPT until State practice in implementing the TPNW can be assessed over a longer period. However, the danger of "forum shopping" in order to escape non-proliferation obligations has been effectively closed off with the requirement to maintain, as a minimum, existing IAEA safeguards obligations. There are no indications that any State would want to withdraw from the NPT in favour of the TPNW, nor is it clear what a State would hope to gain by doing so.

Close analysis shows that claims that the TPNW undermines the NPT do not stand up to scrutiny and/or cannot be substantiated. Rather, they are the expressions of a politically motivated counternarrative from those States who object to the Humanitarian Initiative and the TPNW, because of the challenge they present to the nuclear status quo and a particular interpretation of what the NPT represents in terms of obligations and commitments. As Ritchie concludes, "(t)he NPT has since become an institution used to legitimise the continued possession of nuclear weapons by the five . . . (i)t has become a hegemonic vehicle that constitutes and is used to reinforce a particular conception of the nuclear order".[85]

This conception is demonstrated in the Russian critique of the TPNW as being "at variance with the agreements reached earlier under the NPT, including the 2010 action plan".[86] This interpretation of NPT Article VI is shared by all nuclear weapon States and conditions progress on nuclear disarmament with the maintenance of nuclear deterrence, until a security environment exists that "allows" for a world without nuclear weapons. Until such time, they consider their special role as a nuclear weapon State secure and, as per the indefinite extension of the NPT, legitimate. Viewed from this hegemonic perspective, the TPNW is clearly a challenge and "at variance".

The TPNW codifies the majority of non-nuclear weapons States' longstanding interpretation of the disarmament obligation contained in NPT Article VI, as well as the subsequent commitments reached at the 1995, 2000 and 2010 NPT Review Conferences. Moreover, the TPNW's comprehensive prohibition of nuclear weapons follows the logic that there are "no right hands that can handle the wrong weapons".[87] The prohibition of this weaponry must be comprehensive and based on the horrific characteristics of the weapon, rather than on who possesses them. The nuclear weapon States have not used their *temporary* nuclear weapons possessor status under the NPT to act with sufficient urgency or credibility on the implementation of Article VI, despite having committed themselves to do so. The TPNW is thus intended and needed to facilitate the realisation of the NPT. From the perspective of the TPNW, the States that possess or rely on nuclear weapons are, thus, "at variance" with the NPT in much more fundamental ways.

Addressing other critiques of the TPNW

Once the TPNW was concluded, its opponents had a legal text to criticise, rather than a concept. In addition to their complaint that it undermines the NPT, a number of other points have been raised to discredit it. Claims were made that the TPNW is not clear regarding disarmament verification, for example that the "ban treaty provides a workable framework for verifying the dismantlement of a state's nuclear program is wishful, and indeed simply magical, thinking".[88] Other points raised were that the TPNW lacks clarity on whether it outlaws the possession of nuclear weapons or not. The speed of the negotiations has also been criticised which, it is alleged, resulted in a flawed text, including as regards the treaty's withdrawal clause.

On the disarmament verification argument, the TPNW followed a logical and pragmatic approach. The absence of specific provisions stems from the fact that the nuclear armed States, did not take part in the negotiations. As Giorgou concludes,

> In this respect the text is indeed vague – and legitimately so. Indeed, it would have been neither possible nor appropriate to set one single standard a priori and applicable to all nuclear possessor states, irrespective of differences among nuclear arsenals and of possible future developments in such arsenals prior to the entry into force of the TPNW for the state(s) in question.[89]

The TPNW explicitly provides space to include the input and expertise of adhering nuclear armed States to develop concrete verification measures, once they join the treaty. Therefore, the TPNW does not create a loophole for cheating on nuclear disarmament. Moreover, the TPNW was never meant to be a comprehensive Nuclear Weapons Convention with detailed provisions related to the verification of the complete and irreversible elimination of nuclear weapons. Such provisions are certainly necessary, as recognized notably in Article 4 of the TPNW, to attain and maintain a nuclear weapon free world. However, "whether one likes it or not, this was not the role envisaged for the TPNW by its drafters".[90] Far from being a major weakness, "this pragmatic approach recognises that eventual adherence by nuclear-weapon-possessing states will require their input into how 'irreversible' elimination (admittedly a high standard, but one which all parties to the NPT have affirmed) would take place".[91]

A misleading allegation that claims the TPNW is unclear in outlawing nuclear weapons refers to an alleged tension between Article 1 and Article 4 of the TPNW. In Article 1, State Parties undertake never, under any circumstances, to possess nuclear weapons; Article 4 describes an avenue by which States can join the treaty *before* they have actually eliminated their nuclear weapons. The use of the phrase "notwithstanding Article 1" in Article 4 clarifies that there is no real contradiction between these two articles. The TPNW follows the very same approach – prohibition of possession, but possibility to join before elimination i.e. "join and destroy", that is embodied in other disarmament treaties, such as for example the Chemical Weapons Convention.[92]

As far as withdrawal is concerned, the criticism is that the TPNW makes withdrawal too complicated.[93] The objection is that in an armed conflict, the possession or use of nuclear weapons could become "necessary" for a State. Such a State, fearing an outbreak of armed conflict, would have an incentive to leave the TPNW "in advance", in order to avoid being trapped by the withdrawal delay clause once the war actually started. If the withdrawal takes effect only after 12 months, as stipulated in the TPNW, this would put an excessive burden on said State. This line of thinking contradicts the whole purpose of the TPNW. The possibility to withdraw without any conditions would have severely undermined the credibility of the treaty, whose main obligation (Article I) is for States to never under any circumstances acquire, possess and use etc. nuclear weapons, evidently also in an armed conflict. The TPNW thus makes withdrawal purposefully more difficult than under the NPT, a lesson learned from the example of DPRK's withdrawal from the NPT.[94] Moreover, the withdrawal clause reflects what has become standard wording in newer prohibition conventions, such as the Anti-Personnel Mine Ban Convention and the Convention on Cluster Munitions.[95]

On the haste or otherwise of the TPNW negotiations,[96] it suffices to say that this was a direct outcome of the mandate for the negotiations, which limited the purpose of the treaty to establishing a clear and unequivocal prohibition norm, rather than attempting to solve all issues related to nuclear disarmament comprehensively. The drafting process was built on the wording of similar prohibition treaties, allowing for a comparable quality of the resulting text, as well as on the groundwork accomplished during the 2016 open-ended working group in Geneva. Finally and importantly, there was a high degree of convergence of views between the negotiating parties and an awareness that the negotiations represented a truly historic opportunity. The States participating in the negotiation actually wanted to achieve a treaty prohibiting nuclear weapons.

The effect of these arguments on the TPNW and its supporters

At the time of writing, approximately three years after the TPNW was adopted, tension continues, one could even say "rages on". It is impossible to make an assessment as to which set of arguments has prevailed or will ultimately prevail. Clearly, achieving the TPNW in the face of such opposition from the world's most powerful military States was a remarkable accomplishment. The process leading up to the TPNW can thus be described as a period in which the nuclear status quo was successfully challenged by the Humanitarian Initiative. The opponents of this initiative found it difficult to deal with the humanitarian focus, were not able to halt its momentum and could not hamper the sense of empowerment and agency that the Humanitarian Initiative had created among non-nuclear weapon States. Several tactical mistakes – political and discursive – on the part of the nuclear weapon States and the nuclear umbrella States ended up contributing, rather than extinguishing, this momentum. Once the TPNW was achieved, the dynamic of the discourse changed insofar as the supporters of the new treaty had something to defend and the opponents had a concrete outcome to criticise and attack. In the years since the adoption of the TPNW, the treaty's opponents have wasted no opportunity to do this, with some effect.

On 24 October 2020, Honduras ratified the TPNW and was the 50th State to do so, triggering the conditions for the entry into force of the TPNW on 22 January 2021. Reaching the number of ratifications needed for the TPNW to enter into force was however, slower and more difficult than originally imagined.[97] The number of States that have signed the TPNW to date is lower than the number of States that participated in the negotiations and supported the "Humanitarian

Pledge" and the UN General Assembly resolution that mandated them.[98] Some of this will be for innocuous reasons. In most non-nuclear weapon States, there will be many other legislative and political priorities, which put ratification of the TPNW not necessarily high up on the "to do list". In other States, the number of experts dealing with multilateral nuclear weapon processes is very small; some of whom will have changed positions since the time of the adoption, which could have an impact on the speed with which domestic ratification processes are pursued. A certain "slump" in attention after the high levels given to an issue during treaty negotiations is also to be expected. However, it is also likely that a number of TPNW supporting States have been affected by the fierce opposition to the treaty.

The pressure and lobbying campaigns of nuclear weapon States have continued and intensified.[99] In a particularly unprecedented move, ostensibly to prevent the entry into force, in October 2020 the US wrote to States that had already ratified the TPNW saying that they had "made a strategic error and [you] should withdraw your instrument of ratification or accession".[100] It is difficult for most non-nuclear weapon States to withstand such pressure from the most powerful States. Some TPNW-supporting States may therefore have slowed down the ratification process, rather than risk adversely affecting their relations with the TPNW opponents, given the many other competing priorities for which these relationships are important. Moreover, while nuclear disarmament is certainly an important global issue, in many, if not most non-nuclear weapon States, nuclear weapons are not a domestic political priority. The opposite is true of those States that vehemently oppose the TPNW with its challenge to what they consider their core interests and special status.

The vehemence with which the opposition to the TPNW has been pursued may have taken some supporters of the TPNW aback. The effectiveness of a counternarrative can be measured in the extent to which it creates doubts and insecurity. While the broad range of procedural and substantive criticisms of the TPNW are relatively easy to counter, it is time-consuming to refute each and every one of the barrage of criticisms, warnings and accusations directed against the TPNW, even when these counterarguments are incorrect and predominantly politically motivated. In this context, the accusation that the TPNW undermines the NPT and the nuclear disarmament and non-proliferation regime, clearly had an impact. As a result of what they perceive to be an unjustified and offensive accusation, some TPNW supporters have felt the need to justify and reiterate that the TPNW is not intended to damage the NPT.[101] Arguably, this has also led to more cautious behaviour with regard to promoting the treaty, as would have been the case otherwise. Indeed, the 2017, 2018 and 2019 Preparatory Meetings for the 2020 NPT Review Conference, as well as the UN First Committees in those years were dominated by several other, highly contentious issues. Among them were the deterioration of US/NATO relations with Russia, the increasing competition between US and China, the end of the INF Treaty, the US withdrawal from the Iran Nuclear Agreement and the nuclear weapons program of the DPRK. Nuclear disarmament and the TPNW played a less prominent role in these fora than at the height of the Humanitarian Initiative and the TPNW process. In light of the "undermining the NPT" accusations, some non-nuclear weapon States may have considered it crucial to avoid being blamed for a possible failure of the postponed 2020 NPT Review Conference, by pushing too hard for the nuclear disarmament and the TPNW. Indeed, some TPNW supporters may have found it somewhat of a relief that other problems, in particular the geopolitical antagonisms between the nuclear weapon States are instead on full display. The notion of "sitting out the Trump Presidency" could also have played a role. This administration's antagonistic approach towards multilateralism in general is likely to have contributed to more reticence among non-nuclear weapon States on nuclear disarmament.

After the adoption of the TPNW in 2017, the focus of TPNW supporters shifted from the humanitarian consequences and risks of nuclear weapons towards highlighting the benefits of the treaty and defending it against criticism and opponents. Conversely, the focus of opponents of the TPNW turned from their difficulties in handling the Humanitarian Initiative and preventing the ban, to attacking the TPNW with the counterarguments highlighted in this chapter. Attention to the substantive arguments that underpin the logic of the TPNW was reduced in the post-TPNW adoption period. In my view, this discursive shift has been beneficial for the TPNW opponents. It is simply an easier task for the TPNW opponents to attack the effectiveness of a treaty in which they do not participate. It is much harder to grip the more fundamental questions relating to the sustainability and ethical defensibility of nuclear deterrence, in view of the humanitarian consequences and risks of nuclear weapons. Nuclear weapon States, therefore, have an interest in keeping the discussion focussed narrowly on the Treaty, so as to conceal their lack of substantive answers to the questions and issues which form the basis of the TPNW. "Deflection" from the humanitarian consequences and risk arguments that proved such a counterproductive tactic for the nuclear weapon States before the TPNW was adopted, has since been brought to bear with more effect.

Civil society actors struggle with the same predicament: while it is of key importance for ICAN to emphasise the TPNW, it being the major achievement of their campaign, ICAN, too, has found it difficult to avoid spending much of its time defending the TPNW against the criticisms of its opponents.

For the nuclear weapon States and the nuclear umbrella States, a focus on the TPNW, rather than on its underlying arguments, is tactically easier to handle. This has been aided by the fact that the involvement of the so-called "humanitarian sector"[102] has remained limited in the nuclear weapons debate. While several humanitarian organisations participated in the conferences on the humanitarian impact of nuclear weapons and provided very important substantive contributions,[103] this has not been carried forward in a sustained way, with the exception of the ICRC. One reason for this is that there have not been any significant international events focussing on the humanitarian impact of nuclear weapons at the level of the conferences in 2013 and 2014. Despite some inroads into the "humanitarian sector", nuclear weapons have remained an issue that is dealt with and dominated by traditional security policy. In State bureaucracies as well as in international organisations and NGOs operating in the "humanitarian sector", there is an institutional reluctance and also a lack of capacity to become more deeply involved. Nuclear weapons are politically highly contested and there are many other competing humanitarian priorities and emergencies of a more straightforward nature. The Humanitarian Initiative has shown that the more the nuclear weapons discourse is opened up to include other voices, in particular from a humanitarian perspective, the stronger the impact is on this discourse. A broader set of perspectives makes it more difficult for the States that want to keep nuclear weapons to argue their case. Conversely, as long as the discourse remains firmly in the hands of security policy experts, it is much easier for these States to set the parameters of the debate and to dominate it. The fault here lies also with TPNW supporters who could have done better in keeping other voices and actors more involved in this issue. The discourse has fallen back somewhat into the "comfort zone" of the nuclear status quo.

Future TPNW Meetings of State Parties will provide a designated framework for States, international organisations and civil society to refocus on the humanitarian consequences and risks of nuclear weapons. However, in order to be more widely effective beyond the TPNW supporting States, a broader discourse on nuclear weapons will have to be rekindled. What was initiated as a successful "humanitarian reframing" of the nuclear weapons issue, was not continued sufficiently after the TPNW was adopted. It will be necessary for the TPNW supporters to refocus on this aspect.

Finally, academia and think tanks within the strategic studies community, i.e. those that deal with security policy issues and in particular nuclear weapons, also play a significant role in shaping the nuclear weapons discourse and the perception of the TPNW. The vast majority of actors in the strategic studies community are concentrated in nuclear armed States or nuclear umbrella States. In those States, a certain "nuclear weapons culture" of shared practices and attitudes has developed over a long period of time, and most tend to look at security, nuclear weapons and nuclear deterrence in a certain way. This particular "lens" is overwhelmingly in line with the traditional parameters of the nuclear weapons discourse, as determined by the States that dominate the nuclear status-quo, and is an important reinforcing factor. This community, also referred to as the "non-proliferation complex" by Ruzicka and Campbell to a large extent "propagates a conservative ideology of post – cold war nuclear politics, one that privileges a stable international order dominated by status-quo large nuclear powers, and that has forsaken its original blueprint for a nuclear-free world".[104] As Thompson has characterised it, "the [nuclear] weapons system, and the entire economic, scientific, political, and ideological support system to that weapons system – the social system which researches it, 'chooses' it, produces it, polices it, justifies it, and maintains it in being".[105]

The perspective of non-nuclear weapon States only plays a marginal role in the work of most representatives of the strategic studies community. The small number of researchers who do write with this perspective in mind, cannot compensate for the clear dominance of the orthodox, and in comparison, well-funded, nuclear weapons approach that academia and think tanks are accustomed to follow.

As a consequence, supporters of the TPNW have found it difficult to have an impact on this expert community. There is certainly a significant increase in articles, papers and books about the TPNW and the developments that led to it. However, most of these contributions are either sceptical and critical, or have not taken up in any detail the arguments that the Humanitarian Initiative has put forward. The TPNW tends to be portrayed as a non-nuclear weapon States initiative, borne out of frustration with the slow pace of nuclear disarmament and assessed critically in line with the counternarrative arguments discussed earlier in the chapter. While frustration was certainly one motivating factor for non-nuclear weapon States, the Humanitarian Initiative and the TPNW represent much more. The more fundamental issues of this initiative and the different perspectives on security, legitimacy and responsibility with regard to nuclear weapons and a security system based on nuclear deterrence, are mostly ignored by the orthodox strategic studies community. While there is no evidence to suggest that there is a deliberate strategy of criticising the TPNW,

> one factor may be that it is generally understand within the orthodox strategic studies community that the TPNW should be marginalized. It is good for networking and advantageous for career prospects and the standing within this community if one is seen to be playing the game.[106]

The power structures in the nuclear weapons discourse have, as such, not (yet) changed fundamentally with the arrival of the TPNW. The combined forces of the States opposing the Humanitarian Initiative and the TPNW together with most of the orthodox strategic studies community make for formidable opponents for the supporters of the TPNW. There is a clear imbalance in terms of political weight, public information presence and security policy expert dominance. It can be argued therefore that the Humanitarian Initiative was remarkably successful – against all odds – in developing arguments and building a momentum that led to the TPNW. Sustaining this momentum, however, has been more difficult. The opponents of these initiatives have brought their counterarguments more effectively to bear after the TPNW was adopted than in the period before. However, the supporters of the TPNW have contributed to this to some extent by decreasing their focus on the humanitarian consequences and risks of nuclear weapons. From playing tactically and politically very good offence to achieve the TPNW, the defence of the treaty, since its adoption, has been more of a challenge for supporting States and for civil society.

The key question that may well ultimately determine the importance of the TPNW will be to what extent the supporters of the TPNW can refocus the discourse on the humanitarian consequences and risk arguments the underpin the TPNW and maintain this issue as a political priority. The entry into force of the TPNW will help State parties and civil society organisations in this respect. The process leading to the TPNW has shown that the humanitarian focus provides powerful arguments that give agency to non-nuclear weapon States. It raises valid and important questions related to human security, responsibility and legitimacy in relation to nuclear weapons, which the TPNW opponents have struggled to address. If supporters of the TPNW, States and civil society want to influence and ultimately change the nuclear weapons policies and the belief in nuclear deterrence in the States that rely on these weapons, they will have to continue to build and promote the breadth of the humanitarian consequences, risks and international humanitarian law arguments on which the TPNW rests. These arguments will continue to be resisted forcefully by the supporters of the nuclear status quo.

Notes

1 See Gro Nystuen, Kjølv Egeland, and Torbjørn Graff Hugo, *The TPNW: Setting the Record Straight*, Norwegian Academy of International Law, October 2018, p. 35.
2 See Chapter 1.
3 See for example at the 2011 First Committee of the UN General Assembly. Relatively few non-nuclear weapon States explicitly referred to the humanitarian consequences of nuclear weapons, among them Norway, Austria, New Zealand, Mexico, Philippines, Switzerland, Malaysia and the New Agenda Coalition; available at www.reachingcriticalwill.org/disarmament-fora/unga/2011/statements.
4 See Chapter 2.
5 Ibid.
6 Ibid.
7 Ibid.
8 See "First Committee Monitor", no. 4, 29 October 2012, p. 4, available at www.reachingcriticalwill.org/images/documents/Disarmament-fora/1com/FCM12/FCM-2012-4.pdf.
9 See Chapter 1.
10 See Chapter 2.
11 See statements by China, France, Russia and the US in the Conference on Disarmament on 22 and 29 January 2013, available at and https://documents-dds-ny.un.org/doc/UNDOC/GEN/G13/641/97/PDF/G1364197.pdf?OpenElement and https://documents-dds-ny.un.org/doc/UNDOC/GEN/G14/607/50/PDF/G1460750.pdf?OpenElement.
12 See Chapter 2.
13 Joint explanatory note by China, France, Russia, the United Kingdom and the United States on non-attendance at the Oslo Conference, 2013, available at www.reachingcriticalwill.org/images/documents/Disarmament-fora/oslo-2013/P5_Oslo.pdf.
14 The reference "under any circumstances" stands for a categorical rejection of nuclear weapons use and the practice of nuclear deterrence. Assurance "that nuclear war should never be fought", in fact endorses the practice of nuclear deterrence, with the argument that its purpose is the prevention of (nuclear) war. The formulation is also a variation of the famous Joint Statement by Reagan and Gorbatchev of 7–10 December 1987, which read "They will continue to be guided by their solemn conviction that a nuclear war cannot be won and must never be fought".; available at www.reaganlibrary.gov as well as available at www.washingtonpost.com/archive/politics/1987/12/11/joint-statement-by-reagan-gorbachev/cd990a8d-87a1-4d74-88f8-704f93c80cd3/
15 Joint explanatory note by China, France, Russia, the United Kingdom and the United States.
16 Statements by Russia, UK, France, US and China to the Conference on Disarmament on 5 March 2013, available at https://documents-dds-ny.un.org/doc/UNDOC/GEN/G13/642/17/PDF/G1364217.pdf?OpenElement.

180 *The contest of arguments*

17 Ibid.
18 Ibid.
19 Ibid.
20 Ibid.
21 Joint Statement by China, France, Russia, UK and US to the 2015 NPT Review Conference on 30 April 2015, available at www.reachingcriticalwill.org/images/documents/Disarmament-fora/npt/revcon2015/statements/30April_UKJoint.pdf.
22 See Chapter 3.
23 See Chapter 2.
24 Statement by the US at the Vienna Conference on 9 December 2014, available at www.bmeia.gv.at/fileadmin/user_upload/Zentrale/Aussenpolitik/Abruestung/HINW14/Statements/HINW14_Statement_USA.pdf.
25 Statement by the UK at the Vienna Conference on 9 December 2014, available at www.bmeia.gv.at/fileadmin/user_upload/Zentrale/Aussenpolitik/Abruestung/HINW14/Statements/HINW14_Statement_UK.pdf.
26 Ibid.
27 Ibid.
28 See also Chapter 2.
29 See Paul Meyer, "The Nuclear Nonproliferation Treaty: Fin de Regime?", in *Arms Control Today*, April 2017.
30 Press Statement US Department of State on 7 July 2017, available at www.state.gov/conclusion-of-un-negotiations-on-a-treaty-to-ban-nuclear-weapons/.
31 See for example Chapter 3, p. 23.
32 See Department of Foreign Affairs and Trade, "Australia's Nuclear Non-Proliferation and Disarmament Policy", available at www.dfat.gov.au/international-relations/security/non-proliferation-disarmament-arms-control/nuclear-issues/Pages/australias-nuclear-non-proliferation-and-disarmament-policy.
33 Russian Foreign Minister Sergei Lavrov, "Russia Doesn't Plan to Join the Treaty on the Prohibition of Nuclear Weapons", 19 January 2018, available at https://sputniknews.com/russia/201801191060881071-lavrov-russia-treaty-nuclear-weapons/.
34 Statement by US at First Committee of the UN General Assembly on 14 October 2016, available at www.reachingcriticalwill.org/images/documents/Disarmament-fora/1com/1com16/statements/14Oct_USA.pdf.
35 See also Chapter 1.
36 See also Alexander Kmentt, "How Divergent Views on Nuclear Disarmament Threaten the NPT", in *Arms Control Today*, December 2013.
37 Statement by US at First Committee of the UN General Assembly on 14 October 2016.
38 See Chapter 3.
39 Joint press statement of the US, UK and France on 7 July 2017, available at https://usun.usmission.gov/joint-press-statement-from-the-permanent-representatives-to-the-united-nations-of-the-united-states-united-kingdom-and-france-following-the-adoption/.
40 Statement by France at the First Committee of the UN General Assembly on 14 October 2016, available at http://statements.unmeetings.org/media2/7662311/france.pdf.
41 Statement by France at the First Committee of the UN General Assembly on 4 October 2017, available at https://reachingcriticalwill.org/images/documents/Disarmament-fora/1com/1com17/statements/4Oct_France.pdf; http://statements.unmeetings.org/media2/7662311/france.pdf.
42 Statement by Russia at the First Committee of the UN General Assembly on 27 October 2016, available at www.un.org/press/en/2016/gadis3563.doc.htm.
43 US Statement on 2 May 2014, available at www.reachingcriticalwill.org/images/documents/Disarmament-fora/npt/prepcom14/statements/2May_US.pdf.

44 Statement by Germany on 22 February 2016, available at www.unog.ch/__80256 ee600585943.nsf/(httpPages)/5ee5df8a4a4bfd97c1257fb60054c6ce?OpenDocument &ExpandSection=3%2C2#_Section3.
45 Statement by Australia on 22 February 2016, available at www.unog.ch/__80256 ee600585943.nsf/(httpPages)/5ee5df8a4a4bfd97c1257fb60054c6ce?OpenDocument &ExpandSection=3%2C2#_Section3.
46 Statement by Poland in the Open-Ended Working Group on 9 May 2016, available at www.reachingcriticalwill.org/images/documents/Disarmament-fora/OEWG/2016/Statements/09May_Poland.pdf.
47 Statement by the Netherlands on 14 October 2016, available at www.reachingcriticalwill.org/images/documents/Disarmament-fora/1com/1com16/statements/14Oct_Netherlands.pdf.
48 See Department of Foreign Affairs and Trade, "Australia's Nuclear Non-Proliferation and Disarmament Policy".
49 Joint Statement delivered by Australia on behalf of 17 States, at the First Committee of the UN General Assembly, 21 October 2013.
50 See Chapter 4.
51 Ibid., see also Cesar Jaramillo, "Six Deceptive Arguments Against a Nuclear Weapons Ban", in *OpenCanada*, 31 March 2017, available at www.opencanada.org/features/six-deceptive-arguments-against-nuclear-weapons-ban/.
52 Statement by France at the First Committee of the UN General Assembly, 14 October 2016.
53 Statement by the US Delegation at the First Committee of the UN General Assembly on 14 October 2016, available at http://statements.unmeetings.org/media2/7662304/usa.pdf.
54 Statement by France at the First Committee of the UN General Assembly on 14 October 2016.
55 Joint Statement by China, France, Russia, UK and US to the 2015 NPT Review Conference on 30 April 2015.
56 Statement by US at the First Committee of the UN General Assembly, 12 October 2016, available at https://2009-2017.state.gov/t/avc/rls/2015/248112.htm.
57 Statement by Russia at the First Committee of the UN General Assembly on 3 October 2016; see also Chapter 4.
58 Joint Press Statement from France, UK and US after the adoption of the TPNW on 7 July 2017, available at https://usun.usmission.gov/joint-press-statement-from-the-permanent-representatives-to-the-united-nations-of-the-united-states-united-kingdom-and-france-following-the-adoption/.
59 Statement by Russia in the Conference on Disarmament on 22 August 2017, available at https://undocs.org/CD/PV.1425.
60 See Christopher Ford, "'The Politics of Arms Control' Getting Beyond Post-Cold War Pathologies and Finding Security in a Competitive Environment", speech at International Institute of Strategic Studies, 11 February 2020, available at www.state.gov/the-psychopolitics-of-arms-control/.
61 See Chapter 3.
62 Statement by France at the First Committee of the UN General Assembly on 14 October 2016.
63 Joint Press Statement from France, UK and US After the Adoption of the TPNW on 7 July 2017.
64 See for example Foreword by David Cameron and Nick Clegg, "Securing Britain in an Age of Uncertainty: The Strategic Defence and Security Review", Cm 7948. Cabinet Office, October 2010, p. 5, available at https://assets.publishing.service.gov.uk/government/uploads/system/uploads/attachment_data/file/62482/strategic-defence-security-review.pdf.

65 US Statement by the US delegation at the First Committee of the UN General Assembly on 14 October 2016.
66 See Adam Mount and Richard Nephew, "A Nuclear Weapons Ban Should First Do No Harm", in *Bulletin of the Atomic Scientist*, 7 March 2017, available at https://thebulletin.org/2017/03/a-nuclear-weapons-ban-should-first-do-no-harm-to-the-npt/#.
67 See Christopher Ford, Briefing on the TPNW, Carnegie Endowment for International Peace on 22 August 2017, available at https://carnegieendowment.org/2017/08/22/briefing-on-nuclear-ban-treaty-by-nsc-senior-director-christopher-ford-event-5675.
68 UK Statement Following the Conclusion of Negotiations at the United Nations on a Treaty Prohibiting Nuclear Weapons on 7 July 2017.
69 Statement by Russia in the Conference on Disarmament on 22 August 2017, available at https://undocs.org/CD/PV.1425.
70 See Thomas Hajnoczi, "The Relationship Between the NPT and the TPNW", in *Journal for Peace and Nuclear Disarmament*, 11 March 2020, available at https://doi.org/10.1080/25751654.2020.1738815.
71 The "Irish Resolution", submitted to the UN General Assembly in 1958 is widely regarded as the forerunner of the Nuclear Nonproliferation Treaty (NPT); see for example https://nsarchive.gwu.edu/briefing-book/nuclear-vault/2018-10-29/60th-anniversary-irish-resolution-forerunner-npt; South Africa acceded to the NPT as a non-nuclear weapon state in 1991 and entered into a safeguards agreement, including the Additional Protocol, with the International Atomic Energy Agency (IAEA) the same year; see for example available at www.nti.org/analysis/articles/south-africa-nuclear-disarmament/.
72 See Ramesh Thakur, "Nuclear Disarmament, the NPT and the Ban Treaty: Proven Ineffectiveness Versus Unproven Normative Potential", in *NAPSNet Policy Forum*, 9 January 2018, available at https://nautilus.org/napsnet/napsnet-policy-forum/nuclear-disarmament-the-npt-and-the-ban-treaty-proven-ineffectiveness-versus-unproven-normative-potential/.
73 Ibid.
74 See also Chapter 5.
75 Explanation of Vote by The Netherlands on 7 July 2017, available at www.permanentrepresentations.nl/latest/news/2017/07/07/explanation-of-vote-of-ambassador-lise-gregoire-on-the-draft-text-of-the-nuclear-ban-treaty.
76 Christopher Ford, Briefing on the TPNW, Carnegie Endowment for International Peace.
77 For more information see "IAEA Safeguards Overview: Comprehensive Safeguards Agreements and Additional Protocols", available at www.iaea.org/publications/factsheets/iaea-safeguards-overview.
78 Eirini Giorgou, "Safeguards Provisions in the Treaty on the Prohibition of Nuclear Weapons", in *Arms Control Law*, 11 April 2018, available at https://armscontrollaw.com/2018/04/11/safeguardsprovisionsinthetreatyontheprohibitionofnuclearweapons/.
79 See IAEA Safeguards Overview: Comprehensive Safeguards Agreements and Additional Protocols.
80 Interview with a diplomat conducted by the author on 30 April 2020.
81 Giorgou, "Safeguards Provisions in the Treaty on the Prohibition of Nuclear Weapons".
82 See Chapter 5.
83 Statement by UN High Representative for Disarmament Affairs, Izumi Nakamitsu, at the Closing of the TPNW Negotiations on 7 July 2017, available at www.un.org/disarmament/tpnw/webcast-english.html.

84 The "Forum shopping" accusation means that a state might sign on to a ban treaty that lacks non-proliferation safeguards in order to avoid the more burdensome NPT requirements for international monitoring and transparency, which might allow them latitude to withdraw from the NPT. See for example Adam Mount and Richard Nephew "A nuclear weapons ban should first do no harm".
85 Nick Ritchie, "A Hegemonic Nuclear Order: Understanding the Ban Treaty and the Power Politics of Nuclear Weapons", in *Contemporary Security Policy*, 2019, available at https://doi.org/10.1080/13523260.2019.1571852.
86 Statement by Russia in the Conference on Disarmament on 22 August 2017.
87 Statement from UN Secretary General Kofi Annan on 22 April 2013, available at www.un.org/press/en/2013/sgsm14968.doc.htm.
88 Christopher Ford, Briefing on the TPNW, Carnegie Endowment for International Peace, on 22 August 2017.
89 Giorgou, "Safeguards Provisions in the Treaty on the Prohibition of Nuclear Weapons".
90 Ibid.
91 Paul Meyer and Tom Sauer, "The Nuclear Ban Treaty: A Sign of Global Impatience", in *Survival*, vol. 60, no. 2, 2018, 61–72, available at https://doi.org/10.1080/00396338.2018.1448574.
92 Incidentally, the Chemical Weapons Convention does not even include the clarifying reference "notwithstanding Article I".
93 See for example Carnegie Endowment for International Peace, Christopher Ford, Briefing on the TPNW on 22 August 2017.
94 On 10 January 2003, North Korea announced that it was withdrawing from the PT and that its withdrawal from the NPT left it free from the binding force of its IAEA Safeguards Agreement.
95 See Chapter 15.
96 See also Chapter 5.
97 Per 1 February 2021, 52 States have ratified the TPNW and 86 have signed it.
98 See Chapter 4.
99 See Chapter 4, In most cases, there is only anecdotal evidence of these campaigns as are no public records and officials from States at the receiving end of these diplomatic demarches are mostly reluctant to speak openly about them. One exception is Sweden, where a classified letter by then-US Secretary of Defence to his Swedish counterpart was leaked in August 2017 following Sweden's vote in support of the adoption of the TPNW one month earlier. In this letter, Sweden was warned that accession to the TPNW would "adversely affect Swedish defence cooperation with the US and with NATO". See also available at www.icanw.org/sweden.
100 The full text of the US communication sent to States during the course of October 2020 is available in, Tariq Rauf, "Nuclear-Armed States Panic as Nuclear Weapons Prohibition Treaty Becomes International Law", in *InDepthNews*, 26 October 2020, available at www.indepthnews.info/index.php/opinion/3940-nuclear-armed-states-panic-as-nuclear-weapons-prohibition-treaty-becomes-international-law.
101 The author recalls for example an exchange at a Wilton Park Non-Proliferation Conference in December 2019, when one ambassador from a TPNW supporting State responded to yet another statement from a nuclear weapon State representative that the TPNW damages the NPT by exclaiming: "How often do you want us to say that we support the NPT? This is like an abusive husband who needs to hear that we love him anyway".
102 The "Humanitarian Sector" broadly refers to humanitarian aid and emergency response actors and organisations in States, International Organisations and NGOs.

103 See the description of the three conferences on the humanitarian impact of nuclear weapons, in Chapter 2; see also See also John Borrie and Tim Caughley, *An Illusion of Safety: Challenges of Nuclear Weapon Detonations for United Nations Humanitarian Coordination and Response*, UNIDIR, 2014.
104 See Craig Howard Campbell and Jan Ruzicka, "The Nonproliferation Complex", in *Ethics and International Affairs*, 2013, p. 336, available at https://doi.org/10.1017/S0892679413000257.
105 See Edward Thompson, "Exterminism and Cold War", in *New Left Review, Exterminism and Cold War*, Verso Editions, 1982, p. 20.
106 Interview by the author with a security policy researcher who is sympathetic to the TPNW on 1 May 2020.

Part IV
TPNW impact and outlook

8 What does the TPNW represent and what is its impact?

"Nuclear weapon States can no longer claim that their possession of nuclear weapons has international approval and legitimacy – and that this will continue unchanged into the future".[1]

Both the genesis of the Humanitarian Initiative and the process leading to the TPNW present interesting chapters in the history of nuclear diplomacy. The successful pursuit, by a majority of States, of a legal prohibition on nuclear weapons, against the determined opposition of the most powerful States, represents a radical shift in multilateral diplomacy on nuclear weapons, a policy field heretofore dominated by those few powerful States. It is a significant development and a challenge to the nuclear order because the Humanitarian Initiative and the TPNW change the ways in which nuclear weapons are dealt with in international affairs.

The Humanitarian Initiative and the TPNW have exposed the pre-existing divisions in the international community on nuclear weapons and nuclear disarmament and challenged the nuclear order. This has yet to result in much change of the actual behaviour or policies of nuclear weapon States. To date, the Humanitarian Initiative and the TPNW represent possibilities or rather opportunities and a clear mandate for change. They represent a "fork in the road" for global efforts to deal with nuclear weapons.

It is too early to assess the long-term significance and impact of the Humanitarian Initiative and the TPNW on the nuclear weapons discourse and the policies of nuclear armed States. This can only be determined over time. The level of legal and political support that the new norm attracts will provide a useful marker to assess its impact. Another gauge will be to what extent, if at all, the TPNW's underlying arguments permeate into the political and security discourse in nuclear armed States and nuclear umbrella States and bring about change to nuclear weapon policies. This would require a broader societal discussion on nuclear weapons and of nuclear deterrence in those States, which, in turn, will be influenced by the support and strength the TPNW norm gathers. Can the TPNW play a transformative role in achieving the goal of a world without nuclear weapons? Or, is it a determined but ultimately unsuccessful attempt by a majority of

States to counter an inevitable trend towards a new and possibly even more dangerous nuclear arms race among the major military powers?

This chapter explores some of these different possibilities and trends. It assesses the divergence in the nuclear weapons debate and addresses the, in my view, profound shift the Humanitarian Initiative and the TPNW represent. It discusses the impact on the nuclear weapons discourse that is already discernible from these initiatives. The chapter considers their possible longer-term influence on the nuclear weapons regime and the overall prospects for multilateralism in this field.

The deepening divide

While nuclear weapons and nuclear disarmament have always been very contested issues,[2] the divide in the international community on these issues has deepened since 2011 over the Humanitarian Initiative and in 2017, over the TPNW. The divergences are profound, and it may now be impossible to brush over them in the international nuclear weapons debate.

Firstly, there is division over the way the nuclear weapons issue is addressed in multilateral fora. This is especially felt in the structures of the NPT-based nuclear disarmament and non-proliferation regime which are perceived by those on the one side of the divide as hierarchical and undemocratic. This phenomenon might be referred to as a democratic divide. Secondly, there is division over the rationale for nuclear disarmament. Here we see differences of understanding in what constitutes nuclear disarmament and why, under which conditions, and with what degree of urgency it should be pursued. Thirdly, there is a fundamental divergence of perspectives on the security value of nuclear weapons and the practice of nuclear deterrence. The Humanitarian Initiative and the TPNW are pertinent to all three aspects.

Democracy and disarmament

One of the key objectives of the Humanitarian Initiative was to re-frame the nuclear weapons discourse in a humanitarian direction. This would make the discourse more accessible, for more States, and for a broader set of stakeholders than the usual restricted circle of security policy experts. In the years 2011–2017, the Humanitarian Initiative, through its many and varied efforts, did provide a framework with which to address nuclear weapons from the perspective of humanitarian consequences and risks. As a result, the character of the nuclear weapons debate changed. It became more inclusive.

Many more States, including those that usually take a less visible role or voice in multilateral disarmament efforts, participated in and made substantive contributions to these discussions.[3] A diplomat who did not feel comfortable engaging in a discussion on nuclear deterrence doctrine in the past, now had a set of pertinent points to make regarding the consequences on food security, public health or the economy of his/her country that a nuclear weapon explosion would have. States were now equipped to argue more clearly and more forcefully that they too have a justified stake in the nuclear weapons debate, given the fact that they too will suffer the consequences and risks of a nuclear weapon explosion.

A focus on human security provided non-nuclear weapon States with additional arguments with which to oppose nuclear weapons. The possession of these weapons by nine nuclear armed States and the lack of progress on nuclear disarmament pose legitimate security concerns and perceptions of threat also in non-nuclear weapon States. While these concerns existed and were known before, the Humanitarian Initiative articulated them and brought them into sharper focus. As a result, a security debate conducted solely in and between nuclear armed States and their allies has become unacceptable. The non-nuclear weapon States can no longer be disenfranchised; the human security of all must be considered. Stressing the human security of all enables non-nuclear weapon States to articulate a different case, based on their own valid security needs. This has the potential to cut through in a way that the tired, oft-repeated demands for nuclear weapon States to follow through with their NPT disarmament promises has never done. As discussed in Chapter 7,[4] nuclear weapon States and nuclear umbrella States find it difficult to provide credible counterarguments to these humanitarian consequence and risk arguments and choose to deflect from, rather than engage in, this discussion.

Another striking, if not defining characteristic of the entire process leading to the TPNW was the openness to and involvement of civil society organisations and academia, in which ICAN played a pivotal role. In other multilateral fora where nuclear weapons are discussed, the participation of civil society organisations is much more restricted, such as for example in the Conference on Disarmament. In the three humanitarian conferences, the meetings of the open-ended working group and the TPNW negotiations, NGOs and academic experts' participation and contributions were invited and welcomed. Not only did this contribute to a dynamic atmosphere in these meetings, it also reflected an understanding by a majority of States, that nuclear weapons necessitate a broad and societal discourse that also involves stakeholders beyond the confines of the diplomatic and security policy expert community.

In 2011, the UN High Representative for Disarmament, Sergio Duarte told the UN First Committee of the General Assembly that the

> evidence that democracy is coming to disarmament is 'indisputable' in light of the actions by mayors, grass-roots organizations and civil society groups in promoting progress in nuclear disarmament. . . . It is apparent in the persisting and growing expectations voiced in the General Assembly for new progress in disarmament.[5]

It is probably too much to say that democracy has "come to nuclear disarmament" through the Humanitarian Initiative and the TPNW. The nuclear disarmament and non-proliferation regime, as epitomized by the NPT and the Conference on Disarmament, remains hierarchical and discriminatory. Fierce opposition to these initiatives on the part of the nuclear weapon States is evidence of their unwillingness to accept any change to the status quo. Nevertheless, the

Humanitarian Initiative and the TPNW represent a democratic *shift* in the nuclear weapons debate that was long overdue. Firstly, non-nuclear weapon States have been prepared to pursue their interests through the UN General Assembly, the central democratic body of the United Nations, and seek a mandate for the TPNW negotiations and conclude this Treaty. Secondly, the comprehensive and unequivocal prohibition of nuclear weapons in the TPNW, containing no exceptions for any actor, are a further manifestation of the demand for a more egalitarian approach to nuclear weapons.

Multi-stakeholder participation is more in line with the ways in which other global issues are addressed internationally today, such as climate change, sustainable development, the environment, or global health. The nuclear weapons debate in the traditional multilateral nuclear weapons fora looks anachronistic and reminiscent of the Cold War. It is undemocratic in comparison with the debate on other global topics and non-nuclear weapons States are no longer prepared to accept that it is conducted in this manner. Support for the Humanitarian Initiative and the TPNW is unequivocal evidence of this. Nuclear weapons are an existential threat to the survival of all humankind and should be dealt with as such. These weapons are not only a national security prerogative of a select few States. We watch with interest to see how the nuclear weapon States react and respond to our demands for more democracy in the nuclear weapons debate, as their response will largely determine the future of the multilateral nuclear disarmament and non-proliferation regime.

Is nuclear disarmament a priority, or not?

As discussed in the previous chapters, fundamental differences exist in the international community over how nuclear disarmament and the implementation of NPT Article VI should proceed. Moreover, a significant trust and credibility deficit has built up over time among non-nuclear weapon States regarding the sincerity and urgency with which the goal of nuclear disarmament is being pursued.[6] This deficit is increased by the failure of the nuclear weapon States to implement their disarmament commitments and obligations, notably those contained in the 2010 NPT Action Plan and by the alarming fact that all nuclear armed States are currently engaged in nuclear weapons modernisation and upgrading programmes. The allocation of significant budget resources to these programmes in recent years, indicates more than anything else, the intent of maintaining nuclear weapon and nuclear deterrence for a long time to come.[7] This is particularly pronounced in the modernization programmes taking place in the US and Russia against the background of a deteriorating bilateral relationship.[8] Together, these two States own over 90 percent of all global nuclear weapons. Even though the US currently denies it,[9] it is difficult not to assess these modernisation programmes as anything other than a new nuclear arms race.[10] Recent years have also seen a marked increase in dangerous nuclear rhetoric, as well as outright threats to use nuclear weapons.[11] Rising geopolitical tensions between nuclear-armed States is noticeable as is a general re-emphasis of the importance of nuclear weapons in those States.

As proof of progress on nuclear disarmament, nuclear weapon States tend to invoke their general affirmation of the goal of nuclear disarmament (once a future security environment allows it), a limited reduction in numbers of warheads, or other complementary steps such as increased transparency or confidence building measures.[12] As important as these steps are, for non-nuclear weapon States, this approach to nuclear disarmament is hardly credible anymore.[13]

How can nuclear disarmament be made an urgent priority when nuclear armed States deem their nuclear weapons essential to the maintenance of international peace and security? Could they ever consider "real" nuclear disarmament, as it would strip them from what they consider their "ultimate security guarantee".[14] As long as nuclear weapons are considered essential, it is difficult to see these States wanting to take transformative steps to move away from relying on these weapons and towards a security environment in which they no longer consider these weapons as necessary.[15] Hence nuclear disarmament is mired in an unsolvable contradiction, managed conceptually by viewing nuclear disarmament as an aspirational goal, achievable in a peaceful, but as yet wholly undefined international security environment in a distant future.[16]

Different perspectives on nuclear disarmament have existed since the entry into force of the NPT in 1970. The adverse developments of recent years have strengthened the non-nuclear weapon States' perceptions of discontent and disenfranchisement with the nuclear status quo. As a consequence, the idea of adherence to Article VI of the NPT and an associated disarmament process has effectively ceased. It is now difficult to uphold the notion that all NPT State parties share a broadly compatible interpretation of the objective of nuclear disarmament and of what the disarmament obligation of Article VI means in concrete terms. Credible nuclear disarmament requires taking discernible steps away from a reliance on nuclear weapons as a foundation for security. No credible and transformational, let alone urgent steps, are forthcoming from the nuclear weapon States.

The reasons why a norm-setting approach to prohibiting nuclear weapons through the TPNW emerged as a viable route forward for a majority of non-nuclear weapons States are twofold: firstly, it was the only potentially transformational step achievable without the engagement of the nuclear armed States. Secondly, it emerged precisely because nuclear weapon States were themselves unable or unwilling to demonstrate the necessary sense of urgency and leadership for nuclear disarmament, let alone formulate any vision of how a world without nuclear weapons could be achieved.

The adoption of the TPNW is a legally binding clarification on the part of the non-nuclear weapon States that nuclear disarmament is an urgent priority and that the implementation of disarmament obligations and commitments by the nuclear weapon States has been far from satisfactory or credible. Obfuscation of this fact and vague and the issuing of aspirational affirmations regarding nuclear disarmament will no longer be satisfactory.

What are the consequences of this deepening rift and why does it even matter, given that the divide on nuclear disarmament has, in reality, always been there? It matters because this rift is problematic for the future of the multilateral nuclear disarmament, arms control and non-proliferation regime and the NPT in particular. Despite its weaknesses, this regime continues to enjoy strong support in the international community. This still holds true but cannot be taken for granted. Ultimately, the value of and support for legal frameworks is not set in stone. Such frameworks need to be continuously reconfirmed and be grounded in a core understanding of credibility and fairness that is shared among States. There is for every international treaty a finite level of inconsistencies, contradictions or credibility deficits that can be absorbed, before the fundamental equilibrium is disturbed.[17] The so-called nuclear disarmament pillar of the NPT may have now reached such a crossroads.

The TPNW is intended to give urgency to nuclear disarmament and to strengthen and shore up support for the NPT and the nuclear disarmament and non-proliferation regime as a whole. Thus far, there are few signs that the message of the TPNW has been received by the nuclear weapon States and is creating a heightened sense of urgency for nuclear disarmament. Their reactions are predominantly dismissive and/or hostile.[18] Regrettably, this also demonstrates that the continued reliance on nuclear weapons counts much more than the maintenance of the global norms of the NPT and the nuclear disarmament and non-proliferation regime. The further loss of legitimacy and a potential disintegration of the nuclear disarmament and non-proliferation regime should be of concern to all. As long as the contradictions and double standards of the nuclear disarmament issue are not addressed and resolved, the danger to the integrity of these crucial global norms and multilateral frameworks will grow.

The challenge to nuclear deterrence

Assessments of the security value of nuclear weapons and the practice of nuclear deterrence vary amongst States. The TPNW has provided legal clarification on these topics as it prohibits the use and the threat of use of nuclear weapons under any circumstances. Irrespective of the question of whether the TPNW becomes customary international law,[19] it is no longer possible to argue – or to pretend – that a policy of nuclear deterrence based on the threat of inflicting unacceptable humanitarian devastation, is considered legal or legitimate by a majority of States. The Humanitarian Initiative and the TPNW have provided a rationale, not only for the legal consideration of nuclear weapons and the practice of nuclear deterrence, but also to challenge the very substantive foundation on which the nuclear deterrence calculus is based. The impact of the humanitarian consequences and risk arguments on the security value calculus of nuclear weapons may well prove the most significant long-term impact of the Humanitarian Initiative and the TPNW. A broader discussion on nuclear deterrence and the security value of nuclear weapons, in light of their humanitarian consequences and risks, now needs to be taken forward with urgency.

Humanitarian consequences of nuclear weapons: what does this mean in concrete terms?

Nuclear deterrence rests on the credible threat of inflicting unacceptable destruction on an adversary. The mutual knowledge of vulnerability to such destruction, enforces restraint and rational behaviour on everyone, so the theory goes. Nuclear deterrence requires credible nuclear strike and counter-strike capabilities "to impose costs on an adversary that would be unacceptable and far outweigh the benefits that any adversary could hope to achieve".[20] It also requires that all actors believe in the resolve that nuclear weapons would be used. Without the double credibility of both capabilities and resolve, nuclear deterrence theory does not work. At the same time, all nuclear weapon States assume, believe and hope, that the threat alone will suffice to deter and that these capacities will never have to be deployed, leading to "the crazy reality that nuclear deterrence is a scheme for making war less probable by making it more probable".[21] As the key tenets of nuclear deterrence are the threat of use and the actual use of nuclear weapons, rather than assuming non-use, it is important and warranted to consider the full range of concrete implications and consequences of actual nuclear weapons explosions.

A lot has been done in the context of the Humanitarian Initiative to present new research and to provide new facts and findings of what the actual humanitarian consequences of nuclear weapons explosions would be. Arguably, the most important new findings come from research into climate change. The findings on temperature drop and consequent large-scale global famine as a result of even a limited nuclear war,[22] are highly influential new contributions to the humanitarian discourse.[23] New scientific research has considered the impact on health from a nuclear weapons explosion, including the gender dimension,[24] as well as on the environment, socioeconomic development, migratory movements, food security, social cohesion and the global economy.[25] More research is needed to better understand how the different consequences would interrelate. The "Humanitarian Pledge" recognised the complexity and the possible interrelationship of these different consequences and the subsequent TPNW is a particular legal response to these findings. One can agree or disagree with the legal dimension of the TPNW, but as the research and the findings on the consequences of nuclear explosions are based on empirically demonstrable facts, they should be considered seriously in any cost-benefit analysis underpinning prevailing assumptions on nuclear deterrence. The breadth of consequences and the risks of nuclear weapons should be weighed against the posited security benefit of nuclear weapons. What is the *balance of probability* between the belief that nuclear weapons deter and prevent large-scale wars and the knowledge that deterrence, including nuclear deterrence, can fail and the measurable ensuing humanitarian and other consequences?

If the short-, mid- and long-term consequences of nuclear weapon explosions and the interrelationship of these consequences are not only grave but graver than previously realised[26] and not yet fully understood, does this impact on the above-mentioned analysis? What is the impact of these graver humanitarian consequences on the credibility of nuclear deterrence? It could make nuclear deterrence more effective in the sense asserted by the former Australian foreign minister that "the horrendous humanitarian consequences of nuclear weapons are precisely why deterrence has worked".[27] Or, it could undermine nuclear deterrence credibility, because the necessary resolve to use nuclear weapons falters, the graver, more global and interrelated the consequences are. Graver and potentially global consequences mean that the use of nuclear weapons results in unacceptable consequences, including for the State that deploys its nuclear weapons first. Leaving aside the problematic moral and ethical dimension of maintaining such a policy, it simply does not square with the underlying foundation of nuclear deterrence, namely that it is based on the rational behaviour of all actors involved. A credible threat of using nuclear weapons requires a readiness to act in a gravely self-harming or even suicidal manner, so rational analysis could not allow this to happen. This renders any decision to use nuclear weapons irrational, thus, undermining the credibility of the threat. Given the escalatory danger of using nuclear weapons, this also applies to an initial, more limited use of these weapons. If the consequences of nuclear weapons use are gravely harming, if not suicidal, for friend and foe alike, the threat itself becomes *incredible* and the logic of the nuclear deterrence calculus collapses.[28]

Although this reasoning is unlikely to convince nuclear deterrence believers, an important discussion could and should be had about the level of self-inflicted harm that would lead to a "self-deterrence" effect. At what stage and at which level of impact on the economy, public health, migratory movements and food security, or in terms of aggregate combination of such consequences would the equation start to change? What in terms of humanitarian consequences is acceptable and for whom? Are there objective criteria to gauge this and can they be discussed and assessed? In a nuclear conflict, how exactly do the nuclear armed States integrate the humanitarian consequences on their own population, the presumptive opponent's population and on the rest of the world, innocent bystanders to this conflict, into their calculations?

It is relevant to note that nuclear deterrence is discussed predominantly in the abstract. Different threat perceptions and scenarios are assessed and addressed with various nuclear weapons use scenarios as a response. The underlying rationale is based on assumptions of credible threat, mutual restraint and deterrence stability and not that nuclear weapons will actually be used or, at least, not be escalated into a nuclear war. To what extent does nuclear planning go beyond this assumption of non-use and its corollary, namely an abstract consideration of the consequences of the use of nuclear weapons? Are counterforce and countervalue[29] targeting assessments considered in terms of what the consequences on human beings and societies would really mean? Even the horrendous concept of "mutually assured destruction" (MAD) is used colloquially, in the abstract, and as an argument in favour of nuclear deterrence and deterrence stability and its assumed outcome, i.e. the non-use of nuclear weapons. As long as nuclear deterrence and nuclear weapons use scenarios in nuclear doctrines stay in the abstract and remain limited to evaluations of strategic stability and military "necessities", the consideration of the consequences of these weapons is also likely to remain abstract. This abstraction is deliberate.

> In order to make nuclear weapons acceptable to political leaders, public opinion . . . there has been a systematic effort to play down the appalling side effects and 'overkill' problem associated with even the smallest modern nuclear weapons. . . . What is at stake from the failure of nuclear deterrence is the devastation and poisoning of not just the belligerents but potentially most forms of life on Earth.[30]

It is at least possible, if not likely, that the validity of nuclear deterrence as a concept and any cost/benefit analysis of it would be assessed differently, if the breadth of consequences of nuclear explosions were assessed in more concrete terms. The more such concrete assessments involve the participation of practitioners and stakeholders beyond the military and security elites, the greater the potential for change would be. However, as discussed in Chapter 7, despite the Humanitarian Initiative which advocates exactly for this, engagement by the nuclear armed States and their allies in any concrete consideration on the humanitarian consequences remains very limited.

Compliant with international humanitarian law; how exactly?

Nuclear armed States address the legality of the use of nuclear weapons in a limited and predominantly abstract manner. The 1996 Advisory Opinion of the International Court of Justice declared

> the use or threat of use of nuclear weapons to be generally contrary to the rules of international law applicable in armed conflict, and in particular the principles and rules of humanitarian law [but could not] conclude definitively whether the threat or use of nuclear weapons would be lawful or unlawful in an extreme circumstance of self-defence, in which the very survival of a State would be at stake.[31]

Some nuclear weapon States have stated publicly that their plans for using nuclear weapons would observe "the fundamental principles of the Law of Armed Conflict, and will apply the principles of distinction and proportionality and will not intentionally target civilian populations and civilian objects".[32] Others prefer not to engage in this discussion at all.

There are some scenarios in which nuclear weapons use may not automatically amount to a violation of international humanitarian law. This could be the case, for example, in the deployment of nuclear weapons against an aircraft carrier in the middle of the ocean or a nuclear weapon "warning shot" in an uninhabited area. However, these scenarios do not account for the danger and the likelihood that such a use of nuclear weapons would trigger a nuclear escalation. In a nuclear deterrence context, practically all realistic nuclear weapon use scenarios are based on the idea of causing or threatening to cause massive and unacceptable consequences to the adversary. Many scenarios foresee the large-scale destruction of infrastructure and the gravest consequences to non-combatant civilian populations as collateral. The credibility of nuclear deterrence is therefore based – de facto and almost by definition – on the threat of severe violations of international humanitarian law, a point that has been underscored repeatedly by legal experts.[33] Nevertheless, the actual use and targeting policies of nuclear weapons are as much shrouded in secrecy as any assessment as to how the principles of international humanitarian law would be observed in concrete terms. Just as the consideration of the humanitarian consequences of the use of nuclear weapons remain in the abstract, so do declarations of how and in which circumstances such weapons would be used and how this could be undertaken in a lawful manner.

A broader and more transparent discussion on how nuclear weapons could be deployed in compliance with international humanitarian law would probably conclude that only a very narrow range of predominantly *hypothetical* or, at best very limited, scenarios remain, leaving aside the subsequent risks of further nuclear escalation. This discussion would necessarily expose the illegality of most *realistic* scenarios for nuclear weapons use, under today's nuclear deterrence doctrines. Such a discussion should therefore have a significant effect on policy conclusions regarding nuclear deterrence, especially as the extremely curtailed scenarios in which nuclear deployment could possibly be compliant with international humanitarian law would likely lead to a different cost-benefit analysis of nuclear deterrence.

What are the circumstances of extreme self-defence in which international humanitarian law principles would not apply or be overturned, and with which legal reasoning? How exactly do nuclear planners weigh a military target against collateral damage and what are the parameters for this, for example in the case of a major city? Given the probable transboundary consequences of nuclear weapons use, how are the principles of distinction and proportionality applied vis-à-vis populations in third countries that are not party to the conflict? What about the responsibility and the ability to clean up after an accident or use of nuclear weapons and to provide compensation? To what extent is this responsibility included in the decision-making process and in nuclear doctrines in nuclear armed States? Once these issues are discussed in concrete terms – here the humanitarian consequences and the question of the legality of nuclear weapons use naturally converge – the rationalisation of nuclear deterrence and the balance of arguments may shift significantly.

The distinct link between humanitarian consequences and international humanitarian law came to the fore in the context of the Humanitarian Initiative and is the foundation of the TPNW. This link is clearly expressed in its preamble. Again, nuclear armed States, thus far, have not engaged on this *in concerto* discussion. They do not want to take any nuclear scenario "off the table" for fear of weakening the credibility of their nuclear deterrence posture. Ultimately, they must believe that the question of legality will not arise, because the weapons will not actually be used. Given that nuclear deterrence requires the readiness to use these weapons, this is an untenable and disingenuous position.

Weighing the risks of nuclear deterrence

Given the enormous consequences of nuclear weapon explosions, the importance of minimising and eliminating the risks associated with the existence of these weapons cannot be overstated. Nuclear risk reduction is one area which currently receives much international attention and where a higher degree of political convergence seems to exist. Who could possibly be against reducing the risks posed by nuclear weapons? However, here too, we see differing views of what actually constitutes a nuclear risk and, consequently, what nuclear risk reduction should entail. Perceptions of nuclear risk change and different stakeholders assess this risk differently. Views will vary on whether nuclear risk stems from the possession of nuclear weapons, use scenarios, intent, the safety and security of nuclear weapons, the prevention of accidents, from policies and doctrines or from strategic nuclear risks. Moreover, probabilistic assessments about these risks are difficult to make, owing to the limited empirical data available with which to measure them.

One of the key contributions of the Humanitarian Initiative and the TPNW is the increased focus on risks associated with the possession of nuclear weapons and the practice of nuclear deterrence per se, rather than from the actions of individual States. It provides an aggregated view of the nuclear weapons practices of all nuclear armed States and the resulting risk for all of humanity. This defines the perspective of non-nuclear weapon States regarding nuclear risks today.

For non-nuclear weapon States, the grave humanitarian consequences that would result from nuclear explosions, are the risks to which they are exposed, against their will and outside their control. These risks stem from the fact that nine States in the world possess nuclear weapons and the security policies of those States are based on nuclear deterrence. The risks could be realised through deliberate use of nuclear weapons, a miscalculation leading to deterrence failure that results in a nuclear conflict, or indeed any form of accident. Nuclear weapon States' threat perceptions are generally intertwined and mutually reinforcing. Given the conflicts and tensions involving nuclear armed States with multiple deterrence relationships, the potential for escalation with resulting nuclear risks is considerable. Overconfidence in the stability of nuclear deterrence or the perceived need to demonstrate the credibility of nuclear deterrence, at all times, could lead some actors to overly aggressive rhetoric and reckless nuclear posturing, as seen more frequently in recent years.[34]

The Humanitarian Initiative[35] has brought multiple examples of past "near misses" to light, demonstrating the worrying degree to which good fortune or "dumb luck"[36] has prevented nuclear war. While the probability of these situations occurring and the risks materialising is difficult to assess and may be considered low, the risks exist and are certainly very serious given the scale of the consequences.

Nuclear deterrence is therefore seen by non-nuclear weapon States not only as a high-risk practice due to the grave consequences of nuclear weapons but also because it is practiced by humans and relies on machines and processes designed by humans. The risks are inherent in possessing and maintaining nuclear weapons. The actions and the behaviour of one State or one leader in a nuclear armed State may be assessed to be more risk prone than that of another. However, from the perspective of non-nuclear weapon States, these differences are not the central issue. The collective nuclear weapons policies and actions of all nuclear armed States and their allies create an aggregated and interconnected set of global nuclear risks. From this perspective, the nuclear risk lies in the fact that the consequences of these weapons are too catastrophic and existential, the practice of nuclear deterrence too precarious and, consequently, no human being or government should be given or assume such a responsibility. Not surprisingly, the prohibition and elimination of nuclear weapons are considered the gold-standard of risk reduction measures.

With regard to other risk reduction measures, non-nuclear weapon States want to reduce the likelihood of any nuclear weapons explosions whether intentional, inadvertent, unintentional or from accidents owing to human or technical reasons. In addition to progress on nuclear disarmament and the elimination of nuclear weapons, which evidently is the gold-standard, they request measures that take nuclear weapons as far away from use or accidents as possible. Such measures include de-alerting, taking weapons out of operational service, more transparency about postures and actual use scenarios, further reductions of stockpiles, confidence building measures and political and legal steps aimed at strengthening the nuclear disarmament and non-proliferation regime. In the eyes of non-nuclear weapons States, the findings of the Humanitarian Initiative have made these risk reduction measures significantly more urgent.

Nuclear armed States, on the other hand, appear to have a different risk reduction perspective. They look primarily at nuclear risks coming from other nuclear armed States and their impact on the strategic relationship they have with those States. Their perspectives on nuclear risks are conditioned by national security considerations and the primacy of maintaining stable nuclear deterrence relationships.

While there is either limited transparency or none at all regarding the management of nuclear weapons, presumably all of the "nuclear nine" undertake serious efforts to limit nuclear risks. Individually, nuclear armed States will have a certain level of confidence in their own nuclear weapons decision-making procedures and policies and the safety and security of their nuclear weapons stockpile. This level of confidence has thus far led these nine States to conclude that their own nuclear risks are manageable and warranted because of their belief in the benefit and necessity of nuclear deterrence.

The nine nuclear armed States perceive risk in the other, potentially adversarial, nuclear armed States. In this rendering, risk stems from a lack of knowledge of the other's nuclear weapons capabilities, intent and policies, or doubts about decision making processes or security and safety procedures. This perspective has a significant bearing on how risk reduction measures are considered. In addition to preventing the proliferation of nuclear weapons, it gives dominance to "strategic risk reduction"[37] i.e. countering risks that could undermine nuclear deterrence relationships. Risk reduction measures are geared towards avoiding or managing crisis situations and to achieving a better understanding of the policies and intentions between adversaries, so as to maintain stable and less risky deterrence relationships. In short, the focus of this form of risk reduction is to make nuclear deterrence work better, rather than consider the risks of the practice of nuclear deterrence itself.

As such, the range of measures available to reduce nuclear risks is necessarily limited. Risk reduction measures that restrict the ability to use nuclear weapons, such as de-alerting, limiting nuclear weapons postures, a "no first use" declaration[38] or removing nuclear weapons from operations are assessed as having a negative impact on the credibility of nuclear deterrence. This leads to a reluctance among nuclear armed States to consider such measures. Risk reduction measures are considered only insofar as they do not impact the nuclear deterrence calculus. Here we see the inherent contradiction and conundrum posed by the necessity to maintain nuclear weapons in a manner that demonstrates readiness and resolve to always use them, as required for the credibility of nuclear deterrence, and a more comprehensive approach to risk reduction measures aimed at ensuring that they will never be used, intentionally or unintentionally, or through human or technical error.

A good illustration of this conundrum can be seen in a notable reluctance to take nuclear weapons off a "launch on warning" alert level. De-alerting has been urged by experts for a long time.[39] Giving decision makers more time in a crisis greatly reduces the danger of miscalculations, when compared to a time-pressured situation and/or faulty information. The "launch on warning" practices

> remain in place today [note: by the US and Russia], they are a continuing source of strategic instability. They run an unacceptable level of nuclear risk, offer inadequate warning and decision time to support rational decision-making, and severely constrain the flexibility of national leaders during crises and conflict.[40]

Nevertheless, taking nuclear weapons off a high-alert status is rejected by these nuclear weapon States. In a crisis, so the argument goes,[41] nuclear weapon States would want to put nuclear weapons back on high alert so as to not be vulnerable to an attack, resulting in a "re-alerting race", which could effectively exacerbate the crisis. This leads them to the conclusion that it would be better to keep nuclear weapons permanently "on high alert" rather than "de-alerting" them. For non-nuclear weapon States, this demonstrates the worrying and overarching imperative for nuclear armed States of maintaining the perceived credibility of nuclear deterrence at all costs, which trumps all other risk reduction considerations.

Emerging technologies such as cyber weapons, hypersonic weapons and artificial intelligence (AI) in weapons systems add yet more layers of risk.

The extent to which these technologies could exacerbate (strategic) nuclear risks and negatively impact nuclear deterrence stability is currently a subject of intense debate.[42] There is widespread agreement on both sides of the disarmament/deterrence argument that the implications of these technologies for nuclear deterrence and strategic stability are likely to be considerable; the conclusions from this differ somewhat. For sceptics of nuclear deterrence, these emerging technologies increase existing concerns regarding the security calculation on which nuclear deterrence is based as they "heighten the existing risks of nuclear weapons use, in both predicted and unpredicted ways. As emerging technologies are increasingly incorporated in military operations, the potential for unintended consequences or mistakes will continue to grow".[43] Supporters of nuclear deterrence focus primarily on the impact of emerging technologies on strategic stability and, consequently, on how best to integrate and rationalise these challenges into existing (nuclear) deterrence concepts.[44] Wherever one stands on this issue, the emerging technologies have undeniably added another layer of risks to the nuclear weapons debate.

The Humanitarian Initiative and the TPNW have brought the nuclear risk issue to the fore but the nuclear armed States have yet to engage on the broader nuclear risk dimension and on the consequent risk reduction measures that are required. The TPNW is underpinned by an assessment of the humanitarian and other consequences of nuclear weapons explosions and the legality of nuclear weapons use scenarios in a concrete, rather than abstract, manner. Nuclear risks are considered from the perspective of the aggregate risks stemming from the possession of these weapons and the practice of nuclear deterrence by all nuclear armed States. Scrutiny of the consequences, legality and risks associated with nuclear weapons, leads to the legal, ethical and rational conclusions contained in the TPNW. These reject arguments that posit the security value of nuclear weapons and/or find wisdom in maintaining the practice of nuclear deterrence.

Assumptions and beliefs in the disarmament/deterrence divide

Nuclear deterrence is credited by its advocates of having "helped maintain peace between the great powers and have not led their few other possessors into military adventures".[45] Its rationale as "guarantor" for international security and stability and as the "ultimate insurance policy"[46] for nuclear armed States remains, today, the backbone of defence policies of all nuclear armed States and their allies. Extended nuclear deterrence, such as US nuclear security guarantees to nuclear umbrella States is also intended to convince an "allied government it does not need to develop weapons of mass destruction".[47]

At the same time, the soundness of nuclear deterrence theory has been contested and critiqued since its inception. One of the key arguments against it is on moral and ethical grounds,[48] given the destructive and indiscriminate characteristics of nuclear weapons. The effectiveness of nuclear deterrence in preventing major

What the TPNW represents and its impact 201

conflict or nuclear war and having maintained a "long nuclear peace"[49] is also questioned: the evidence is at best anecdotal and impossible to prove, whereas several actual examples show that nuclear weapons have not deterred conflicts involving nuclear armed states or even deterred non-nuclear armed States from attacking nuclear armed States.[50]

Nuclear deterrence theory's assumption of a universal rationality is also challenged as "irredeemably flawed"[51] given that one "simply do(es) not know whether a common rationality will hold among the decision-makers involved to prevent nuclear weapon use".[52] In addition, an "adversary may not be the rationally calculating actor presupposed in the deterrence scenario".[53] When compared with the bi-polarity of the Cold War,[54] the nine nuclear actors of today increase the complexity of nuclear deterrence, at the same time as the relevance of nuclear weapons and the effectiveness of nuclear deterrence to address the security threats of the twenty-first century is ever more doubtful.[55]

How can these diametrically opposed perspectives be reconciled? What is the prudent and less risky course of action? Betting on a precarious nuclear deterrence-based stability under the *sword of Damocles*[56] with the risks of potentially catastrophic consequences for all, or face the potentially higher risks of instability and large-scale war in a world without nuclear deterrence? Is the "nuclear quiet" preferable to a more "nervous world", as Schelling[57] has suggested? Or does prudence demand the urgent removal of the existential threat of nuclear weapons, since a world without them is in any case safer, as the TPNW contends?

The majority of non-nuclear weapon States supporting the Humanitarian Initiative and the TPNW have given their clear answer to this question. This answer is not based on definite proof but comes after weighing the risks, uncertainties and possible outcomes. It concludes that the humanitarian consequences of nuclear weapons explosions are grave and potentially existential and the risks of their deliberate, inadvertent or accidental use are unclear but considerable and certainly not negligible. On balance, they have found that nuclear weapons threaten the security of all much more than their presumed security value adds to it. When weighing the different contingencies, States that rely on nuclear weapons thus far reach the opposite conclusion. Nuclear weapons are what has been described as a "wicked problem",[58] one in which there is agreement neither on the problem itself, nor on its solution. These seemingly irreconcilable differences are argued forcefully along the nuclear disarmament – nuclear deterrence divide with no resolution in sight.

There is one important aspect where a degree of convergence exists however, namely that no definitive proof exists for either side of the argument. It can neither be proven that deterrence has worked in the past or will work in the future, just as much as it cannot be proven that it has not prevented large scale conflict in the past or will not do so in the future. Moreover, how would a deterrence "success" in any particular crisis scenario prove that in the next, different one, it would work again? Sceptics have characterised nuclear deterrence theory and deterrence stability as "an article of faith" and a "myth".[59] Some nuclear deterrence advocates also acknowledge the "faith dimension" of nuclear deterrence, while reaching the opposite conclusion namely that

> all nuclear weapons possessors in the real world – and a good many of their friends and allies – seem to think deterrence works, and they indeed have long acted as if it does. Even if we believe in nuclear deterrence only in the same sense that Pascal famously suggested one should believe in God[60] – that is, because the cost of doing so in error is lower than the cost of not doing so in error – I'd say we have every reason to keep on believing.[61]

Weighing the risks, uncertainties and consequences related to nuclear weapons and nuclear deterrence, against all possible implications for security and humanity's survival, is certainly extremely difficult. A good place to start, however, would be to acknowledge the lack of certainty and proof and the fact that there are no absolutes on either side of the deterrence/disarmament argument. In any case, it should be acknowledged that "like any human belief system nuclear deterrence depends on a nest of assumptions".[62] Given the unparalleled high stakes, these assumptions need to be examined with utmost care. All subjective assessments carry the inherent risk of overconfidence in one's own views, which could lead to confirmation bias and a reluctance to consider alternative arguments, a risk that, again, applies for both sides of the disarmament/deterrence divide. Identifying possible "sources of overconfidence in the controllability and predictability of those futures as well as relabelling the claims of knowing the future as bets"[63] is crucially important. Difficult as it is, the key question is to define what policy conclusions should be drawn from "not knowing", from the fact that in reality, we are dealing with "bets, beliefs and assumptions"? Given the existential threat that nuclear weapons pose to the survival of humanity, a posited belief in nuclear deterrence seems a very unwise wager and students of Pascal had rather ask: "what harm will come to you if you gamble on the truth of nuclear deterrence and it proves false?"

To answer this question, the set of arguments built in the context of the Humanitarian Initiative provide a crucially important contribution. Unlike the predominantly subjective assumptions that underpin the arguments pro or contra nuclear deterrence, the breadth of humanitarian and other consequences of nuclear weapons use can be studied and assessed, as can questions about legal implications of use or threat of use of nuclear weapons. Similarly, a variety of risk drivers and combinations of risks in conjunction with the possession of nuclear weapons and the practice of nuclear deterrence can be identified and analysed. The difficulty lies more in the limited empirical data to measure nuclear weapons risks and the resulting challenges to make predictions about the risks and the likelihood of them coming to pass.

The contentious nature of the debate on the security value of nuclear weapons and on the pros and cons of nuclear deterrence means that it is impossible to convince the other side of one's argument. With regard to stances on nuclear deterrence or disarmament, experience shows a tendency on both sides of the argument to integrate facts into pre-existing constructs and political preferences. Only a transparent, concrete and inclusive discussion, covering all measurable implications, consequences and risks of nuclear weapons would allow a realistic cost/benefit analysis of nuclear deterrence. A more concrete assessment of the *legality* of nuclear weapons use also has the potential to lead to a more objective and less posited consideration of its effectiveness. This would be a discussion that weighs these elements against the assumed security and stability benefits of nuclear deterrence. A broader acknowledgement on the part of all stakeholders of the lack of ultimate proof of the veracity of the assumptions – on either side of the argument – is necessary and would be a major step in the right direction. The Humanitarian Initiative and the TPNW have opened the door for such engagement. The TPNW, in legal force represents a clearly expressed expectation for such a discussion to take place.

Futile or transformative

NPT meetings and the UN General Assembly have certainly been shaken up by the Humanitarian Initiative and the TPNW, making these less comfortable settings for the nuclear weapon States and the nuclear umbrella States. However, there are few signs that the message has been received, neither in the sense of creating a heightened sense of urgency for nuclear disarmament, nor in a willingness to consider the TPNW's underlying rationale and the considerations described above. Nuclear weapons States remain resolutely attached to their belief in nuclear deterrence and the indispensable value of nuclear weapons. It seems that the Humanitarian Initiative and the TPNW have not (yet) reached the nuclear weapons/nuclear deterrence establishment that shapes the relevant policies in these States. Can the TPNW and its human security rationale generate a transformative effect, beyond energising the disarmament-minded non-nuclear weapon States? Ultimately, its relevance will be measured over time and by the extent to which it impacts on the nuclear policies of nuclear weapon States to move away from their reliance on nuclear weapons as an instrument of security.

Two scenarios seem possible: one where the TPNW is notable and determined challenge to the nuclear status quo but is not successful in impacting the resurgence of "nuclearism"[64] and the new and possibly even more dangerous nuclear arms race among the major military powers. A more transformative scenario would be one in which the TPNW leads to greater engagement on the part of the nuclear armed States on the humanitarian consequences, risk and international humanitarian law arguments on which the TPNW is based. The result of this second scenario could be more momentum and more serious efforts to move away from the reliance on these weapons and a serious (re)commitment to the goal of a world without nuclear weapons. Both scenarios will depend on what happens to the momentum created by the TPNW after its entry into force in January 2021. We are now at a crossroads which leads either to opportunities and transformational change or to more of the same and these opportunities for change are missed.

Supporters of the TPNW hope to see a steady growth of States joining the treaty, keeping the momentum going beyond its entry into legal force.[65] It is obvious but necessary to point out that the legal and political weight generated by the treaty is in direct relationship to the number of States who are party to it. Mounting international pressure for the prohibition of nuclear weapons together with continued communication of the humanitarian consequences and risks associated with them, will also lead to more public discourse in nuclear weapon States and nuclear umbrella States. Every additional ratification of the TPNW, even by small States, is an opportunity to demonstrate that a delegitimization of nuclear weapons and nuclear deterrence is taking place and that the TPNW norm is taking hold.

The interplay between multilateral frameworks, such as the United Nations and NPT meetings, where arguments can be made and their strength demonstrated, and national political processes is very important. The role of civil society to bring and keep the TPNW arguments in the public eye is essential. The extent to which this can be achieved will vary between countries. The critical voice of civil society will be heard more in democratic societies than in autocratic ones. It is likely that public discourse in nuclear umbrella States, already more sceptical towards nuclear weapons, will be most open to the humanitarian consequences and risk arguments.[66] In some States that host US nuclear weapons under nuclear sharing arrangements, for example Germany[67] and the Netherlands,[68] an increasing debate on these issues is already taking place. The contradictions between professed support for a world without nuclear weapons and the actual policies of reliance on nuclear weapons and nuclear deterrence is more apparent in those States than in others. These debates take place at the same time as discussions within NATO on the need to strengthen deterrence, including nuclear deterrence owing to heightened threat perceptions regarding Russia[69] and looming fears of a weakening transatlantic alliance.[70]

Supporters of the TPNW calculate that a broader debate on these issues, one outside narrow security policy expert circles, will generate more receptiveness for the argumentation that underpins it. Correspondingly, the growing strength of the norm and the increasing debate on the humanitarian consequences and risks of nuclear weapons, as well as the illegality of their use, will challenge nuclear deterrence tenets and create a positive and transformative political dynamic.

Opponents of the TPNW are intent on limiting the impact of the TPNW, as much as possible. By criticising the TPNW as well as pressuring States not to join the treaty,[71] the nuclear weapons States and nuclear umbrella States hope to weaken its normative, and hence political, impact. The smaller the number of State parties the TPNW gains, the less consequential challenge to the nuclear order remains. As long as the number of State parties remains relatively low, the normative force can be more easily dismissed and political pressures for nuclear disarmament, especially within democratic nuclear umbrella States, can be better withstood. Opponents hope to keep any discussion on the humanitarian consequences and risk arguments of the TPNW at best within the narrow confines of expert circles, and in any case, as far away as possible from the general public. A broad and public discourse beyond the security policy expert community is best avoided. Containing the issue within multilateral frameworks to which the media and the public pay less attention makes this easier.

The national security experts in nuclear weapon States who deal with nuclear weapons, the so-called nuclear weapons establishment, operates quite separately from multilateral nuclear disarmament, arms control and non-proliferation fora. Multilateral diplomacy only plays a secondary or subordinate role to the nuclear weapon States' domestic decision-making processes on nuclear weapons policy and strategy.[72] Nuclear weapon States consider multilateral fora neither relevant nor desirable frameworks in which to hold a discussion on nuclear weapons policy. Since most of the Humanitarian Initiative and the TPNW process took place in these multilateral fora, the exposure of these nuclear weapons establishments to the human security arguments is limited. The perspectives on nuclear weapons policy issues and on nuclear deterrence expressed in multilateral fora by non-nuclear weapon States and civil society organisations are probably considered of little relevance to national nuclear policy decisions. Indeed, the nuclear weapons establishments in nuclear weapon States appear immune to or unpersuaded by arguments of the Humanitarian Initiative and the TPNW thus far.

When non-nuclear weapons States engage in multilateral meetings, they may think that nuclear weapons policies in a broader sense are on the agenda. This belief is mistaken. At these meetings, the diplomats representing nuclear weapon States have no mandate and consequently no particular interest in discussing nuclear deterrence and nuclear weapons policy, things considered strictly national security issues by their governments. Their briefs, priorities and expertise are primarily focussed on non-proliferation and managing and controlling multilateral processes, to ensure that nothing happens, and no decisions taken which run counter to their national interests.

The tactics of the opponents of the TPNW can confidently be said to comprise the following: firstly, to try to keep the TPNW norm as weak as possible by exerting pressure on States not to ratify it. Secondly, to criticise the treaty and keep any discussion of it contained in expert circles where it can be more easily controlled and is less visible to the "outside" world. Lastly, to avoid engaging on the TPNW's underlying humanitarian consequences, risk and international humanitarian law arguments, in order to prevent any public discourse on and possible domestic political challenges to their nuclear weapons policies.

Such tactics, irrespective of whether they are successful, carry the considerable risk of exacerbating the divide in the international community. As long as nuclear weapon States and their allies see the TPNW as an irritant, to be opposed for being contrary to their national interests and their preferred way of handling the nuclear weapons issue at the international/multilateral level, they will not have fully understood the message that these developments represent. It is a message of loss of legitimacy in the nuclear status quo, of loss of credibility in the sincerity with which treaty obligations and commitments on nuclear disarmament are implemented. It is a message of concern about multilateralism and support for a different – human – collective security paradigm. It is also a verdict on current nuclear weapons policies and the practice of nuclear deterrence both of which have been found irresponsible and illegitimate by a large part of the international community.[73] As former UN High Representative for Disarmament Angela Kane stated, "nuclear weapon States can no longer claim that their possession of nuclear weapons has international approval and legitimacy – and that this will continue unchanged into the future".[74]

The consequence of an exclusively dismissive and negative approach is more, not less, acrimony and a deeper divide in the international community. Opponents of the TPNW must weigh the risks involved in maintaining their categorical opposition to it against further undermining their credibility and with it, that of the wider nuclear regime. From their perspective, more constructive engagement with the TPNW's underlying arguments risks the potential negative effects of a wider discussion on nuclear weapons policies and on nuclear deterrence. To date, nuclear weapon States clearly prefer opposition to the TPNW over engagement with its underlying rationale. The perceived security value of their nuclear weapons carries more weight than the perspectives of a large part of the international community and is put ahead of cohesion and support for the global nuclear disarmament and non-proliferation regime.

The Humanitarian Initiative and the TPNW have created a new landscape in the global nuclear weapons discourse. The process that brought the Treaty about and the legal reality that it now represents and binds large parts of the international community to, is evidence of this. Determined efforts to strengthen the significance of this new landscape are ongoing and there are equally determined efforts by those who believe in the security value of nuclear weapons to suppress it. The outcome of this contest of arguments will be determined over time. It is undeniable that the TPNW and its underlying rationale have created new spaces and new opportunities for dialogue and thus moved the dial on nuclear weapons. The TPNW supporters are rightly proud of the historical significance of what they have achieved, given the considerable obstacles they faced and continue to face. They have every reason to look forward to the contest of arguments with confidence, provided that the opponents of these initiatives are prepared to engage in this conversation.

A multilateral outlook

The discourse on nuclear weapons and the contestation around the NPT and the TPNW do not take place in isolation. They are integral elements of wider geopolitical developments and the dynamic environment of international relations. It is increasingly understood that international cooperation is essential to tackle global challenges in an interconnected and globalised world. Climate change, environmental protection, or global health issues, such as the response to the Covid-19 pandemic, are prime examples. Tension exists on most of these issues between multilateral cooperation that achieves mutually beneficial outcomes, and national sovereignty considerations with their narrower, often diverging, national interests. This tension is particularly prominent in the field of security, where state centrism and national security considerations dominate, and shared, cooperative and multilateral security perspectives are much more difficult to achieve. The nuclear weapon issue lies very much at the heart of this tension.

The nuclear weapon issue, rightly understood, is a security challenge for all humanity and a key element of the TPNW's message is a call for a cooperative and multilateral solution to it. This is at odds with the national security prism, through which nuclear armed States and their allies view this issue. Non-nuclear weapon States supported the TPNW specifically to push for progress on the nuclear weapon issue and to keep the multilateral flame alive in the field of nuclear weapons and nuclear disarmament. This is an important signal when all other multilateral nuclear disarmament, arms control and non-proliferation processes and institutions stagnate or are paralysed by great power competition, conflicting priorities and inflexible rules of procedure. Arguably, the support for the TPNW is also evidence for the wish of these States to strengthen the principle of a multilateral, cooperative and international law-based approach to international relations and international security.

What is then the outlook for a multilateral approach to solve the contested nuclear weapons issue and to achieve real progress towards a world without nuclear weapons? Can the TPNW be expected to bring transformative momentum in this direction, when multilateralism is severely challenged in its "normative foundations and its operational capacity"[75] on virtually all global issues? There is ground to be both pessimistic and, at least somewhat, optimistic.

The multilateral glass half empty

Increasing geopolitical competition between major powers and the subsequent negative impact on multilateral frameworks for cooperation provides grounds for pessimism. Multilateralism describes international cooperation between States that leads to the dynamic development of international law and improved conditions and standards of behaviour of States globally. It has been a defining principle in the quest for global peace and prosperity, promoted in particular by the US after World War II. This no longer holds true to the same extent. The US has increasingly relinquished its traditional role as "a benevolent hegemon championing the multilateral system and Western universalism"[76] and in part now openly disavows multilateral institutions and approaches. While this trend may have been most visible under President Trump's "America First" policy of not "entering America into any agreement that reduces our ability to control our own affairs",[77] the US has "long been simultaneously both the lynchpin of multilateral order and deeply sceptical of the project".[78] The US move towards unilateralism takes place against growing geopolitical competition between the US and China, as well as with Russia, both of which "increasingly are working to bring multilateral architecture into closer alignment with their own authoritarian norms".[79] China especially, but also Russia, champion anti-liberal and anti-Western trends and rhetoric.[80] This is part of a growing competition between democratic and authoritarian systems and world views that are opposed to, if not incompatible with, the liberal values on which the multilateral system has been built. The European Union, a traditional promoter of multilateralism, is often internally divided and has, thus far, not been able to assert itself sufficiently on the international scene in order to counterbalance these trends. The same can be said for other regional organisations in Africa, Latin America and Asia. Increasing geopolitical tensions in combination with unilateralist and anti-multilateral trends in the US and growing anti-liberal assertiveness of China and Russia sparks "questions about the very the future of multilateralism"[81] and puts cooperation within multilateral frameworks increasingly at risk.

Multilateral cooperation on disarmament, arms control and non-proliferation is very much impacted by these trends; this is especially true of nuclear weapons. Of late, discussions in relevant multilateral fora such as the First Committee of the UN General Assembly, the NPT or the Conference on Disarmament have seen an increase in aggressive exchanges and frequent spats, in which accusations and recriminations are traded. This more confrontational atmosphere follows 20 years of paralysis and stagnation in the multilateral nuclear disarmament efforts in these fora. The Conference on Disarmament, set up in 1978, is supposed to serve as the "single multilateral disarmament negotiation forum"[82] but has utterly failed to live up to its mandate and has not seen any multilateral negotiations on nuclear disarmament (nor on any other topic) since the mid-1990s. The lack of political will on the part of the nuclear armed States, coupled with different strategic interests and the stringent consensus requirement, makes such negotiations look even more out of reach and hopeless in today's more confrontational geopolitical environment.

Beyond their shared interest of trying to manage and control multilateral processes and to maintain the – for them beneficial – NPT-based hierarchical nuclear status quo,[83] not much in terms of new multilateral ideas or initiatives is to be expected from the US, China or Russia, nor from any other nuclear armed States for that matter. As observed by an expert: "In this situation, the TPNW is a godsend for the nuclear weapon States. It gives them at least something to agree upon".[84] Against the background of these trends and given their opposition to any multilateral pro-nuclear disarmament initiative in recent years, it seems difficult to see how these States will be ready in the foreseeable future to engage constructively in the UN or other multilateral frameworks to achieve progress on nuclear disarmament.

In essence, however, this situation is neither new nor fundamentally different to the multilateral approach the nuclear weapon States/five permanent members of the UN Security Council have always taken. In the past, multilateral initiatives in the disarmament, arms control and non-proliferation fields were promoted and supported by these States essentially for two main reasons. The first reason is that the respective weapons or related activities were no longer considered necessary to their own national security. The second reason is to stop other States getting the weaponry they already have. This is done by establishing legally binding restrictions on the purchase or development of these weapons for anybody except themselves. Once such restrictions are codified through multilateral treaties, their enforcement, including through action of the UN Security Council, becomes the focus, as evidenced for example by the many resolutions in conjunction with the nuclear programmes of North Korea and Iran.[85] In the field of nuclear weapons, support for any multilateral disarmament is hard to find.

The CTBT is an example for both reasons. Only after each of the five nuclear weapon States concluded that they had conducted enough nuclear tests to be able to maintain their arsenals without further testing,[86] were they ready to countenance such a ban. This was in 1996. After their own "security needs" were satisfied, the non-proliferation aspect of prohibiting nuclear weapons development in other States gained importance and facilitated the multilateral negotiation process to codify a prohibition on nuclear testing. Secretary of State Madeleine Albright stated this openly when she made the case for US ratification of the CTBT:

> We have conducted more than 1,000 nuclear tests – hundreds more than anyone else. We do not need more tests to protect our security. Would-be proliferators or modernizers, however, must test if they are to develop the kind of advanced, compact nuclear weapons that are most threatening.[87]

Multilateral nuclear disarmament aspirations, thus, had very little to do with the CTBT. The resurfacing of a debate in the US about the need to resume nuclear testing,[88] underscores this, as does its refusal, thus far, to ratify the treaty.

A similar dynamic can be detected in the long-standing attempts to negotiate a treaty prohibiting the production of fissile material for nuclear weapons (FMCT). The nuclear weapon States like to cite this project as the "next logical step to advance the multilateral nuclear disarmament and non-proliferation agenda".[89] The nuclear weapon States, however, all possess large stockpiles of fissile materials[90] for nuclear weapons, enough to build and replace nuclear weapons long into the future. They oppose the notion of including their existing stocks into negotiations and want to limit the FMCT to the future production of fissile material only. The start of negotiations in the Conference on Disarmament has been blocked by Pakistan for the past several years, which considers its own fissile material stockpile still insufficient for its long-term nuclear weapons programme. Through a multilateral codification of something they no longer need themselves, nuclear weapon States clearly want to retain their own fissile materials while blocking the production and stockpiling for others. Notwithstanding the importance of such a future ban, it has little to do with a commitment to multilateral nuclear disarmament. The start of FMCT negotiations will remain elusive, until such moment when all nuclear armed States feel that their own fissile material stockpile needs are fully met. Or, to put it in another way, the FMCT will become a reality, only when its actual nuclear disarmament value has disappeared, and it has become exclusively a non-proliferation measure.

The much-celebrated disarmament commitments that have been agreed to by consensus in the NPT in 1995, 2000 and 2010 are themselves examples for the, at best, half-hearted commitment to multilateral nuclear disarmament. These commitments are formulated in vague or ambiguous ways and without concrete timelines and benchmarks. They are also hopelessly qualified. Such qualifications are usually made with the seemingly innocuous formulation that disarmament actions should "promote international stability, peace and undiminished and increased security".[91] Since nuclear weapon States decide for themselves how they interpret what "promotes international stability" and what constitutes "undiminished and increased security", any action can be and usually is postponed indefinitely, because the current security environment is always deemed unfit. In reality, these endlessly flexible qualifiers are de facto code to avoid nuclear disarmament and maintain nuclear weapons and nuclear deterrence policies in perpetuity.

While the prospects for multilateralism in the field of nuclear disarmament appear bleak, it can, thus, be argued that multilateral engagement on the part of the nuclear weapon States never really existed, beyond their non-proliferation agenda. This is demonstrated perhaps inadvertently but clearly by the 2018 US Nuclear Posture Review, which criticizes the TPNW as seeking "to inject (sic) disarmament issues into non-proliferation fora, potentially damaging the non-proliferation regime".[92] Pessimism is therefore justly warranted for anyone expecting the nuclear weapon States to promote a multilateral approach to nuclear weapons issues beyond nuclear non-proliferation, let alone to assume a leadership role on nuclear disarmament. Such leadership and grounds for cautious optimism is found elsewhere.

The multilateral glass half full

One reason for cautious optimism is the changing nature of international relations. Despite the Cassandra calls heralding the demise of multilateralism and the undoubtable structural weaknesses of multilateral institutions and processes, the quantity and quality of international cooperation is today, higher than it has ever been. There is virtually no policy field where international and regional frameworks of cooperation have not increased significantly in recent years, facilitated by growing mobility, economic cooperation and communication technologies. This is a logical reflection of the growing understanding that for most issues in today's globalized and interconnected world, sustainable solutions can only be found in a cooperative manner. The magnitude and complexity of pressing global issues such as climate change, global health, migration flows, global economic shocks, environmental degradation, cybersecurity or dealing with humanitarian emergencies, to name but a few, all require international cooperation. In addition to States, non-State actors, international organizations, civil society and advocacy groups, economic actors, such as international corporations, and academic and scientific networks play increasingly prominent and decisive roles in international relations and on global issues. International relations and multilateral cooperation are in a process of change and will see much higher levels of multi-stakeholder participation. This trend is evidenced, for example, by the climate change issue, where efforts at the multilateral level, such as the 2015 Paris Agreement,[93] are complemented by civil society action, local and regional initiatives, changes in corporate practices, and global scientific cooperation. Undoubtedly, the level of awareness and interest in climate change is dramatically higher than it was just a few years ago.

Certainly, many societies experience counter-reactions to these trends towards more international cooperation and witness anti-globalization tendencies that result in populist, protectionist and nationalist strands and policies. In some countries, governments pursue such policies. However, while anti-globalist sentiments and unilateralist policies may be understandable on a human level, they offer no pathway to solve any of those global challenges. There is a certain inevitability towards an overall trend of more, rather than less, international cooperation to address global challenges. This has been underscored in the most indisputable way by the Covid-19 pandemic.

There is no plausible conceptual reason why the issue of nuclear weapons, with its inherent risks to all of humankind, should not be addressed as a global challenge, similarly to climate change. In fact, there is a powerful connection between these two issues.[94] True, security matters and military affairs continue to be predominantly the prerogative of States and State sovereignty, dealt with by a closed circle of security policy experts, but this situation is also in flux. The Humanitarian Initiative and the TPNW are themselves examples of a changing and more dynamic, multi-stakeholder, international environment. With respect to global security issues and in line with other global issues, this dynamism will increase and necessarily also affect the way nuclear weapons are approached. A national security perspective that is based on the mutual assurance of complete destruction with catastrophic global consequences for humankind and the planet will – or at least should – be considered increasingly anachronistic and contestable.

Another reason for cautious multilateral optimism comes from the power of international law and the desire of most States to act within the boundaries of international law and international legitimacy. This is where the TPNW can play a major role. The Treaty makes it crystal clear that the overwhelming majority of States no longer considers the possession of nuclear weapons and the practice of nuclear deterrence to be lawful or legitimate. While the TPNW is only legally binding for its State parties, it can also generate an indirect normative and political impact on States that remain outside of its legal scope. The more the TPNW membership grows and the treaty is implemented, the more legal and political questions relating to nuclear weapons come to the fore. These are questions about the legality of the use or threat of use of nuclear weapons, the applicability of and compliance with international humanitarian law, questions about the actions that would constitute assisting, encouraging or inducing, all of which are prohibited by the TPNW,[95] or the legal issues regarding liability and compensation in the case of nuclear weapons use or accidents, as well as the personal responsibility of decision makers with respect to nuclear weapons.

Even if nuclear weapon States, along with nuclear umbrella States, try to avoid or deflect from this legal discussion, as well as from a broader discussion that weighs the consequences and risks of nuclear deterrence against its assumed security benefits, these questions and issues are present. The TPNW provides a framework to address them, raising the pressure for nuclear weapon States as well as nuclear umbrella States to engage and provide legal and other justifications and counterarguments. As more States join the TPNW, the more problematic an avoidance and "ostrich" approach will become, both internationally, as well as in domestic political discourse. Ideally, a broader, more inclusive, and more intense domestic debate in nuclear weapon States and nuclear umbrella States will now take place.

This debate is particularly relevant for nuclear umbrella States, especially those NATO allies[96] on whose territory US nuclear weapons are stationed. The compatibility of these so-called "nuclear sharing" policies with the non-proliferation provisions contained in Article I and II[97] of the NPT has been frequently challenged.[98] The unambiguous prohibition of nuclear weapons in the TPNW, based on a humanitarian rationale, further raises the pressure on these nuclear umbrella States to justify the compatibility of the practice of nuclear sharing with their own nuclear disarmament obligations under Article VI of the NPT. The NPT was negotiated in the late 1960s. The legal interpretation of that treaty which justifies nuclear sharing today,[99] is increasingly considered anachronistic, and, as the TPNW proves, at odds with the legal view of a significant part of the international community. Nuclear umbrella States, however, all consider themselves to be strong proponents of multilateralism and rules-based global order.[100] The increasing legitimacy and credibility deficit on the issue of nuclear weapons can, thus, result in challenging domestic political discussions about their nuclear sharing "security needs". In particular as it can be contrasted with the desire and declared self-image of these States of defending the credibility of multilateralism and international law.

Moreover, while major military powers such as the US, China and Russia may be sceptical of multilateral approaches with regard to the nuclear weapons issue, the legality and legitimacy of their policies vis-à-vis the rest of the international community are important to them. The power of permanent members of the UN Security Council may be sufficient to enforce non-proliferation measures in the short run, but international law is crucial to secure broad international support in proliferation scenarios, such as those of Iran or North Korea. The agreement between Iran and the E3/EU+3 on a Joint Comprehensive Plan of Action (JCPOA), for example, enjoyed broad support by the international community when it was concluded in 2015 and endorsed by the UN Security Council.[101] Clearly, the international community does not want to see a nuclear-armed Iran. The entire rationale of the JCPOA was based on international law, namely the NPT and the legally binding prohibition of nuclear proliferation. The international community supported the JCPOA because of its basis in international law and notwithstanding the supreme irony that those States leading the charge to prevent Iran from acquiring nuclear weapons capability, continuously stress the importance of these weapons for their own security. Actions by the permanent members of the UN Security Council based on coercion alone would be possible, but they would not be considered legitimate by the international community. The TPNW not only highlights this double standard. It has created a new legal standard of behaviour against which the nuclear weapon policies of the permanent members of the UN Security Council, i.e. the NPT nuclear weapon States, look increasingly wanting. The TPNW sheds a bright legal and political spotlight on their "do as I say not as I do" policies and in the eyes of large swathes of the international community, their omissions with regards to "respect for the obligations arising from treaties and other sources of international law",[102] as far as nuclear disarmament and NPT Article VI are concerned. This should be of concern for these States, as the repercussions go well beyond the nuclear weapons issue and touch upon the legitimacy of their special responsibility under the UN Charter, as permanent members of the Security Council.

The possible, more optimistic multilateral outlook is, thus, based on broad longer-term trends and currents in international relations. One such trend is towards more international cooperation out of necessity and in the face of global challenges. The second trend sees a growing recognition that international cooperation on global issues is only possible within the boundaries of international law and international legitimacy. From my perspective, it is to be hoped, that the TPNW and its humanitarian rationale will play an incremental and transformative role in moving the nuclear weapons issue more in the direction of these trends and anchor nuclear disarmament firmly within multilateral and global human security frameworks, rather than in predominantly national security perspectives.

A different, negative development is also possible, one in which nationalist trends grow, and the narrow perspectives of national interests lead to more retraction from multilateral cooperation. This can result in zero sum approaches to global challenges and to international security, where one side wins and the other loses and, consequently, to missed opportunities to address complex global challenges in a collective manner. Such approaches can edge the world towards more confrontation, thus creating more insecurity dynamics. These, in turn, may be used to provide the justification and rationale for the continued retention of nuclear weapons and reliance on nuclear deterrence, as well as for the proliferation of nuclear weapons. Some of these dynamics are on display today.

On the nuclear weapons issue, leadership is unlikely to come from those States who have, at best a selective approach towards multilateral cooperation, and who consider the nuclear status quo beneficial to them. It is also unlikely to come from States whose perspective on national and international security is also largely dominated by "nuclearism". Leadership that prevents negative developments and edges the nuclear weapons issue towards progress and more international cooperation, needs to come from those States that have most to lose from a slide into power geopolitics and the demise of multilateral cooperative frameworks. Fortunately, the vast majority of States fall into this category and the TPNW is evidence of this.

The TPNW and its rationale based on humanitarian consequences, nuclear risks and international humanitarian law has provided the international community with a lever to push for a broader discourse on nuclear weapons. It is based on arguments that can enable the international community to take steps away from "nuclearism" and the belief in nuclear deterrence. Whether or not this transformative opportunity is grasped will depend on the extent to which discourse now takes place. Progress will require a much broader engagement on the nuclear weapons issue than is the case today, and multi-stakeholder pressure to see this issue addressed as a global challenge, requiring urgent international action. For this to happen, the involvement by an informed citizenry demanding leadership and progress from their governments will be essential. Maybe the Humanitarian Initiative and the TPNW show that the time is now finally ripe to heed the warning expressed by Albert Einstein in 1947 that

> (t)he basic power of the universe cannot be fitted into the outmoded concept of narrow nationalisms. For there is no secret and there is no defense; there is no possibility of control except through the aroused understanding and insistence of the peoples of the world. We scientists recognize our inescapable responsibility to carry to our fellow citizens an understanding of the simple facts of atomic energy and its implications for society. In this lies our only security and our only hope – we believe that an informed citizenry will act for life and not death.[103]

Notes

1 See Angela Kane, "Between Aspiration and Reality: Treaty on the Prohibition of Nuclear Weapons", in *Friedrich Ebert Stiftung – Peace and Security*, April 2019, p. 7, available at https://library.fes.de/pdf-files/iez/15401.pdf.
2 See for example Lawrence S. Wittner, *Confronting the Bomb: A Short History of the World Nuclear Disarmament Movement*, Stanford University Press, 2009.
3 See for example the statements in and working papers for the 2016 open-ended working group discussed in Chapter 4.
4 See Chapter 7.
5 Sergio Duarte, UN High Representative for Disarmament, Statement by to the First Committee of the General Assembly on 3 October 2011, available at https://news.un.org/en/story/2011/10/390212-un-official-highlights-impact-democracy-and-rule-law-advancing-disarmament.
6 See for example the implementation of the 2010 NPT Action Plan discussed in Chapter 1 and the 2015 NPT Review Conference discussed in Chapter 3.
7 See Chapter 3.
8 Russia is said to develop new nuclear weapon systems, which include a nuclear-powered cruise missile and a nuclear weapon underwater "doomsday" drone and new ballistic missile submarines, strategic bombers, submarine-launched ballistic missiles (SLBMs), and intercontinental ballistic missiles (ICBMs). The US is said to invest the staggering amount of 2 trillion USD over the next 30 years to overhaul its entire nuclear weapons complex. In addition, the US is developing low yield tactical nuclear weapons and, after the demise of the Intermediate Forces Treaty (INF) in 2019, a new ground-launched intermediate-range cruise missile; see "Nuclear Weapons Ban Monitor: Tracking Progress Towards a World Free of Nuclear Weapons", p. 24, available at https://banmonitor.org/.
9 See for example US Strategic Command "MythMonday" campaign of Twitter, e.g. Tweet on 13 July 2020, available at https://twitter.com/US_Stratcom/status/1282690143418298370.
10 See B. Zala, "How the Next Nuclear Arms Race Will Be Different from the Last One", in *Bulletin of the Atomic Scientists*, 2 January 2019, available at https://thebulletin.org/2019/01/how-the-next-nuclear-arms-race-will-be-different-from-the-last-one/#.
11 For a collection of such incidents between 2015–2019 involving US/NATO, Russia, Israel, North Korea, India and Pakistan, see "Nuclear Weapons Ban Monitor", p. 22.

12 See for example statements by Russia and UK at the 2019 NPT Preparatory Meeting on 2 May 2019, available at www.un.org/disarmament/wmd/nuclear/npt2020/prepcom2019/.
13 The US has acknowledged this to some extent in its statement at the 2019 NPT Preparatory Meeting on 2 May 2019 when it declared that "the traditional, numerically-focused 'step-by-step' approach to arms control has gone as far as it can under today's conditions. The dramatic reductions in nuclear arsenals that took place when Cold War tensions eased have largely run their course, and security conditions have become much less favorable", available at www.un.org/disarmament/wmd/nuclear/npt2020/prepcom2019/.
14 See for example Bruno Tertais, "Going to Zero: A Sceptical French Position – Nuclear Abolition: Neither Desirable, nor Feasible . . . at Least for Now", in *Moving Beyond Nuclear Deterrence*, Nuclear Abolition Forum Issue 2, 2013, available at www.worldfuturecouncil.org/wp-content/uploads/2016/01/NAF_2013_Moving_beyond_nuclear_deterrence_to_a_nuclear_Weapons_free_World.pdf.
15 See Chapter 7.
16 As an example for this conceptual contradiction see the NATO statement that "As Long as Nuclear Weapons Exist, NATO Will Remain a Nuclear Alliance", in *Active Engagement, Modern Defence: Strategic Concept for the Defence and Security of the Members of the North Atlantic Treaty Organisation*, adopted by Heads of State and Government in Lisbon, 23 May 2012, available at www.nato.int/cps/en/natolive/official_texts_68580.htm.
17 See also Alexander Kmentt, "How Divergent Views on Nuclear Disarmament Threaten the NPT", in *Arms Control Today*, December 2013.
18 Discussed in Chapter 7.
19 See Chapter 2.
20 See for example "NATO Brussels Summit Declaration", issued by the heads of state and government participating in the meeting of the North Atlantic Council in Brussels, 11–12 July 2018, available at www.nato.int/cps/en/natohq/official_texts_156624.htm.
21 See Robert Green, *Security Without Nuclear Deterrence*, Astron Media, 2010, p. 40.
22 See Chapter 2; Ira Helfand, "Nuclear Famine: Two Billion People at Risk? Global Impacts of Limited Nuclear War on Agriculture, Food Supplies, and Human Nutrition", in *IPPNW and Physicians for Social Responsibility*, 2nd ed., briefing paper, November 2013, available at www.ippnw.org/nuclear-famine.html.
23 Incidentally, this led to an interesting scientific debate with competing studies. One study in 2018 used a different model and concluded that the effect would be somewhat less serious, whereas another study in 2019, concluded that the results would likely be even more severe. For the 2018 study see J. Reisner et al., "Climate Impact of a Regional Nuclear Weapons Exchange: An Improved Assessment Based on Detailed Source Calculations", in *Journal of Geophysical Research: Atmospheres*, vol. 123, 2018, 2752–2772, available at https://doi.org/10.1002/2017JD027331; for the 2019 study see Owen B. Toon, Charles G. Bardeen, Alan Robock, Lili Xia, Hans Kristensen, Matthew McKinzie, R. J. Peterson, Cheryl Harrison, Nicole S. Lovenduski and Richard P. Turco, "Rapid Expansion of Nuclear Arsenals by Pakistan and India Portends Regional and Global Catastrophe", in *Science Advances*, vol. 5, no. 10, 2 October 2019, available at https://doi.org/10.1126/sciadv.aay5478; https://advances.sciencemag.org/content/5/10/eaay5478.abstract.
24 See for example Mary Olson, "Disproportionate Impact of Radiation and Radiation Regulation", in *Interdisciplinary Science Reviews*, vol. 44, no. 2, 2019, pp. 131–139, available at https://doi.org/10.1080/03080188.2019.1603864, see also available at www.genderandradiation.org/.
25 See description about the three conferences on the humanitarian impact of nuclear weapons in Chapter 2.

26 See Humanitarian Pledge.
27 Julie Bishop op-ed, see Chapter 2, note 66.
28 See Alexander Kmentt, "The Development of the International Initiative on the Humanitarian Impact of Nuclear Weapons and Its Effect of the Nuclear Weapons Debate", in *International Review of the Red Cross*, vol. 97, 2015, p. 706.
29 Counterforce targets are an adversary's military and military installations. A countervalue target includes an adversary's population and population centres, knowledge, economic or political resources.
30 See Green, *Security Without Nuclear Deterrence*, p. 40.
31 See the 1996 Advisory Opinion of the International Court of Justice, "Legality of the Threat or Use of Nuclear Weapons", 8 July 1996, available at https://web.archive.org/web/20171118183503/www.icj-cij.org/files/case-related/95/7497.pdf.
32 See for example the "Report submitted by the United States of America pursuant to actions 5, 20 and 21 of the Final Document of the 2010 Review Conference of the Parties to the Treaty on the Non-Proliferation of Nuclear Weapons", submitted on 1 May 2014, available at https://undocs.org/NPT/CONF.2015/PC.III/16.
33 See for example the conclusion by the International Committee of the Red Cross that "(t)he ICRC finds it difficult to envisage how any use of nuclear weapons could be compatible with the rules of IHL", available at www.icrc.org/en/document/weapons.
34 See above note 11.
35 See Chapter 2; see also Patricia Lewis et al., *Too Close for Comfort: Cases of Near Nuclear Use and Options for Policy*, Royal Institute of International Affairs, April 2014, available at www.chathamhouse.org/publications/papers/view/199200.
36 See Robert McNamara interview in the documentary "The Fog of War", see 19 December 2003, also Film Review, "McNamara Looking Back at Vietnam and Other Battles", in *New York Times*, 19 December 2003, available at www.nytimes.com/2003/12/19/movies/film-review-mcnamara-looking-back-at-vietnam-and-other-battles.html; see also Benoit Pelopidas, "Power, Luck, and Scholarly Responsibility at the End of the World(s)", in *International Theory*, May 2020, p. 8, available at https://doi.org/10.1017/S1752971920000299.
37 See for example para. 22 of the "G7 Statement on Non-Proliferation and Disarmament" of 6 April 2019, "Strategic risk reduction efforts would include transparency and dialogue on nuclear doctrines and postures, military-to-military dialogues, hotline agreements among nuclear weapon possessors, 'accident measure' agreements, transparency, and notification exercises, as well as missile launch notification and other data exchange agreements"; available at www.g8.utoronto.ca/foreign/190406-disarmament.html.
38 China is the only nuclear weapon State to maintain an unconditional no-first use policy. See also Ankit Panda, "No First Use and Nuclear Weapons", in *Council on Foreign Relations*, 17 July 2018, available at www.cfr.org/backgrounder/no-first-use-and-nuclear-weapons.
39 See Global Zero Commission on Nuclear Risk Reduction, "De-Alerting and Stabilizing the World's Nuclear Force Postures", April 2015, available at www.globalzero.org/wp-content/uploads/2018/10/Global-Zero-Commission-on-Nuclear-Risk-Reduction-Full-Report.pdf.
40 Ibid., p. 2.
41 For example, at a briefing for NPT State parties organized by the US Delegation during the 2015 First Committee of the UN General Assembly on the issue of "de-alerting" attended by the author.
42 See for example: Vincent Boulanin (ed.), "The Impact of Artificial Intelligence on Strategic Stabilityand Nuclear Risk", in *Euro Atlantic Perspectives, Stockholm International Peace Research Institute (SIPRI)*, vol. I, May 2019, available at www.sipri.org/sites/default/files/2019-05/sipri1905-ai-strategic-stability-nuclear-risk.pdf; or

Christopher A. Bidwell, J.D. and Bruce W. MacDonald, "Emerging Disruptive Technologies and Their Potential Threat to Strategic Stability and National Security", in *Special Report, Federation of American Scientists (FAS)*, September 2018, available at www.fas.org; or Beyza Unal, Yasmin Afina, and Patricia Lewis (eds.), *Perspectives on Nuclear Deterrence in the 21st Century*, Chatham House, April 2020, p. 13, available at www.chathamhouse.org/sites/default/files/2020-04-20-nuclear-deterrence-unal-et-al.pdf; or Matthew Kroenig and Bharath Gopalaswamy, "Will Disruptive Technology Cause Nuclear War?", in *The Bulletin of the Atomic Scientist*, 12 November 2018, available at https://thebulletin.org/2018/11/will-disruptive-technology-cause-nuclear-war/.

43 See ICAN Briefing, "Emerging Technologies and Nuclear Weapon Risk", available at www.icanw.org/briefing_emerging_technologies_and_nuclear_weapon_risks.

44 See for example Bidwell et al., "Emerging Disruptive Technologies and Their Potential Threat to Strategic Stability and National Security", p. 6.

45 See Kenneth Waltz, "The Spread of Nuclear Weapons: More May Be Better", in *Adelphi Papers*, no. 171, International Institute for Strategic Studies, 1981.

46 Lisa Gordon-Hagerty US National Nuclear Security Administration chief, quoted in Susan Montaya-Bryan, "Official: Nuke program Serves as 'Ultimate Insurance Policy'", in *Associated Press*, 7 August 2019, available at https://abcnews.go.com/Technology/wireStory/official-nuke-program-serves-ultimate-insurance-policy-64816002.

47 See Justin V. Anderson, Jeffrey A. Larsen, and Polly M. Holdorf, "Extended Deterrence and Allied Assurance: Key Concepts and Current Challenges for U.S. Policy", in *INSS Occasional Paper 69*, USAF Institute for National Security Studies USAF Academy, September 2013, p. XII, available at www.usafa.edu/app/uploads/OCP69.pdf.

48 See for example statements made by Pope Francis in Hiroshima and Nagasaki in August 2019, available at www.japantimes.co.jp/news/2019/11/24/national/full-text-of-pope-francis-nagasaki/#.XjBL62iTJPY see also Chapter 1, p. 46.

49 See Alexei V. Fenenko, "Long Peace and Nuclear Weapons", in *Russia in Global Affairs*, vol. 17, no. 1, 2019, available at https://eng.globalaffairs.ru/articles/long-peace-and-nuclear-weapons/.

50 See for example David P. Barash, "The Deterrence Myth", in *Aeon*, 9 January 2018, available at https://aeon.co/essays/nuclear-deterrence-is-more-ideology-than-theory; see also Ward Wilson, *Five Myths About Nuclear Deterrence*, Houghton Mifflin Harcourt, 15 January 2013.

51 Bradley A. Thayer, "Thinking About Nuclear Deterrence Theory: Why Evolutionary Psychology Undermines Its Rational Actor Assumptions", in *Comparative Strategy*, vol. 26, no. 4, 2007, pp. 311–323, 317, available at https://doi.org/10.1080/01495930701598573.

52 See John Borrie, "Human Rationality and Nuclear Deterrence", in *Perspectives on Nuclear Deterrence in the 21st Century*, Beyza Unal, Yasmin Afina, and Patricia Lewis (eds.), Chatham House, April 2020, p. 13, available at www.chathamhouse.org/sites/default/files/2020-04-20-nuclear-deterrence-unal-et-al.pdf.

53 See for example Peter Rudolf, "US Nuclear Deterrence Policy and Its Problems", in *SWP Research Paper*, October 2018, p. 22, Stiftung Wissenschaft und Politik -SWP-Deutsches Institut für Internationale Politik und Sicherheit, available at https://nbn-resolving.org/urn:nbn:de:0168-ssoar-60517-9; see also Chapter 4, p. 6.

54 See for example Michael Krepon, "Can Deterrence Ever Be Stable?", in *Survival*, vol. 57, no. 3, 2015, pp. 111–132, available at https://doi.org/10.1080/00396338.2015.1046228.

55 See for example George P. Shultz, William J. Perry, Henry A. Kissinger, and Sam Nunn, "Deterrence in the Age of Nuclear Proliferation", in *The Wall Street Journal*, 7 March, 2011, available at https://media.nti.org/pdfs/NSP_op-eds_final_.pdf.

56 John F. Kennedy, Address Before the General Assembly of the United Nations, New York City, 25 September 1961: "Every man, woman and child lives under a nuclear

sword of Damocles, hanging by the slenderest of threads, capable of being cut at any moment by accident or miscalculation or by madness. The weapons of war must be abolished before they abolish us", available at www.jfklibrary.org/archives/other-resources/john-f-kennedy-speeches/united-nations-19610925.

57 See Thomas Schelling, "A world Without Nuclear Weapons?", in *Daedalus Journal of the American Academy of Arts and Sciences*, Fall 2009, pp. 124–130, available at www.amacad.org/sites/default/files/academy/multimedia/pdfs/publications/daedalus/world.pdf.
58 See Patricia M. Lewis, "Nuclear Weapons as a Wicked Problem in a Complex World", in *Nuclear Disarmament: A Critical Assessment*, Bård Nikolas, Vik Steen, and Olav Njølstad (eds.), Routledge, 2019, p. 67.
59 See Michael Krepon, "A Nuclear Myth", in *Dawn*, 3 August 2014, available at www.dawn.com/news/1122887/a-nuclear-myth.
60 French Philosopher Blaise Pascal (1623–66) famously answered the question whether it would be better to bet that God exists or does not exist by stating "Belief is a wise wager. Granted that faith cannot be proved, what harm will come to you if you gamble on its truth and it proves false? If you gain, you gain all; if you lose, you lose nothing. Wager, then, without hesitation, that He exists".
61 See Christopher Ashely Ford, "Conceptual Challenges to Nuclear Deterrence", in *Nuclear Abolition Forum*, no. 2, 2013, available at www.worldfuturecouncil.org/wp-content/uploads/2016/01/NAF_2013_Moving_beyond_nuclear_deterrence_to_a_nuclear_Weapons_free_World.pdf.
62 See Borrie, "Human Rationality and Nuclear Deterrence", p. 20.
63 See Pelopidas, "Power, Luck, and Scholarly Responsibility at the End of the World(s)".
64 "'Nuclearism', a category that connects the theory and practice and institutions of nuclear deterrence, the attendant willingness to wage nuclear war, the rejection of international law, and the hierarchical ordering of states in the world system, which helps explain much of nuclear weapons policy and politics". C. Dahlgren, *On Nuclear Weapons: Denuclearization, Demilitarization and Disarmament: Selected Writings of Richard Falk*, S. Andersson (ed.), Zia Mian (foreword), Cambridge University Press, 2019, pp. ix–xvi, available at https://doi.org/10.1017/9781108675796.020.
65 The TPNW entered into force on 22 January 2021.
66 See "Polls: Public Opinion in EU Host States Firmly Opposes Nuclear Weapons", available at www.icanw.org/polls_public_opinion_in_eu_host_states_firmly_opposes_nuclear_weapons.
67 See "Streit über US-Atomwaffen in Deutschland", in *Tagesschau*, 3 May 2020, available at www.tagesschau.de/inland/nukleare-teilhabe-streit-101.html.
68 See Susi Snyder, "Dutch Government Sets a (Qualified) Timeline to End the Nuclear Task", 8 July 2019, available at https://nonukes.nl/dutch-government-sets-a-qualified-timeline-to-end-the-nuclear-task/.
69 See for example NATO Parliamentary Assembly, "A New Ear for Nuclear Deterrence? Modernisation, Arms Control, and Allied Nuclear Forces", in *General Report (Joseph A. Day General Rapporteur)*, 12 October 2019, available at www.nato-pa.int.
70 See for example Dick Zandee, "The Future of NATO – Fog Over the Atlantic?", in *Strategic Monitor 2018–19*, available at www.clingendael.org/pub/2018/strategic-monitor-2018-2019/the-future-of-nato/.
71 See Chapter 7, note 100.
72 See for example the 2018 US Nuclear Posture Review, where the chapter on non-proliferation and arms control (without mentioning the word *disarmament*) appears at the end of the document almost as an afterthought; available at https://fas.org/issues/nuclear-weapons/nuclear-posture-review/.
73 See Chapter 6.
74 See Kane, "Between Aspiration and Reality".

75 See "Multilateralism Is in Crisis – Or Is It?", in *The Graduate Institute Geneva, Global Challenges Issue*, no. 7, April 2020, available at https://globalchallenges.ch/issue/7/multilaterism-is-in-crisis-or-is-it/.
76 Ibid.
77 Donald J. Trump, "Trump on Foreign Policy", transcript of a speech in Washington, DC on 27 April 2016, in *The National Interest*, available at https://nationalinterest.org/feature/trump-foreign-policy-15960.
78 See Will Moreland, "The Purpose of Multilateralism", in *Foreign Policy at Brookings*, September 2019, p. 4, available at www.brookings.edu/research/the-purpose-of-multilateralism/.
79 Ibid., Executive Summary, p. 1.
80 See for example Reuters, "China's Propaganda Chief Warns Against 'Seduction' of Western Values", in *South China Morning Post*, 17 November 2017, available at www.scmp.com/news/china/policies-politics/article/2120330/chinas-propaganda-chief-warns-against-seduction-western.
81 See for example "Paralysis Constricts Security Council Action in 2018, as Divisions Among Permanent Membership Fuel Escalation of Global Tensions", in *United Nations Annual Round-Up Release 2018*, 10 January 2019, available at www.un.org/press/en/2019/sc13661.doc.htm.
82 The Conference on Disarmament, was recognized by the first Special Session on Disarmament of the United Nations General Assembly (SSOD-I) (1978) as the single multilateral disarmament negotiating forum of the international community. See United Nations Office Geneva, Introduction to the Conference (on Disarmament), available at www.unog.ch/80256EE600585943/(httpPages)/BF18ABFEFE5D344DC1256F3100311CE9?OpenDocument; see also Chapter 1, p. 4.
83 See Chapter 6.
84 Remark by an expert to the author in the margins of the P5-process meeting with civil society on 12 February 2020 in London, UK. For the P5-process, see also Chapter 3, note 30.
85 See Security Council Report, "UN Documents for DPRK (North Korea)", available at www.securitycouncilreport.org/un-documents/dprk-north-korea/; "UN Documents for Iran", available at www.securitycouncilreport.org/un-documents/iran; another example of this coercive aspect are the UN Security Council resolutions in advance of the US-led invasion of Iraq in 2003, which were largely built on arguments of Iraqi non-compliance with previous resolutions and other legally binding non-proliferation instruments, such as IAEA safeguards. See for example UN Security Council Resolution 1441 (2002) of 8 November 2002, available at https://undocs.org/S/RES/1441(2002).
86 France and China in fact conducted their last nuclear tests series still in January and July 1996 respectively while the Soviet Union (1990), the UK (1991) and the US (1992) already had moratoria in place. India and Pakistan conducted nuclear tests in 1998 and have not signed the CTBT.
87 Madeleine Albright, "A Call for American Consensus", in *Time*, 22 November 1999.
88 See for example Daryl Kimball, "Nuclear Testing, Never Again", in *Arms Control Today*, July–August 2020, available at www.armscontrol.org/act/2020-07/focus/nuclear-testing-never-again.
89 See for example G7 Statement on Non-Proliferation and Disarmament, Lübeck, 15 April 2015, available at www.auswaertiges-amt.de/en/newsroom/news/150415-g7-npdg/270870.
90 See International Panel on Fissile Materials, "Fissile Material Stocks", 14 July 2020, available at http://fissilematerials.org/.
91 See for example "Action 5" of the 2010 NPT Action Plan, Final Document of the 2010 NPT Review Conference, NPT/CONF.2010/50 (vol. I), p. 21, available at www.un.org/en/conf/npt/2010/.

92 See 2018 US Nuclear Posture Review, p. 72, available at https://fas.org/issues/nuclear-weapons/nuclear-posture-review/.
93 See "2015 Paris Agreement of the United Nations Framework Convention on Climate Change", available at https://unfccc.int/process-and-meetings/the-paris-agreement/the-paris-agreement.
94 See above note 23.
95 See the discussion of the TPNW prohibitions in in Chapter 5.
96 See above, note 67 and 68.
97 Article I of the NPT states that: "Each nuclear-weapon State Party to the Treaty undertakes not to transfer to any recipient whatsoever nuclear weapons or other nuclear explosive devices or control over such weapons or explosive devices directly, or indirectly". Article II states that "Each non-nuclear weapon State party undertakes not to receive, from any source, nuclear weapons, or other nuclear explosive devices; not to manufacture or acquire such weapons or devices; and not to receive any assistance in their manufacture".
98 For example the statement by Russia at the 2015 NPT Review Conference, 27 April 2015, "Both articles [note: Articles I and I] are violated during so-called 'nuclear sharing' when servicemen from NATO non-nuclear weapon States are trained to apply nuclear weapons and participate in the nuclear planning process". Non-nuclear weapon States have also frequently raised this issue.
99 NATO asserts that nuclear sharing is in compliance with the NPT because it pre-dates the NPT and that it does "not involve any transfer of nuclear weapons or control over them unless and until a decision were made to go to war, at which time the treaty would no longer be controlling". See US Department of State Archive, "Foreign Relations, 1969–1976, Volume E-2, Documents on Arms Control, 1969–1972", available at https://2001-2009.state.gov/r/pa/ho/frus/nixon/e2/83203.htm.
100 See for example the "Alliance for Multilateralism" (https://multilateralism.org) established in 2019 by France and Germany, in which most nuclear umbrella States participate.
101 See Security Council Resolution 2231 (2015) of 20 July 2015, available at https://undocs.org/S/RES/2231(2015); at the time of writing, the future of the JCPOA is in severe doubt due to the US announcement on 8 May 2018 to withdraw from the agreement.
102 See preamble of the Charter of the United Nations, available at www.un.org/en/sections/un-charter/preamble/index.html.
103 Letter of the Emergency Committee of Atomic Scientist, signed by Albert Einstein (Chairman) of 22 January 1947, available at https://fas.org/sgp/eprint/einstein.html.

Post scriptum
Some final thoughts on constructive engagement and bridge building . . .

What are the chances of overcoming the fundamental divide that characterises the nuclear weapons discourse? Are the divergences not too profound and have they not now become insurmountable with the legal clarification of the prohibitions contained in the TPNW and the *message* of the Humanitarian Initiative? That may be so. It is, however, also possible and certainly desirable that these new developments are taken seriously and lead to a genuine effort to build bridges across the divide in the international community on these complex and contentious issues. Supporters of the TPNW would welcome such engagement on the part of nuclear weapon and nuclear umbrella States, as they are well aware that the TPNW alone is no panacea for solving the nuclear weapons issue, but one of many necessary steps to achieve a world without nuclear weapons. In their view, the TPNW should facilitate, if not compel, the kind of engagement on the part of the nuclear weapon States that has hitherto been missing.

From the perspective of supporters of the TPNW, any "bridge-building" discussions would, arguably, be seen as incomplete or miss the key point without also addressing the veracity of nuclear deterrence and the security value of nuclear weapons, as laid out in the concluding chapter.

To paraphrase a US official speaking about a US nuclear disarmament initiative, constructive engagement with the non-nuclear weapon States and the message expressed by the Humanitarian Initiative and the TPNW would presumably demonstrate "that the international community is now finally at a point where it can start asking the right questions".[1] If this were the case, some of the *right* questions that arise from the Humanitarian Initiative and the TPNW would be:

- What are the limits of knowledge about nuclear deterrence, about whether it works or does not work? What is the role of subjective assessments on both sides of the deterrence/disarmament argument and the possibility of overconfidence in the respective assumptions?
- What conclusions should be drawn from the fact that much in the nuclear weapons debate is based on subjective assessments, leading to the possibility of overconfidence in the respective arguments? To what extent can the "not knowing" whether nuclear deterrence works or does not work be a point of convergence?

- How can one weigh the belief that nuclear weapons deter and prevent large-scale wars with the knowledge that deterrence, including nuclear deterrence, can fail with the risk of unacceptable humanitarian and other consequences?
- How do the "nuclear deterrence risks" compare with the "risks of nuclear weapons elimination"?
- What would security in a word without nuclear weapons look like? Can the following two statements be at all assessed objectively: "A world without nuclear weapons cannot be today's world without nuclear weapons" versus "A world without nuclear weapons would in any case be more secure as the existential threat to humanity is removed"?
- How does/can one think of an end of the nuclear age? In the context of post-disarmament, post-use of nuclear weapons, post-existence of nuclear weapons, with a replacement deterrence system or in a future security environment whose outlines are not clear today?
- Does a more concrete and scenario-based assessment of the actual humanitarian and other consequences of nuclear weapon use undermine or strengthens the credibility of nuclear deterrence? What are the knowledge and the uncertainties as regards either assumption?
- Moreover, would such a focus on measurable humanitarian and other consequences and of risks associated with nuclear weapons have the potential for changing the nuclear deterrence calculus and its cost-benefit analysis? If not now, what would be the changed parameters, such as consequences and risks, where this would be the case?
- To what extent do nuclear deterrence doctrines and targeting plans go beyond a predominantly abstract consideration of the consequences of the use of nuclear weapons due to the assumption of ultimate non-use because deterrence will not fail? How concretely do nuclear armed States, therefore, integrate the humanitarian and other consequences on their own population, the presumptive opponent's population and on populations in third countries into their nuclear weapons use scenarios?
- How, and in which concrete scenarios, do nuclear deterrence doctrines and targeting plans ensure compliance with IHL and the principles of distinction and proportionality? In this context, what exactly do notions of "existential threat", "extreme self-defence", "undiminished security" and "unacceptable damage" mean today, for whom?
- How are international humanitarian law principles considered in relation vis-à-vis populations in third countries that are not party to the conflict, given likely or possible transboundary humanitarian consequences of nuclear weapons?
- How are issues such as the responsibility and the ability to clean up after an accident or use of nuclear weapons included and considered in the decision-making process and in nuclear doctrines in nuclear armed States?
- What actually constitutes nuclear risk reduction? Is it related to possession/elimination? Use scenarios? Intent? Safety and security? Doctrine and policies? How do different stakeholders in the nuclear weapons discourse

subjectively accept conceptions of risks related to the possession of nuclear weapons and the practice of nuclear deterrence?
- To what extent does nuclear deterrence require a readiness to take risks in order to underscore its credibility, possibly resulting in a propensity towards probing and dangerous behaviour and a false sense of security?
- What is the impact of new technologies on nuclear deterrence? At what stage and with which new technological development would the current assessments behind nuclear deterrence change?
- How do different types of legitimacy regarding the possession of nuclear weapons and the practice of nuclear deterrence interrelate and how and why are they challenged? At what point could one conclude that, over time, the legitimacy as regards possession and nuclear deterrence has diminished, the situation has changed?[2]

A broad dialogue and engagement on a range of questions such as those would certainly be a difficult affair for all sides of the disarmament/deterrence divide, given the acrimonious history of the nuclear disarmament debate and the strongly held views on the nuclear weapons issue. They are, however, among the legitimate and pertinent questions derived from the arguments made in the context of the Humanitarian Initiative and the TPNW. Opposing, dismissing or deflecting from these issues, as has been the tactic of opponents of the TPNW thus far, exacerbates existing disagreement. While the different perspectives may ultimately prove very difficult to resolve, a more constructive dialogue between proponents of the deterrence/disarmament camps would in itself be a positive contribution to nuclear weapons discourse and, hence, strengthen the cohesion of the multilateral nuclear disarmament and non-proliferation regime. This important conversation should take place more broadly, more inclusively and with urgency.

Notes

1 US State Department, "Creating an Environment for Nuclear Disarmament (CEND) Working Group Kick-Off Plenary Meeting", press release on 19 July 2020, available at www.state.gov/forty-two-countries-seek-common-ground-at-the-creating-an-environment-for-nuclear-disarmament-cend-working-group-kick-off-plenary-meeting/.
2 These questions were raised and discussed in the context of two workshops that I organised in cooperation with Chatham House and the Friedrich Ebert Foundation (FES) in December 2019 and October 2020, entitled "Bridge Building in the Nuclear Disarmament Discourse – Nuclear Deterrence and the Humanitarian Approach to Nuclear Weapons".

Annex I
Austrian Pledge

VIENNA CONFERENCE ON THE HUMANITARIAN IMPACT OF NUCLEAR WEAPONS 8–9 DEC. 2014

Pledge presented at the Vienna Conference on the Humanitarian Impact of Nuclear Weapons by Austrian Deputy Foreign Minister Michael Linhart

Having hosted and chaired the Vienna Conference on the Humanitarian Impact of Nuclear Weapons from 8–9 December 2014 and in light of the important facts and findings that have been presented at the international conferences in Oslo, Nayarit and Vienna, Austria, solely in her national capacity, and without binding any other participant, wants to go beyond the summary just read out. After careful consideration of the evidence, Austria has come to the following inescapable conclusions and makes the subsequent pledge to take them forward with interested parties in available fora, including in the context of the NPT and its upcoming 2015 Review Conference:

Mindful of the unacceptable harm that victims of nuclear weapons explosions and nuclear testing have experienced and recognising that the rights and needs of victims have not yet been adequately addressed,

Understanding that the immediate, mid- and long-term consequences of a nuclear weapon explosion are significantly graver than it was understood in the past and will not be constrained by national borders but have regional or even global effects, potentially threatening the survival of humanity,

Recognizing the complexity of and interrelationship between these consequences on health, environment, infrastructure, food security, climate, development, social cohesion and the global economy that are systemic and potentially irreversible,

Aware that the risk of a nuclear weapon explosion is significantly greater than previously assumed and is indeed increasing with increased proliferation, the lowering of the technical threshold for nuclear weapon capability, the ongoing modernisation of nuclear weapon arsenals in nuclear weapon possessing states, and the role that is attributed to nuclear weapons in the nuclear doctrines of possessor states,

Cognizant of the fact that the risk of nuclear weapons use with their unacceptable consequences can only be avoided when all nuclear weapons have been eliminated,

Emphasizing that the consequences of a nuclear weapon explosion and the risks associated with nuclear weapons concern the security of all humanity and that all states share the responsibility to prevent any use of nuclear weapons,

Emphasizing that the scope of consequences of a nuclear weapon explosion and risks associated raise profound moral and ethical questions that go beyond debates about the legality of nuclear weapons,

Mindful that no national or international response capacity exists that would adequately respond to the human suffering and humanitarian harm that would result from a nuclear weapon explosion in a populated area, and that such capacity most likely will never exist,

Affirming that it is in the interest of the very survival of humanity that nuclear weapons are never used again, under any circumstances,

Reiterating the crucial role that international organisations, relevant UN entities, the Red Cross and Red Crescent Movement, elected representatives, academia and civil society play for advancing the shared objective of a nuclear weapon free world,

Austria regards it as her responsibility and consequently pledges to present the facts-based discussions, findings and compelling evidence of the Vienna Conference, which builds upon the previous conferences in Oslo and Nayarit, to all relevant fora, in particular the NPT Review Conference 2015 and in the UN framework, as they should be at the centre of all deliberations, obligations and commitments with regard to nuclear disarmament,

Austria pledges to follow the imperative of human security for all and to promote the protection of civilians against risks stemming from nuclear weapons,

Austria calls on all states parties to the NPT to renew their commitment to the urgent and full implementation of existing obligations under Article VI, and to this end, to identify and pursue effective measures to fill the legal gap for the prohibition and elimination of nuclear weapons and Austria pledges to cooperate with all stakeholders to achieve this goal,

Austria calls on all nuclear weapons possessor states to take concrete interim measures to reduce the risk of nuclear weapon detonations, including reducing the operational status of nuclear weapons and moving nuclear weapons away from deployment into storage, diminishing the role of nuclear weapons in military doctrines and rapid reductions of all types of nuclear weapons,

Austria pledges to cooperate with all relevant stakeholders, States, international organisations, the International Red Cross and Red Crescent Movements, parliamentarians and civil society, in efforts to stigmatise, prohibit and eliminate nuclear weapons in light of their unacceptable humanitarian consequences and associated risks.

+++++

Note:

On 18 May 2015, Austria informed the NPT Review Conference that the "Austrian Pledge" was "no longer a national pledge". The "Austrian Pledge" was renamed into "Humanitarian Pledge". The text was identical to the "Austrian Pledge" except that all references to "Austria" were replaced by "We, the States supporting and/or endorsing this pledge".

The "Humanitarian Pledge Document" is available at www.hinw14vienna.at or www.bmeia.gv.at/fileadmin/user_upload/Zentrale/Aussenpolitik/Abruestung/HINW14/ HINW14vienna_Pledge_Document.pdf

Annex II
Text of the Treaty on the Prohibition of Nuclear Weapons

General Assembly

Distr.: General 7 July 2017

Original: English

United Nations conference to negotiate a legally binding instrument to prohibit nuclear weapons, leading towards their total elimination
New York, 27–31 March and 15 June–7 July 2017
Agenda item 9
Negotiations, pursuant to paragraph 8 of General Assembly resolution 71/258 of 23 December 2016, on a legally binding instrument to prohibit nuclear weapons, leading towards their total elimination

Treaty on the Prohibition of Nuclear Weapons

The States Parties to this Treaty,

Determined to contribute to the realization of the purposes and principles of the Charter of the United Nations,

Deeply concerned about the catastrophic humanitarian consequences that would result from any use of nuclear weapons, and recognizing the consequent need to completely eliminate such weapons, which remains the only way to guarantee that nuclear weapons are never used again under any circumstances,

Mindful of the risks posed by the continued existence of nuclear weapons, including from any nuclear-weapon detonation by accident, miscalculation or design, and emphasizing that these risks concern the security of all humanity, and that all States share the responsibility to prevent any use of nuclear weapons,

Cognizant that the catastrophic consequences of nuclear weapons cannot be adequately addressed, transcend national borders, pose grave implications for human survival, the environment, socioeconomic development, the global economy, food security and the health of current and future generations, and have a disproportionate impact on women and girls, including as a result of ionizing radiation,

Acknowledging the ethical imperatives for nuclear disarmament and the urgency of achieving and maintaining a nuclear-weapon-free world, which is a global public good of the highest order, serving both national and collective security interests,

Mindful of the unacceptable suffering of and harm caused to the victims of the use of nuclear weapons (hibakusha), as well as of those affected by the testing of nuclear weapons,

Recognizing the disproportionate impact of nuclear-weapon activities on indigenous peoples,

Reaffirming the need for all States at all times to comply with applicable international law, including international humanitarian law and international human rights law,

Basing themselves on the principles and rules of international humanitarian law, in particular the principle that the right of parties to an armed conflict to choose methods or means of warfare is not unlimited, the rule of distinction, the prohibition against indiscriminate attacks, the rules on proportionality and precautions in attack, the prohibition on the use of weapons of a nature to cause superfluous injury or unnecessary suffering, and the rules for the protection of the natural environment,

Considering that any use of nuclear weapons would be contrary to the rules of international law applicable in armed conflict, in particular the principles and rules of international humanitarian law,

Reaffirming that any use of nuclear weapons would also be abhorrent to the principles of humanity and the dictates of public conscience,

Recalling that, in accordance with the Charter of the United Nations, States must refrain in their international relations from the threat or use of force against the territorial integrity or political independence of any State, or in any other manner inconsistent with the Purposes of the United Nations, and that the establishment and maintenance of international peace and security are to be promoted with the least diversion for armaments of the world's human and economic resources,

Recalling also the first resolution of the General Assembly of the United Nations, adopted on 24 January 1946, and subsequent resolutions which call for the elimination of nuclear weapons,

Concerned by the slow pace of nuclear disarmament, the continued reliance on nuclear weapons in military and security concepts, doctrines and policies, and the waste of economic and human resources on programmes for the production, maintenance and modernization of nuclear weapons,

Recognizing that a legally binding prohibition of nuclear weapons constitutes an important contribution towards the achievement and maintenance of a world free of nuclear weapons, including the irreversible, verifiable and transparent elimination of nuclear weapons, and determined to act towards that end,

Determined to act with a view to achieving effective progress towards general and complete disarmament under strict and effective international control,

Reaffirming that there exists an obligation to pursue in good faith and bring to a conclusion negotiations leading to nuclear disarmament in all its aspects under strict and effective international control,

Reaffirming also that the full and effective implementation of the Treaty on the Non-Proliferation of Nuclear Weapons, which serves as the cornerstone of the nuclear disarmament and non-proliferation regime, has a vital role to play in promoting international peace and security,

Recognizing the vital importance of the Comprehensive Nuclear-Test-Ban Treaty and its verification regime as a core element of the nuclear disarmament and non-proliferation regime,

Reaffirming the conviction that the establishment of the internationally recognized nuclear-weapon-free zones on the basis of arrangements freely arrived at among the States of the region concerned enhances global and regional peace and security, strengthens the nuclear non-proliferation regime and contributes towards realizing the objective of nuclear disarmament,

Emphasizing that nothing in this Treaty shall be interpreted as affecting the inalienable right of its States Parties to develop research, production and use of nuclear energy for peaceful purposes without discrimination,

Recognizing that the equal, full and effective participation of both women and men is an essential factor for the promotion and attainment of sustainable peace and security, and committed to supporting and strengthening the effective participation of women in nuclear disarmament,

Recognizing also the importance of peace and disarmament education in all its aspects and of raising awareness of the risks and consequences of nuclear weapons for current and future generations, and committed to the dissemination of the principles and norms of this Treaty,

Stressing the role of public conscience in the furthering of the principles of humanity as evidenced by the call for the total elimination of nuclear weapons, and recognizing the efforts to that end undertaken by the United Nations, the International Red Cross and Red Crescent Movement, other international and regional organizations, non-governmental organizations, religious leaders, parliamentarians, academics and the hibakusha,

Have agreed as follows:

Article 1 Prohibitions

1   Each State Party undertakes never under any circumstances to:

   (a) Develop, test, produce, manufacture, otherwise acquire, possess or stockpile nuclear weapons or other nuclear explosive devices;
   (b) Transfer to any recipient whatsoever nuclear weapons or other nuclear explosive devices or control over such weapons or explosive devices directly or indirectly;

(c) Receive the transfer of or control over nuclear weapons or other nuclear explosive devices directly or indirectly;
(d) Use or threaten to use nuclear weapons or other nuclear explosive devices;
(e) Assist, encourage or induce, in any way, anyone to engage in any activity prohibited to a State Party under this Treaty;
(f) Seek or receive any assistance, in any way, from anyone to engage in any activity prohibited to a State Party under this Treaty;
(g) Allow any stationing, installation or deployment of any nuclear weapons or other nuclear explosive devices in its territory or at any place under its jurisdiction or control.

Article 2 Declarations

1   Each State Party shall submit to the Secretary-General of the United Nations, not later than 30 days after this Treaty enters into force for that State Party, a declaration in which it shall:

(a) Declare whether it owned, possessed or controlled nuclear weapons or nuclear explosive devices and eliminated its nuclear-weapon programme, including the elimination or irreversible conversion of all nuclear-weapons-related facilities, prior to the entry into force of this Treaty for that State Party;
(b) Notwithstanding Article 1 (a), declare whether it owns, possesses or controls any nuclear weapons or other nuclear explosive devices;
(c) Notwithstanding Article 1 (g), declare whether there are any nuclear weapons or other nuclear explosive devices in its territory or in any place under its jurisdiction or control that are owned, possessed or controlled by another State.

2   The Secretary-General of the United Nations shall transmit all such declarations received to the States Parties.

Article 3 Safeguards

1   Each State Party to which Article 4, paragraph 1 or 2, does not apply shall, at a minimum, maintain its International Atomic Energy Agency safeguards obligations in force at the time of entry into force of this Treaty, without prejudice to any additional relevant instruments that it may adopt in the future.
2   Each State Party to which Article 4, paragraph 1 or 2, does not apply that has not yet done so shall conclude with the International Atomic Energy Agency and bring into force a comprehensive safeguards agreement (INFCIRC/153 (Corrected)). Negotiation of such agreement shall commence within 180 days from the entry into force of this Treaty for that State Party. The agreement shall enter into force no later than 18 months from the entry into force of this Treaty for that State Party. Each State Party shall thereafter maintain such

obligations, without prejudice to any additional relevant instruments that it may adopt in the future.

Article 4 Towards the total elimination of nuclear weapons

1 Each State Party that after 7 July 2017 owned, possessed or controlled nuclear weapons or other nuclear explosive devices and eliminated its nuclear-weapon programme, including the elimination or irreversible conversion of all nuclear – weapons-related facilities, prior to the entry into force of this Treaty for it, shall cooperate with the competent international authority designated pursuant to paragraph 6 of this Article for the purpose of verifying the irreversible elimination of its nuclear-weapon programme. The competent international authority shall report to the States Parties. Such a State Party shall conclude a safeguards agreement with the International Atomic Energy Agency sufficient to provide credible assurance of the non-diversion of declared nuclear material from peaceful nuclear activities and of the absence of undeclared nuclear material or activities in that State Party as a whole. Negotiation of such agreement shall commence within 180 days from the entry into force of this Treaty for that State Party. The agreement shall enter into force no later than 18 months from the entry into force of this Treaty for that State Party. That State Party shall thereafter, at a minimum, maintain these safeguards obligations, without prejudice to any additional relevant instruments that it may adopt in the future.

2 Notwithstanding Article 1 (a), each State Party that owns, possesses or controls nuclear weapons or other nuclear explosive devices shall immediately remove them from operational status, and destroy them as soon as possible but not later than a deadline to be determined by the first meeting of States Parties, in accordance with a legally binding, time-bound plan for the verified and irreversible elimination of that State Party's nuclear-weapon programme, including the elimination or irreversible conversion of all nuclear-weapons-related facilities. The State Party, no later than 60 days after the entry into force of this Treaty for that State Party, shall submit this plan to the States Parties or to a competent international authority designated by the States Parties. The plan shall then be negotiated with the competent international authority, which shall submit it to the subsequent meeting of States Parties or review conference, whichever comes first, for approval in accordance with its rules of procedure.

3 A State Party to which paragraph 2 above applies shall conclude a safeguards agreement with the International Atomic Energy Agency sufficient to provide credible assurance of the non-diversion of declared nuclear material from peaceful nuclear activities and of the absence of undeclared nuclear material or activities in the State as a whole. Negotiation of such agreement shall commence no later than the date upon which implementation of the plan referred to in paragraph 2 is completed. The agreement shall enter into force no later than 18 months after the date of initiation of negotiations. That State

Party shall thereafter, at a minimum, maintain these safeguards obligations, without prejudice to any additional relevant instruments that it may adopt in the future. Following the entry into force of the agreement referred to in this paragraph, the State Party shall submit to the Secretary-General of the United Nations a final declaration that it has fulfilled its obligations under this Article.

4 Notwithstanding Article 1 (b) and (g), each State Party that has any nuclear weapons or other nuclear explosive devices in its territory or in any place under its jurisdiction or control that are owned, possessed or controlled by another State shall ensure the prompt removal of such weapons, as soon as possible but not later than a deadline to be determined by the first meeting of States Parties. Upon the removal of such weapons or other explosive devices, that State Party shall submit to the Secretary-General of the United Nations a declaration that it has fulfilled its obligations under this Article.

5 Each State Party to which this Article applies shall submit a report to each meeting of States Parties and each review conference on the progress made towards the implementation of its obligations under this Article, until such time as they are fulfilled.

6 The States Parties shall designate a competent international authority or authorities to negotiate and verify the irreversible elimination of nuclear-weapons programmes, including the elimination or irreversible conversion of all nuclear – weapons-related facilities in accordance with paragraphs 1, 2 and 3 of this Article. In the event that such a designation has not been made prior to the entry into force of this Treaty for a State Party to which paragraph 1 or 2 of this Article applies, the Secretary-General of the United Nations shall convene an extraordinary meeting of States Parties to take any decisions that may be required.

Article 5 National implementation

1 Each State Party shall adopt the necessary measures to implement its obligations under this Treaty.
2 Each State Party shall take all appropriate legal, administrative and other measures, including the imposition of penal sanctions, to prevent and suppress any activity prohibited to a State Party under this Treaty undertaken by persons or on territory under its jurisdiction or control.

Article 6 Victim assistance and environmental remediation

1 Each State Party shall, with respect to individuals under its jurisdiction who are affected by the use or testing of nuclear weapons, in accordance with applicable international humanitarian and human rights law, adequately provide age- and gender-sensitive assistance, without discrimination, including medical care, rehabilitation and psychological support, as well as provide for their social and economic inclusion.

2   Each State Party, with respect to areas under its jurisdiction or control contaminated as a result of activities related to the testing or use of nuclear weapons or other nuclear explosive devices, shall take necessary and appropriate measures towards the environmental remediation of areas so contaminated.
3   The obligations under paragraphs 1 and 2 above shall be without prejudice to the duties and obligations of any other States under international law or bilateral agreements.

Article 7 International cooperation and assistance

1   Each State Party shall cooperate with other States Parties to facilitate the implementation of this Treaty.
2   In fulfilling its obligations under this Treaty, each State Party shall have the right to seek and receive assistance, where feasible, from other States Parties.
3   Each State Party in a position to do so shall provide technical, material and financial assistance to States Parties affected by nuclear-weapons use or testing, to further the implementation of this Treaty.
4   Each State Party in a position to do so shall provide assistance for the victims of the use or testing of nuclear weapons or other nuclear explosive devices.
5   Assistance under this Article may be provided, inter alia, through the United Nations system, international, regional or national organizations or institutions, non-governmental organizations or institutions, the International Committee of the Red Cross, the International Federation of Red Cross and Red Crescent Societies, or national Red Cross and Red Crescent Societies, or on a bilateral basis.
6   Without prejudice to any other duty or obligation that it may have under international law, a State Party that has used or tested nuclear weapons or any other nuclear explosive devices shall have a responsibility to provide adequate assistance to affected States Parties, for the purpose of victim assistance and environmental remediation.

Article 8 Meeting of States Parties

1   The States Parties shall meet regularly in order to consider and, where necessary, take decisions in respect of any matter with regard to the application or implementation of this Treaty, in accordance with its relevant provisions, and on further measures for nuclear disarmament, including:

   (a) The implementation and status of this Treaty;
   (b) Measures for the verified, time-bound and irreversible elimination of nuclear-weapon programmes, including additional protocols to this Treaty;
   (c) Any other matters pursuant to and consistent with the provisions of this Treaty.

2. The first meeting of States Parties shall be convened by the Secretary-General of the United Nations within one year of the entry into force of this Treaty. Further meetings of States Parties shall be convened by the Secretary-General of the United Nations on a biennial basis, unless otherwise agreed by the States Parties. The meeting of States Parties shall adopt its rules of procedure at its first session. Pending their adoption, the rules of procedure of the United Nations conference to negotiate a legally binding instrument to prohibit nuclear weapons, leading towards their total elimination, shall apply.
3. Extraordinary meetings of States Parties shall be convened, as may be deemed necessary, by the Secretary-General of the United Nations, at the written request of any State Party provided that this request is supported by at least one third of the States Parties.
4. After a period of five years following the entry into force of this Treaty, the Secretary-General of the United Nations shall convene a conference to review the operation of the Treaty and the progress in achieving the purposes of the Treaty. The Secretary-General of the United Nations shall convene further review conferences at intervals of six years with the same objective, unless otherwise agreed by the States Parties.
5. States not party to this Treaty, as well as the relevant entities of the United Nations system, other relevant international organizations or institutions, regional organizations, the International Committee of the Red Cross, the International Federation of Red Cross and Red Crescent Societies and relevant non-governmental organizations, shall be invited to attend the meetings of States Parties and the review conferences as observers.

Article 9 Costs

1. The costs of the meetings of States Parties, the review conferences and the extraordinary meetings of States Parties shall be borne by the States Parties and States not party to this Treaty participating therein as observers, in accordance with the United Nations scale of assessment adjusted appropriately.
2. The costs incurred by the Secretary-General of the United Nations in the circulation of declarations under Article 2, reports under Article 4 and proposed amendments under Article 10 of this Treaty shall be borne by the States Parties in accordance with the United Nations scale of assessment adjusted appropriately.
3. The cost related to the implementation of verification measures required under Article 4 as well as the costs related to the destruction of nuclear weapons or other nuclear explosive devices, and the elimination of nuclear-weapon programmes, including the elimination or conversion of all nuclear-weapons-related facilities, should be borne by the States Parties to which they apply.

Article 10 Amendments

1. At any time after the entry into force of this Treaty, any State Party may propose amendments to the Treaty. The text of a proposed amendment shall be

communicated to the Secretary-General of the United Nations, who shall circulate it to all States Parties and shall seek their views on whether to consider the proposal. If a majority of the States Parties notify the Secretary-General of the United Nations no later than 90 days after its circulation that they support further consideration of the proposal, the proposal shall be considered at the next meeting of States Parties or review conference, whichever comes first.
2   A meeting of States Parties or a review conference may agree upon amendments which shall be adopted by a positive vote of a majority of two thirds of the States Parties. The Depositary shall communicate any adopted amendment to all States Parties.
3   The amendment shall enter into force for each State Party that deposits its instrument of ratification or acceptance of the amendment 90 days following the deposit of such instruments of ratification or acceptance by a majority of the States Parties at the time of adoption. Thereafter, it shall enter into force for any other State Party 90 days following the deposit of its instrument of ratification or acceptance of the amendment.

Article 11 Settlement of disputes

1   When a dispute arises between two or more States Parties relating to the interpretation or application of this Treaty, the parties concerned shall consult together with a view to the settlement of the dispute by negotiation or by other peaceful means of the parties' choice in accordance with Article 33 of the Charter of the United Nations.
2   The meeting of States Parties may contribute to the settlement of the dispute, including by offering its good offices, calling upon the States Parties concerned to start the settlement procedure of their choice and recommending a time limit for any agreed procedure, in accordance with the relevant provisions of this Treaty and the Charter of the United Nations.

Article 12 Universality

Each State Party shall encourage States not party to this Treaty to sign, ratify, accept, approve or accede to the Treaty, with the goal of universal adherence of all States to the Treaty.

Article 13 Signature

This Treaty shall be open for signature to all States at United Nations Headquarters in New York as from 20 September 2017.

Article 14 Ratification, acceptance, approval or accession

This Treaty shall be subject to ratification, acceptance or approval by signatory States. The Treaty shall be open for accession.

Article 15 Entry into force

1. This Treaty shall enter into force 90 days after the fiftieth instrument of ratification, acceptance, approval or accession has been deposited.
2. For any State that deposits its instrument of ratification, acceptance, approval or accession after the date of the deposit of the fiftieth instrument of ratification, acceptance, approval or accession, this Treaty shall enter into force 90 days after the date on which that State has deposited its instrument of ratification, acceptance, approval or accession.

Article 16 Reservations

The Articles of this Treaty shall not be subject to reservations.

Article 17 Duration and withdrawal

1. This Treaty shall be of unlimited duration.
2. Each State Party shall, in exercising its national sovereignty, have the right to withdraw from this Treaty if it decides that extraordinary events related to the subject matter of the Treaty have jeopardized the supreme interests of its country. It shall give notice of such withdrawal to the Depositary. Such notice shall include a statement of the extraordinary events that it regards as having jeopardized its supreme interests.
3. Such withdrawal shall only take effect 12 months after the date of the receipt of the notification of withdrawal by the Depositary. If, however, on the expiry of that 12-month period, the withdrawing State Party is a party to an armed conflict, the State Party shall continue to be bound by the obligations of this Treaty and of any additional protocols until it is no longer party to an armed conflict.

Article 18 Relationship with other agreements

The implementation of this Treaty shall not prejudice obligations undertaken by States Parties with regard to existing international agreements, to which they are party, where those obligations are consistent with the Treaty.

Article 19 Depositary

The Secretary-General of the United Nations is hereby designated as the Depositary of this Treaty.

Article 20 Authentic texts

The Arabic, Chinese, English, French, Russian and Spanish texts of this Treaty shall be equally authentic.

DONE at New York, this seventh day of July, two thousand and seventeen.

Index

accidental use of nuclear weapons 31, 39, 45, 144, 201
Acheson, Ray 19, 115
acquisition of nuclear weapons (TPNW prohibition of) 117, 174
Additional Protocol, IAEA 121–122, 128
Africa 208
African Group 75, 99, 103–104, 112, 127
Albright, Madeleine 209
Algeria 60, 66, 112, 127
Amano, Yukio 121
Amersham 41
Amersham group 38, 41, 46, 55, 71
Amersham strategy meeting 28–32
Anti-Ballistic Missile Treaty (ABM Treaty) 10
Anti-Personnel Mine Ban Convention 12–13, 124–125, 131, 174
Argentina 95
Arms Trade Treaty 13
Article 36 (NGO) 28, 38, 91
artificial intelligence 199
ASEAN 61, 75, 98, 103–104, 112
Asia 208
assistance (TPNW prohibition of) 117–120
Australia 32, 56, 61, 75, 91, 95, 98, 99–102, 160, 162
Austria 4, 13, 18–19, 32, 33–35, 40–46, 54, 57, 59–61, 66, 68–69, 72–75, 90–92, 94, 99, 101–102, 111, 117–118, 120, 122, 125, 126–127
Austrian Pledge 4, 46, 54–57, 59, 61, 65
Aviano, NATO military base 43

Belgium 118
Berkshire Group 56, 91
Berkshire meetings 38, 41

Biological and Toxin Weapons Convention (BWC) 53, 55, 162; verification regime 10
Bishop, Julie 40
Blair, Bruce 39
Bolton, John 10, 11
Bolton, Matthew 63, 146
Brazil 93–94, 95, 98, 101, 111, 122, 126–127
Broadly Likeminded Group 91, 95
Browne, Desmond Lord of Ladyton 58
Bush, George W. 10, 14

Cabactulan, Libran 16
Campbell, Craig Howard 177
Canada 12, 69, 96, 102
CARICOM 61, 103
Casey-Maslen, Stuart 119–120, 123, 125
CELAC 56, 61, 75, 99, 103–104, 112, 119, 127, 129; Third Summit (2015) 56
Chatham House Royal Institute of International Affairs 38
Chemical Weapons Convention 53, 123, 162
Chile 59, 115, 126, 126–127
China 2, 12, 19, 157, 175, 207, 212
climate effects 31
cluster munitions 13, 124–125
Cluster Munitions Convention 131, 174
Cold War 1, 2, 9, 10, 177, 190, 200
collateral damage 44, 159, 196
Collective Security Treaty Organization (CSTO) 118
Commissario, Pedro 115, 120
Common Article 1 Geneva Conventions 40
Community of Latin American and Caribbean States (CELAC)

Index

Comprehensive Nuclear Test Ban Treaty (CTBT) 9, 10–11, 19, 58, 96, 116, 117–118, 120, 127, 129, 160, 209
comprehensive safeguards agreement, IAEA 122
Conference on Disarmament 9–10, 12, 13, 33–35, 58–59, 101, 111, 156–157, 160, 189, 208–209; programme of work 11; Revitalizing the Work 18
confidence building measures 191, 198
Convention on Certain Conventional Weapons (CCW) 13; Protocol V 124
core group 111, 120, 126–128
Costa Rica 56, 59, 94–95, 111
Covid-19 pandemic 206, 211
customary international law 37, 96, 192
cyber risks 39, 43, 45, 144; cyber weapons 199

de-alerting 160, 198–199
de-legitimisation of nuclear weapons 104
destroy and join 122–124
develop nuclear weapons (TPNW prohibition of) 118, 120
Diana Princess of Wales 12
disarmament and non-proliferation regime 116, 121, 145–146, 150, 166, 168–169, 175, 188, 192, 198, 206, 223, 229
disarmament machinery 18, 33
double standard NPT 11
Duarte, Sergio 189

E3/EU+3 11, 75, 212
Ecuador 95, 120, 127
effective legal measures (to prohibit and eliminate nuclear weapons) 53, 57, 60, 62, 64, 77, 79, 89, 91, 92, 95, 98
Egeland, Kjølv 145
Egypt 120, 122, 125, 129
Eide, Espen Bart 36
Einstein, Albert 214
emerging technologies 199–200
encourage (TPNW prohibition) 117
environmental remediation 124–125, 130
error, human or technical 38–39, 45, 95, 144, 175, 199
Estonia 102
ethical imperatives for a nuclear-weapon-free world, resolution UN General Assembly (2015) 75, 79

Feroukhi, Taous 60, 68
Fihn, Beatrice 113, 151

Fiji 95, 99, 124, 127
financing (of nuclear weapons) 120–121, 130
First Committee of the UN General Assembly 10, 12, 32, 208; (2010) 18; (2011) 18, 189; (2012) 32–33, 156; (2013) 32, 35; (2014) 32; (2015) 4, 68, 73, 75–78, 89, 143; (2016) 102–104
Fissile Material Cut-Off Treaty (FMCT) 9, 18, 96, 160, 209
Focus Group, NPT Review Conference (2015) 65–68, 72
France 10, 19, 33, 37, 63, 75, 78, 102, 104, 113, 151, 157, 162, 164–165

Germany 75, 96, 102, 118, 162, 204
Giorgou, Eirini 173
Global Zero (NGO) 39, 162
Gorbachev, Mikhail 9
Griffen, Vanessa 113
Guatemala 95, 99, 120, 127
Guterres, Antonio 150

Hajnoczi, Thomas 72, 103, 150, 168
Haley, Nikki 113
Harrington de Santana, Anne 142
Hibakusha 38, 43, 116, 124, 126, 151
Higgie, Dell 118
Hiroshima 15, 38, 40, 75, 92, 126, 151
Holy See 59, 103–104, 127
Honduras 174–175
humanitarian consequences 2, 13–16, 27–28, 30–32, 34–39, 41–46, 52–55, 57–60, 62–64, 67, 70–71, 73–76, 79, 91, 103, 116, 125, 132, 143–147, 151, 155–156, 158–161, 164–166, 176–179, 188–189, 192–198, 200–205, 211, 213, 222; climate consequences 31, 38, 44, 143, 155, 193; food security consequences 36, 38, 116, 143, 188, 193–194; gender dimension 43, 45, 116, 193; human health 36, 38, 44–45, 116, 143, 146, 188, 190, 193–194; lack of response capability 31, 36–38, 45, 55, 116, 143, 158–159; migratory movements 146, 193, 196, 210; nuclear testing 37, 45; social order 36, 38, 44, 143, 193, 224; socio-economic 36, 38, 44, 116, 143, 146, 188, 193–194; transboundary effects 37–38, 43–44, 143, 158, 196, 222
humanitarian consequences of nuclear weapons, resolution UN General Assembly (2015) 75, 79

humanitarian disarmament 4, 13–14, 125, 131
Humanitarian Pledge 54, 65–66, 71, 72, 90, 93, 143, 147, 169, 193; Humanitarian Pledge resolution UN General Assembly (2015) 74–75, 79
human security 2, 12, 111, 116, 143–146, 159, 179, 189, 205
hypersonic weapons 199

IAEA 123, 170–171; Additional Protocol 170–171
ICAN, International Campaign to Abolish Nuclear Weapons 1–2, 28, 30, 37, 39, 42, 52, 54, 56–57, 64–65, 68, 71–72, 90–91, 101, 104, 110, 113, 118–120, 125–126, 128, 129–130, 147, 150–151, 176, 189
inadvertent use of nuclear weapons 38–39, 164, 198, 201, 210
India 12, 19, 34, 90; India-US nuclear agreement 11
Indonesia 59, 95, 115, 126–127
INF Treaty 175
International Atomic Energy Agency (IAEA) 121
International Campaign to Ban Landmines (ICBL) 12
International Committee of the Red Cross (ICRC) 12, 14–16, 112, 114, 118, 124, 127, 176; International Red Cross and Red Crescent Movement 4, 36, 117
international cooperation and assistance 124–125
International Court of Justice (ICJ) 1996 Advisory Opinion 195
international humanitarian law 15–16, 28–31, 43, 46, 71, 112, 116, 127, 146, 195–196, 203, 205, 211–213, 222
International Law and Policy Institute (ILPI) 28, 92, 122
International Physicians for the Prevention of Nuclear War (IPPNW) 31, 155
Iran 10, 11, 14, 75, 112, 119–120, 122, 125, 129, 175, 209, 121; Effective measures on nuclear disarmament, resolution UN General Assembly (2015) 76–79; Iran Nuclear Agreement (Joint Comprehensive Plan of Action, JCPOA) 2, 75–77, 129, 212
Iraq 10
Ireland 13, 59, 64, 70, 72–75, 90–92, 99, 101, 111–112, 115, 120, 122–123, 126–127, 169

Israel 90
Italy 43, 96, 118

Jamaica 127
James Martin Center for Nonproliferation Studies 19
Japan 1, 15, 32, 100
join and destroy 122–124, 173

Kane, Angela 206
Kazakhstan 119–120, 127
Kellenberger, Jakob 14–15
Kenya 12, 98
Kissinger, Henry 14
Kleib, Hasan 115
Kongstad, Seffen 16
Kurz, Sebastian 32, 61

Labbé, Alfredo 115, 124
Laggner, Benno 62–64, 66, 68, 156
Latin America 208
Law of Armed Conflict 195
legal gap (for the prohibition and elimination of nuclear weapons) 46, 52, 55, 57, 60, 70–71, 96
Liechtenstein 99
Lomonaco, Jorge 97

Main Committee One, NPT Review Conference (2015) 61–65
Malaysia 59, 94–95, 126–127
Marschik, Alexander 17
Marshall Islands 124
Martens Clause 116
Maurer, Peter 112, 150
Mexico 12–13, 18–19, 33–35, 38, 56, 59, 72–75, 76–79, 90–91, 95, 97–98, 101, 111, 117, 120, 122–123, 126–127
Middle Eastern Zone free of Weapons of Mass Destruction (MEZFWMD) 69
military preparations for use of nuclear weapons (prohibition of) 118
Minty, Abdul 64–65
miscalculation 38, 77–78, 144, 165, 197, 199
modernisation of nuclear arsenals 2, 20, 58, 190
Mozambique 115, 120, 127
Mueller, Harald 17
Mukhatzhanova, Gaukhar 19
mutually assured destruction (MAD) 194

Nagasaki 38, 40, 75, 92
Nakamitsu, Izumi 171

NATO 2, 32, 37, 43, 104, 118–119, 126, 128, 162, 175, 204, 212; NATO Deterrence and Defence Posture Review (2012) 119; NATO Nuclear Planning Group 118
Nauru 95
Nayarit Conference 38–42, 46
negative security assurances (NSAs) 18, 160
negotiation mandate 89, 171
neoconservatives 10
Netherlands 96, 104, 116, 118, 121, 125–126, 128–129, 162, 204
New Agenda Coalition 52–54, 55, 57, 60–62, 64, 68, 73
New Strategic Arms Reduction Treaty (New START) 14, 19, 58
new technologies 223
New Zealand 12, 59, 118, 120, 122, 126–127
Nigeria 101, 111, 119, 126–127
Nobel Peace Prize (2017) 1, 4, 54, 151; Nobel Committee 54, 151
no first use declaration 199
Nolan, Helena 115, 122, 127
Non-aligned movement (NAM) 15, 33, 94, 98
non-aligned states 9
Non-Proliferation and Disarmament Initiative (NPDI) 61
non-proliferation complex 177
North Korea 2, 10, 14, 90, 170, 174, 209, 212; 2006 nuclear test 11
Norway 13, 16, 18–19, 27–28, 33–35, 38, 119, 128, 131, 155
Norwegian People's Aid 28
NPT Preparatory Committee (2012) for the Review Conference (2015) 31, 155
NPT Preparatory Meetings for the 2020 NPT Review Conference 175
NPT Review and Extension Conference (1995) 10, 20, 58, 64–65, 141, 166, 172, 209
NPT Review Conference (2000) 9, 10, 11, 58, 65, 141, 172, 209
NPT Review Conference (2005) 10
NPT Review Conference (2010) 14–18, 27, 31, 58–59, 61, 64, 141, 155, 172, 209
NPT Review Conference (2015) 4, 32, 41–43, 52, 56–57, 59, 60–70, 71–75, 89, 143, 158

nuclear deterrence 1–3, 29, 32, 35, 44–45, 63, 66–67, 72, 102–104, 116–117, 119, 128, 132, 141, 142–147, 155, 159, 162–168, 170, 172, 176–179, 187–188, 190, 192–206, 210–211, 213
nuclearism 203, 213
Nuclear Nonproliferation Treaty (NPT) 116, 127; 2010 Action Plan 20, 30, 34, 41–42, 57, 58, 146, 156–157, 160, 172; Action One 16–17; NPT Article I 212; NPT Article II 11, 169, 212; NPT Article IV 10–11, 169; NPT Article VI 9, 52–54, 59–60, 62–63, 66, 72, 92–93, 142, 145–146, 161–162, 166–167, 169–170, 190–191, 212–213; NPT grand bargain 11; NPT indefinite extension 10, 64, 166
nuclear risks 2, 38–39, 41, 43–46, 52, 54–55, 57, 59–60, 62–64, 67, 71, 74, 76, 116, 132, 141, 143–147, 158–160, 162, 164, 166, 176–179, 188–189, 192–193, 196, 197–200, 201–204, 206, 211, 213, 222–223, 225; reduction 197–200
Nuclear Suppliers Group 11
nuclear testing 95, 117–118
nuclear umbrella States 32, 38–40, 42–44, 52, 54, 56, 61, 66–67, 74, 76–78, 90, 94–98, 100–102, 110, 113, 118–119, 121, 123, 128, 144–145, 148–149, 159–160, 162, 164, 167, 168–170, 174, 176–177, 187, 189, 200, 203–204, 211–213, 221
nuclear weapon free zones 15, 95
nuclear weapons accidents 29, 38–39, 197–198, 211, 222
Nuclear Weapons Convention 28–29, 53, 94, 98, 173
nuclear weapons establishment 205, 222
nuclear winter 31
Nunn, Sam 14
Nystuen, Gro 119

Obama, Barack 14; Prague speech 14, 43
open-ended working group (2013) 4, 33–35, 46, 156; discussion at 2015 NPT Review Conference 68, 73–74, 76–79; open-ended working group (2016) 89–101, 102–104, 123, 126, 131, 143, 161, 174, 189
Organisation for the Prohibition of Nuclear Weapons in Latin America and the Caribbean (OPANAL) 61

Oslo Conference 36–40, 42, 128, 147, 156–157, 160
Ottawa-Process 12

P5 (permanent five members of the UN Security Council) 37, 77, 158; P5 Process 58
Pakistan 12, 19, 34, 90, 95, 209
Palau 95, 99
Paris Agreement on Climate Change (2015) 210
Pascal, Blaise 201
PAX 120
Perry, William 14
Peru 120, 127
Philippines 16, 59, 95, 120, 126–127
Plasai, Virachai 115
Poland 162
Pope Francis 44, 112–113, 127
possession of nuclear weapons (prohibition of) 34, 45, 96, 117, 119, 170, 172–173, 211
Potter, William 66
Prague agenda 14, 19
Preamble TPNW 111, 114, 116–118, 143, 160, 169, 196
production of nuclear weapons (TPNW prohibition of) 45, 117, 120
progressive approach 95, 167

radiation exposure 43
Reaching Critical Will 19, 28, 35, 61
Reagan, Ronald 9
re-alerting race 199
Reykjavík Summit (1986) 9
Ritchie, Nick 172
rogue states 10
rules of procedure 11–12, 14, 32–34, 74, 77, 110–111, 207
Russia (Russian Federation) 3, 9–10, 13–14, 19, 33, 58, 102, 104, 157, 160, 162, 165, 175, 190, 199, 204, 207–208, 212
Ruzicka, Jan 177

safeguards 121–122, 132, 170–171
Samoa 95, 99
San Marino 99
Schelling, Thomas 200
Schlosser, Eric 39
Shultz, George 14
Singapore 115, 125
small arms and light weapons: illicit trade 13

South Africa 13, 41, 64, 71–75, 90–91, 100–101, 111–112, 117, 120, 122, 126–127, 169
Southeast Asian Nuclear Weapon Free Zone 120
South Korea 32
Soviet Union 9
Sri Lanka 98
stationing of nuclear weapons (TPNW prohibition of) 117
step-by-step approach to nuclear disarmament 27, 32, 43–44, 147, 156–158, 160, 162
stockpiling of nuclear weapons (TPNW prohibition of) 115
Støre, Jonas Gahr 27, 31
strategic risk reduction 199
strategic stability 142–143, 164, 194, 200
strategic studies community 177–178
Subsidiary Body I, NPT Review Conference (2015) 61–65
Sweden 12, 59, 74, 120–121, 125–128
Switzerland 13, 16, 31, 59, 74, 120–121, 125–128
Syria 112

Taking Forward Multilateral Nuclear Disarmament Negotiations, resolution (2011) 18, 33
Taking Forward Multilateral Nuclear Disarmament Negotiations, resolution (2012) 33–35, 156
Taking Forward Multilateral Nuclear Disarmament Negotiations, resolution (2015) 74–79, 90, 92
Taking Forward Multilateral Nuclear Disarmament Negotiations, resolution (2016) 101–104, 110
testing of nuclear weapons (TPNW prohibition of) 117–118, 125, 128
Thailand 70, 91, 115, 120, 126–127
Thakur, Ramesh 170
Thirteen practical steps (2000 NPT Review Conference) 9, 10, 11, 17, 58
Thompson, Edward 177
Thongpakdi, Thani 91, 98, 101, 102
threat of use of nuclear weapons 62, 117, 130, 192–193, 195, 202, 211
Thurlow, Setsuko 126, 151
TPNW Preamble 111, 114, 116–118, 143, 160, 169, 196; prohibitions Article (I); Article I (a) develop nuclear weapons 118, 120; testing of

nuclear weapons 117–118, 125, 128; produce nuclear weapons 45, 117, 120; acquisition of nuclear weapons 117, 174; stockpiling 115; I (b) transfer of nuclear weapons 34, 45, 117; I (d) use of threat of use 117, 130, 192–193; I (e) assist 117–120; encourage 117; I (g) stationing of nuclear weapons 117; transfer of nuclear weapons 34, 45, 117; Article III safeguards 121–122, 132, 170–171; Article IV (destroy and join) 122–124; (join and destroy) 122–124, 173; Article VI victim assistance and environmental remediation 124–125, 130; Article VII international cooperation and assistance 124–125; Article XVII withdrawal 115, 125–126
transit (of nuclear weapons) 114–115, 117, 119–120, 130, 163
transparency measures 17, 66, 89, 91, 95, 115, 191, 198
Trinidad and Tobago 126
Trump, Donald 131, 176, 207
Turkey 102, 118
Tuvalu 95

UN Charter 117, 213
UN Development Programme (UNDP) 36
UN disarmament machinery 12, 18, 33, 159
unequivocal undertaking (2000 NPT Review Conference) 10
UN General Assembly 4, 12, 18–19, 32–33, 35, 55, 60, 70, 73–76, 79, 89, 91, 95, 97–101, 110, 121, 131, 150, 156–157, 161, 163, 175, 189–190, 203; first resolution (1946) 1, 104; rules of procedure 11–12, 74, 110
UN High Commissioner for Refugees (UNHCR) 36
unintentional use of nuclear weapons 144, 198–199

United Kingdom (UK) 19, 33, 37, 39, 43–44, 56, 63, 65, 102–104, 113, 151, 157–159, 162, 165
United Nations Disarmament Commission 59
United Nations Institute for Disarmament Research (UNIDIR) 38, 92, 122
United States of America (US) 2, 9–10, 12, 17, 19, 32–33, 37, 39, 43–44, 56, 58, 63, 69–70, 77, 90, 00, 102–104, 113, 118, 128–129, 151, 157–158, 161, 165, 175, 190, 200, 207, 212
UN Office for the Coordination of Humanitarian Affairs (OCHA) 36
UN Secretary General 18
UN Security Council 11, 142, 144, 208, 212–212
US Nuclear Posture Review (2018) 210

Vatican 44
Venezuela 122
verification (nuclear disarmament) 53, 76, 94, 96, 114–115, 121, 167, 170, 172–173
victim assistance 124–125, 130
Vienna Conference on the Humanitarian Impact of Nuclear Weapons (2014) 4, 41–46, 52, 54–57, 64, 149, 158–159
Vienna Convention on the Law of Treaties 125
Viet Nam 127

Wall Street Journal 14
Washington Post 71
Western European and Others Group (WEOG) 155
Whyte Gómez, Elayne 111, 114, 121, 125
Wildfire 147–149
Williams, Jody 12
withdrawal from TPNW 115, 125–126
World Food Programme (WFP) 36
World Health Organization (WHO) 43
World War II 207

Zambia 95

Printed in Japan
落丁、乱丁本のお問い合わせは
Amazon.co.jp カスタマーサービスへ